Published by

Heaney Media

First printing: October 2016

Caricature by Stevie Conroy

 All enquiries to: heaneymedia@btinternet.com
A CIP catalogue for this title is available from the British Library.

ISBN: 978-1-5262-0637-4

DEDICATION

Dedicated to my wife Bernie, sons Bryan and Damian
and grandchildren, Jane and Ben

She's ma peerie, weerie, winkle
Ma jeely an' ma jam
Ma fairy, ma canary
An' ma bonnie wee bit spam
She's ma bunch o' soorocks
An' ma laughing cockatoo
An' I'll be Maggie's cockabendie
Cockie leekie loo

They say when we get merried
In a year or two or three
We'll settle up the Vennel
Or maybe doon the Quay
An' when the ebbing tide is low
And we've got nowt tae dae
We'll play at bee baw babbity
To pass the time away

Old Dumbarton folk song

* *Soorocks: Scots word for sorrel from AJ Cronin's Hatter's Castle*
Your dumpling tastes like soorocks

Cover photographs: *A selection of photographs of landmarks and people from the Lennox. Back cover: Bill Heaney interviewing Clint Eastwood, Tony Blair, Ally McCoist and Murdo MacLeod, Working at Westminster and at the Scottish Executive in Edinburgh, and Bill and Bernie Heaney pictured in the throne room at Hillsborough Castle, the official residence of HM the Queen and the Royal Family in Northern Ireland.*

CONTENTS

ACKNOWLEDGEMENTS

I am indebted to my wife, Bernadette, and our sons, Bryan and Damian, who have put up with my life-long obsession with newspapers and journalism, the trade I have followed for 55 years from copy boy to editor. I am grateful for the encouragement to produce this book from my good friend, former US ambassador Frank Meehan; the late Daniel Lynch JP., sage of Dumbarton, and Dick Dickson JP, my fisherman friend, angling correspondent and kenspeckle figure on the banks of the River Leven and Loch Lomond. Petra McMillan, owner of the Dumbuck House Hotel in Dumbarton, asked me to assist her with the production of a nostalgic newspaper to hang on the walls of that august establishment.

Kirsty Wark inspired me with a talk she gave at the Edinburgh Book Festival about everyone having a book in them. Alison Shaw kindly gave me permission to use her obituary of the Queen of the Loch, the inimitable centenarian Hannah Stirling; Ian Bruce, Herald geo-political editor wrote the obituary of his friend John Easton, campaigner for PS Waverley; Donald Fullarton assisted me with photographs and information from Helensburgh, and Tom O'Neill has been generous with his football reminiscences and old photographs. I am the editor of this book, not the author, although many of the articles and pictures are mine and every effort has been made to trace the others and credit them where possible. My former colleague, the accomplished veteran, Brian Averell took a number of the photographs published here and I collected copies of many of them from West Dunbartonshire Council and readers over the years.

Bernie and I are proud of our sons. Bryan is an advocate in Edinburgh, and Damian, a senior school teacher in the West Highlands. Our grandchildren, Jane and Ben, bring so much happiness into our lives and drag me away from my books and laptop in this often solitary writer's life. I am indebted to Gerry Fitzgerald, Bill Owens and Craig M Jeffrey, who brought me into the newspaper trade. Thank you to the readers and staff of the *Lennox Herald*, who are forever helpful with encouragement, ideas and information for stories and photographs for my columns in Dunbartonshire's oldest and most popular weekly newspaper.

Over the years the *Lennox Herald* staff has included some now famous names. Talented journalists who started out as trainees with me include

Kamal Ahmed, Economics Editor of BBC News; David Livingstone, golf presenter on Sky Sports; Samantha Poling, investigative reporter of BBC *Newsnight*; author and television scriptwriter Sergio Casci; Scottish Parliament head of media affairs, Annette McCann; Crown Office spokesperson Lorraine Davidson; Lorraine Herbison, Head of News and Sport at Radio Clyde; John McGarry, sports writer of the *Scottish Daily Mail*; Archie Fleming, of the *Scottish Daily Express*; Jim McGhee, of the *South China Morning Post;* Eric Wishart, *Agence France Presse;* Martin Hannan, *The Scotsman;* Lynn Cochrane, *Sunday Times;* Audrey Davis, Hazel Reilly, Michelle McMenemy, Annette Rankine and Amanda Graham. I like to think they embraced my motto: 'What High Street does today, Fleet Street does tomorrow.'

THE EDITOR

Bill Heaney fishing on Loch Lomond. *Picture by Dick Dickson.*

Bill Heaney was brought up in Dumbarton, where he continues to live in Round Riding Road and write two columns each week for the *Lennox Herald*, the leading weekly newspaper. He was born in Airthrey Castle in Bridge of Allan, now part of Stirling University, and raised by his grandmother in Brucehill. A newspaper delivery boy from the age of 12, a copy boy at 16, a *Scottish Daily Express* reporter at 17 and an editor from the age of just 21, printer's ink runs through his veins. Heaney has won the Scottish Weekly Newspaper Journalist of the Year Award three times, along with a number of other UK industry honours. He has also worked in Edinburgh as a special adviser for Scotland's First Minister and at Westminster as personal assistant and media adviser to the chair of the Treasury Select Committee. He worked for more than a year with the Vice President of the European Parliament.

Heaney said: 'I enjoy everything to do with newspapers. I have come through 55 years of remarkable change in the industry, from the excitement and intricacies of hot metal production through to the present digital age. I hope that readers of this collection of reports, features, obituaries and photographs enjoy reminiscing, and that it brings them pleasure, particularly over Christmas and New Year when families traditionally get together to talk about old times. Hopefully, it will also bring a wider understanding of journalists and journalism. Veterans can thumb through the pages and look back over a golden era for newspapers. This is a book to dip into and slowly read when the house is quiet and you want simply to relax and remember the past. Conversely, it can be a catalyst for one of those 'do you remember' discussions around the fireside or dinner table that we all love. Please have a care also then for those who cannot remember the past, the unfortunate amongst us who suffer from dementia or those who for health reasons are confined to the house.'

FOREWORD

Nothing pleases us more than nostalgia. However, is it good for us to trawl through the past? Are the 'good old days' just a myth, and is it because they were actually so bad - and the way we live now is so good by comparison - that we enjoy these trips down memory lane? An excellent article on this subject in the *Scottish Review*, an on-line magazine, set me wondering about this – and, at the same time, reminiscing yet again. The writer, Paul Tritchler, was looking back at the 'Sixties when we were teenagers. He 'escaped' to London and I ran off to Glasgow. Tritchler writes: 'I paid rent to a shady landlord … in exchange for a dimly lit room with mice, metered gas, and a tabletop electric cooker that took an hour to bring a can of tomato soup to bubbling point. It was the dreariest place in W11, the batteries in my cassette player drained constantly, I went to bed early to stay warm. I was lonely, hungry and homesick.' For me, add the word scared to those last three adjectives because my own experience in that era of the Townhead area of Glasgow was much the same.

While working as a copy boy for the *Scottish Daily Express* in Albion Street, I lived in a single-end tenement flat off Dobbie's Loan and slept on a creaking sofa with no cushions and broken springs. A shilling in the meter kept the small electric fire going for just 20 minutes. There was no bath or shower and the lavatory was outside on the stair head. Since gang fights were commonplace in that part of the city at that time, I went to sleep shivering with a rug pulled over my clothes and a ladder jammed up against the door to keep the Fighting Tongs out. While he was away, Tritchler's parents had the gas and electricity cut off at their home, which meant they spent one Christmas in the dark. My parents too were having a tough time because a fly-by-night construction company offered my step-father a highly-paid job on the Kariba Dam in Rhodesia, which is now Zimbabwe, with an airline ticket thrown in. The job did not materialize, but the return airline ticket did, as did the bill for it, which brought Sheriff Officers to the door looking for the money. The messengers at arms poinded the furniture, the television set and even the forks in the kitchen drawer. This was at a time when my wages were £4.7.6 a week.

Tritchler tells us that dwelling on the past was once linked to depressive states, but there is today a growing body of research that suggests nostalgia is a unique asset. And that it enables us to make sense of our existence, to improve psychological health, and to reduce fears about death. Regardless of age or culture, nostalgia narratives are never absent from our lives. They might be tinged with sadness and triggered by negative thoughts or loneliness, but in the end they are always positive experiences, and frequently socially oriented. The universality of nostalgia as a discrete aspect of memory suggests it evolved as part of selective pressures in our environment. It appears as an adaptive neurological protection system that strengthens neural pathways and builds resilience and motivation by reminding us who we are and where we are coming from.

Tritchler quotes research conducted by psychologists Constantine Sedikides and Tim Wildschut, who have concluded that nostalgia has three main functions. It increases positive - but not negative – mood; it defends our sense of self, and it reinforces social connectedness. Their empirical studies also suggest the centrality of nostalgia's place in increasing relationship satisfaction, of strengthening belongingness and empathy, and of preserving a sense of meaning in life. It does this, says Wildschut, by connecting the past with the present to point optimistically to the future. Not surprisingly there are now multi-disciplinary teams looking at ways of developing nostalgia narratives as therapeutic interventions for post-traumatic stress, depression and early stage Alzheimer's. Tritchler's conclusion is that far from being a dark, depressive indulgence, nostalgia is a remarkable attribute of memory that helps dissolve barriers and give structure and meaning to our life. Just as the brain is set up for metaphor, nostalgic experiences operate as an emergency generator when the power is cut. Writing about the past certainly makes me feel good and to learn now that it is considered to be an antidote to Alzheimer's is a bonus.

Like every other place on earth, what really makes Dunbartonshire is its people. And to create a true picture of any community one has to look not just at the living, but the dead. That is why I have used so many obituaries in this book. And photographs too of not just who we are but who we were. James Joyce did this in his remarkable short story *The Dead*, which contains this wonderful observation of how the dead are never far away from us: "It had begun to snow again. He watched sleepily the flakes, silver and dark, falling obliquely against the lamplight ... snow was falling upon every part of the lonely churchyard on the hill ... it lay thickly drifted on the crooked crosses and headstones ... he heard the snow falling faintly through the universe and faintly falling, like the descent of their last end, upon all the living and the dead."

Chapter 1

THE WAVES

The hugely impressive, Clyde-built Queen Mary.

Every one of us has a story to tell. We may not think that our lives are all that interesting, but there are people out there who would devour our every word. And maybe, if they are talented, intelligent and clever, pull their own words together and have them published in book form. Kirsty Wark told a large audience at the Edinburgh Book Festival to get their pencils, notebooks and laptops out and write a memoir. And she added that the usual 'I'm far too busy for that stuff' excuse does not hold water. There may even be a best-seller happening all around you. You may only have to raise your eyes and look or just sit down and recall and reminisce. Family histories, old photographs, things that happen at work and play, in the street where you live, your own town or your holiday hideaway, are a valuable resource for writers. What takes place in your own home

– and in the homes of your friends, relatives and neighbours – is a rushing, gurgling burn where nuggets of literary gold can be panned. Busy is just another four-letter word to Kirsty Wark, presenter of BBC *Newsnight*, who specialises in the Arts and politics.

Feminist Kirsty runs the family home in Scotland, where she is not averse to hoovering and high dusting. Her feminism stems from a genuine concern for women and equal rights. It is not based on wearing badges declaring 'Women make policy, not coffee' or mouthing slogans. Kirsty feeds her husband, Alan, and grown up children on her own legendary *cordon bleau* cooking and widely-acclaimed home baking. I have seen television footage of her working in the kitchen of her Glasgow home with her sleeves rolled up, before going into the garden to cut the grass. She absolutely adores gardening and zipped round with the mower before nipping off to carry the Commonwealth Games baton through her part of the city she loves. For Kirsty, filling public engagements is an honour, not a chore.

At the Edinburgh Book Festival, Kirsty appeared for a photo call and uncomplainingly stood out in the rain, while the media took photographs of her. She looked trim and attractive in jeans and even, as my wife declaimed, lovely, and she has the personality to go with that. Kirsty's smile is disarming. Little wonder then that the people she interviews open up to answer the hard questions she puts to them on *Newsnight* in her distinctive Ayrshire brogue, while gazing at them inquisitively over her horn-rimmed specs. There was no doing the prima donna on it at that photo call, no appeal against having to brave the wind and rain. 'Just look at me,' she said in dismay, as she stepped out into yet another downpour and faced a battery of cameras and flashguns. 'Someone just said that my sweater looks like the Celtic away strip,' she said, smiling all the while. One usually grumpy photographer – and there are many - said: 'If Celtic had had Kirsty in their team, they would have won.' This was a reference to a football match which had taken place the previous evening.

Kirsty was appearing at the Book Festival to give a talk entitled *The Changing Clyde* to a packed audience in a large Charlotte Square marquee. The talk was based on her novel, *The Legacy of Elizabeth Pringle*, which tells the story of two women from very different backgrounds, whose experiences highlight a century of change in the West of Scotland. With beautifully drawn characters, Wark maps out two captivating personal journeys that unexpectedly overlap. Two women, one young and one old, are drawn together by a beautiful house in the holiday island of Arran, which the younger one wants to own. Not just the women but the male characters are interesting too, with one of them based on Kirsty's solicitor father from Kilmarnock, and another on the inimitable Leonard Cohen. The book is full of beautiful birds, of the feathered variety, and war planes soaring over a busy Firth of Clyde. This story hugs love and memory of households and holidays and happiness and heartache. It brought back so many memories of those halcyon summer days long ago when the waves were a huge attraction for us children. We went down to the Clyde shore on long, hot summer days to escape the baking heat, melting tar on the roads, and 'the sun splitting the cossies'. Then, everyone used to wait for big ships and small boats passing in the river to 'catch' the waves as they swept into Havoc shore and up to the mouth of the River Leven at Levengrove Park or under Dumbarton Rock. The bigger the ship, the higher the waves, the more we loved them. And this was despite the fact that few of us could afford a pair of swimming trunks to go diving into them. Never mind though, a few brave lads stripped off and dived into the water in the buff. The more mature people, the mothers and fathers, uncles and aunties and grandparents, went for a paddle.

When did the biggest waves ever coming rolling in at Dumbarton? There is a story; apocryphal possibly, that this happened in 1936 after the Queen Mary was launched from John Brown's shipyard in Clydebank. The great Cunarder was making its journey down the Clyde for the first and last time to do time trials over the measured mile off the island of Arran. There was talk in our house for years afterwards of the waves from the great ship coming up to the foot of the cliffs at Brucehill and Clerkhill and washing on to the railway track at Westcliff, between Dalreoch and Cardross. People spoke exaggeratedly of waves 'splashing half way up the Castle'. Certainly, the day the Queen Mary sailed down the Clyde was a day to remember. It wasn't just the children of Dumbarton, Helensburgh and Cardross who recalled this event for many years afterwards, however. One of the finest descriptions of this great day is included in Kirsty Wark's novel in which the fictional Miss Pringle was a schoolteacher on Arran for a time. In the novel she recalls the circumstances of the launch and sea trials of the great ship.

Kirsty Wark at the Edinburgh Book Festival.
Picture by Bill Heaney

This was one of the passages from her book which Kirsty chose to read at the Edinburgh Book Festival: 'The children in my class knew all about ships. The Firth of Clyde was the gateway to the world and the waters off Arran teemed with every kind of vessel, from the grandest liners to coal ships and steamers, Navy frigates, magnificent ocean going yachts, fishing boats and skiffs, but there was nothing as thrilling as the prospect of the sailing of the Queen Mary.

'I made her our class project and the children wrote politely to John Brown and Company at Clydebank requesting information about the new liner. When packages of drawings and diagrams arrived along with copies of the draughtsmen's measurements for the hull and the stern and the cross sections, we pinned them up on friezes on the classroom wall. We painted and cut out pennants and the flags of John Brown, and Cunard and White Star, and the Red Ensign, all of which we hung on string from one side of the classroom to the other. It was almost unimaginable to us that the biggest object in the world was being built on the Clyde and that we would see it before it commanded the waves.

'On April 15, 1936, the Queen Mary sailed for Arran. It was a beautiful ice clear day, and the whole school headed for Clauchlands Point. The children were beside themselves with excitement, and were awestruck when they heard her three whistles blowing from ten miles away, heralding her arrival. Small aircraft roared overhead, glinting in the sunshine and circling over the great ship as she sailed forth, tipping their wing at us as they flew back and forth from ship to shore like frenzied flies. All manner of craft, decked in bunting, blew their own tinny whistles as they sailed out to greet her, taking care to keep clear of the wash, and soon we saw the vast black hull and smoke billowing from the forward funnel, which was painted the bright orange of the Cunard Line. Boys and girls alike were jumping up and down waving hats and flags, and then, overawed by her sheer size as one thousand feet of ship seemed to bear down on us, they were suddenly silent, transfixed and open-mouthed. Soon we could see craftsmen, engineers, officers and seamen dotted all over the decks, waving to us, proud men who had created this magnificent object of beauty and power ...'

This is just beautiful writing by Kirsty, who went to school in Ayr and cut her broadcasting teeth with BBC Scotland in Glasgow.

* *The Legacy of Elizabeth Pringle by Kirsty Wark is published by Two Roads and is available from all good bookshops.*

QE2 launch at Clydebank

After a long and illustrious career, the Queen Mary was retired to become a hotel in Long Beach, California, USA, but she is still very much part of our history. The QE2 came later. I reported on her construction and launch from John Brown's shipyard in Clydebank and it was not without incident. Her Majesty the Queen had sent the champagne bottle crashing against her hull, but the other queen cheekily refused to budge. Step forward then George Parker, the immaculately dressed, bowler-hatted shipyard manager. Gentleman George gave the QE2 a gentle push and the huge vessel slipped away into the river and shipbuilding history. Sadly, the QE2 was the last of the great Cunarders to be built on the Clyde.

The QE2. *Picture by Cunard*

Chapter 2

THE CLYDE STEAMERS

PS Jeanie Deans, a favourite with passengers on the River Clyde.

It was the highlight of our year. A trip ***Doon the Watter*** was what everyone and his granny looked forward to when you said farewell to winter and the better weather came in, usually around Easter. Families from a' the airts and pairts arrived by train at Craigendoran Station to join the famous steamers, the paddle steamers Jeanie Deans, PS Waverley and the MV Clansman, you name it. You wouldn't call the king your aunty if you were lined up on the platform in your best clothes and your granny had bought the train tickets from Joe O'Neill, Hans Glover or Bill Campbell or stationmaster Johnny Mann at Dalreoch Station. Perhaps the young clerk Tommy Moy was still there dishing out train tickets before going on to become the boss of one of the biggest logistic companies in Europe and Russia? There were no foreign holidays for us in those days. This was your holidays and everyone was filled with excitement and determined to enjoy the day that was in it.

Boarding the old steam trains was always a thrill. You searched for an empty carriage and slung what bags you had on to the luggage racks. The carriages were comfortable and decorated with photographs of some of the magnificent views you might see along the way. The first tummy tickler was going through the "dark tunnel" under Clerkhill Convent, past the Skittery Widds and Lovers' Lane and emerging at Havoc, near Wallace's Cave. You were soon shielding your eyes from the sun shining above the hills of Greenock and Port Glasgow and reflecting off the wide expanse of the River Clyde. Or you shrunk back sheltering from the sheets of rain your granny dismissed as "just a wee shower". You were warned not to pull the leather strap or lean out the carriage window lest you had your head chopped off at a signal box or a spark from the fire of the steam locomotive entered your eye.

The *Song of the Clyde*, sung by the Scots tenor Kenneth MacKellar, lists the exotic destinations of the steamers – Rothesay, of course, Dunoon and Innellan, Campbeltown and the Kyles of Bute. Soon you were at Cardross and then Craigendoran Junction as it was at that time. This is where the West Highland Railway really begins and the line heads out from there towards Garelochhead and emerges alongside the north westerly shores of Loch Lomond. Significant points on the journey include Crianlarich, an important Highland junction of both road and rail where the line crosses - and is linked to - the Callander and Oban Railway and Tyndrum, the smallest place in Scotland to boast two railway stations. After Tyndrum, the line climbs on upwards to Rannoch Moor.The station at Corrour on the moor is one of the most remote stations in Britain. Carrying on northwards, the final stop before Fort William is Spean Bridge. A branch line was constructed from Fort William to Banavie Pier at the southern end of the Caledonian Canal.

Craigendoran Station was a favourite steamer connection point for Dumbartonians heading Doon the Watter.

But back to Craigendoran whose name in Gaelic: is Creag an Dòbhrain, which means "the rock of the otter". At one time this station had five platforms, two of them island platforms on the West Highland Line - sometimes called Craigendoran Upper – and one called Craigendoran Pier serving the Clyde steamers. The era of the Clyde steamer began in August 1812 with the very first successful commercial steamboat service in Europe, when Henry Bell's *Comet* began a passenger service on the River Clyde between Glasgow and Greenock. The Comet undertook her official trial run on 6 August 1812. Henry Bell, who later owned the Queen's Hotel in Helensburgh, was himself on board along with John Robertson, maker of *Comet's* engine and William McKenzie, formerly a schoolmaster in Helensburgh, acting as skipper. The journey was completed in three and a half hours and after this success, other operators sprang up in competition and the Firth of Clyde became immensely popular with holidaymakers.

By 1900 there were over 300 steamers operating and going *Doon the Watter* was still in full swing in the early 1960s. Then competition from new forms of holiday travel brought the era almost to a close, but PS Waverley continues to provide the leisurely delights of Clyde steamer excursions. From the outset steamboat services were aimed at holidaymakers, with a stop at Helensburgh Pier, bringing passengers to Bell's Baths Hotel, the name the Queen's was known by at that time. Within ten years there were nearly 50 steamers on the Firth of Clyde, sailing as far as Largs, Campbeltown and Inveraray, and the Glasgow Magistrates had introduced a £5 fine for services running late. This was to prevent "the Masters of steam boats, from improper competition and rival ships, postponing their departure for considerable and uncertain periods, after the times they had previously intimated to the public".

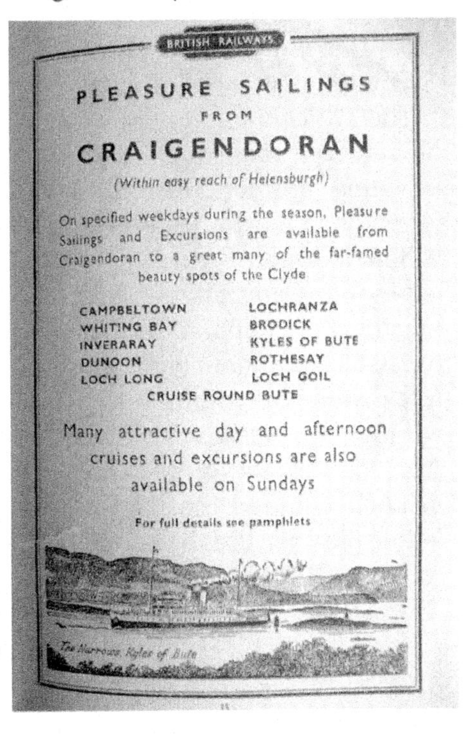

Steamer services were also introduced onto the inland lochs, with the Marion appearing on Loch Lomond in 1816.

With the rapid industrialisation and population growth of 19th century Glasgow great numbers were eager to be released from the grimy city on holidays and during the annual Glasgow Fair fortnight. Workers escaped from the shipyards and factories and went on a cruise down the Clyde to clean unspoilt scenery.

Tiny villages, perhaps with a stone jetty, soon became resorts with wooden piers and villas, hotels and public houses. Local residents would let out rooms, and boarding houses developed. Established towns like Dunoon and Rothesay became major resorts.

Wealthy people – tobacco and whisky barons amongst them - built sandstone villas at places such as Kilcreggan, Blairmore and Innellan to which they could commute daily, or weekly, during the summer.

The first turbine powered merchant vessel, the Clyde steamer *TS King Edward*, was built in 1901. Her successor, the *TS Queen Mary* of 1933, was a floating restaurant on the River Thames in London until 2009. The *PS Waverley*, built in 1947, is the last survivor of these fleets, and the last sea-going paddle steamer in the world. Immensely popular, the *Waverley* sails a full season of cruises every year from places around Britain, and has sailed across the English Channel for a visit to commemorate the 1940 sinking of her predecessor, built in 1899, at the Battle of Dunkirk.

The *PS Jeanie Deans* was also a paddle steamer, built in 1931 for the London and North Eastern Railway. She was a popular boat, providing summer cruises from Craigendoran until 1964. Built for the London and North Eastern Railway in 1931 to compete with the CSP turbine steamer, *Duchess of Montrose*, she was built by the Fairfield Shipbuilding and Engineering Company, Govan, as a paddler, rather than the more popular turbine steamer, allowing her a shallow draught to visit Craigendoran and Helensburgh. She took the name of an earlier fleet member, continuing the tradition of the North British Railway naming their vessels after characters from Sir Walter Scott's novels. The 1900 steamer *SS Sir Walter Scott* still sails on Loch Katrine, while on Loch Lomond the *PS Maid of the Loch* is being restored by the Paddle Steamer Preservation Society at Balloch Pier.

Ian Campbell MP with the finalists of the Miss Dunbartonshire competition at Helensburgh swimming pond in 1970. *Picture courtesy Stewart Walker*

Local businessman and blues band enthusiast Robert Ryan was brought up at Craigendoran and remembers watching from the windows at his home the steamers coming and going from the pier there. People from all over the world have been in touch with Robert on his *Ben Lomond Free Press* website reminiscing about the old days. One wrote: "I remember being on the Craigendoran steamers. I was born too late for the Broomielaw ones. We used to get the steam train from Drumry to Craigendoran, then the boat. The dads would disappear to 'see the engines', which meant they were off to the bar, and the mums would sit up on the deck. Then kids like me would run amok, playing hide'n'seek in the lifeboats and throwing things at the porpoises. Everybody seemed to survive. Then it was Kilcreggan and Dunoon. If dad was flush it was Rothesay after Innellan."

Another correspondent wrote to Robert saying he was really sad to see the decrepit state of Craigendoran Pier today. Mention of *Doon the Watter* days almost always bring tears to the eyes of exiles, people who emigrated from Dunbartonshire after the Second World War. One of them, Peter Jelsby, who had spent a long time in America, wrote: "We would go down to Craigendoran for the day and spend lots of time on the shore there. When I was 15, my dad and I built a wooden hut that started off as a one room hut and ended up the size of a two bedroom and parlour house where we would spend our weekends and summers. These week-ends and summers, I loved very much and I often sit back and think of those days gone by. I can honestly say, I learned to swim right at the Craigendorn Pier, which brings great pleasure in my life and memories that I will forever treasure."

Happy days at Helensburgh seafront when maw, paw and the weans enjoyed themselves on the esplanade.

Jeanie Deans was the first Clyde steamer with a three-crank engine, giving her an impressive speed of 18.5 knot in trials. As built, she had two small deckhouses, one forward, supporting the open bridge and one aft of the twin funnels, covering the companionway. After her first season, a large first class observation saloon was built forward on the promenade deck, providing welcome shelter during poor weather. Her funnels were lengthened to reduce the cinders deposited on passengers. After war service, she was extensively refitted, including a new deckhouse, increasing tonnage to 814. During the winter of 1956/7, she was converted to oil and she had radar fitted in 1960. Lochgoilhead and Arrochar were ports of call for her and on Sundays, she provided cruises down the Firth. These lower Firth cruises were extended from the 1932 season, visiting Ayr and offering cruises around Ailsa Craig and bringing her into direct contact with the *Duchess of Hamilton*. By the outbreak of war, she was the longest and fastest paddle steamer on the Firth. She was requisitioned by the government and saw war service as a minesweeper and then as an anti-aircraft vessel on the River Thames.

Returning to her peacetime duties, she launched the popular Round Bute cruise in the 1950s. The *Jeanie Deans* was withdrawn after the 1964 season and sold for further cruising on the River Thames. As *Queen of the South,* she operated for the Coastal Steam Packet Company until 1967, but technical problems made the new venture a failure. Sadly, in December 1967, she left the Thames for breaking up at Antwerp.

The Queen Mary II spent her "retirement" as a floating restaurant on the River Thames in the heart of London.

Chapter 3

THE PUFFERS

The great Scottish actor Duncan Macrae with the Vital Spark.

Apart from the old paddle steamers, which took most of us *Doon the Watter* for our holidays or days out, the Clyde puffers are the vessels of which we in the West of Scotland are most fond. The short Para Handy stories which Neil Munro first published in the *Glasgow Evening News* in 1905 appeared in the newspaper for more than 20 years. They achieved widespread fame, with collections issued in book form from 1931 still in print today. There are some interesting photographs of puffers and the men who built them on the walls of the recently revitalised Dumbuck House Hotel in Dumbarton. With the continuing popularity of these Munro stories, the puffers became film stars in *The Maggie*, and *Para Handy* which, with his *Vital Spark*, was the subject of three popular BBC television series dating from 1959 to 1995. The Clyde puffer is a type of small coal-fired and single-masted cargo ship built mainly at shipyards on or near the Forth and Clyde canal and locally at Scott's of Bowling. These puffers provided a vital supply link around the west coast and Hebridean islands of Scotland. Stumpy little steamboats, they achieved an almost mythical status thanks largely to the short stories Munro wrote about the Vital Spark and her captain Para Handy. These produced three television series and starred initially Duncan Macrae (of *Wee Cock Sparra* fame) and later Roddy McMillan as the enigmatic ship's captain. Characteristically, these boats had bluff bows, crew's quarters with table and cooking stove in the focsle, and a single mast with derrick in front of the large hold, aft of which the funnel and ship's wheel stood above the engine room, while the captain had a small cabin in the stern. When publication of the *Vital Spark* stories began in 1905 the ship's wheel was still in the open, but later a wheelhouse was added aft of the funnel giving the puffers their distinctive image. Their flat bottom allowed them to beach and unload at low tide, essential to supply remote islands in places from Barra to Benbecula without suitable piers. Typical cargoes would include coal and furniture, with farm produce and sand and gravel often being brought back brought back to the mainland. History tells us the puffers were developed from the gabbert, small single-masted sailing barges which took most of the coastal trade. The original puffer was the *Thomas*, an iron canal boat of 1856, less than 66ft (20 m) long to fit in the Forth and Clyde Canal locks, powered by a simple steam engine without a condenser. This was because it drew fresh water from the canal and there was no need to economise on water use. Once steam had been used by the engine, it was simply exhausted up the funnel in a series of puffs as the piston stroked. As well as the visual sight of a series of steam puffs following the boat, the simple engines, fired up by crewmen such as Dan ('more steam, MacPhail') made a characteristic puffing sound. By the 1870s, similar boats were being adapted for use beyond the canal and fitted with condensers so that they no longer puffed, but the name stuck. From this basic type of puffer, three varieties developed: inside boats continued in use on the Forth and Clyde canal, while shore-head boats extended their range eastwards into the Firth of Forth and westwards as far as the Isle of Bute and from there up the length of Loch Fyne, their length kept at 66ft (20m) to use the canal locks. Both these types had a crew of three. Puffers of a third type, the outside boats, were built for the rougher sea routes to the Hebridean islands with a crew of four and the length

A group of workers outside the engine shop at Scott's of Bowling on Clydeside.

increased to 88ft (27m) still allowing use of the larger locks on the Crinan Canal which cuts across the Kintyre peninsula.

There were more than 20 builders in Scotland, mainly on the Forth and Clyde canal at Kirkintilloch, Maryhill and Bowling on the Clyde. During the First World War, these handy little ships showed their worth in servicing warships, and were used at Scapa Flow, and for the Second World War, the Admiralty (Ministry of Defence) placed an order in 1939 for steamships on the same design, mostly built in England, with the class name of VIC, standing for 'Victualing Inshore Craft'. After the war a number of VICs came into the coasting trade. The *Innisgara* was fitted with an internal combustion engine in 1912, and while puffers generally were steam-powered, after the Second World War new ships began to be diesel engined, and a number of VICs were converted to diesel. The coasting trade to serve the islands was kept up by the Glenlight Shipping Company of Greenock until in 1993 when the then government withdrew subsidies and, unable to compete with road transport using subsidised ferries, the service ended. A small number of puffers survive as conservation projects, though most of these have diesel engines. The 1940s brought an upsurge in business to Clyde shipbuilding yards. The wartime Admiralty needed 100 victualling boats in a hurry, most of which were built in England. No new designs were needed as the perfect boat existed in a Clyde puffer.

Scott's of Bowling foreman Jackie Woods (left) with Jim Sharp.
Photographs courtesy Margaret McWilliams.

Steam sailings on one old puffer, the *VIC 32*, have been available to the public from 1979, latterly as cruises on the Caledonian Canal. From 2004 she underwent extensive refitting at Corpach Boatyard at the west end of the canal near Fort William, funded by donations and lottery funds. The VIC 27 was renamed *Auld Reekie*, which starred as the *Vital Spark* in the third BBC TV Para Handy series, was berthed at Crinan Basin for 14 years, all the while deteriorating. She was purchased by the owner of the Inveraray Maritime Museum, who carried out some work on her but she has since been resold to a new owner who has already started on her major restoration work. As she is the oldest surviving steam-powered puffer in existence, she is being restored and preserved as part of Scotland's heritage afloat. VIC 72, renamed *Eilean Eisdeal,* continued in operation as the last of the true working puffers into the mid-1990s. In 2006, she was again renamed as *Vital Spark* of Glasgow. She is now accessible to the public, alongside the *Arctic Penguin* at the Inveraray Maritime Museum, and continues to make sailings. The *Spartan*, another diesel-engine puffer, is on display at the Scottish Maritime Museum at Irvine. It has recently undergone restoration work on her hull, and is still being refitted. The museum also features the diesel-powered motor coaster *MV Kyles*, which is an early Clyde built coaster, not a puffer.

Pibroch, sadly left to rot at the pier in Connemara, Ireland.

My own relatives, namely Jackie Woods, Mick Ward and Aeneas McFall, worked on *Pibroch,* which was built at Scott's of Bowling in 1957 as a diesel-engined boat for the Scottish Malt Distillers Limited to carry malt whisky from the distillers on Islay. On my annual trips to Connemara in the West of Ireland, I would see *The Pibroch* lying at the pier at Letterfrack in County Galway, where she had been in desperate need of restoration since 2002. The puffer steadily deteriorated on that rain and gale-lashed coastline and, as time passed, her bulkheads began to give way. In 2010, she was sold and was subsequently scrapped. I miss her now since *Pibroch* was a sign that I had almost come to the end of a long, long journey to my adopted home at the back of beyond. *Pibroch's* sister ship, the *Julia T.*, lies in 30m of water in Killary Bay, a vast Norwegian-type fjord, some 300 yards off Lettergesh. There have also been reproduction puffers built to a smaller size, most recently the *MV Mary Hill* for tourist traffic on the Forth and Clyde canal.

Smoke's up on the puffer Dorothy at Dumbarton Quay.

Chapter 4
THE ENGINEER

Robert Napier

Like so many Dumbartonians, the sea and ships are in my DNA. I recall lying in my bed at night in the house high above the River Clyde, listening to the ships' horns on foggy winter nights. And on sunny days too when we flocked to the Clydeshore and the red sands and squelching black mudflats of Havoc. My ambition from a very young age was to go to sea. This had something to do, no doubt, with the fact that my father was a marine engineer, and that, round the Clyde shore in summertime, we got close enough to touch the ships that passed along the dark, deep channel. Tom Gallacher in his wonderful book *Hunting Shadows* tells us about the ships: 'We knew them all. Holts blue funnel with black top (The Blue Flue), Donaldson's all black smoke stack, the two red bands ringing the top of the Clan Line, Brocklebanks's blue and white bands. 'They towered above us. The sand under our bare feet trembled to the vibration of their engines. Yelling and waving we pranced about. They were OUR ships. Their engine rooms were manned by OUR uncles and brothers and cousins.'

Denny's shipyard pictured from Levengrove Park.

The street where my family lived up a close in Napier Crescent, Brucehill, was named after a remarkable man who was recognised world-wide as the greatest ship's engineer of his time. Robert Napier was born in Dumbarton at the height of the Industrial Revolution, to James and Jean Napier. His father was of a line of esteemed bell-wrights, blacksmiths, and engineers, with a brother, also named Robert, who served as blacksmith for the Duke of Argyll at Inveraray Castle. Robert was educated at Dumbarton Academy, where he took an interest in drawing, which reflected in his later life in an interest in painting and fine arts. Against his father's hopes that he would become a minister in the Church of Scotland, he developed an interest in the family business. At age 16, he was confronted by a Royal Navy press gang who intended to conscript him into service during the Napoleonic Wars. Instead of allowing his son to be conscripted, James Napier signed a contract of formal indenture with his son, making him immune to conscription. Robert's apprenticeship with his father lasted for five years, after which time he moved to Edinburgh and worked for Robert Stevenson, builder of the Bell Rock Lighthouse. In 1823 he won a contract to build a steam engine for the paddle steamer *Leven*. The engine was so good that it was later fitted to another ship, the paddle steamer *Queen of Beauty*. The *Leven* engine – his first engine – now rests at the Denny Ship Model Experiment Tank branch of the Scottish Maritime Museum in Dumbarton. In 1827, Robert Napier had the unique distinction of having built the engines of both of the two fastest ships to compete in the Rhu-based Northern Yacht Club's August Regatta. These were the paddle steamers *Clarence* and *Helensburgh.* This distinction earned him a reputation as a shipbuilder, which furthered his career, as did also his co-operation on hull design with Thomas Asheton Smith. In 1828, Robert Napier established Glasgow's Vulcan Foundry.

Many of Scotland's most esteemed shipbuilders apprenticed under Robert Napier, including James and George Thomson, who founded the J & G Thomson shipyard, which became known as John Brown & Company in Clydebank, and John Elder, of the Fairfield Shipbuilding and Engineering Company in Govan. Robert Napier continued building steamship engines, eventually expanding into steam engines for ocean-going vessels. In 1835, he procured a controversial contract with the East India Company to build an engine for their ship, the paddle steamer *Berenice* which, built by David Napier, his cousin, and using Robert's engine, proved faster than her sister ship, the paddle steamer *Atalanta,* beating her to India by 18 days on their maiden voyage.

In 1838, Robert Napier was contracted by the Admiralty to produce 280 NHP engines for two of their ships, the first class paddle steamer sloops *Stromboli* and *Vesuvius* but after that, orders ceased. When Napier had this queried in Parliament, the reply proved that Napier's engines were cheaper and more reliable than those built in the Admiralty's usual shipyards on the Thames. Thereafter, Robert Napier was the Admiralty's primary engine builder. Napier's largest success, however, came from his business deals with Samuel Cunard. Together with Cunard, James Donaldson, Sir George Burns, and David MacIver, he co-founded the British and North American Royal Mail Steam Packet Company and decided the colours since the vermilion colour and black hoops were already used on earlier Napier-engined ships. This was evidenced by the shipbuilder's model of *P.S. Menai* of 1830, which was exhibited in the Scottish Transport Museum in Glasgow. In 1841, he expanded his company to include an iron shipbuilding yard in Govan and the Parkhead Forge Steelworks, and in 1843 they produced their first ship, the *Vanguard.* Napier also procured a contract with the Royal Navy to produce vessels, notably the *Jackal,* the *Lizard*, and the *Bloodhound*, which became the first iron vessels in the Royal Navy. He also allowed naval officers in training to visit the shipyard to familiarise themselves with the new vessels.

The Parkhead Forge was acquired by William Beardmore and Company in 1886. Napier's Shipyard in Govan was also later acquired by

Beardmore's in 1900 before being sold on to Harland & Wolff in 1912 – they built the *Titanic* - before finally closing in 1962. The Parkhead Forge would eventually close in 1976 and the site is now one of the biggest retail centres in Glasgow. Like so much of Dumbarton's history and the achievements of its accomplished sons and daughters, the Napier Engine was not appreciated by some ignoramuses in the town. It was incorporated into the design for the new Town Centre in the 'Sixties and placed in a pond and fountain, which was vandalised frequently by louts who thought it funny to throw packets of washing powder into it. The subsequent foam spread across the shopping area from College Way down to the High Street. It was moved from there to the park overlooking the River Clyde at Dumbarton Castle and eventually to its present site at the Scottish Maritime Museum in Castle Street. There were tears in the eyes of Provost Ian Campbell, who was later to become the Member of Parliament, when Denny's shipyard closed in 1963. Denny's had been synonymous with Dumbarton as far back as 1811. By 1823 the company name had changed to William Denny & Son, whose first launch was the paddle steamer *Superb*. From 1845 the company became Denny Brothers, and in 1849 the firm was reconstituted as William Denny & Brothers, this being William, James and Peter Denny, a statue to whom stands proudly to this day in the gardens of the Municipal Buildings in the town's College Park Street. Although the Denny yard was situated near the junction of the River Clyde and the River Leven, the yard was on the Leven. The founder developed the company's interests in ship owning and operation with interests in the British & Burmese Steam Navigation Company, the Irrawaddy Flotilla Company and La Platense Flotilla.

The Company built all types of ships but were particularly well known as producers of fine cross-channel steamships and ferries. It was a pioneer in the development of the ship's stabiliser in conjunction with Edinburgh-based Brown Brothers & Company. In 1913, the Channel steamer *Paris* was one of the first ships to use geared turbine engines utilising new Mitchell tilting-pad fluid bearing. It also undertook experimental work in hovercraft and helicopter-type aircraft. A marine engineering company, also based in Dumbarton, was formed by Peter Denny, John Tulloch and John McAusland in 1850 as Tulloch & Denny. In 1862 the company was renamed Denny & Co. The company manufactured a wide range of types of marine engines and was absorbed into William Denny & Brothers in 1918. My own father, the late Douglas Hay, a former pupil of Dumbarton Academy, was one of many young men from Dumbarton to become marine engineers after being apprenticed at Denny's. Douglas joined the Merchant Navy and survived a remarkable three times when his ship was torpedoed and sunk during the Second World War.

There had been hopes that shipbuilding in Dumbarton would continue to thrive after the war. Denny's at first enjoyed a period of boom conditions with contracts for building merchant and passengers ships to replace those lost by U-boat sinkings and those too old for service. The Denny-Brown stabiliser and the hovercraft both showed Denny's in its traditional role as an initiator of new developments. But the difficulties besetting shipbuilding across Britain proved in the end fatal to the company, which closed down both shipyard and engine works suddenly in 1963. Not only Provost Campbell wept at the news which spread quickly through the town, where the workers were used to lay-offs when a ship was launched or went out on sea trials, but never to closure. More than 2,000 people were employed in the yard at one time and whole housing developments had been built for them at Dennystown in West Bridgend and Clyde and Leven Streets in the Newtown. The managers were housed in and around Knoxland Square and the directors in Oxhill and Kirktonhill. It was the worst of times for these families who watched their livelihoods sailing down the river with the launch of the last ship from Denny's yard. Dumbarton has never really recovered from that crushing blow which saw the beginning of the de-industrialisation of Clydeside on both banks of the river from Dumbarton to Glasgow.

Launches taking place at Denny's Leven shipyard in different eras.

Dennystown is pictured (bottom) from the air on the banks of the River Leven.

Barefoot children in Dennystown during the Hungry Thirties.

Dennystown Forge, Dalreoch Station, Dennystown, William Street and the Squares.

Ever anxious workers leaving after a day in the shipyards.

Former Our Lady and St Patrick's High School janitor Pat Connelly (right) and a mate working in Denny's shipyard.

Welders at Denny's shipyard, including Eddie McKinley and Davie Rainey, working on the ill-fated Irish ferry, Princess Victoria, in 1947. The ship sank with the loss of 133 lives in a storm off Stranraer in 1953.

The Denny Institute in Church Street, next door to the Lennox Herald office.

The Denny's ladies football team of the 1950 included Lily McAllister Shaw (second right, back row) and a member of the Trainer family, extreme right front row.

Chapter 5

THE MANAGERS

John T Robertson and Paddy O'Connell.

It is remarkable that two men with Dumbarton connections are writ large in the history of two of the world's most famous football clubs. One was Paddy O'Connell who played for Dumbarton just after the First World War and who later became manager of FC Barcelona. Paddy has been credited with saving the many times European champions from bankruptcy and extinction during the Spanish Civil War in 1935. It was while gathering information for an obituary on Stewart Campbell for the *Lennox Herald* that I discovered that his grand uncle, the Rangers and Scotland international John Tait Robertson was the first ever manager of Chelsea FC. Chelsea, which started from humble beginnings, were English Premier League champions, owned by the Russian oligarch Roman Abramovitch and managed by Josie Maurinho, the most controversial, outspoken and probably richest football manager in the world. He has now been signed up by Manchester United in controversial circumstances.

I have trawled through the Stamford Bridge club's history to find out about the Robertson connection. It appears that on the evening of 10 March, 1905, in an upstairs room at the Rising Sun pub, Chelsea FC was formed by a small group of men. Among the founding directors were millionaire owner Henry Augustus 'Gus' Mears, his brother Joseph, their brother-in-law Henry Boyer, publican Alfred Janes and his nephew Edwin, who ran the Rising Sun. The club was the brainchild of another founder, Frederick Parker, and started from scratch to fill Gus Mears's ambitious stadium project in Fulham, being built across the road by the famous architect Archibald Leitch. Robertson, who came from Dumbarton but appears not to have played for the then Boghead Park-based team, was engaged as the fledgling club's player-manager. In collaboration with Parker, who also engineered Chelsea's admission to Football League Division Two, Robertson constructed a squad, including larger-than-life goalkeeper Willie Foulke. Robertson was ordered to hire football's first ball-boys to emphasise the 23-stone goalkeeper's presence. Robertson was well acquainted with the game by this time. He played as a central defender and won 16 caps for his country, scoring three goals. Having started his career at Greenock Morton, Robertson moved to Everton and then Southampton before returning home to Rangers, where he won three consecutive league titles in his first three seasons. Robertson was the first player signed by Chelsea, in 1905, and he scored their first competitive goal. He made his debut for Scotland on 2 April, 1898, while at Everton, beating England 3–1.

John T Robertson of Rangers and Chelsea

His second cap came on 8 April of the following year, while at Southampton and all of his 14 remaining caps came during his time at Rangers. My friend, the late Stewart Campbell, a graphic designer who created the coat of arms of West Dunbartonshire, was rightly proud of the family's connection with Chelsea and was predictably interested in the design of their club badge. He said: 'Chelsea Football Club was formed by Scottish ex-pats living and working in London, hence the blue shirts and the lion rampant on the club badge.'

Success for Chelsea came spectacularly fast: the table-top clash with Manchester United on Good Friday 1906, attracted a staggering attendance of 67,000. Promotion to the First Division was achieved with Robertson in charge and in 1907 and over the ensuing campaign the newly nicknamed 'Pensioners' attracted the biggest crowds ever known in Britain. For the first few seasons the Chelsea players wore Eton Blue, the horse racing colours of club President Lord Cadogan, a much lighter hue than the shirts of today. Blue was, and is still, the colours of Robertson's old team, the famous Glasgow Rangers, and to this day Ibrox aficionados have a close association with Chelsea. In just a few short years the personality of Chelsea FC was being established by a club that was wealthy, ambitious, and fashionable and with immense drawing power.

John Tait Robertson, to give him his full name, was replaced by William Lewis and then David Calderhead and their heirs, most famously Tommy Docherty and Jose Mourinho. The fiery Portuguese hit the headlines again and again, almost as often as his strikers hit the crossbar, when he branded rival Premier League managers 'stupid'.

The so-called beautiful game has come a long way over the past century and football pitches, the ball and kit have changed beyond recognition. Mourinho has criticised those who he believes are overly-focused on their own philosophy and possession football. It's no longer a question of booting the ball up the park and hoping someone gets a head or a boot to it to score a goal.

'There is no new generation of managers,' Mourinho said. 'What it is, is people who have got some idea, some philosophy, and want to create something like, "we build very well from the back, we have a very good ball possession, and we don't play counter-attack". But if you don't play counter-attack then it's because you are stupid. Counter-attack is a fantastic item of football, an ammunition that you have, and when you find your opponent unbalanced you have a fantastic moment to score a goal. I think people are creating illusions and it has influenced public opinion. But football will never change. Football is to win.'

Jose Mourinho, the Manchester United manager, at a coaching session with Dumbarton man Stevie Woods, the goalkeeping coach for Glasgow Celtic.

I wonder what his predecessor John Tait Robertson, who cut his footballing teeth on Dumbarton Common, would have thought of that. Meanwhile, Barcelona FC has its heroes in spades with Messi, Naymar and Suarez right up there as the lodestars of world football, but they would be nowhere today were it not for a Dubliner who once played for Dumbarton FC.

Meanwhile, Barcelona FC has its heroes in spades with Messi, Naymar and Suarez right up there as the lodestars of world football, but they would be nowhere today were it not for a Dubliner who once played for Dumbarton FC. The story of Paddy O'Connell'sn journey from Boghead to Barcelona is both fascinating and tragic. He was born in March 1887, so there will be some people still alive who will have had this story passed down to them by local people who may even have watched him play for Dumbarton in the season 1918-19. There will almost certainly be still with us senior citizens who recall the colourful Paddy O'Connell being installed as first team coach at the Nou Camp in 1935. Paddy, who was a predecessor of the likes of Jose

Paddy O'Connell on the bench at FC Barcelona.

Mourinho, Pep Guardiola and the current head coach of the Barcelona squad, Luis Enrique, managed the team from 1935 - This was when he saved them from financial disaster and being wiped out under the regime of General Franco.

During the 1936-37 season La Liga was suspended because of the Spanish Civil War. However, clubs in the Republican area of Spain competed in the Mediterranean League and, under O'Connell, FC Barcelona won this title. During the summer of 1937, O'Connell took the club on tour to North America. In Mexico they played against, amongst others, Club America, Atlanta F.C. Necaxa and a Mexican XI. In the USA, they played against Brooklyn Hispano, Brooklyn St. Mary's Celtic, and an American Soccer League XI. They finished the tour with a game against a Hebrew XI. In financial terms this tour saved the club, but O'Connell managed to return to Catalonia with only four players after the others were forced by Franco's regime to go into exile in Mexico and France. By the 1937-38 season the Republican area was reduced in size and a second Mediterranean League was impossible to organise. However, a Liga Catalana, featuring just Catalan teams, was organised and, despite his depleted squad of players, O'Connell and FC Barcelona won both the Liga Catalana and the Campionat de

Catalunya. It is for these reasons, O'Connell is still remembered and honoured by the Catalans and FC Barcelona followers, who worship him as a hero. This is despite the fact that, like so many Irish and Scottish sporting stars of that era, Patrick O'Connell, who was also known as Don Patricio O'Connell, died destitute and alone from alcoholism in London in 1959, aged just 72.

During the early 1900s he had a distinguished career as a strong and talented defender, playing for various clubs in Ireland, England and Scotland. O'Connell captained Ireland and was a member of the team that won the 1914 British Home Championship. His success with Ireland saw him join Manchester United where he again became captain. After retiring as a player he moved to Spain where he managed a number of clubs and in 1935 he led Real Betis to their one and only La Liga title. O'Connell played as junior with Dublin team Stranville Rovers before joining Belfast Celtic. He then joined Sheffield Wednesday in 1908 and Hull City in 1912 before transferring for a season to Manchester United, making 34 league appearances and scoring twice. O'Connell signed for Leyton Orient in April, 1915, but the First World War interrupted his career. During the war he played as a guest player for both Rochdale A.F.C. and Chesterfield FC and, of course, Dumbarton, where he spent the 1919-20 season at Boghead Park.

In 1922 O'Connell was appointed manager of Racing de Santander. He subsequently guided the team to five regional titles and in 1928 they became founding members of La Liga This success attracted the interest of FC Barcelona who appointed him as successor to Franz Platko for the 1935-36 season when he guided them to the Campionat de Catalunya and the Copa de España final. O'Connell went on to manage Sevilla FC between 1943 and 1945 before serving a second term as Racing de Santander coach between 1947 and 1949. O'Connell's story is contained in an article for *El Pais* by the famous Spanish football expert Jimmy Burns who has also written a great deal about the Spanish Civil War with which the Dunbartonshire village of Renton has a special connection, about which you can read later in this book.

Burns wrote: 'Football in the Spanish-speaking world owes a great deal to foreigners, not least those of an Anglo-Saxon or Gaelic background. The game in South America and in Spain, like the railways and the mines, followed the flag of British colonialism with traders and colonisers of English, Scottish, Welsh, and Irish origin helping to form the first football clubs as part of their social engagement with the natives.

'While Latin American countries south of the Río Grande, led by Brazil and Argentina, would see a new home-grown style of football emerging from local talent, the involvement in Spanish football of Ingleses, as the northern foreigners came to be generically referred to, proved more enduring. Of those overseeing the development of clubs, nowadays associated with Spain's Primera Liga, few characters have earned as much belated recognition as Patrick O'Connell.'

Burns added: 'There is a sense in which O'Connell's life on the sharp political edge of Iberian football is a chronicle of a story foretold. It is difficult to separate his arrival in Barcelona in the 1930s from his birth into the Ireland of the 1880s. O'Connell was born into a working class family whose nationalist politics and emigration were influenced by the Irish potato famine of 1845-9. To this day little is known about O'Connell's background. It is safe to assume however that the fate of his relations on both sides of the Atlantic was sealed by the deeply disturbing events of those years.

'For the young Patrick, from the outset football provided both an escape and a sense of identity. He played as a junior for the Dublin team Stranville Rovers before joining Belfast Celtic during a period when the politics of sectarianism and religious bigotry were beginning to cast a long shadow across the island of Ireland.

'It was at Belfast Celtic during the early years of the 20th century that O'Connell began to make his mark as a tough and talented defender. The club was by then the leading light in Irish soccer, as popular if not more so than some of the more traditional Gaelic football teams. Founded in the traditionally Catholic Falls Road of Belfast in 1891, it was named after Glasgow Celtic which it wished to emulate in the style of its play and the passionate loyalty of its supporters. Football, or soccer, as they liked to call it, allowed working- class Irish nationalists to reach out across the Irish Channel, and find common cause with those of similar ancestral roots on the British mainland.'

However, as in politics, as in sport, so many careers end in disappointment. Despite famously captaining Ireland with a broken arm and being part of the team that won that 1914 Home Championship with ten men, O'Connell's stint at Manchester United coincided with a slump in the club's fortunes. It was on the eve of a match between Manchester United and Liverpool that O'Connell met up with a group of players from both sides in a pub and agreed to lay an 8-1 bet that United would win by 2-0. Jimmy Burns has revealed that this was indeed the score-line when it fell to O'Connell to take a penalty.

'He took the penalty and the ball went very wide. The day was Good Friday and no doubt a sense of guilt and subsequent contrition took hold of the still relatively young O'Connell. Years later his picaresque inventiveness reaped a rich reward at FC Barcelona. Yet on the eve of the so-called Great War, it brought him shame at Manchester United, even though he escaped criminal charges. Like millions of his generation, O'Connell subsequently had his controversial stay at the club brought to an abrupt end by the First World War …

'O'Connell managed to save himself from the worst horrors of the Belgian trenches, and played on throughout the rest of the war and its immediate aftermath in lesser known amateur clubs on both sides of the Scottish border, including two seasons as a 'collier' with the non-league Ashington AFC. This was one of the oldest clubs in Northumberland, where the legendary Charlton brothers, Jack and Bobby, would later begin their footballing careers as ball boys.'

Jimmy Burns was born in Madrid in 1953. His father, the late Tom Burns, met his mother Mabel Maranon while working in the British embassy in Madrid during the Second World War. His latest book is La Roja: a journey through Spanish football, is by a man who knows his subject inside out.

Chapter 6

THE RENTON

Smollett, the novelist, features on the welcome sign at Renton.

All the best places have 'The' in front of their name. The Gorbals in Glasgow, The Raploch in Stirling and *The* Renton in West Dunbartonshire are but three of them. These legendary places all have something in common. They have produced great sportsmen and writers, musicians and artists. World champion boxer Benny Lynch in the case of The Gorbals; Billy Bremner, the irascible but great football captain of Scotland and Leeds United, from The Raploch, and Alex Jackson, of the Wembley Wizards, who brought fame and recognition to The Renton. These places also share a colourful history of unemployment, poverty, immigration, deprivation – and achievement. Any Gaelic form of the name Gorbals is conjecture, but since none survives from medieval times, *Gort a' bhaile* (garden of the town) is the most popular of these.

In the 19th and 20th centuries, The Gorbals was home to large numbers of immigrants from the Scottish Highlands, Italy and Ireland, attracted by the work available from shipbuilding to textiles and factory work. It also housed the new wave of Jewish immigrants from eastern and central Europe, and was home to the great majority of Scotland's Jewish population. The Jewish population moved out of the area towards Whitecraigs and Newton Mearns as it rose in education and improved economic circumstances. Although the Irish-Catholic population of Gorbals has diminished to a great extent, many of them have remained there since the area was redeveloped with town houses and modern flats.

The Raploch or The Raptap as it is sometimes known in Stirling, is a council estate which came into being in the middle of the 20th century, when council housing replaced the decrepit accommodation in the old town. Billy Bremner is joined on The Raploch role of honour by Duncan Ferguson, who became the most expensive player to move between two British football clubs when he left Dundee United for Rangers for £4million in 1993. The Raploch was the subject of a 2002 BBC Scotland documentary presented by arts correspondent Pauline McLean, from Dumbarton, entitled *Raploch Stories*, and in a 2007 sequel *Raploch Stories Revisited*. Another Dumbarton connection with the Raploch has been through Francis Cummings, a marvellous musician and conductor, who was brought up in Brucehill, and went to school nearby at St Patrick's. In 2008 the Raploch became the home of the UK's first El Sistema children's orchestra, called *Big Noise Raploch*. Under Mr Cummings' direction, a children's orchestra with over 100 members, performed with Gustavo Dudamel and the Simón Bolívar Symphony Orchestra of Venezuela and on a BBC Scotland Christmas eve programme.

And then there is The Renton, birthplace of Tobias Smollett, father of the novel. Smollett was a poet and author, best known for his picaresque novels, such as *The Adventures of Roderick Random* (1748) and *The Adventures of Peregrine Pickle* (1751), which influenced later novelists such as Charles Dickens. George Orwell admired Smollett very much. Smollett was born at Dalquhurn, the fourth son of Archibald Smollett of Bonhill, a judge and land-owner who died about 1726, and Barbara Cunningham, who died about 1766. He was educated at the University of Glasgow, where he qualified as a surgeon. His career in medicine came second to his literary ambitions and in 1739 he went to London to seek his fortune as a dramatist. Unsuccessful, he obtained a commission as a naval surgeon on *HMS Chichester* and travelled to Jamaica, where he settled down for several years. In 1742, he served as a surgeon during the disastrous campaign to capture Cartagena. On his return, he set up practice in Downing Street and married a wealthy Jamaican heiress, Anne 'Nancy' Lascelles, in 1747.

Renton's Alex Jackson was perhaps the greatest footballer of his era, a hero for Scotland, Huddersfield and Chelsea – until, aged only 26, it all went wrong. He was the hat-trick- scoring hero of Scotland's greatest ever victory over England, considered by some the finest player in the world and named 'the most-discussed footballer of the century' by the *Mirror*, albeit after only a third of it.

He revolutionised the role of the winger, was traded for enormous fees, won league titles and scored in cup finals, and he was handsome, charismatic and wildly popular with supporters. Alex Jackson, in short, ascended to the very pinnacle of the sport. And then he fell.

Alex Jackson, the Wembley Wizard, behind the bar of his London public house.

The man they called The Gay Cavalier was only 26 when he played his last league game. By his 27th birthday he was turning out in the Cheshire County League, and though he generated plenty of headlines when his career was at its peak he earned little more than a footnote in the papers when he died, aged just 41. Jackson was born in Renton in 1905 -- 'Typical of hundreds of Scottish villages, Renton has been football-mad for generations,' Jackson wrote. 'It is just a small agricultural district where every boy and every girl plays football all year round. That football madness may seem somewhat crude to the civilised south, but there's no question that it bred footballers.' Two of these were in his family alone and Jackson spent a single season playing for Dumbarton before, in 1923, he and an older brother, Walter, travelled to the US to visit another sibling, John, and both ended up playing football there.

The *New York Times* reported from a match there that 'young Jackson showed the speed of a deer despite the condition of the field and his dexterous footwork enabled him to carry the ball to within striking distance of the goal several times.' Jackson signed for Aberdeen and then Huddersfield, the English champions, who got their man – ahead of Bolton, Everton, Aston Villa, Sunderland and Liverpool – for a club record fee of £5,000 and one big bar bill. Before the deal went through the Huddersfield manager and future Arsenal legend, Herbert Chapman, travelled to Renton to get the blessing of the player's father. 'When all the business had been done, Chapman and my father went to the only pub in town to seal the contract with a nice glass of Scotch,' Jackson told the French magazine *Paris Match* several years later.

The Central Bar in Main Street, Renton.

The 'only pub in town' was the Central Bar in Main Street which is today still standing and serving drinks to the villagers and anglers, who fish the nearby River Leven. Alex Jackson, who became a publican himself in London, added: 'The entire population of the village, upon learning that such a famous man was in town, went down to the pub to see him. Mr Chapman, generous as always, made a sweeping gesture with his hand, inviting everyone for a drink. And, according to old Scottish custom, everyone ordered a whisky and a pint of beer. Mr Chapman might have drunk the finest champagne in all the Ritz Hotels of the world, but I'm certain that he never bought a more expensive round of drinks.'

From one artist of the greatest game in the world to another artist, who creates remarkable work with a paint brush, a canvas and a palette of oils. Stephen Conroy, because he lived in a local authority house in Station Street, Renton, became known as 'the council house painter,' but what a remarkable painter he is. He hit the newspaper headlines when Bob Geldof took a liking to his work and came to Renton with a view to purchasing some of it. Conroy, who went to St Patrick's High School, where he was mentored by art teacher John Lyons, is what is called a contemporary Scottish figurative painter. He was born at Braeholm in Helensburgh, in 1964, and studied at the Glasgow School of Art between 1982 and 1987. By 1989, Conroy's work had already gained much recognition and praise in the United Kingdom and internationally. The artist has remained in Scotland, where he currently lives and works from a studio at the house which he shares with his mother, Elizabeth and sister, Ele[illegible] overlooking the River Clyde in Cardross.

One of the highlights of his career is that in 1998, Conroy won the Grand Prize of Rainier III, Prince of Monaco. He is represented by the distinguished London gallery Marlborough Fine Art, and through the gallery has had solo exhibitions in London, Manchester, Glasgow, New York and Madrid, and has shown in museums in Aix-en- Provence and Johannesburg. I am delighted to say I have been to one of these exhibitions, but I am disappointed not to be up there with Bob Geldof and the Aberdeen oil magnate Sir Ian Wood as one of the proud owners of a Stephen Conroy painting. I am though the proud possessor of some of the work of his father, Stevie, who was a welder in John Brown's shipyard in Clydebank and an excellent caricaturist whose work decorates a few houses, public and private, in Dunbartonshire. Stevie used to draw cartoons and caricatures on the bulkheads of the great ships on which he was working in John Brown's shipyard. Some of these must still be there today, a floating gallery sailing the seven seas unseen in dark corners of the hold. Stephen Conroy's work is part of a number of public and private collections including The British Council, London; The Contemporary Art Society, London; Frissiras Museum, Athens; The Metropolitan Museum of Art, New York; National Portrait Gallery, London; Robert Fleming Holdings Ltd., London; The Royal College of Surgeons of England; Scottish National Gallery of Modern Art, Edinburgh; Scottish National Portrait Gallery, Edinburgh, and the Whitworth Art Gallery in Manchester.

Artist Stephen Conroy photographed in his place of work.
Picture by Eleanor Conroy.

Chapter 7

THE WORLD CUP

The World Cup won by Renton.

Why are you so good? I think it was my former colleague Jim White, a sports presenter on Sky Television who asked this remarkable question of the Rangers' star player, Brian Laudrup. Or maybe it was Hazel Irvine, a starry-eyed young commentator at the time, who asked it of Ally McCoist, also of Rangers. It sounds daft, but then again, why are some footballers so good compared with so many others who are, as the fans would have it, duff, red rotten, dirty, slow or clueless? These are just a few of the unkind adjectives – often accompanied by expletives – which filter their way down from the terracing and grandstands and even into our living rooms via radio and television. One of the stories attached to Renton's world championship winning team of 1888 is that their success was down to its diet. The players were said to be fed on 'chicken bree,' a heady mixture of free range chicken soup, barley and a generous glass or ten of sherry or other 'fortified wine'.

There has been a great deal in the *Lennox Herald* in recent times about Renton and its footballing history, but Valeman David Currie, of BBC Scotland's sports desk in Glasgow, seems to have captured the actuality of what happened in an insightful article on BBC Scotland's website. David says football's first World Championship trophy is an unimpressive piece of work. It is around a foot high and made of inexpensive pewter. The trophy's permanent home, as one would expect, is somewhat grander - a museum dedicated to the game in one of football's sporting cathedrals. But what's it doing in the Scottish Football Museum at Hampden Park? The trophy was won by the Dunbartonshire village team of Renton in 1888 in the heyday of the amateur game in Scotland. Renton were one of several in the Dumbarton area - others include the Vale of Leven and Dumbarton. Sandy McBain of the Scottish Football Museum outlines one reason for the popularity of football in the area.

He said: 'Queens Park did an exhibition game in the area and perhaps the locals decided it was a better game than rugby. They would also have seen that football was a simpler game; whatever the reason football was extremely popular in Dunbartonshire.' Renton, Dumbarton and the Vale of Leven were all early winners of the Scottish Cup. Indeed it was Renton's 6-1 thrashing of Cambuslang in the cup final of 1888 that started them on the road to becoming the first world champions. According to the myth that now surrounds the story, Renton were challenged to a match by the English FA Cup winners West Bromwich Albion. Whatever the circumstances, a game was subsequently arranged to determine who were the 'Champions of the United Kingdom and the World'. The venue was Lesser Hampden at Cathkin Park, home of Third Lanark no more. The date: the 19 May 1888, although the match nearly didn't take place at all.

Sports specialists David Currie (left) and the late Bob Crampsey.

David Currie writes: 'Newspapers of the time report that the game was played in the foulest of conditions. A thunder storm had wreaked havoc in Glasgow, claiming the lives of four people. Perhaps, unsurprisingly, West Brom wanted the game postponed - but the hardy Rentonians insisted the game go ahead.' Around 6,000 spectators watched the Renton dark blues beat their challengers by four goals to one. Two of Renton's goals were scored by the McCall brothers, Jamie and Archie - both Scottish internationals. Indeed, Renton's dominance of the Scottish game in 1888 is highlighted by the fact that eight of the team represented Scotland that year. Renton also beat both Sunderland and Preston in 1888. Perhaps they were justified in describing themselves as champions of the United Kingdom - with apologies to Wales and Ireland, pre-partition of course. But Champions of the World?

Historian and broadcaster, the late Bob Crampsey was not convinced: 'The claim has been vastly overplayed. It started off as a bit of a joke. After all, if you don't play anyone else how can you be Champions of the World?' Crampsey said: 'Market forces entered football. Professionalism entered the sport and players began to gravitate towards metropolitan teams both in Scotland and down south. Even before the advent of professionalism, players could be lured away with the promise of well-paid jobs arranged by the bigger clubs. There are even stories around that English scouts would be giving a good soaking in the local river if they were seen sniffing around a match in Scotland.'

In the same year as Renton were crowned 'World Champions' one of the Scottish game's biggest clubs was born in the East End of Glasgow. And soon two of Renton's star players were on their way to Celtic, as Neil McCallum and James Kelly swapped the dark blue of Renton for green and white hoops. Renton soldiered on, however. They were one of the founder members of the football league in 1890, although they were expelled after just a handful of games. That was because they had played a friendly match against a 'professional' team, the Edinburgh Saints. Renton were re-admitted the following season and continued as a Scottish Football League side until 1898 when they resigned from the league. Twenty four years later they folded completely. Renton's place in Scottish football's history is but a brief chapter. Their story is one of a village team triumphant in an age of amateurism, yet unable to survive long after the birth of professionalism. The club's legacy is part myth, part historical fact. But worthy of a place in the Scottish Football Museum.

Even today the Renton question keeps coming up in pub quiz games. Carol Eastaugh, nee O'Neill, told friends on social media: 'My brother used to often win bets in Scottish and English pubs when he posed the question of who won the first World Cup. He said he always paid for his pints courtesy of that piece of football trivia.' A Dumbarton fan tried to steal Renton's thunder. Gordon Kirkpatrick said: 'It should be noted that in 1883, following Dumbarton's Scottish Cup win, they played Blackburn Olympic, the new English cup holders, and beat them 6-1, preceding Renton's achievement by five years. The only difference being that Dumbarton FC did not proclaim themselves world champions.' Modest as ever, or what?

Renton Football Team

"Champions of the World"

R. Kelso, half-back A. Hannah, back J. Lindsay, Goal A. McCall (Captain), back D. McKechnie, half-back
N. McCallum and H. Campbell, right-wing J. Kelly, centre half back J. Campbell, centre J. McCall and J. McNee, left-wing
Winners of the Scottish and Glasgow Charity Cups

Renton football team 'Champions of the World' pictured are R Kelso, half back, A Hannah, back, J Lindsay, goal, A McCall, captain, back, D McKechnie, half back, N McCallum and H Campbell, right wing, J Kelly, centre half back, J Campbell, centre, J McCall and J McNee, left wing. Winners of the Scottish and Glasgow Charity Cups.

Pictures by courtesy of West Dunbartonshire Libraries.

Renton in the away strip.

Chapter 8

THE BROTHERS

Hugh Ryden, brought up in the shadow of the Smollett monument.

Snowy was the nickname given to Hugh, the youngest of the footballing Ryden brothers from Renton. But it could easily have applied to all three, John, George and Hugh, a hat-trick of handsome, six-foot soccer stars of the Fifties and Sixties. The Rydens, all of whom had striking blond, almost white, hair made it all the way from Dunbartonshire schools football to the highest echelons of senior football in Scotland and England.

George was so famous at Dundee FC that he was invited to sing along with his namesake George Harrison, plus John Lennon, Ringo Starr and Paul McCartney, when the Beatles visited Dundee. He joined his Dens Park team-mate Hugh Robertson, who 'borrowed' George Harrison's guitar, at Caird Hall for a photo call with Liverpool's finest at the east coast city's Caird Hall. Those were the days when the Vale of Leven, Renton and Dumbarton produced so many good players that it was known far and wide as 'the cradle of Scottish football'. Renton were once declared champions of the world and the most famous player ever to grace the Tontine turf was none other than Alex Jackson of the Wembley Wizards. Jackson was the hat-trick-scoring hero of Scotland's greatest ever victory over England, considered by some the finest player in the world and named 'the most-discussed footballer of the century' by the Daily Mirror. He revolutionised the role of the winger, was traded for enormous fees, won league titles and scored in cup finals, and he was handsome, charismatic and wildly popular with supporters. Alex Jackson, in short, ascended to the very pinnacle of the sport. The Ryden brothers, who followed in Jackson's footsteps, weren't half bad either, especially John who had the chalice of greatness dashed from his lips when Bill Nicholson became manager of Tottenham Hotspur.

John, who died in 2013, was a stalwart of the White Hart Lane team in 1950s and was the team captain. Pundits said he was 'within touching distance of footballing immortality – but it passed him by 'when Nicholson took over from Jimmy Anderson as manager of the north Londoners, and the new manager rated Ryden as no more than an ordinary centre-half. He therefore excluded the big Scot from his plans as he constructed the beautiful team which, in 1960-61, would become the first in the 20th century to lift the League and FA Cup double, captained by none other than Danny Blanchflower. John Ryden had made his entry to the senior game as a part-timer with Scottish second-tier club Alloa Athletic in 1950, spending three mid-table seasons at Recreation Park and compiling a century of appearances before a £1,000 deal took him across the border to Accrington Stanley of the Third Division North in February 1954. The hardy, industrious local man flourished at Peel Park and, after 80 consecutive League outings, he was sold to Spurs for £8,500, a colossal sum to impecunious Stanley. Ryden made a bright start in the top flight, deputising for the injured veteran stopper Harry Clarke at Preston in April 1956 and scoring one of his rare goals in a 3-3 draw.

John Ryden, skipper of Tottenham Hotspur, and one of the finest players to come out of Renton.

He was granted his first settled run in the team before being displaced by the younger Maurice Norman, who was bigger, younger and destined to play for England. For 1957-58 he bounced back, replacing Tony Marchi as captain and making 35 appearances, easily the most of his Tottenham career, as Spurs finished a creditable third in the title race. But clouds were looming on Ryden's horizon and though he played and scored in the first game of the Nicholson regime – a remarkable 10-4 home triumph over Everton – soon the No 5 shirt was handed to the rapidly improving Norman. Ryden was tough, tenacious and dedicated, but Nicholson was not sufficiently impressed, and after Dave Mackay was recruited from Hearts in March 1959 there was no way back for the Renton man. He remained at White Hart Lane as a reserve until summer 1961 when, with Tottenham celebrating their historic double, he moved to Third Division Watford. Later John Ryden, a popular, modest man, lived in Kent and worked in the finance industry and insurance industry in London.

George Ryden (back row) with John, Paul, George and Ringo and team-mate, Hugh Robertson, on the guitar.

Pictures by courtesy of DC Thomson, Dundee

George Ryden, who is 75, played for Dundee, St Johnstone and Stirling Albion, and was in the Dens Park team which took part in the 1964 Scottish Cup Final, which they lost 3–1 to Rangers. This was a classic tie that was watched by 120,982 spectators on the first occasion that Dundee and Rangers had met each other in a Scottish Cup Final.

Few would dispute that the Dundee side of the early Sixties, of which George Ryden was an integral part, was the finest in the Club's 150 year history. League Champions in 1961/62 and European Cup semi-finalists the following year, their Scottish Cup quarter-final with Rangers in 1963 had been almost universally regarded as the 'final before the final'. Two controversial and dramatic ties were finally decided by a last minute winner from Ralph Brand at an Ibrox Stadium packed with 81,190 spectators inside and thousands more locked outside. This was the Dark Blue side of legends such as Alex Hamilton, Bobby Cox, Andy Penman, Alan Cousin and Alan Gilzean while Rangers had the likes of Jim Baxter, John Greig, Willie Henderson, Jimmy Millar and Davie Wilson, who later became manager of Dumbarton FC, in their ranks. Hugh Ryden, the youngest of the brothers all three of whom went to St Patrick's High School in Dumbarton, played as an inside forward for Bristol Rovers, Stockport County, Chester City and Halifax Town. Hugh said: 'I had four older brothers who were my football idols. There was Tommy, John, Eddie, George and myself. Tommy and Eddie played at junior level in Scotland which is open-age football, just below the professionals, and John and George played at the highest level.'

Chapter 9

THE ROOTER

John Madden in Scotland cap and football shirt.

Here is a question for the people who still attend football matches or who enjoy a pub quiz. Try it on the person standing next to you at Millburn or in the stand at the Rock or Parkhead or Ibrox: Who scored Celtic's first ever goal and is buried in the grounds of Bonhill Parish Church in Alexandria? Follow it up with this one: Who kicked the first ball in the first official match in Celtic's history? The answer to the first question is that it was a Valeman, Neilly McCallum, who once played for Renton, and the second that it was a Son of the Rock, Johnny Madden, who played for Dumbarton before signing for Celtic. Both men were in the team for Celtic's inaugural match against a Rangers XI, the Inauguration match of 28 May, 1888, which Celtic won 5-2. The expert source for information on these two very famous footballers is Tom O'Neill, formerly of Poindfauld and Westcliff and now of Woodyard Road, Dumbarton.

Tom has also drawn my attention to a story which will raise eyebrows in Old Firm circles and is right up there with Maurice Johnston and Alfie Conn, who played for both Celtic and Rangers. It seems that Madden posed as a Rangers player to get himself a job in Prague. Up until World War One, situated in Bohemia, Prague had been part of the Austro-Hungarian Empire. Founded in the late 1800s, Slavia, which eventually became a multi-sports club, had its roots in a Czech Nationalist oratorical society. Slavia claim to be the first honorary member of the English FA, and also to be the only football club in the world that still wears its original match day strip. In 1988 reporting on a ceremony to mark the 40th anniversary of

his death, a Prague newspaper posed the question as to how, Madden, described as 'this average Scot' came to be involved with Slavia. A club historian speculated that Madden had been recommended to Slavia by an Englishman, George Payne, who as well as having business interests in Prague, had, in the late 1890s, been a team mate of Madden's at Tottenham Hotspur. Madden had a business card.

John Madden and that Rangers business card.

The card itself, with its 'John Madden Glasgow Rangers' legend, lends credence to a story from nearer home. In late 1904, Slavia were in the market for a Scottish coach, preferably John Tait Robertson of Rangers. Born in Dumbarton High Street, Robertson, with hopes of a career in journalism, was not particularly interested in a job in Prague. Apparently Madden, Robertson and Finlay Speedie, another Dumbarton man with Rangers connections, colluded to deceive Slavia. Finlay Speedie was the uncle of Mrs Annie McKay of Brucehill Road, wife of Joe McKay and mother of Christopher and Archie, who died aged 102. Madden was photographed dressed in a Rangers' jersey and international cap belonging to either Speedie or Robertson and made off to Prague with this 'proof 'of his Rangers identity. Around about 1910, Robertson became the first professional manager of Chelsea. Eventually as coach of the Rapide and MTK clubs of Vienna and Budapest, he met up with Madden on the continent where Madden informed him that coaching in Prague was infinitely preferable to hammering down hot rivets in a Clydeside shipyard. Robertson's story is contained in chapter 4 of this book. But back to McCallum. Vale historian Willie Scobie tells us that when he retired from work with the local council, he was engaged by the Rev Ian Miller to write a history of Bonhill Parish Church. He said: 'It was while researching this with the help of the librarian, we located a copy of the Lennox Herald from the 13th of November, 1920, in which there was to be found the obituary of one Neilly McCallum. McCallum had been a Bonhill man who played outside-right for the Renton on that glorious day when they beat English Cup-Winners, West Bromwich Albion, to become 'Champions of the World'. Neilly promptly left the Renton to join the formative Glasgow Celtic. The club's first game had been against the Rangers and McCallum had truly scored the first goal in Celtic's history. According to the obituary he had died at the age of 51 … and he was buried in Bonhill churchyard.' At that time, there was no room for him at Our Lady and St Mark's burial place.

Willie said: 'I urgently availed myself of a photocopy of this precious report. Quite apart from its obvious significance in terms of sporting history, and the importance with which it would be regarded by the Celtic-supporting element of the Scottish populace, there was an amazing coincidental factor which enhanced this story. By some strange chance it so happened that the minister at Bonhill was probably the only genuine Celtic-supporting Church of Scotland minister in the land. I couldn't wait to hear what he made of this. Less than an hour later, I sat in the cramped and cluttered church office. My minister was absolutely delighted in a kind of too-good-to-be-true sort of way. He scratched his head, scrutinised the obituary for the third time and put a hand to his chin in a thoughtful gesture and said I suppose this could be of some local interest.'

Renton man Alec Brady, who played for Celtic and Everton.

Understatement wasn't the word for it. Church member Willie said: 'Ian, this story will make the nationals.' The Rev Ian swung around on his chair and threw a questioning glance at Alice, the church secretary. She said: 'I think Willie's right, Ian.' So that's how the Church of Scotland minister and Willie Scobie came to be standing in the churchyard waiting to be interviewed for BBC Scotland. Ian Miller and Eddie Docherty, of the local council's Cemeteries Department, managed to find Neilly McCallum's unmarked grave and sometime later a tasteful stone was placed there by the Celtic Graves Society in a quiet and dignified ceremony. Celtic Lisbon Lions Jim Craig and Stevie Chalmers attended that service conducted by Father Martin Kane, then of St Patrick's, Dumbarton. Jim Craig was back in the village again recently to honour another Renton footballer.

It is not for nothing that the Vale of Leven village of Renton is known as the cradle of Scottish football. Alec Brady was honoured by the Celtic Graves Society, who came to the village to commemorate the life and mark the final resting place of one of the Renton soccer legends. The poignant event took place at tiny Millburn Cemetery in the village Main Street kirkyard, where the now abandoned Renton Parish Church has crumbled to a pile of grey sandstone rubble and the graves have for years been neglected and overgrown. The event was held in conjunction with the Everton FC Heritage Society – Alec Brady also played for the Liverpool club - and members of the Brady family were represented. Members of the Brady family, whose last home in Renton was in Hall Street, included John Brady and his wife, Margo, of Alexandria; Stephen Brady, Pat Brady, Sister Elizabeth Brady SND, formerly head teacher of St Michael's PS in Dumbarton's West End; Jackie Black and Mark Brady, who works at the Clyde Naval Base at Faslane. Renton councillor Jim Bollan and the Rev Ian Miller, of Bonhill Parish Church, a life-long Celtic supporter, were also present in the large gathering of friends, relatives and Celtic fans. Alec Brady was a former Everton forward who moved to Scotland in 1891 to join Celtic, and his signing was a major coup for the then fledgling Glasgow club. He had already won the English League Championship with Everton in 1891 – the first time they had won the title – before he helped Celtic to their first ever Scottish Cup triumph in 1892, scoring six goals during that campaign. In total, he played 24 games for the Celts, scoring 10 goals before he moved back to England, joining Sheffield Wednesday where he helped them win the FA Cup for the first time in 1896. He returned to Scotland in 1899, joining Clydebank before moving to Renton two years later. He died in 1913 at the age of just 43. Alec Brady was born in Glasgow in April, 1870, and moved to Renton with his family. He was a man of many clubs and played inside forward for Newcastle West End, Sunderland, Burnley, Everton, Celtic, Sheffield Wednesday and Renton, who were Champions of the World in 1888.

Lisbon Lion Jim Craig with the family of Alex Brady in Millburn Churchyard, Renton. Picture by Colin Garvie

He began his career with his local junior side Renton Thistle and played for various clubs before, in August 1989 Brady he was persuaded to join Everton by their then captain Andrew Hannah, who was also Renton. However a dispute with his player registration meant he was given a two month suspension. After scoring twice on his debut against Stoke and a hat-trick in the 11-2 win against Derby in the FA Cup, Everton's record victory they narrowly missed out on winning the league trophy to Preston North End. In his second season with Everton they were crowned English League Champions. In 1891, Alex was lured back to Scotland to play for Celtic in the second Scottish Football League Championship. Despite narrowly missing out on the league title to Dumbarton, Celtic went on to win the Scottish Cup, the clubs first ever major trophy. Brady spent just one season at Celtic before moving to Sheffield Wednesday for seven seasons. He was a part of the Wednesday side that won the FA Cup in 1896, making Brady one of the first players to win both the Scottish and English trophies at a time when they were considered the pinnacle of football competitions.

He returned Scotland to play with Clydebank in 1899 before returning to his hometown team, Renton where he ended his playing career. And so we return to John William Madden, who was also known as Jake Madden, Johnny Madden and The Rooter, the last a nickname because the centre forward hit the ball so hard that he once uprooted a goalpost. April 2016 saw the 70th anniversary of the death in Prague of John Madden, who was born in Dumbarton and played for Grimsby Town, Dundee, Dumbarton, Celtic and Scotland. Madden, who to this day has relatives in Dumbarton – the Quinns, McQuades, McGinns and many others –was the first man to ever lead a Celtic forward line. Prior to Celtic, he was a riveter in the shipyards, most probably Denny's in Dumbarton. Madden is a legend in what is now the Czech Republic. He is regarded by some as 'the Father of Czech football'. His dressing room reign is seen as the great era in the history of Slavia. Madden brought over new tactics and views on football from Scotland which helped to cement the club's progress. He was one of the first Scottish players to work as a coach on the European continent, and was said to be a disciplinarian who stopped players smoking and drinking before and after matches, while pushing them to train with gymnastic and athletic exercises. He managed to set up a golden age for the club for a long 25 years, where, under Madden, Slavia won an incredible 134 domestic matches from a possible 169. In June, 1930, Madden retired from Slavia and professional football at the age of 66, though he remained in Prague for the rest of his life. Remarkably, he was still coaching teams from his wheelchair at 73. He spoke fluent Czech after just 12 months in Prague and married a local woman, Francesca Chekhov. He almost lost his ability to speak English because he had been out of the country for so long.

The Madden-driven revolution of Czech football was no accident. As a player, Johnny had always kept himself at the peak of physical fitness. Over the years, the self-taught Madden trained ballet dancers, tennis and ice hockey players to be utterly as fit as required in their various spheres. He was years ahead of his time in matters of physiotherapy and football psychology. Madden was fastidious in personal appearance and always dressed in the latest styles from Britain.

John Madden (left) pictured with his Slavia team that had just won the league championship, was the first man to kick a ball for Celtic FC against the Old Firm.

Olsany Cemetery Prague. Members of Slavia's youth team, flank Madden's coffin.

John Madden (left front) and Neilly McCallum (second right) in the Celtic team, which beat Rangers in the first Old Firm match.

He applied the same meticulousness to coaching and training. He designated rest days between matches. For routine training sessions, players' boots had to be properly laced-up, the pitch accurately lined and goal nets hung whenever possible. Individual training regimes were laid down in writing for different members of the squad. Oddly enough, Johnny, the fitness fanatic, thought nothing wrong with standing in the dressing room issuing pre-match instructions while puffing on his chibouk (pipe). John William Madden, once of the High Street in Dumbarton, remains a hero in Prague, where on anniversary of his death the 'Friends of Slavia' put flowers on his grave in the rambling Olsany cemetery as a mark of respect and remembrance. Willie Maley Celtic's first manager claimed that a major feat of his club's early days, was that of becoming the first side to defeat the four Dunbartonshire teams, Alexandria, Dumbarton, Renton and Vale of

Leven in one season, Madden never acquired a Scottish Cup winner's medal. However, in 1893, he was a regular in the Celtic side that won three League Championships in the early 1890s.

A huge turnout of mourners attended John Madden's funeral.

Slavia player Kubik lays flowers on the 40th anniversary of Madden's death.

John Madden with son, Harry, and wife, Francesca Chekhov and the immaculately kept grave of John Madden in Olsanay Cemetery, Prague.

Pictures courtesy Tom O'Neill and Elizabeth McQuade

Page 67.

1865. BIRTHS in the Burgh of Dumbarton in the County of Dumbarton

No.	Name and Surname. (1)	When and Where Born. (2)	Sex. (3)	Name, Surname, & Rank or Profession of Father. Name, and Maiden Surname of Mother. Date and Place of Marriage. (4)	Signature and Qualification of Informant, and Residence, if out of the House in which the Birth occurred. (5)	When and Where Registered, and Signature of Registrar. (6)
109	Robert Boyle	1865 June Twelfth 5h 0m a.m. 46 High St. Dumbarton	M.	John Boyle Ship Carpenter (Journeyman) Margaret Boyle M.S. Drennan 1863, July 22nd Millisle, County Down (Ireland)	Jn Boyle Father (Present)	1865 June 13th at Dumbarton Wm Jardine Registrar
200	John Madden	1865 June Eleventh 3h 0m a.m. 71 High St. Dumbarton	M.	Edward Madden Engine Keeper Agnes Madden M.S. Avery 1847 April County Derry (Ireland)	Edward Madden His + Mark Father (Present) Wm Jardine Registrar Witness	1865 June 14th at Dumbarton Wm Jardine Registrar
201	Felix Beattie	1865 June Tenth 0h 30m a.m. 156 High St. Dumbarton	M.	Felix Beattie Boiler Maker (Apprentice) Rose Beattie M.S. Scullion 1852 County Derry	Felix Beattie His + Mark Father Wm Jardine Registrar Witness	1865 June 14th at Dumbarton Wm Jardine Registrar

John Madden's birth certificate from 1865 when he was registered in Dumbarton. His mother was from Derry in the North of Ireland. Sharp-eyed Dumbarton people will note that the name immediately below Madden's is that of Felix Beattie, whose family owned a well-known slater and plasterer business in Church Street, Dumbarton.

Chapter 10

THE QUIET MAN

Maureen O'Hara at *The Quiet Man* cottage and her sister, Peggy, who worked at St Margaret's Hospice in Clydebank.

Who doesn't remember going to 'the pictures' on a Friday night and on a Saturday? In those halcyon days of the 1950s, we had four cinemas in Dumbarton – the Picture House in High Street, the Rialto in College Street, the Regal in Church Street and the La Scala in Glasgow Road. On Saturday mornings we also had the ABC Minors in College Street and, if you were flush, or had run into by design rather than accident, a generous uncle, in my case it was my Uncle Jock, walking down the Vennel, then you might have the money for a matinee. He always kept a single shilling in his waistcoat pocket for me. When that occasional but memorable event came to pass you could jouk through Kane's Pend and down MacInnes the Butcher's Close to the Picture House in the High Street. And, if you were really lucky, John Wayne or Maureen O'Hara, or both, would be starring on the big screen that afternoon. For me it was a case of good luck heaped on good fortune since I might get in for nothing since I had a relation who worked there. Annie McKinney, my mother's cousin, was an usherette in the Picture House and if the cashier, Elsie

Scullion, was in good form we got the nod to take our free seats in the balcony. Ecstasy would be piled on good fortune when Annie came round with her tray at the interval and gave each of us one of those big ice lollies from Lyons Maid. We thought we had died and woke up in heaven. Angels might look heavenly but even more attractive to my ten year old eyes was Maureen O'Hara. I saw her in *The Quiet Man*, which had people queuing for metaphorical miles along Artizan and down the High Street to watch herself and the Duke, the inimitable John Wayne. The queue in Artizan past Cooper's grocery shop and the old Town Clock – it used to be on the wall there, facing towards the Bridge - was inevitably the longest since that was the line-up for the (cheaper) seats in the stalls. The High Street queue, which sometimes stretched on a good day past Sam Graham the Baker's and maybe even as far as Cocozza's Central Café was for seats in the more expensive balcony. All these memories came rushing back when in 2016 Maureen O'Hara sadly died aged 95 at her home in Boise, Idaho, USA, and I was writing her obituary for the Scotsman and the *Connacht Tribune* in Ireland. Almost always when I am writing anything at all, I come across and interesting local angle for my articles in the *Lennox Herald*. The Maureen O'Hara story was no exception. Not only did she appear frequently in our midst to colour our memories here, O'Hara's sister, Peggy, was a nun who helped the Irish Sisters of Charity to pioneer the hospice movement in Clydebank. The St Margaret of Scotland Hospice celebrated its 60th birthday in 2016 and was praised globally for the magnificent work it does for the people from West Dunbartonshire. A good friend told me about this connection when Maureen O'Hara's name came up in conversation just days before her death. He said asked if I knew that Maureen O'Hara's sister worked at the Hospice and that she had the same stunning good looks. If anything she was even more attractive than her film star sister. I contacted Sister Rita Dawson at St Margaret's who confirmed that Sister Margaret Mary Fitzsimons had indeed worked there – 'I think she was one of the first to go to Scotland. She used come here whenever she was over on holiday.'

Who would have thought then that while we sat spellbound in the stalls at the Picture House watching *The Quiet Man* - or stamping our feet and singing *The Shores of Tripoli* with John Wayne - that Maureen O'Hara's sister was up the road in Clydebank nursing our sick and dying relations and friends? Like her sisters and brothers, Peggy Fitzsimons, who died in California, was born in Dublin in May 1919. Sister. Margaret Mary was the name she chose when she joined the Sisters of Charity in 1938. She worked in both Ireland and Scotland before going to the United States, where she came to California in 1957, and ministered as a teacher and principal in St. Cornelius School in Long Beach and other schools until 1968. In 1978, Sister Margaret Mary earned her certification and began her work as administrator of Marycrest Manor, a skilled nursing facility in Culver City, and served there until 1988, after which she worked in development for Marycrest Manor until 2003. In failing health, she became a resident of the nursing home in 2007, where she died March 9, 2013. A friend said of Sister Margaret Mary, who must have been known to many local families: 'She was known as a kind and gracious woman who gave her life in service to others. She was proud of her Irish heritage and spent over seventy-five years of her life as a Religious Sister of Charity serving the people of God with great love and respect.'

Sister Margaret Mary looks from her photograph to be a kindly, quiet and reserved woman, unlike Maureen whose nicknames included Big Red, the Pirate Queen and the Queen of Technicolor, which she was in an era when there were many princesses around competing for that crown. Maureen was born on August 17, 1920. Her mother, Marguerita Lilburn FitzSimons, was an accomplished contralto. Her father, Charles FitzSimons, managed a business in Dublin and also owned part of the renowned Shamrock Rovers football team. The film star to be was the second of six FitzSimons children - Peggy, Florrie, Charles F. FitzSimons, Margot Fitzsimons and James O'Hara completed the family. In her personally approved biography, she said she loved playing rough athletic games as a child and excelled in sports. She combined this interest with an equally natural gift for performing. In 1968 Maureen found personal happiness when she married General Charles Blair, who was a famous aviator whom she had known as a friend of her family for many years. Blair was the real-life version of what John Wayne had been on the screen. He had been a Brigadier General in the Air Force, a Senior Pilot with Pan American, and held many incredible record-breaking aeronautic achievements. Maureen retired from films in 1973 after making the TV movie *The Red Pony*

(1973) and with Blair, she managed Antilles Airboats, a commuter sea plane service in the Caribbean. She not only made trips around the world with her pilot husband, but owned and published a magazine, writing a monthly column for it. Tragically, Charles Blair died in a plane crash in 1978. People will remember her as one of the most beautiful women in the world in the 20th century. Her vivid auburn hair, sparkling green eyes, perfect white teeth, generous red lips, flawless features and hour-glass figure made her the queen of the cinema. Apart from *The Quiet Man*, in which the chemistry between O'Hara and her co-star Wayne was enough to melt the ice creams of the patrons in the stalls in the Picture House, she made a total of five movies with Wayne, whom she admired and adored. O'Hara once said: 'I was tough. I was tall. I was strong. I didn't take any nonsense from anybody. He was tough, he was tall, he was strong and he didn't take any nonsense from anybody. As a man and a human being, I adored him.' She was as forthright in real life as she was passionate on screen. She trained at the Abbey Theatre in Dublin and was spotted, after a London screen test by Charles Laughton. Her first film was *Jamaica Inn*, made in 1938 and directed by Alfred Hitchcock. Laughton was so pleased with her performance that he cast her opposite him in *The Hunchback of Notre Dame* in 1939. She then starred in *How Green Was My Valley*, which won the 1941 Academy Award for Best Picture. Six years later she made *Miracle on 34th Street*, which became a Christmas Day classic. O'Hara loved the Irish and the Irish loved her, especially the Irish at home and the millions who are part of the diaspora in Scotland, across Europe and the United States and Australia for whom *The Quiet Man* has become a cult movie. The New York Fire Brigade have it on hand for watching through their breaks. *The Quiet Man* cottage, located at Maam Cross in Connemara, which featured in the film, was at the centre of a planning row when proposals to demolish it were revealed in the press. It was saved however after a worldwide internet petition to Galway County Council, who designated it a protected structure. It will now stand as a permanent memorial to Maureen O'Hara and the other stars who made *The Quiet Man*, the most popular film ever to have been made in Ireland.

The Picture House in Dumbarton High Street where people flocked every weekend to see Maureen O'Hara and John Wayne movies.

Chapter 11

THE AMBASSADOR

Frank Meehan, the US Ambassador in Prague with film star Elizabeth Taylor.

Dumbarton-educated 92-year-old Frank Meehan, the last but one United States ambassador in East Germany, kept his ever-attentive ears and gimlet eyes on full alert as Steven Spielberg's film *Bridge of Spies* unfolded on the big screen. Meehan, who was brought up in Clydebank and went to school at St Patrick's High was a major player in in this remarkable Cold War espionage story. He was at Checkpoint Charlie in occupied Berlin when one of the most important secret prisoner exchanges in history took place there - and at Glienicke Bridge on the River Havel in 1962, the *Bridge of Spies*. Meehan is one of only a handful of people still alive and able to give a first-hand account of this nerve-wracking drama, which saw American U2 spy-plane pilot Gary Powers swapped for a Russian spymaster, Willie Fisher, aka Rudolf Abel, a lieutenant colonel of the Soviet intelligence service. A third alleged spy who turned out to be entirely innocent was involved as an integral part of the deal. He was American student Frederic Pryor, an economics student doing research in the Russian sector of divided Berlin and was arrested by the Stasi. Pryor was delivered simultaneously into the arms of his grateful parents at Checkpoint Charlie by Ambassador Meehan.

Tom Hanks plays Brooklyn lawyer and aspiring politician James B. Donovan, a man thrust unwillingly into the middle of the Cold War when he is handed a brief to defend Abel in a spectacular New York show trial. And later to fly to Berlin to negotiate the spy-swap involving Rudolf Abel and Gary Powers, whose espionage aircraft was shot down over the Soviet Union. 'I wonder who will play me,' said Frank Meehan mischievously, sitting back on the sofa in the comfortable lounge of his home overlooking the Firth of Clyde in Helensburgh. The morning sun streams through the large picture window looking out on a stunning autumnal view of the Gareloch towards Rosneath Peninsula and the far off Renfrewshire Hills. Meehan entertains himself these days mainly by reading *The Economist* and watching the passing pageant of sailing yachts and puffers from his window, although he is brushing up on his Russian and learning Spanish while he waits to apply for 'eternity leave', an asset which shows he retains a sense of humour in his old age. Warships, including a Trident nuclear submarine, slip past on the loch through Rhu Narrows to the Clyde Naval Base at Faslane. The Cold War may be on hold for the moment but the presence of submarines, battleships and those controversial nuclear missiles looms large over this part of Scotland.

How then did a young man who was brought up just 15 miles away in Clydebank and educated in Dumbarton and Glasgow find himself in the US embassy in Moscow when the U2 story broke? This was the biggest geo political news story of its time. Meehan was born of Scottish parents in East Orange, New Jersey, in 1924, but his mother was unable to settle in America and returned home to Clydebank just a few months after her son's birth. Young Frank went to school first at St Stephen's Primary School in Dalmuir and then to St Patrick's High School in Dumbarton, where he was a star pupil. He was about to sit his Higher Leaving Certificate exams when, on the nights of March 13 and 14, 1941, Clydebank was brutally blitzed by Luftwaffe bombers. The famous shipyard town suffered the worst destruction and greatest loss of civilian life in Scotland in the Second World War. More than 528 people died, 617 people were seriously injured, and hundreds more were injured by blast debris and shrapnel in what has become universally known as the Clydebank Blitz. Out of approximately 12,000 houses, only seven remained undamaged — with 4,000 completely destroyed and 4,500 severely damaged. The Meehan family escaped when their house in Dalmuir was rendered uninhabitable. Like thousands of their fellow townsfolk, Meehan's parents and his elder sister, Agnes, were evacuated to live with a family in Coatbridge, Lanarkshire.

St Patrick's High School at Castlehill, Dumbarton.

Frank's parents wanted him to finish his education at St Patrick's however and they arranged to have him boarded out with friends near his school in Dumbarton. This was the Ward family, who lived in a small council flat at Firthview Terrace in Brucehill in the town's West End. The Ward children included James, who was to become a bishop, and David, a world class opera singer who was later to star as Wotan in Wagner's *Ring Cycle* at Covent Garden. The other members of the family became teachers. Meehan was dux medallist at St Patrick's. He was a brilliant student whose academic achievements included an MA and an LLD (Hon) from Glasgow University and later an MPA from Harvard. He worked hard during his summer holidays from university as a builder's labourer carrying a heavy wooden hod laden with bricks and mortar up scaffolding to the tradesmen employed on rebuilding his beloved Clydebank.

Time off for Frank – there was not a lot of it - was spent courting his wife, Margaret Kearns, who was also a victim of the Blitz. Margaret's family were evacuated from Clydebank and billeted out with the Blackie publishing family in their Charles Rennie Mackintosh-designed mansion, the Hill House in Helensburgh. Margaret was a Post Office telephonist who joined the Army and was stationed at Fort George in Inverness. She and Frank enjoyed hill walking and musical gatherings with their friends.

Meehan's professor at Glasgow University recommended him to the editor of the old *Glasgow Herald* in Mitchell Street, where he became a down-table sub editor until he received his conscription papers for the Army – the US Army. He was sent to Fontainebleau in France for infantry training and from there to Bremen in Germany where he employed his recently-found journalistic skills as a radio reporter and news reader on the American Forces Network. Meehan was commissioned in the US Foreign Service in 1951 and was a Clerk in the US Consulate in Bremen.

The Charles Rennie Mackintosh designed The Hill House.

He was one of a number of junior officers employed on the Marshall Plan administration. He specialised in the Foreign Service in Central and Eastern European communist affairs with assignments in USSR, Hungary, Czechoslovakia, Poland and East Germany.

A skilled linguist, Meehan was US Ambassador to Czechoslovakia from 1979-80 and in Poland from 1980-83. In Warsaw, he dealt with the ongoing crisis there involving world figures and has written a book about it. They included the Solidarity shipyard trade unionist Lech Walesa and General Wojciech Jaruzelski, who finally imposed martial law and was the last leader of the Communist People's Republic of Poland. All the while the Polish pope, Pope John Paul II, who later became a saint of the Roman Catholic Church, kept a close watch on the distressing and dangerous happenings in his native land, and he spoke face to face with Meehan who went to Rome for a meeting.

Frank Meehan and his wife, Margaret, being introduced to Pope Saint John Paul ll in the Vatican.

Frank Meehan became involved in the U2 affair almost by accident while working as a young diplomatic officer at the US embassy in Moscow in 1960. 'There was tension in the embassy when the news came through that the Powers plane had been brought down,' he said.

Meehan added: 'Russian party leader Nikita Khrushchev was going to attempt to humiliate the United States over their denial that such spy planes ever existed. He had put the U2 on display in the Hall of Chess in Moscow's Gorky Park and invited the public to view the proof of what the United States had been denying – that they had been successfully spying on the Soviet Union for fully four years.'

Khrushchev had condemned as despicable this US behaviour which had put in jeopardy the planned summit of world leaders in Paris to discuss an end to the Cold War. He had become frustrated with his own failed attempts to pin a spying charge on the Americans and had plunged himself desperately into a propaganda war with the West. The shooting out of the sky of the U2 and its pilot by a Russian missile from a remarkable 70,000ft was the vital evidence of espionage that Khrushchev had been so anxious to obtain, especially since the Americans had claimed all along that they were merely doing weather research. And when it dropped into his lap the Russian leader suddenly lost his 'fetish for secrecy,' which he was accused of by US President Dwight D Eisenhower, and embraced passionately a new enthusiasm for publicity and propaganda.

Ambassador Frank Meehan, his wife, Margaret, and a poster for Bridge of Spies.

The engine of Article 360 – the official name for the highly secret U2 - was hauled out of a swamp at Sverdlovsk, where it had crashed, and returned to Moscow along with the shaken pilot by a phalanx of senior Soviet air force officers and heavily armed KGB men. The dismantled aircraft was put on public display with large captions in Russian and English, maps of its route, cameras and an explanation of its deadly purpose which was to identify Russian military installations.

Pilot Gary Powers' pressure suit, which protected him as the U2 soared to heights of 75,000 feet and more – it was a space suit in all but name – was also displayed as were his pistol, parachute and the poison pin with which he was to inject himself if he chose to take his own life. A delighted Khrushchev took it upon himself to accompany the world's media on a tour of the exhibits of US espionage and then paraded Powers who pretended he had never seen the plane before but examined it closely. Powers was later driven back to the Lubyanka, where he spent his nights in gloomy anticipation of a secret trial and a bullet in the head - but emerged later to become the focus of one of the show trials of the century. The US pilot noticed there were no scorch marks on the aircraft's tail or even scratches on the paint of U2 and rightly concluded he had been the victim of a near miss – not a direct hit. Giles Whittell's book *Bridge of Spies* says the Moscow public formed queues that snaked endlessly through Gorky Park, and the squads of military attaches at the US embassy were as curious as anyone to go down and have a look. Professionally the Americans needed to find out if it was genuine and what had brought the U2 down. Personally they were fascinated by an aircraft that even top people in the Pentagon had not been security cleared to know about. Whittell wrote: 'But they were also known to the KGB and did not want to give Mr Khrushchev any more excuses for grandstanding.'

This is where Frank Meehan came in – 'So instead of going themselves they sent a young political officer who had good Russian, an open, friendly manner and next to zero knowledge of aeronautics. His name was Frank Meehan.' Meehan, who is fit of body and sharp of mind despite his great age, recalled: 'The line seemed miles long. I knew I could go right up to the top of the queue and show my diplomatic ID and they would let me in. Then I thought to myself that maybe they would try to make a show of me. They were not averse to that kind of thing and were perfectly capable of doing it.'

He says he then 'did a Hamlet' – 'I argued with myself. I walked down the queue on and on asking myself, will I do it, won't I do it, should I do it. I finally got my courage up and went to the head of the line where there was this big cop, a huge man, a *militsianer*, towering above me. He looked down at me and I produced my wallet with my ID and he looked again at me some more, taking in my suit and my American clothes and shoes. That look was cold and he had some questions. I thought he was going to throw the book at me and then he lightened up a bit. "Pozhalusta' – it's your plane. Be my guest.'

Meehan made his way into the Hall of Chess, looked around and noted in Russian and English the contents of the captions attached to the U2 parts before going back to the American embassy and writing up his notes. Modestly he says: 'I did my best, but what did I know about any plane? What I produced was an ignoramus's report on what it looked like. Without those captions attached I would not have known which bits were which.'

In the movie, James Donovan played by Tom Hanks, is given the credit for brokering the terms of the deal which saw Gary Powers swapped for Willie Fisher, aka Rudolf Abel, whose father is believed to have come from Greenock, a Clydeside town which these days Meehan can see across the river from his living room.

Donovan did have a major role in this, but it was Moscow-based Meehan, who was assigned to Berlin to look after the student Frederic Pryor's family. Meehan and his good friend and invaluable contact, Wolfgang Vogel, an East German lawyer – he was dismissed by Donovan as a KGB puppet - set the ball rolling on the negotiations and did the ground work.

US Ambassador Frank Meehan watching the ships go by near his at home in Helensburgh. Picture by Bill Heaney.

This involved the essential third element, which was young Pryor's release. Meehan and Vogel had negotiated over long days and months with the Germans secret police and these two men became more and more significant players in the drama. This climaxed with Pryor being released from Stasi custody to Meehan at Checkpoint Charlie while Powers and Abel were swapped simultaneously away from the glare of publicity on Glienicke Bridge. The world's media had been subject to a news blackout and were not around when Meehan took Fred Pryor by the arm from Vogel's Mercedes and handed him over to his relieved parents, Millard and Mary. Nor were the press there for the Abel-Powers swap on that cold, misty February morning in 1962. This was despite the fact there had been regular media speculation about this for nearly 20 months with news editors rubbing their hands at the prospect of a cracking story involving a wrecked meeting of world leaders, a master spy and the disgraced pilot of the U2.

But the story broke – as stories will – when a native Berliner, a lowly Reuters News Agency copy-taker and editorial assistant, Annette Von Broeker, after the reporting staff had gone home for the night, suggested to her boss that the Powers swap might take place at Glienicke Bridge - not at Checkpoint Charlie. Shaking with nerves, the blonde, blue-eyed Von Broeker sped off in a taxi to Glienicke Bridge, where a large contingent of military police were guarding the barrier.

She decided to ignore them and to talk instead to a young regular West German policeman who walked with her out of sight of the others and gave her the full details for the biggest scoop of her life in journalism. Soon the telegraph wires from Berlin were buzzing and, as the news of the successful spy swap filtered through to him in Washington, President John F Kennedy raised a glass of champagne and called an impromptu press conference at the White House. Sometime later Frank Meehan also negotiated successfully the release of the Russian dissident Anatoly Shcharansky and in February, 1986, delivered him personally into the West in another spy swap deal, again at Glienicke Bridge. A rising star of the diplomatic world, Meehan, whose ambassadorial appointments were confirmed by Presidents Ronald Reagan and Jimmy Carter, now lives quietly far from the world of spies and diplomats with just a passing interest in politics.

Frank Meehan, the last but one US ambassador in East Berlin, and Billy McNeil, ambassador in chief at Celtic FC.

Picture by Bill Heaney

He keeps an eye on the progress of Celtic Football Club and attends the occasional important match at Parkhead, where he was introduced to another ambassador - Celtic's ambassador in chief, Lisbon Lions captain Billy McNeil. Meehan told him he had once played at Celtic Park for St Mary's Boys Guild in Duntocher, West Dunbartonshire, where he was a team mate of Alec Boden, who was later to become Celtic's left back. 'But that was about 75 years ago,' he said.

That Boys Guild team won a national trophy against, Meehan thinks, Holy Cross High School from Hamilton, at Celtic Park. Meehan also played for the Rest of Scotland Schools against Glasgow Schools at Brockville, Falkirk. To celebrate his 90th birthday on February 14, 2014, Frank Meehan went as a guest of the SFA to see Scotland vs USA at Hampden Park in Glasgow and stood hand on heart for the American national anthem. He was once again in a VIP seat in the stand when Scotland met Poland in a 2-2 draw in Glasgow. He enjoys short breaks in the Highlands and Islands, nights out at the theatre in Glasgow, Italian food and reading, especially long evenings translating from Russian to Spanish.

Diplomatic chess game that prised dissident Shcharansky from Siberian prison

Ambassador Meehan with the Russian Anatoly Shcharansky

The successful Berlin spy-swap involving the Russian refusenik Anatoly Shcharansky was a different game of chess from the one in which the two main players were US pilot Gary Powers and Soviet spymaster Rudolf Abel. However, the Shcharansky deal might never have happened had it not been for the close friendship between US Ambassador Frank Meehan and Wolfgang Vogel, the East German lawyer who became Berlin's spy trader extraordinaire. That friendship was forged 20 years earlier when these two men co-operated in achieving the release of American economics student Frederic Pryor, who was an essential pawn in the remarkable spy-swap at Glienicke Bridge and Checkpoint Charlie. Basically, the Americans told the East Germans that if Pryor's release was not part of that deal then the Powers-Abel swap was a non-starter. Meehan is described in the book *Bridge of Spies* by author Giles Whittell as having been 'born in New Jersey but grew up in Scotland and spoke English, German and Russian with the same soft Celtic inflection'.

Whittell who was the Moscow correspondent of *The Times* met Meehan at Vogel's funeral in Bavaria in 2008, nearly 50 years after the two men had been involved in the Powers-Abel swap. He wrote: 'Meehan and Vogel found they could trust each other. They were both Catholics, serious about faith but less so about doctrine. They actually looked similar, and they got along.' He said the existence of the channel between Meehan and Vogel may have been 'the clincher' in getting Frederic Pryor out of the Stasi prison at Hohenschonhausen. Vogel, who worked closely with the East German secret police, convinced them he was getting a good deal by handing over Pryor. He claimed the Meehan connection was more valuable – 'Here was a political officer from the US mission cultivating the next best thing to diplomatic relations. 'From the point of view of the German Democratic Republic, it was not a bad reward for trading in a perfectly innocent economist.' So valuable to the Powers-Abel deal was Pryor that for the days before he was freed, his Stasi interrogators stood guard to make sure the student didn't kill himself. Fast forward then to 1986 when a much softer Communist line was being taken by Mikhail Gorbachev and the Shcharansky swap at last took place.

By this time spy trading was almost commonplace in Berlin and on occasion it was literally done by the busload. A familiar site on Glienicke Bridge was a gold-coloured Mercedes driven by Wolfgang Vogel, who had been earning a king's ransom acting for clients who were desperate to escape to the West side of the Berlin Wall. Craig R Whitney, a *New York Times* reporter wrote in his book *Spy Trader* that 'Vogel was always immaculately dressed in formal double-breasted suits cut of Western cloth. He looked like a diplomat and moved with confident ease. He appeared to be popular and seemed equally relaxed with American and West German officials and the East German secret police with whom he was on first name terms.' No less than 25 imprisoned Western spies and four Communist ones were released at Glienicke Bridge under Vogel's auspices in 1985 – 'Chartered buses brought them up to the barriers, television cameras focused in on their faces for a brief moment, and then they disappeared back into the secret world – but into freedom, on their own side after months or years of imprisonment by their adversaries.'

The heavily guarded Iron Curtain held no terrors for Vogel who was as familiar with Checkpoint Charlie as with the Glienicke Bridge, and where the guards let him pass without ever asking to see his papers. He is reported to overseen the release of more than 30,000 East German political prisoners over a period of 25 years. These people were his clients for whom he bartered with the West German government, which paid the Communists billions of marks to release the prisoners and their families. Whitney reported: 'The number of people who owed their freedom to Vogel's unique practice eventually reached nearly a quarter of a million.' The successful Anatoly Shcharansky swap sealed Vogel's reputation as a *spy trader*. It was probably more difficult than any of the others – and the world was watching every move.

Shcharansky, whose championship of human rights made him a martyr and a cause celebre in the West, was never a spy at all. But it took nearly seven years of steady work for Vogel, ably assisted by Meehan, to obtain freedom from a stark Siberian prison for the man the Stasi and the KGB insisted had been an American intelligence agent. The Communists held on to Shcharansky because they considered he would be a useful tool when it came to reaping diplomatic benefits from the West. Success in having Shcharansky released only came at the end of a series of spy swaps involving the release of scores of agents on three continents. This was made possible by the reactivation of the informal channel between Vogel and Frank Meehan, the career diplomat with whom he had been friendly since 1962. Meehan had been following the Shcharansky case as deputy chief of the US diplomatic missions in Vienna and Bonn and now finally he was involved as US ambassador to East Germany.

Observers believe the secret of their success, in the end, lay in its diplomatic ambiguity with, on the one hand, the US insisting that Shcharansky was not a spy but, on the other, with Vogel bargaining for his freedom with captured Communist agents as if he were. In the end, Shcharansky, who had been accused of passing on secrets to American journalists and joining forces with the 'refuseniks' who were Soviet Jews who had been denied permission to emigrate to Israel, was freed. A child chess prodigy who claims to have maintained his sanity by playing chess against himself in his mind while he was in jail in Siberia - he beat the world chess champion Garry Kasparov in an exhibition game in 1996. – Shcharansky was allowed to travel to Israel where he became a government minister.

Ambassador's visit to the Scottish Parliament

Former US Ambassador Frank Meehan with Jackie Baillie MSP at the Scottish Parliament in Holyrood, Edinburgh.

Dumbarton MSP Jackie Baillie was host to a special visitor in the Scottish Parliament in Edinburgh. Frank Meehan, the former United States ambassador in Warsaw, Prague and Budapest presented Jackie with a copy of his recently published memoir, *Polish Reflections.*

It was Frank's first visit to the Scottish Parliament at Holyrood. He said: 'I had been to Edinburgh on a number of occasions, but I never managed to fit in a visit the Scottish Parliament. Jackie Baillie kindly arranged for me to have a tour of the debating chamber and other areas of interest in the Holyrood building.

"I was greatly impressed by much of what I saw there. I am very grateful to her for her kindness. I had a wonderful day out. Ms Baillie and her staff were very kind to me.'

The way they were on foreign postings

Frank and Margaret Meehan with their baby daughter, Anne, in Europe, where he worked in US embassies in Moscow, Prague, Budapest and East Berlin.

Chapter 12

THE SOLDIER

GLEN'S

ALEXANDRIA

Lennox Herald

CLACKERS

IAN TYRRELL SPORTS

LOCAL SOLDIER IS IRA BLAST VICTIM IN BELFAST

Bonhill mother flies to son's bedside

by William Heaney

All the horror of Ulster was brought home to West Dunbartonshire this week when a local soldier lost his right eye following a terrorist bomb attack in Belfast.

John Whittle — lost an eye.

Balloch actor is school dux

by James McGhee

Chemists o

of 5 leaders

lessey men

Sergeant John Whittle, a Scots Guard who survived an IRA bomb attack in Belfast in 1971, died peacefully in London in October, 2015. He was 73. Whittle, who was Glasgow-born and lived in Vale of Leven in Dunbartonshire, was 29 when he was seriously wounded and lost his right eye. His fellow soldier, Guardsman Brian Hall, 22, from Dunfermline, Fife, was killed in Cupar Street, off the Falls Road, when a bomb was planted by the Official IRA. Two other soldiers and two housewives passing the scene were also injured as political situation worsened and the IRA stepped up their campaign to drive British troops out of Northern Ireland. The Army had taken over a three-storey house with the RUC and created a listening and observation post to cover the so-called Peace Line near the Springfield Road. A high wall was later built there to keep apart the then warring Republican communities of the Falls Road and the Loyalist stronghold of Shankill Road. It is believed that terrorists approached the Army post along a back alley and forced a woman working in a baker's shop into a car which they parked near the scene. They then left a suitcase packed with 100lbs of gelignite on the floor of the shop against a wall next door to the Army post. A local grocery shop owner said: 'The bomb exploded and the building collapsed like a pack of cards. It seemed no one could come out alive.'

Sergeant John Whittle of the Scots Guards

Sergeant Whittle, who was educated at Vale of Leven Academy and served his time as a plumber with Duncan Rodger in Alexandria before deciding to join the Scots Guards, was taken to the Royal Victoria Hospital in in Belfast. A single man, he had been in the Guards for almost nine years at the time of the IRA incident and had served in Malaya, Borneo, Kenya and Sharjah, Persia. Northern Ireland was a posting Sgt Whittle and most other Service personnel did not want to receive at that time since Belfast was extremely dangerous, besieged by terrorists and blighted by tragedy and turmoil. Sgt Whittle had been caught up in a number of near rifle shot misses and bomb explosions but with his fellow Scots Guards stuck bravely to the task of trying to keep the peace in one of the most dangerous parts of Belfast.

His mother, Lucy, and sister, Olga, were flown out from their home at 62 Napierston Road, Bonhill, to see John in hospital. An Army spokesperson said: 'unfortunately Sgt Whittle took most of the explosion on his head and has lost his right eye. He is now apparently well and sitting up in bed. His life is no longer in danger.' His aunt, Mrs Elsa Thomson, expressed her concern about the safety of British troops caught up in the Troubles in Belfast at that time. She said there appeared to be no prospect of an end to the violence and added: 'The terrorists are killing soldiers, children and innocent people, and the Army's presence is not having the desired effect – peace.' Even in the Royal Victoria Hospital, soldiers like John Whittle were not safe from terrorist gunmen. When I went to the hospital to interview him, a Black Watch soldier from Stornoway, red hackle in his cap and automatic rifle clutched across his chest, stood guard at the injured sergeant's bedside. Not even in hospital were soldiers safe to sleep peacefully as IRA gunmen wearing white overall coats and passing themselves off as medical staff had shot at least one of them in his hospital bed. When the Black Watch armed guard went off to inform a senior officer about a suspicious object smouldering in a litter bin in the Falls Road, just below the window of the ward, he passed his weapon to Sgt Whittle in the bed. Despite having lost his eye, Sgt Whittle's morale was at a peak. He told me: 'I was lucky to get out with my life. Although I am due to leave the Army in six months' time, I won't be quitting.'

The only place he wanted to get out of at that moment though was the hospital, where everyone was on edge, but he had to stay there until after an operation to remove fragments of glass from his body. He said: 'I've lost all my kit. All I am left with is my camera which, by some miracle wasn't broken, and a pair of blood-stained boots.' Sergeant Whittle kept to his pledge to stay on in the Scots Guards and took up duties as an Army recruitment officer in Scotland before retiring and joining a company of commissionaires and concierges in London. His friend and colleague, Kevin Gorman, paid tribute to him at Sgt Whittle's funeral in Hendon, London, where he lived latterly in a care home. He said that John Whittle had been a brave soldier, respected colleague and good friend who would be sadly missed by everyone connected with the Scots Guards. His funeral was a dignified and moving service and Sgt Whittle's coffin was draped with the Union Flag with his Scots Guard's cap and belt on top. An Army piper played a final farewell – 'It was a fitting send-off for an old soldier,' said Kevin Gorman. Sergeant John Whittle never married and his parents, Lucy and Joseph, predeceased him, as did his sister, Olga. A memorial service was arranged by Scots Guard colleagues to take place in London and was held before Sergeant Whittle was brought home for a military burial at which a piper played a traditional lament in Vale of Leven Cemetery.

Bill Heaney on patrol in Belfast with Argyll infantryman John Healy from Alexandria.

Chapter 13

THE US MARINE

Sergeant Alex Chisholm, killed in action in Vietnam.

The two minutes' silence at 11 o'clock on Remembrance Day morning rightly took many local families down memory lane to recall loved ones lost in conflict.

In the morning
And at the going down of the sun
We will remember them ...

Remember them we do, not just here in Dumbarton but across the world. It wasn't just Scots who gave their lives for our country, soldiers from the Commonwealth made the ultimate sacrifice for democracy. These young people didn't 'fall' nor did they 'pass away' but were

cruelly killed in battle. They died. Their lives were extinguished, snuffed out like candles in the wind. They died so that we could live in peace and freedom. But peace comes dropping slowly even in the 21st century – far too slowly. From the fact that millions lost their lives and millions more were driven out of their homes and became refugees the world learnt nothing. War and terror tops the schedule of every television and radio news bulletin and state of the art ordnance and other sophisticated weaponry continue to reap a grim harvest of death, destruction, injury and limbs lost 'in action'. All those terms such as 'passed away,' 'the fallen,' and 'in action,' are used by journalists and government spin doctors to lessen the impact of the bloodshed and carnage brought by war. Isn't it time we called a spade a spade and looked death in the eye since no softer words can really ameliorate the impact of it? Only then might people realise war is not about the bravery and glory of going over the top to the sound of blood stirring pipe tunes, but death and devastation. And young people being denied the chance to live, work and marry and bring up a family and look after their parents and grandparents in their old age. How heart aching must it have been especially for those parents and wives and sweethearts of soldiers who got through four years of war only to receive those dreaded telegrams at the end telling them their nearest and dearest had perished just as the fighting ended?

These thoughts came to mind as I walked round the neatly kept avenues between the graves in God's Acre at the foot of Garshake on Remembrance Day morning. I had been looking earlier through the records of the Commonwealth War Graves Commission at the number of Service personnel buried in our local cemeteries. There are hundreds of names of men and women carved on war graves and cenotaphs from Dumbarton through Renton (Millburn Parish Church), Alexandria and Bonhill, Cardross, Helensburgh, Faslane, Garelochhead and Rosneath and Kilcreggan, far more than I ever imagined. People come from all over the world to pay their respects and to search out the last resting place of their relatives who died, people they never have known but love just the same. The poem and poppy are prominent Remembrance Day symbols throughout the Commonwealth, particularly in Canada, where *In Flanders Fields* is one of the nation's best-known literary works.

Fresh poppies and tiny crosses have been laid on the graves of four young Canadians and two English persons who were killed on the 13th of September, 1944, when their plane, an Avro Lancaster bomber of 101 Squadron RAF, crashed on Conic Hill, near Balmaha on Loch Lomondside. The aircraft – piloted by a young woman, Flying Officer Claire Edwards Brooks, of the Royal Canadian Air Force and her colleague Flying Officer Lloyd George Peardon, was on a training flight from Ludford Magna in Lincolnshire when the tail broke off and it dived into a bog. The other members of the crew who were killed were two air gunners, a navigator and a wireless operator. The youngest person to die in the crash was Sergeant James Watt, of Banff, Alberta, who was just 18 years old. James was amongst the youngest RCAF airmen in Bomber Command to be killed in action. Few reports exist of this crash or of the subsequent funeral at Dumbarton, most probably because the Official Secrets Act was in place at that time and details of those involved are hard to come by. A second reason for this of course may have been that the Government did not wish the public to know that women pilots were being trained to go on bombing missions. So, let's simply pay tribute here to this young woman and five men who died tragically in one of the loveliest places in the world, Loch Lomond's Bonnie Banks. At some future date, it is hoped that a memorial to the airmen who died can be sited in the village of Balmaha on the West Highland Way at the foot of Conic Hill. This well-known poem is by one of their own, Canadian John McCrae:

In Flanders fields the poppies blow
Between the crosses, row on row,
That mark our place: and in the sky
The larks still bravely singing fly

Scarce heard amid the guns below.
We are the dead: Short days ago,
We lived, felt dawn, saw sunset glow,
Loved and were loved: and now we lie
In Flanders fields!

Take up our quarrel with the foe
To you, from failing hands, we throw
The torch: be yours to hold it high
If ye break faith with us who die,
We shall not sleep, though poppies grow
In Flanders fields

That poem is from the First World War, of course. Local soldiers from that war are buried here, but there is a grave at Dumbarton Cemetery of one of our own who was killed in the Vietnam War on September 10, 1967. He was Alex Chisholm from Quarry Knowe in Castlehill, Dumbarton. Alex had trained as an engineer and draughtsman at the Dewrance factory in Glasgow Road, Dumbarton, before emigrating to New York. I knew him well from Dewrance where I was the tea boy and he was an intelligent, handsome young man of just 24 years of age on the road to success in his chosen profession. Alex, a member of a large and well-known local family, was a hardworking former pupil of Dumbarton Academy and a nice guy with it. An only son, he was the apple of his mother's eye and dearly loved by his five sisters. He became an American citizen and was called up by the US Marine Corps where he moved swiftly through the ranks to become a sergeant. Sergeant Chisholm 2242793 was called into action in South Vietnam where he was killed by enemy rocket fire. Poignantly, he was due to finish his year's service with the troops in Vietnam just a month after he was killed. His body was flown back to the United States and from there to Scotland where he was buried with full military honours at Dumbarton Cemetery. Sadly, Alex, had he lived would probably have been married with a family of children and grandchildren.

Many older people will have forgotten about Vietnam and wonder why it happened and some of our younger readers will never have heard of it. That is why it is important to remember the horrors of war and all our war dead who were mostly members of the Argyll and Sutherland Highlanders, the Highland Light Infantry, the Cameronians and Black Watch, regiments which recruited locally. They didn't 'fall' or 'pass away' as the news readers have it. They died. Their young lives were stolen from them. They gave their lives for us, our country and our freedom. Peace be with them.

Conic Hill at Balmaha on Loch Lomondside, where four Canadians and two English persons perished when their plane crashed.

An Avro Lancaster bomber.

Poppies mark the graves of the Canadians and English Service personnel at Old Dumbarton Cemetery. Pictures by Bill Heaney

Chapter 14

THE PLAYERS

Hughie Gallacher and Tim Whalen

Hugh Gallacher, who was the leading goal scorer for Dumbarton Football Club during a period of league reconstruction in the 1950s when the club's future was in jeopardy, died in the St Margaret of Scotland Hospice in Clydebank in June, 2013, aged 82. He played a huge part in the revival of the club which had been relegated to 'C' Division in 1954 and, after just one season, was elected to 'B' Division where, for the first time in many years, they would consistently finish in the top half of the league. This was thanks mainly to goals scored by Gallacher, who was a local boy, born and brought up in the Vale of Leven and educated in Dumbarton at St Patrick's High School. He went from school football to play in the junior ranks for Duntocher Hibs at Glenhead Park and went on to join Arbroath. However he was somewhat surprisingly given a free transfer from the Gayfield club, most probably because of his slight build of less than 11 stone and small stature of 5ft.7in. He was immediately snapped up and brought to Boghead Park by Dumbarton manager Peter McGown, quickly endearing himself to the Sons' faithful and finding himself in a battle with John Coyle of Dundee United for the Second Division's top goal scorer title. Sons, a once proud and highly successful Scottish club formed in 1872, were struggling at the time to pay mounting debts of £2,700. But a share issue raised £7,000 and allowed them to carry on playing under the chairmanship of James T Fitzgerald, an executive of the giant Burroughs Machines Company, which had opened a factory at Strathleven on the outskirts of Dumbarton.

The smooth talking American put the board room affairs of the club in order while out on the field of play, in less than eight seasons, Gallacher scored 205 goals in major competitions, making Dumbarton once again a footballing force to be reckoned with. Hugh Gallacher's goal scoring achievements were quite remarkable given that he only played a total of 220 games for the club. The centre forward finished Scotland's top scorer with 35 goals in the league in 1955. In total that year he scored 46 goals in three major competitions, which is a club record to this day.

Crowds in their thousands flocked to 'Fatal Boghead' during that golden era when Gallacher and his team mates turned on the style. In January, 1957, Celtic came to Boghead to mark the switch on of the floodlights, but Gallacher and his Sons' colleagues were beaten 5-2 by the First Division club, who had Charlie Tully and Bobby Evans in their team that night. Gallacher led a Dumbarton forward line which included Leslie Brown, Tim Whalen, Bob Gibson and John Heaney. Eventually Lisbon Lion Bertie Auld who had been loaned to Sons by Celtic joined the squad. The Scottish Cup was the highlight of that season when they knocked out two leading sides – Queen of the South and Motherwell – before eventually succumbing to Raith Rovers, whose line-up included the famous Scotland centre half Willie McNaught. The match was played in front of a packed crowd of 18,000 fans, a record crowd for The Scottish Cup at Boghead.

Hughie Gallacher (centre, front row) in a team which included Tommy Irwin, John McColl, Don Cornock, Jackie McMillan, Benny Cairns, Leslie Brown and John Heaney.

The Fifers coasted to a 4-0 victory in the seventh round tie. Gallacher suffered a broken ankle in the 1958/59 season, but his goal scoring exploits continued when he returned to fitness.

He scored a remarkable four goals against his old club, Arbroath, but ended up on the losing side when Dave Easson netted all five goals for the home team at Gayfield. A month later, Gallacher again netted four goals in a 6-3 win over Hamilton Academicals at Boghead. He was surprisingly sold to Clyde at the end of 1960 and played briefly for Queen of the South before returning to Boghead to play out his career, which ended with him receiving a well-merited benefit match against the Shawfield club. Hugh Gallacher was a modest, self-effacing

individual, a truly quiet man who avoided the limelight at all times. He lived and worked in the Dumbarton area all his life at various factories including Burroughs and Diamond Power.

His first wife, Eileen, died in 1973 and he later married his second wife, Paddy, who predeceased him last year. He spent his retirement holidaying from time to time in Donegal with Paddy, gardening and playing golf at Dumbarton Golf Club, where he was a keen member for many years. He did lots of work for charity and was an accomplished handyman who could turn his hand from plastering to decorating or whatever. Hugh had been ill for some time after being diagnosed with leukaemia and died at the St Margaret of Scotland Hospice in Clydebank.

The respect and affection in which he was widely held in Dumbarton was reflected in the large attendance of friends, family, football officials and fans at his Requiem Mass which was concelebrated by Monsignor James Clancy, Father Eddie Kelly and Father Alfred McKenzie at St Michael's RC Church and funeral thereafter at Dumbarton Cemetery.

Man of the match – Sons' star goal scorer Hughie Gallacher, the Boghead fans' favourite third from left back row with Chairman James Fitzgerald centre front row.

Pictures from the Official History of Dumbarton FC.

Meanwhile, Hugh Gallacher's forward line partner and friend, Thomas (Tim) Dunion Whalen died peacefully at his home in Newark, California, in 2014 with his family by his side. He was 83. Born in Dumbarton, Whalen was the son of Anne Dunion and Michael Whalen, who was employed at William Denny and Sons' Leven shipyard in the town. Tim spent the first 30 years of his life in

Dumbarton, where he was educated at St Patrick's High School and where he would meet the love of his life, Margaret Neeson Whalen, and go on to play professional football for Dumbarton FC. He was part of the Dumbarton team of the mid to 1950s who became known as 'The Nearly Men'. This was because they frequently flattered only to deceive and despite their often brilliant football never won a cup or a league title. The surviving Dumbarton supporters from that era still drool at the memory of the players of the day. Whalen was one of them, inside right to the 'immortal' Hughie Gallacher, Dumbarton's record goal scorer to this day with 205 goals to his credit. Their team mates included players like John McColl, Tommy Craig, Leslie Brown, John Heaney and later Bertie Auld, who went on to win a European Cup medal with Celtic in 1967. The fans still ask how Dumbarton did not win promotion at that time. Several times it was within their grasp and they were drawing to Fatal Boghead, as the club's stadium became known, record crowds. A cup-tie against Raith Rovers, captained by Scotland skipper Willie McNaught, on March 3, 1957, attracted an official attendance of 18,001. However those of us who squeezed on to the terracing, and other schoolboys who 'jouked in' that day, reckoned there more than 20,000 in the stadium. According to the club's official history, compiled by Jim McAllister and Arthur Jones, there was one occasion in January 1956 when Sons' fans claimed the team had intentionally lost 2-0 to St Johnstone. In response, at the end of the season, the board offered a trip to the USA, home of chairman James T Fitzgerald, if promotion was won the following season. Fitzgerald, who was the manufacturing director of Burroughs Machines Limited at Strathleven Industrial Estate in Dumbarton, had been influential in getting all the Dumbarton players jobs at the Burroughs adding machine factory. Whalen was one of those who took advantage of the offer and became a highly skilled toolmaker at the factory.

Despite the fact that 101 goals were scored by Sons the following season - many of them 'laid on' by Whalen for Gallacher and company - the club once again failed to win promotion, coming only ninth in the league. Whalen, who was no slouch himself when it came to putting the ball in the net, once scored four goals against East Stirlingshire. In 1961, disappointed that the America trip bonus had not come his way, Whalen moved to San Francisco with his wife, Margaret, and their three children, Thomas, Patricia and Caroline. Whalen continued his professional football career successfully with the San Francisco Scots, where he continued to lay on the goals for his team mates. Described as a hard-working, dedicated man at his funeral service in Fremont Memorial Chapel, Whalen spent over 10 years as a tool and die maker at Lenkurt, before settling at United Airlines, where he worked as a machinist for 20 years. The pastor added: 'Thomas lived a life defined by his generous, caring and compassionate spirit. He was always the first to offer his help – whether that was his time or his money, he never said 'no' when someone needed a favour.'

Described by his family as understanding and a great listener, he was always willing to lend an ear and offer advice. Tim had the ability to light up any room with his dazzling smile and his ability to make those around him laugh. He was a fun-loving person who will be missed dearly by all his friends and family, but remembered forever for his warm and jovial nature. Tim is survived by his wife of 60 years, Margaret Neeson Whalen, son Thomas, daughters Patricia and Caroline, grandchildren, Ryan, Chris, Sean, Erin, Laura, Julia, Erica and Mollie, and seven great-grandchildren, as well as his sisters Mary McMillan, Helen Robb and Margaret Whalen.

Chapter 15

THE CLIMBER

Ben Humble, a pioneer of the Mountain Rescue Service.
Picture courtesy Roy Humble.

We are so lucky here to live close by some of Scotland's finest mountains, but as with so much that is beautiful in this world danger is often to be found lurking nearby. Climbing can have tragic consequences, especially when freak weather conditions set in and even the most experienced climbers can be caught out. Mountain rescue teams, like the one at Arrochar, near the Cobbler, are relatively new however, less than a century old. And it is thanks to a Dumbarton man that they are here at all. Ben Humble was born on Oxhill Road, Dumbarton, in 1903, the seventh in a family of eight brothers, and fated to completely lose his hearing by his early thirties. Despite this handicap however, Ben Humble left a unique mark on the Scottish outdoors as an author, journalist and photographer and as one of the early pioneers of Mountain Rescue in our country.

The breadth of Ben's legacy is remarkable. Nearly 40 years after his death his books and photographs remain in demand. One of the books is accepted as the definitive history of The Cuillin of Skye. Photographic slides from his lectures on mountain rescue are in the care of the Scottish Mountaineering Club. His restored 16mm cine films of the Civil Defences of the City of Glasgow during the Second World War are held by Scottish Screen Archive, who also have custody of his pioneering climbing films. They include the classic 'In Days of Old' made in 1953 to commemorate the fiftieth anniversary of the Scottish Ladies Climbing Club. Travelling the length and breadth of the country, in the early days mostly on foot, little escaped Ben's notice or his pen during years when outdoor activities were steadily burgeoning. His 'One man's view of Scotland' can be explored by visitors to our National Library in Edinburgh, where under the title Humble Collection all his published contributions are stored alongside his equally valuable scrapbooks of early hill-walking and climbing accidents. In a totally different sphere of interest the lasting results of his fascination and skill with heathers and alpine plants can still be seen today at Glenmore Lodge in the Cairngorms. There the Ben Humble Memorial Garden guards the entrance to Scotland's National Outdoor Training Centre.

At a higher elevation, visitors taking a walk round the Wild Mountain Garden at the Base Station of the Cairngorm Mountain Railway can learn more about this aspect of his story. 'Not bad, not bad' was a common phrase Ben used. These words might well serve as his epitaph, for despite his inability to hear any lectures he had originally qualified in Dentistry at the University of Glasgow. Later Ben became one of the first specialists in Dental Radiology in Scotland. He was an early pioneer also in Forensic Dentistry where his method of identifying human bite marks was the accepted standard in criminal cases for over two decades. All this he eventually had to abandon, enjoying telling his friends 'I couldn't hear my patients screaming!'

The Voice of the Hills, the story of Ben Humble, MBE, written by Ben's nephew Roy Humble, was published in 1995. Added to immeasurably by contributions and humorous stories from old students, friends and climbing colleagues, and using Ben's words wherever possible, this book tells the story of the lasting contributions of a proud and independent Scot. Ben's whole life was a response to the challenge of his deafness and to the one voice he did hear – the voice of the hills. A limited number of copies of the book are still available and may be obtained through the Arrochar, Tarbet and Ardlui Heritage Group, with whom the author has kindly agreed to share the remaining royalties. This award winning voluntary organisation may be contacted either by e-mail at group@arrocharheritage.com or by telephone at 07879 486742.

Chapter 16

THE TAILOR

John Scullion, manager of Burton's in the High Street receiving a sales trophy from area manager, William Appleby.

Suits you, sir. Burton's was just one of a number of bespoke tailors in Dumbarton High Street. This was where the young bucks of the 'Fifties and 'Sixties got their gear. It was all 'on tick', of course. Ten bob down and five bob a week. If you didn't pay up you got a letter from Charlie Williamson, the Sheriff's Officer. That soon put the frighteners on you to pay up whatever was outstanding of the £15 it cost at the time for that beautiful Italian mohair suit. You know the one. Arctic blue mohair, three buttons (covered), brightly-coloured silk lining in the jacket. Trousers with 14 inch or maybe 16 inch bottoms. Twelves were thought to be outrageous, skin-tight even. These were put together with a shirt – button down collar or pin-fastened – purchased from Edwards Sir Shops, manned by Jimmy Travers, Bobby Cawley and Philomena Heaney, in the style the Seekers might have worn, or the Beatles. A very slim tie and a pair of black winkle pickers and you were all set for Arcari's on a Friday night. That's where all the girls who dressed like Cilla Black, God rest her, hung out. Draped around the walls they were like brightly coloured flowers in a gorgeous garden, waiting to be danced. Dumbarton and Vale of Leven girls were fussy when it came to taking the floor. They didn't dance with just anyone, you know. Sometimes nervous young men who asked 'Are ye dancing?' were rebuffed. Smart-assed sirens would sometimes reply: 'Naw, it's jist the way I'm staunin.' Rejected and despondent, the men returned to the balcony to some ribbing from their mates and another Coca Cola. Refreshed by that however they went back into the fray determined and undaunted. Arcari's in Balloch was where many couples now heading for their golden wedding first met. It was either there or in the Roxy in Renton or the Lennoxbank Hotel, which later became the Lido that they met. I don't recall ever going to the Burgh Hall or the Hibs Hall or the Masonic in College Street. The generation ahead of me met up and the danced the night away in these places. If you were lucky back then you came out with your shoes covered in Slipperene – that white powder that made you glide across the floor – and a girl on your arm. If not then it was a fish supper and the bus home. And the inevitable ribbing from your pals – 'Ye didnae get a lumber then?' Some smart guys would reply: 'Unlike you, I never sat out a ladies' choice in my life!' But back to those suits from Burton's and John Collier and Claude Alexander, all three big shops and big names on the High Street. Nearly everyone got his suit made to measure with all the trimmings, two inch lapels, no turn-ups and those covered buttons, of course. Burton's was managed by my father-in-law, John Scullion, who was forever winning prizes for having the best sales figures in Scotland. Some of the people who worked with him included David McIntyre, Pat Hannaway, Jim Mooney, Jim Carson, Joe McCann, Rodger and Damian Scullion, Peter Cummings, Robert Mair and George Wilson. Bernadette Lindsay, May Mooney, Helen McKeever and Rena Philpott worked looked after the books and worked behind the cash desk. There were other 'Saturday men' there too, of course. Burton's even had its own janitor, John Heanue, who washed the display windows and kept the place spotless. The shop was a palace of highly polished windows, wood and bright lights, a cathedral of couture where the bowlers and other sportsmen from across the district bought their blazers and flannels. They wore these proudly with their club badges emblazoned on the breast pocket. The school children's parents bought their uniforms from the Co-op of course in anticipation of the promised dividend. Burton's was the biggest and most imposing building on the High Street, positioned right at Dumbarton Cross at its junction with Quay Street. They say location, location and location is everything when it comes to opening a shop and Burton's had the best location in Dumbarton. Inevitably, there are some humorous stories about the place. There was often a queue to get served and some shuffling, as in the barber's, to see who would get whichever salesman to look after you. 'No' him, please, he couldnae measure ye for a tie, that fella,' was what one customer advised his mate within earshot of the staff. However, it is still generally agreed that Burton's was the best for something to wear at funerals and weddings and on high days and holidays. And at the dancing, of course. Suits you, Sir.

Best and busiest tailor on the High Street – Burton's in Dumbarton.

Chapter 17

THE LITTLE SHIPS

Sergeant James Gillies

Dunkirk veteran, salesman, yacht restorer and centenarian
Born: Dumbarton on April 10, 1914
Died: Erskine, Renfrewshire, February 28, 2015

James Gillies, who fought at Dunkirk and Monte Cassino in the Second World War and later restored one of the 'little ships' which rescued hundreds of British soldiers from certain death on the beaches of Normandy, has died, aged 100, on February 28, 2015, at Erskine Hospital and care home for veterans of the Armed Forces. Gillies was born in the Dennystown area of Dumbarton to Archie Gillies, a boilermaker's labourer in Denny's shipyard, and Maggie Mooney, a housewife and mother to five children, of which Jimmy was the third. His father served in the First World War and on his return home found a son who had hardly known him and who had been brought up at the feet of older men in the community, most of whom were too old for call-up to the Forces. In his own words, Jimmy was a 'bit of a lad'. He regularly skipped school, which he finally left at 14, and started working in Denny's beside his father as an apprentice engineer. His time there came to an abrupt halt when he threw a snowball and hit the gateman who had locked him and other latecomers out of the yard. Apparently the timekeeper's procedure was to sound the horn for one minute and close the gates as soon as the horn stopped. If you were late for work by one minute or more in that era you were locked out for the day. Jimmy moved on to farm labouring at Ardoch Farm, near Cardross, which was owned by the Cunninghame Graham family and tenanted by farmer Jock Kinloch. He was on full board at the farm – sleeping in the hayshed – and one of his memories is walking a plough horse from Drymen to Ardoch, a distance of 12 miles. He moved on to Filshie's farm, near Renton, before deciding that his career lay in driving cars, which became his hobby before he passed his test at 18,

Jimmy married his wife, Jessie Cooley, in 1936 and they had five children together, Jessie, James, Margaret, June and Carol. He is now a grandfather to 12 and a great grandfather to 17 children. After his wedding Jimmy probably felt he had to secure a more permanent job and paid for PSV training at a company named Bone Brothers in Glasgow, obtained his licence in 1937 and found a job driving buses for SMT from their depot in Gavinburn in Old Kilpatrick. He also owned his first car around this period - an old Austin 7 - which he says he picked up cheaply and renovated with parts acquired from various sources. It was unusual for ordinary workers such as Jimmy to own a car at this time but he was rarely without one. He would buy cars which needed attention and nurse them back to life, building a reputation for himself as talented motor mechanic.

However, the Second World War intervened and Jimmy was called up for action on 1 September 1939 having been with the Territorial Army (TA) since 1937. He became a gunner in the 54th Light A.A. Regiment R.A. (TA). With his interest in vehicles and driving, he was also eventually assigned motor transport duties. He was shipped to Cherbourg from Southampton in September, 1939, and the next few months were spent guarding installations and training. By May, 1940, his unit became involved in action against German aircraft and providing cover for infantry units. Many of his oft told stories however related mainly to the retreat to Dunkirk in May, 1940, and the battle for Monte Cassino in Italy from January to May, 1944.

The trek through France towards Dunkirk followed a command to withdraw on the basis of 'every man for himself' and Jimmy and a few colleagues joined together to do just that. He rarely mentioned though that they had no rations or equipment, simply a weapon each and the clothes they stood up in. The soldiers raided farms and orchards for food and Jimmy had a hilarious story of about having to use schoolboy French to borrow a pot from a farmer's wife in which to cook a hen – 'Avez vous a wee stewpot.' Jimmy returned the favour of the by helping French people, who were abandoning their homes to escape advancing German troops. He used his mechanical skills to identify that their truck engine's air filter was blocked and promptly discarded it, restarted the engine and sent them on their way.

Veterans James Gillies and Frank Hannaway with Councillors David McBride, John Miller and Martin Rooney on Remembrance Sunday. Picture by Bill Heaney

On arrival at Dunkirk Jimmy met a British sailor and exchanged his weapon for food because he and his mates were again starving. He didn't remember much about the evacuation from the beaches other than that he was uplifted and safely taken back to the UK. Monte Cassino is described as one of the hardest fought battles of the Second World War, where some 250,000 people were killed or wounded. Again Jimmy told his family little about the horrors of the battle except that it was the worst campaign he was engaged in during his military service. Gillies was demobbed in November, 1945, having reached the rank of Sergeant, and returned home to Dumbarton. His records show that his character was 'exemplary' and he was mentioned in Despatches. He received a Bronze Oak Leaf Emblem in recognition of this achievement.

Military service did not come to an end though as he continued with the TA after the war, eventually serving with the 8th Battalion, the Argyll and Sutherland Highlanders. One of his tasks he remembers well was to take over the running of the bar at their HQ in Latta Street, Dumbarton, which was not profitable at the time. He turned the business around and the branch was able to purchase a coach from the proceeds with the families of the soldiers benefiting by enjoying many day trips around Scotland. He finally left the forces in March, 1967, due to reorganisation, 30 years after first joining as a lad of 23.

Back in Civvy Street at the end of 1945, he had to again earn a living to support his family and returned to his love of driving and mechanics. He drove for a number of firms in the post war years such as George Young at Dalmoak Farm. He also drove for the Dumbarton Co-op, the Scottish Gas Board and Walter Hubbard, which later became the City Bakeries. He was popular a van salesman for bakery produce and with City Bakeries. He was known from Glasgow through Dumbarton to Balloch and Helensburgh and won a number of rewards for his high level of sales. The company also supported him in passing his Advanced Driving Test and in becoming a member of the Institute of Advanced Motorists, an achievement of which he was rightly proud.

Sergeant James Gillies with colleagues from the Argylls.

Jimmy's was promoted to sales manager and his success was, to a large extent, down to his natural flair for sales, an ability to charm customers and to make sure that they added a few cakes and pies to their order. During his time with the City Bakeries, Jimmy also developed an interest in visiting auction sales in Glasgow and regularly helped out the auctioneers during the sales. He also bought a number of items himself and had a keen eye for antiques that would make a profit. His special interest was in watches, which he sometimes sold on his bakery rounds. He remained with City Bakeries until 1978 after 25 years' service. Instead of retiring, Gillies took a job as storeman at McAllister's Boatyard at Sandpoint in Dumbarton, where the Cutty Sark had been built. Remarkably, Jimmy noticed a boat which was partly submerged with other wrecks in the River Leven and inquired if it was available for sale. He found the owners, bought the boat and set about restoring it to its former glory. The boat was one of the 'little ships' of Dunkirk fame, the Cordelia, a 35ft motor yacht of 11 tons built in Hull in 1934.

Centenarian James Gillies, who fought at Monte Cassino and escaped through France to Dunkirk with members of the Argyll and Sutherland Highlanders Association at Erskine Hospital. The 'little ship' Cordelia which Jimmy Gillies saved and restored.

Ship shape - the Cordelia which was restored by Jimmy Gillies

James Gillies with colleagues from the Argylls

It which ferried around 300 soldiers from the beaches of Dunkirk to the safety of off-lying ships before being towed back to Dover to be restored to its former glory. The renovation of the Cordelia turned out to be a major project for Jimmy and he managed to make the boat seaworthy again and to make a few trips 'doon the watter' – short journeys to start with but eventually a trip to Rothesay under the command of the self-appointed and untrained Captain Gillies.

Jimmy sold the Cordelia, which is now owned by the Association of Dunkirk Little Ships, in 1986 and finally left the boatyard and went into retirement in 1988 at the age of 74 when he took up new hobbies, sequence dancing and travel. For the next 20 years he met up with a number of dance partners and joined a range of clubs. Jimmy never forgot his war years and his fallen friends and colleagues. He faithfully attended the annual Remembrance Sunday parade at the Cenotaph in Levengrove Park, Dumbarton. Sadly, the Second World War veterans who attended the service with him gradually faded away, leaving just Jimmy and his old friend, Frank 'Batch' Hannaway, as the sole survivors who attended from that era. Both men have been honoured by the Scottish artist Tom McKendrick, who has started a project to paint the portraits of 100 war veterans for posterity, and has already captured the images of both Jimmy and Batch on canvas. Sergeant

Gillies was eventually admitted to Erskine Hospital for Ex-Services personnel in November 2013 and celebrated his 100th birthday there with family friends and colleagues last April. He died there peacefully in McKellar House with the family around him. His remains were received into St Patrick's Church, Dumbarton, where the Requiem Mass was a celebration of Jimmy's life. The burial service with a large turnout of relatives and friends from the military took place thereafter at Dumbarton Cemetery. Jimmy was predeceased by his wife, Jessie, from whom he was divorced in 1995, and their daughter, also Jessie, and is survived by his four other children and 29 great grandchildren and grandchildren.

Jimmy and daughters Carol Gow and June Moy on his 100th birthday.

The Gillies Clan – members of Jimmy's extended family at his 100th birthday party. Pictures by Bill Heaney.

Chapter 18

THE KNIGHT OF THE ROAD

Champion of the World – Sir Jackie Stewart.

Motor racing legend Sir Jackie Stewart is having to share the distinction of being three-time Formula 1 world champion with that relatively new and very flash young man on the starting grid, Lewis Hamilton. It is 50 years since the then young buck from Dumbuck's remarkable career shot forward against all the odds – and still he holds pole position in the record-breaking success stakes. Lewis Hamilton may have drawn alongside the only Brit to have scored a hat-trick of grand prix championships, but he has not overtaken him and Milton's Jackie Stewart is still the top man. So, is Sir Jackie, at the ripe old age of 77, ready and willing to pass on the F1 crown? Both Stewart and Hamilton have cautioned motor racing pundits to wait until Hamilton's career has ended to make the full judgment on where he sits in the pantheon of brilliant Formula One drivers. Stewart insists he has never shared a 'proper conversation' with Hamilton. To be honest, I have never shared a proper conversation with Stewart since I was never really interested in F1 motor racing or clay pigeon shooting, which are his great sporting loves. We have mostly been like passing ships although I did share an ear with him on the same 'Sixties jukebox in Dino's Café in Helensburgh 'when we were young and sure to have our way'. On one occasion in Edinburgh earlier this century I had the pleasure of meeting Sir Jackie after a business dinner with Jack Nicklaus and Fred (The Shred) Goodwin. Golfing great Nicklaus and Stewart were reputed to be £1 million a year ambassadors at that time for the ill-fated Royal Bank of Scotland. I never understood why Fred Goodwin almost always looked cold, grim and semi-detached – but I do now. If ever a man needed a couple of highly-paid ambassadors to do his glad handing for him it was sour-faced Fred. 'I don't think he (Lewis Hamilton) can yet be a great driver,' said Stewart, who was awarded his knighthood only in 2002, 29 years after his third title. He told reporters before an F1 race in Austin, Texas: 'That is no disrespect because no one achieves that level until later, even Jimmy Clark was only fully appreciated later.' Stewart feels Borders man Jim Clark, the two-time champion who died at Hockenheim in 1968, will always be the greatest British driver, in part because of his smoothness behind the wheel. The grizzled veteran says Hamilton, when on form, can be incredibly precise, but it is when he is up against it that everything becomes more frenetic. It seems obvious from the media coverage that Stewart and Hamilton are not exactly best buddies and that Sir Jackie is mildly put out that Lewis hasn't come to him for advice. The Scot feels Hamilton has been unwise not to seek the counsel of the older generation over the years – 'I have invited Lewis up to the house many times. I don't know why but I haven't had any time with him.' But he does not deride Hamilton's ability behind the wheel, despite the cars being vastly different to 40 years ago. 'The animal is still the same as when I was racing,' Stewart said. 'The Formula One driver mentality and skills are no different.' I have never been much involved in reporting the career of Sir Jackie Stewart, and I must have been elsewhere when his autobiography was published in 2006. It was only when a friend raised with me some of the revelations in that book about Stewart's dyslexia and his early days at school that I dipped into it for the first time. It's truly inspirational for anyone who finds themselves in the predicament he did. Sir Jackie says that his teacher at Dumbarton Academy dismissed him as 'a stupid, lazy boy' because he stumbled over reading out loud in front of the class. He said: 'Everyone was saying I was dumb, stupid and thick – the teachers said so in the classroom and other children said so in the playground – and, in the absence of any other explanation, I started to believe they must be right. I was made to feel inferior day after day. I began to dread going to school and started to look for any excuse to stay at home.' He added he had felt inadequate since he was nine years old and that his inability to read, write and count was a heavy burden he had to shoulder right up until he was 41 and he discovered he had dyslexia. He then sought advice and with expert help became the articulate and literate commentator he is today. Stewart said: 'The fact is that, even when I became a Formula 1 world champion, even when I was mixing with the rich and famous, even when I was closing major deals, I still felt hopelessly inadequate in any matters relating to the three R's – reading, writing and arithmetic. Ever since my schooldays I have had the idea that other people were better than me. I thought I was stupid, and it took me more than 40 years to realise to realise that. I am not, and never have been, stupid. I am dyslexic and there's nothing wrong with that.' Stewart says he had a burning desire to get to Dumbarton Academy secondary school but the fact that he failed the 11-plus exam twice didn't help and he went to Hartfield, the town's junior secondary, where he was consigned to the woodwork class. He added that he got in with the wrong crowd – 'I began to drift towards the periphery of our Dumbarton community. While clever students were socialising at the Denny Institute, named after the local shipbuilders, my friends and I would usually be found at a billiard hall up a close off the High Street. It was a rough place and fights were common: the cues became weapons, and billiard balls were hurled in all directions. Yet, however rough, however unsophisticated, this was starting to feel like my proper station in life. I was 14-years-old and this mere survival seemed to be the limit of my ambition.' That was until one night when he got a kicking on his way to the bus stop. Stewart said: 'I turned to find a bunch of them, maybe four or five youngsters, bearing down on me, and I saw nothing but a blur of fists and boots. The attack was brief and brutal and, not more than a minute later, I was left lying on the pavement, a few yards away from my bus stop, with a fractured collar bone, three cracked ribs and a broken nose.' Sir Jackie still hasn't had that broken nose fixed but what he did change was his ways and the company he kept then. The penny dropped and he took up with another crowd from Milton who socialised in the village Co-op Hall. He gave up the billiard hall, took up an apprenticeship in his father's Dumbuck garage. Sir Jackie's message to young people who find themselves suffering from dyslexia or having lost confidence at school that there are nowadays special services they can tap into – 'You may have to work a bit harder. You may have to do things in a slightly different way. You may even have to pay extra attention to details, but you can do it.'

Happy days – Sir Jackie Stewart and his wife, Lady Helen.
Picture by PA for Daily Mail

What is not in the Stewart biography is the sad news that his wife, Lady Helen, has dementia. Sir Jackie announced that at the beginning of July 2016 and said that although her long time memory was excellent her short-term memory had all but gone. Sir Jackie has generously donated £1 million to dementia research. 'They update our equipment and technology all the time in the motor racing industry, making improvements and new discoveries. I hope we can help to translate this to medicine and that our contribution can lead to a cure for dementia.'

* *Jackie Stewart's autobiography **Winning is not Enough** is published by Headline and is available from good bookshops and on line.*

Chapter 19

THE CORRESPONDENT

Phil Davison, foreign correspondent for Reuters.

Sometimes in this pleasurable pastime of wandering down Memory Lane you stagger into people and places just by chance. And so it was that I was talking on the telephone to Phil Davison, once of this parish, at his home in London. We are both retired old hacks who pass some of our valuable time in the departure lounge of life writing obituaries for the so-called 'quality' newspapers. And even more of that precious time reminiscing about when we battered out big stories on copy paper guillotined from newsprint using ancient typewriters. We were both Dumbarton schoolboys attracted by the smell of printer's ink and the clatter of hot metal slugs from linotype machines as we passed the Lennox Herald printworks in Church Street.

Some journalists have been around the block, but Phil has been around the world since he did his journalistic training and wrote the Hon Man column for the Sunday Post. He has worked for The Times of London; The Independent, as Latin America correspondent, and Reuters, the world renowned news agency. Phil is best known for his coverage of wars, revolutions and natural disasters from East Germany, Beirut, Kosovo and Iraq to the volcanic mudslide of Armero and Hurricane Mitch. The Armero tragedy was one of the major consequences of the eruption of the Nevado del Ruiz volcano in Colombia, on November 13, 1985. As white hot lava erupted from the volcano's crater, it melted the mountain's glaciers, sending four enormous mudslides down its slopes at 30 miles per hour, engulfing the town of Armero and killing more than 20,000 of its almost 29,000 inhabitants. In 1991, Phil was shot by a Serb sniper and during the Gulf War he travelled through the minefields of Kuwait with US Marines. He was Reuters man in Havana, Panama and Cuba and covered earthquakes and drug wars in Columbia and Chile. Not bad for a wee boy from Greenhead Road, whose family owned Davison's Emporium in Castle Street, Dumbarton. From time to time, he pretends to flatter me – deliberately knowing this gives away the fact I am older than him – by telling people he envied me my job as a journalist when he was just a schoolboy at the Academy and a student at Glasgow University. 'I used to read your stuff and think to myself 'that's what I want to be, a newspaper reporter' he would say. Being a journalist is such a glamorous job. Think of all the girls you could attract just by telling them you are a reporter.'

Think again, says I, but Phil, who, with his dark, handsome looks resembled a young Omar Sharif of Dr Zhivago fame, didn't need the kudos that being a journalist brought to the party. I remember covering the Academy School Show in Dumbarton Burgh Hall in the Sixties when he all but had his pick of the many attractive senior pupils who took part. We had been discussing the possibility of him finding a special photograph of Sir Jackie Stewart to put on display in the comfortable lounge bar of the new look Dumbuck House Hotel. It was then reminiscences began to pour out about the school show and one of these young women who became his girlfriend before he went off to travel the world as a foreign correspondent.

John T Robertson and Dumbarton Academy at Braehead.

The Dumbuck Hotel was their favourite watering hole – as it was for so many of us - when they were teenage sweethearts. Being of a discreet disposition and gentlemen of the press, of course, we didn't linger long on the ladies and moved on swiftly to talk about John T Robertson, the teacher who organised the spectacularly successful annual school show. Phil wrote Johnny Robertson's obituary after he died in Duntocher, aged 87, in 2007. The esteem in which he held him was obvious from the first paragraph: 'John T Robertson was far more than a teacher, not least to me. Without his influence, I might have never have become a foreign correspondent, nor a war reporter, nor an amateur musician, sharing his first love, because 'Johnny' took introverts like me out of their shell and taught us that school need not be hell. Most of his fellow teachers called him John T, or JTR, but I'd be going against the honesty he taught me were I to call him anything other than what I and my classmates called him to his face - Johnny. In the 1960s, that was unusual. But Johnny was unusual. He was one of us. We felt as if he was our age. Unlike the other teachers at Dumbarton Academy, Johnny wore his black robe only at assemblies, never in class, where he preferred his crumpled jacket with leather elbows. Whereas our stated pledge in life was never to end up like the other teachers - God forbid - we all wanted to be like John T Robertson. Although history was his alleged subject, JTR's first love was the arts, notably music, the theatre and humorous writing. For three decades, he wrote comic scripts for DC Thomson's most famous comics - the Beano, the Dandy, the Hotspur, the Rover, the Wizard, Bunty and Judy. He is believed to have created Wee Bandy, Gorgeous Gus and Ugg the Caveman, as well as writing many stories for the comic character Alf Tupper, 'the tough of the track', and other well-known comic strips I cannot mention because of copyright disputes.'

For the pupils, he was by far best known for the school shows he put on over the years, notably at Bellahouston Academy, Dumbarton Academy, Hermitage Academy and Clydebank High, where he ended his formal teaching career as what he called 'the hiedie' in 1984. Phil wrote: 'His best-known shows were The Lost Chord and Transports of Delight. One, in which I performed, included a lengthy Boagheid Symphony, named after Boghead Park, Dumbarton, where our local team used to play and bring tears to our eyes even before the half-time Bovril. 'The music was all from opera, the lyrics pure JTR: (Rossini's 'Lone Ranger' symphony - pit 'im aff, pit 'im aff, pit 'im aff, aff aff'). The school shows were far from amateurish. Johnny would never have accepted that. To be honest, most of his school year was focused on these shows. Quite chubby when I knew him, he'd lose up to a stone during rehearsals.'

One of Robertson's greatest achievements was ensuring that everyone in school was involved. Every teacher, even the most hated, or feared - maths, science, that kind of 'useless' stuff - was obliged to make costumes or props. The most obviously talented pupils - dancers, singers, musicians, extroverts - got the biggest roles. But JTR got the losers and loners to overcome their stage fright. He played the piano, organ, trombone, accordion and would join the pupils on stage to encourage them – 'He started his musical career as a drummer in a jazz band at Glasgow University, until his father, a minister, smelled beer on his breath and put paid to his drumming career.'

While head at Clydebank High, he wrote his last big musical production, Risingest, to mark the town's centenary. His song When the Bombers Came - about the blitz of Clydeside during the Second World War - brought tears to the eyes of those old enough to remember. For that show, Clydebank named him 'Bankie of the Year', an honour that made him immensely proud. Davison recalled one final story about his mentor: 'JTR was fond of a wee dram, the 'wee' always being in the Scottish sense. He threw away the empties but maintained a fantastic collection of whisky bottle labels, notably of rare single malts.

This photograph of Dumbarton Academy teachers and prefects includes Phil Davison who is fourth from the right at the back.
Photograph by courtesy of Linda McCluskey

He was active into his later years, playing the organ regularly at Dalnottar Crematorium, Clydebank, never being able to resist a bit of humour, which always went down well among mourners. If the deceased were a Rangers' supporter, he couldn't resist sticking a couple of bars of Follow, Follow into the usual dirge.' Maybe we'll have a coffee at the Dumbuck Hotel when Phil next comes to Dumbarton, and discuss at our leisure the divergent paths we have taken in journalism and in life.

HOCKEY—3rd and 4th XI's
Back Row (l. to r.)—M. Gunn, S. McFarlane, D. Sinclair, J. Haddow, A. McNee.
Middle Row (l. to r.)—P. McLaughlan, J. Malcolm, K. Williamson, P. Dow, J. MacDonald, B. Barbour, H. Montague, M. Downie.
Front Row (l. to r.)—L. McKean, D. Kenny, V. Stuart, F. Campbell, M. Johnston, M. Ross, J. Kelly, L. John.

The Dumbarton Academy ladies' hockey team from the 1960s.

Who do you know in this photograph from Dumbarton Academy? John Welsh, Billy Grainger, Alex Douglas, Billy Thomson are just a few of these pupils from the 'Fifties.

These 'Sixties Dumbarton Academy soccer teams include Ian Stewart, John Turner, Jake Kelly, Andy Skinner, Stewart Gillies and Ally Rae plus (below) Bobby McKean, Davie Allen and John MacEachran.

Pictures courtesy Linda McCluskey

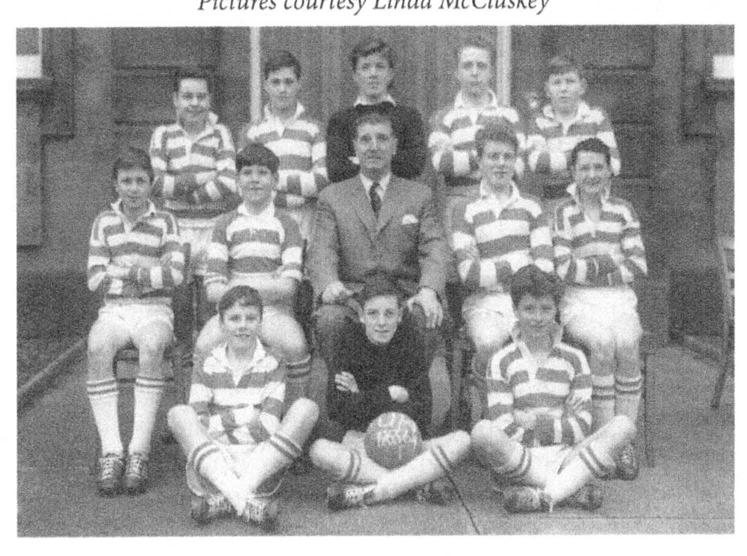

Chapter 20

THE FRUIN

Helensburgh cyclist Bobby Brodie enjoying the hills in Glen Fruin. Picture by Bill Heaney.

Glen Fruin is one of the loveliest, most peaceful places in the whole wide world. For me, it is anyway. It's where I go to relax and gather my thoughts. It may be called The Glen of Sorrows by some, but for me it means silence, beauty, a wide expanse of hopefully blue sky, cotton wool clouds and most of all peace. St Augustine argued that there is no man on this earth who does not wish for peace (nemo est qui pacem habere nolit – City of God, X1X, 12) and in Glen Fruin you will find it in spades amid the wildlife, birds, cattle and sheep, And the rich salmon river which runs through its bright yellow gorse and purple heather-clad hills. When I have done that though, I have usually concentrated mainly on the history of the Battle of Glen Fruin, which led to it being associated with slaughter, deportation and tears. Five hundred years ago the pupils of the Old Dumbarton Academy were taken there by their teachers to witness that bloody battle between the local clans. I always felt however that the story of the Glen must go a lot deeper than that – important though the battle is in our history here - and it would seem that it does.

A Dutch company sent me a small book just before Christmas in 1987, but I must have been too busy with the festivities to open it and so I put it away on my bookshelf. I came across it again just recently and it is called Loch Lomond in Old Picture Postcards, which sold at the time for a princely £6.95. It was published by the European Library in Zatbommel, Netherlands. I am not taking anything away from the book when I say that I found the information in the captions more interesting than the postcards themselves, which are a collection of old and grey images from the 19th century. It appears that there are

numerous ruins and traces of a hamlet at Auchenvennal and of a mansion at Ballevoulin, which at one time belonged to an unknown laird. This is an indication of the once large crofting community there until it became uneconomic to be a small farmer in the 18th and 19th century. Every cloud has a silver lining, however, and this forced the local people into the more lucrative smuggling trade and also illicit whisky making in 'sma' stills'. The licensed house at Cross Keys on the Black Hill, where the roundabout is now on the Helensburgh-Arden road, used to sell some of this 'stark naked' – direct from the still. Ever vigilant excisemen, the forebears of the late, kenspeckle Ferdie Thurgood and his colleagues in HMRC, put a halt to these illegal activities.

In doing so, sadly, they destroyed the livelihood of Glen Fruin's inhabitants and brought about depopulation, the Highland Clearances on a much smaller scale. Further evidence of the large population which resided in the glen between Black Hill and Shandon on the banks of the Gareloch is the fact that at least two churches once existed there, both with graveyards. The first was known as Chapel Diarmid, near Ballevoulin, and the schoolhouse at Kilbride. It was built around 1840 and I noticed as I walked past there that it has a For Sale sign outside it. The house is most probably now sold. This was the site of the other church, dedicated to St Bride or St Bridget. Some of the masonry of the actual church is said to have been built into the schoolhouse and there is evidence of stonework connected with the church at Ballimenoch, including grave slabs near the schoolhouse. According to my book, the Clan Colquhoun and the Clan McGregor had been feuding for generations and many McGregor atrocities took place. These included the cattle raid in 1527 by McGregor of Laggary on Strone Farm, which had been a Colquhoun property in the glen since 1517.

Mary Queen of Scots and a sheep farm in Glen Fruin.

I have never before heard that Mary Queen of Scots was a landowner in Glen Fruin, although her connection with Dumbarton Castle is writ large across Scottish history books. Readers may take this with a pinch of snuff if they wish – or at the very least treat it with some circumspection – but Queen Mary is said to have issued Letters of Fire and Sword against Clan Gregor in 1563. In 1589 the McGregors are said to have murdered Drummond-Ernoch 'under grizzly circumstances', and three years later the Colquhoun Clan chief, Sir Humphry, is said to have been murdered at Bannachra Castle by the Laird of McFarlane. It is alleged that the McGregors were in attendance because the killing was a reprisal for an illicit love affair between Sir Humphry and the Laird of McFarlane's wife. There were raids on Glenmullchen and Glenfinlas in 1562 in which many Colquhouns were wounded and two killed and these are said to have 'brought matters to a head'. The bluidy sarks or shirts of the dead and injured were displayed by the widows of the dead warriors to a queasy James VI at Stirling and the king then gave the Colquhouns the task of controlling the McGregors. The Colquhouns came from the Milton – and today there is a street there named after them there, as there is in Dumbarton off Round Riding Road. The Colquhouns owe all they have to the Lennox, of course, the Earl of Lennox, who granted them something called Umfridus, a charter to the lands of Old Kilpatrick. The original castle of the Colquhouns was at Middleton, north of Milton, then they moved to Dunglass, near the old Esso oil terminal at Bowling. Auchentorlie House now stands on the old Colquhoun estate at Silverbanks, but there is little trace of it today. Sir Humphry Colquhoun, for his loyalty to King Robert the Bruce, obtained a charter for the lands of Luss.

His successor consolidated his inheritance by marrying 'the Fair Maid of Luss,' heiress of the ancient family of Luss and settled down to a 12th century castle on Eilan Rossdhu on Loch Lomond, which was later replaced in the 15th century by a castle on the mainland. One of the visitors to this castle was Mary Queen of Scots on the 15th of July 1563 or, at least that is what it says in the book. It goes on further to say that Oliver Cromwell was rampaging around here in the next century and that he invaded the castle. Whoever wrote these captions either had a previously undiscovered insight into what went on in these parts in the 16th century or I, not he, am a Dutchman. However, his parting words in this interesting chapter about Glen Fruin and Luss are that Lady Helen Colquhoun – after whom Helensburgh was named – shed a tear when she moved from her 'lucky hole' to the mansion of Rossdhu, which is now home to Loch Lomond Golf Club 'where her ghost is said to haunt' the rooms. Much of this history may be apocryphal or even verisimilitude but you can't say it wasn't interesting.

Down the road, Helensburgh is wonderful place to visit. It's not just the fabulous views of the Firth of Clyde and the Argyllshire and Renfrewshire Hills that draw people to this Victorian resort. Nor is it the Charles Rennie Mackintosh designed The Hill House or the comfortable pubs, traditional tearooms and Italian cafes that abound there. However, for many years what Helensburgh residents do when visitors flock to the seafront of this Garden City of the Clyde has been shrouded in mystery. Just ten miles north of the Dumbuck House Hotel, via either the A814 or the A82 Loch Lomondside road, lies beautiful Glen Fruin. That is where local people have for years exposed their milk white torsos to infrequent Scottish sunshine and swam in the freezing waters of Craig's Pool.

Glen Fruin is a dear green and remote place in which to seek tranquillity far from the madding crowds of day trippers. 'Go quietly amid the noise and haste and remember the peace that may be in silence,' says the Desiderata. You can do just that in Glen Fruin where you can enjoy the tranquillity amid the rushy fields and undulating hills, where sheep may safely graze. There you can hear the beat of the wings of herons and raptors and listen to the strange, shrill call of orange-beaked oyster catchers, blown up into the hills from the Gareloch. There is even a Bronze Age burial mound near one of the sheep farms.

Anglers dip their rods in the rushing, tumbling waters of the River Fruin in search of elusive silver salmon that have made their way up there to spawn.

One famous resident of Glen Fruin, who enjoyed the magnificent scenery all year round, was the distinguished Scottish artist, Gregor Ian Smith, who lived at the Old Schoolhouse. Perhaps inspired by the artistic talents of his father, John, a painter, decorator, artist and musician, the young Gregor soon displayed signs of the creativity that was to serve him throughout his life. It is said that Gregor was drawing and painting at the age of three, so it appeared inevitable that he would follow his love of art through his school days. Following his education in Helensburgh, Gregor studied art at the recently fire ravaged Glasgow School of Art from 1926 through to 1931. After finishing his studies at the Art School he moved into teaching at Hartfield School in Dumbarton and eventually into lecturing through the Scottish Arts Council which he continued until his death in 1985.

The memorial stone erected by Gregor Ian Smith to commemorate the Battle of Glen Fruin. Picture by Bill Heaney

He married Kathleen Graham, a fellow teacher at Hartfield School in Dumbarton, and during a long and happy marriage they raised five children - Graham, Charles, Campbell, Kirsteen and Duncan. It was during the early years of raising his family that Gregor revealed another creative string to his bow, that of creative writing. He started writing for the legendary Kathleen Garscadden - 'Auntie Kathleen' of Scottish Children's Hour and BBC Scotland's first radio star. This much loved programme was responsible for launching the careers of great Scottish entertainers such as Stanley Baxter and Rikki Fulton. Gregor authored a series of children's stories, many of which were illustrated by Gregor himself. They included Button: The story of a puppy, Willie Whiskers: the story of Tatterjack, and Bill the Budgie.

Aside from his love of the arts, Gregor's heart lay with the area around Glen Fruin, where he raised a small herd of cattle and tended to his chickens when he was not travelling, lecturing and painting. His love of the Glen led to him erecting the monument to commemorate the Battle of Glen Fruin, which took place between the Colquhouns and the MacGregors in 1603.

Sadly, a group of clerical students from Dumbarton, probably St Mary's College in Church Street, who had assembled to watch the battle, were slaughtered by the MacGregors during the battle. The glen then became known as The Glen of Sorrows.

Glen Fruin contains the Fruin Water which flows into Loch Lomond, and a military bypass road, now the A817, which goes from the A82 over the hills to the Clyde Naval Base at Faslane. Opponents of nuclear weapons have dubbed it The Road to Oblivion, but there are magnificent views from there out over the Gareloch, the Arrochar Alps and Ben Lomond and the islands of Loch Lomond.

Glen Fruin by Edwin Morgan

Our silent love wanders in Glen Fruin with butterflies and cuckoos -
bring me the drowsy country thing! Let it drift above the traffic
by the open window with a cloud of witnesses -
a sparkling burn, white lambs, the blaze of gorse,
the cuckoos calling madly, the real white clouds over us,
white butterflies about your hand in the short hot grass...'

The Second Life, Edinburgh University Press, 1968

Loch Lomond angler Dick Dickson JP at the River Fruin.
Picture by Bill Heaney

Edwin Morgan was particularly brilliant at capturing Scottish landscapes: urban and rural, workaday and spectacular. In this poem, he brings together all of those elements. Stuck in the middle of the city, the speaker yearns to be back in the wild landscape of Glen Fruin. This is a love poem: not just about the love of a partner, but the love of the landscape.

Salmon caught and returned to the River Fruin.
Picture by Dick Dickson

Where sheep may safely graze – shepherds putting their flock on to a hill at Glen Fruin.
Picture by Bill Heaney

Chapter 21

THE WRITER

Archibald J Cronin

Cardross-born novelist Archibald Joseph Cronin was an accomplished storyteller, who practised as a medical doctor over a decade before devoting himself entirely to writing. Cronin gained his fame initially with *Hatter's Castle* (1931). This is the story of the megalomaniac James Brodie, a Dumbarton hat maker. Cronin called the town Levenford in all his books - and his foolish dreams of social acceptance. Cronin, who had his own problems with social acceptance – he was a Catholic in a strong Protestant town - produced several best-sellers drawing from his experiences as a doctor. His most famous character was Dr Finlay Hyslop, which became Dr Finlay's Casebook. Some of his works had religious themes, like *The Keys of the Kingdom* (1942), which was also made into a film, starring Gregory Peck. Cronin continued to write until he was in his eightieth year.

AJ Cronin spent his leisure time between Casci's Café in Church Street and Dumbarton Public Library in Strathleven Place.

'In the recollections of those who, like myself, have ventured into descriptions of their early years, nothing has bored me more than those long, tedious, and particularized listings of the books the author has read and which led, in the end, to the formation of a literary tastes that was demonstrably excellent. For this reason I refrain from presenting a catalogue and state simply that I read everything,' wrote Cronin in *A Song of Sixpence.*

Archibald Joseph Cronin was born in Cardross, the only child of Jessie (Montgomerie) Cronin and Patrick Cronin. His childhood was shadowed by the death of his father and poverty; his mother tried to struggle forward alone. After two years she returned to her parents' home. Cronin was sent to Dumbarton Academy at his uncle's expense. He later transferred to be taught by the Jesuits at St Aloysius College in Glasgow. In 1914 he entered the Glasgow University Medical School, graduating in 1919. During The First World War, Cronin served as a surgeon in the Royal Navy. After the war he worked as a ship's surgeon on a liner bound for India, and then served in various hospitals. He married Agnes Mary Gibson, a fellow medical student, whom he had met at Glasgow University and the couple moved to Tregenny, a small mining town in South Wales, and then to Tredegar, where they spent three years, and where their first child was born. After being appointed Medical Inspector of Mines in 1924, he started to investigate occupational diseases in the coal industry.

These experiences formed the basis of the novels *The Stars Look Down* (1935) and *The Citadel* (1937), which made Cronin famous in the United States, and inspired the director King Vidor's film version of the book. Robert Donat was nominated for an Oscar for his performance in the film. In 1925, Cronin was awarded his M.D. by the University of Glasgow and subsequently he started to practise in Wales and in London. Cronin's health broke down in 1930 and he sold his practice. Whilst convalescing in the West Highlands, he started to write his first novel, *Hatter's Castle*, which is set mainly in High Street, College Street and Round Riding Road, where he lived for a time. He once threw the manuscript away, believing it would not be good. After being encouraged by a local farmer, digging a ditch which his father had dug without finishing the work, Cronin completed his own effort. The book was an immediate success in Britain and was filmed in 1941.

Miller's Farm in Round Riding Road, Dumbarton.
AJ Cronin lived right next door.
Pictures by Bill Heaney

After its publication accusations were made, that Cronin had plagiarized George Douglas's novel *The House with the Green Shutters* (1901). However, the book allowed Cronin to give up practising medicine in favour of writing. *The Stars Look Down* was a socially charged novel, which examined injustices in a North England mining community. Carol Reed's film adaptation, starring Michael Redgrave, was praised by the writer Graham Greene: 'Dr Cronin's mining novel has produced a very good film - I doubt whether in England we have ever produced a better.' Generally it was regarded as the first British film with social relevance.

Vigil in the Night, first published in *Good Housekeeping* in 1939, was filmed by George Stevens in 1940, starring Carole Lombard, Anne

Shirley, and Brian Aherne. In this romantic melodrama, Lombard played a dedicated nurse in a provincial hospital in England, who sacrifices herself for her sister, but then finds work in a large hospital. Cronin's stories inspired also such directors as Victor Saville (*The Green Years*), Philip Leacock (*The Spanish Gardener*), and Jack Cardiff (*Beyond This Place*).

In 1939, Cronin moved to the United States with his family. He wrote *The Keys of the Kingdom*, a story of a Roman Catholic priest, Father Francis Chisholm, who spends years as a missionary in China. Father Chisholm becomes familiar with the teachings of the Chinese philosopher Confucius, adopts a simple way of life, and advocates ecumenical cooperation between all Christians. His tolerance is viewed with suspicion within the institutional Church by his superiors. David O. Selznick had bought the screen rights to the novel in 1941 for $100,000, but he did not want to do the film with Gregory Peck. However, Darryl F. Zanuck, production chief at 20th Century-Fox, was convinced that Peck was right for the Father Chisholm role. Nunnally Johnson had written earlier the screenplay and it was revised by Joseph L. Mankiewicz. The film was shot entirely on the Fox studio lot, but with its $3 million budget it was one of the most expensive pictures of the year. Critical reaction to the film was mixed. In the New York Post Irene Thirer called the picture 'a lengthy, highly dramatic, entrancingly photographed production. Stahl had captured a delicate spiritual quality, and at the same time managed to give the action sequences a biting tang; also he has preserved the wit and subtlety of the manuscript, with each and every performer expertly cast.' Howard Barnes of the *New York Herald Tribune* saw that Mankiewicz and Johnson did not 'succeed in packing a rambling literary narrative into the exigent outlines of a satisfactory film entertainment.'

Cronin himself was satisfied with the result and praised both adaptation and Peck's performance. The actor later said that he had been helped by a Catholic missionary, Father O'Hara, who had lived eight years in China. Peck, who was voted for an Oscar nomination for best actor, is reported to have said: 'I remember particularly in one scene, where I had to preach in Chinese, how Father O'Hara was persuaded to act out the scene for me. I hadn't been able to catch the feeling of it somehow. I couldn't feel natural. So we asked him to try it.

And he did, walking through that crowd of Chinese extras, ringing a little silver bell and talking to each one, in Chinese, after first bowing with the greatest courtesy. He did it as he must have done a thousand times in real life. Then I realized what I had missed in the scene, that courtesy and respect for each person as an individual.'

The Catholic faith was also the central subject in *The Minstrel Boy* (1975). The narrator is Alec, who follows through decades of disasters and triumphs of his friend, Desmond Fitzgerald, a young priest. Alec becomes a doctor and a successful writer. Desmond wins a singing competition and his marvellous voice opens the doors to music for him, and later to Hollywood films. But he also must solve his relationship with the beautiful and wretched Claire, whom he has married, leaving his career within the organization of the Church. Again Cronin's hero must find his true calling in life. Desmond rejects fame and glory, and also the golf club at Bel Air and the Racquet Club at Palm Springs. During his long walks on Malibu Beach he realizes the emptiness of his life: 'Few people use this stretch, far from the swimming beach and bathing huts, and I encounter only the regulars: Charles Chaplin, too enwrapped in his own genius to be conscious of anyone but himself, and a tall, strongly built man who walks slowly, reading, but who occasionally nods and smiles to me as we pass. These apart, one can find solitude, and here I walk, struggling with myself and with my own unhappy thoughts.'

Dumbarton had its own Hatter's Shop in the High Street but there was no connection between the owner and Cronin's fictional figure in his novel.

Eventually Desmond goes to Madras to work amongst the neglected and homeless children of the Untouchables. Although English books were forbidden in Germany during the Second World War, Cronin's works dealing with mining communities were in 1943 on display in Dresden's bookstores for propaganda reasons. After the war Cronin travelled with his family in Europe. In the autobiographical book *Adventures in Two Worlds* (1952) Cronin returned to his experiences as a doctor in Scotland and South Wales, and examined his religious beliefs in the last chapters. Cronin tells how he rediscovered his Catholic background in the 1930s. His father had been Catholic and his mother was from a strongly Protestant family. At school Cronin grew away from religion - he had been teased because of his Catholic faith, and he started to feel disgust for bigotry. Cronin's own dream was brotherhood between people and ecumenical understanding between different churches, not rivalry.

This spirit of conciliation marked all his books dealing with questions of faith. 'Now he perceived how illusory his hopes had been, how all his imaginings had been falsely based on a romantic re-creation of the past. Had he actually expected, after thirty years, to find Mary as on the day he had abandoned her, sweet with the freshness of youth, tenderly passionate, still virginal? God knows he would have wished it so. But the miracle had not occurred and now, having heard the history of a woman who wept for him late and long, who married, though not for love, lost an invalid husband, who suffered hardships, ill-fortune, perhaps even poverty, yet sacrificed herself to bring up her daughter to a worthy profession - knowing all this, he had returned to reality, to the calm awareness that the Mary he would find at Markinch would be a middle-aged woman, with work-worn hands and tired, gentle eyes, bruised and defeated by the battle of life...' (From The Judas Tree, 1961).

By 1958, the sales of Cronin's novels amounted to seven million in the United States. Cronin's humanism and social realism also made him popular in the Soviet Union. Many of Cronin's books were adapted for films or television programs. The television series *Dr Finlay's Casebook* was based on his stories. In the 1960s it was one of the most popular series on British television. For the last 35 years of his life Cronin lived in Switzerland. He died on January 9, 1981, in Montreux. Research carried out by the late Ronnie Armstrong, a head teacher who was well known in the field of amateur dramatics and Dumbarton People's Theatre, also touched on the religion question. Ronnie said Cronin had once written: "*a feeling of social inferiority was immediately communicated to me, a sort of spiritual wound deriving from my religion*'. Armstrong concluded that Cronin, who was the son of a mixed marriage of Protestant mother and Catholic father, and was brought up as a Catholic, attended Dumbarton Academy 'because of his precocious abilities. It is possible that a feeling of alienation from the West of Scotland may have contributed to his long exile from Dumbarton.' Cronin was however an ardent Dumbarton FC fan and listened for their result every Saturday at 4.40pm. A letter expressing his allegiance to the Sons of the Rock hangs on the wall of the entrance to the boardroom in the 'new' stadium at Dumbarton Castle.

Boghead Park and the old Dumbarton Academy building in Church Street.

Chapter 22

THE COALMAN

Coal came by the 'hunnerweight' and was dumped in the cellar by coal merchants such as Eddie Reid, who is pictured here making deliveries in Dumbarton.

Who remembers those long, dark winter nights sitting around a coal fire drinking hot whisky and telling tales of family history, local neighbours and streets, shipyards, shops and factories full of worthies and characters? That is what people used to do before television entered their lives and took over the living room and eventually the kitchen and then even the bedrooms and left no place in the house where peace came dropping slowly. I am pleased to report that good Scottish peat – or turf as it is known in Ireland – is making a comeback in Dunbartonshire in the 21st century. And that people are once again experiencing the pleasant warmth from the glowing sods and smelling the sweet perfume of peat smoke in their homes. Christmas and New Year was a time when families and friends gathered together round the inglenook to reminisce about their Celtic connections and Highland heritage. Do you remember some of the Dumbarton coalmen, the Jacksons, the Thompsons, Paddy Conroy, Paddy and Eddie Reid, Jimmy Bonner, Rab Brown, Wull Conroy, Cuddy Reid and so many more? And how they came round the streets shouting 'Co-ell … Co-ell' with their lorries – and horses and carts - and sacksful of the gleaming black stuff that kept us warm during those long, cold winters? There were the horses too, Jackson's horse, Charlie, was stabled up the chemist's pend in West Bridgend, near their 'rea' at Dalreoch Station. You must remember what the coalmen wore on their backs – strong leather shields sparred with metal strips to keep the sharp black nuggets of coal from cutting into their flesh. Rab Brown, with his muscly arms, his moustache and crinkly brown hair, was a handsome coalman who always had a smile and a kind word for the women.

My grandmother, Elizabeth Healey Heaney (left) and her siblings Annie Lacey, Thomas Healey and Mary McKinney at a wedding in Helensburgh.

It is of my grandmother that these lines from Two Lorries, a poem by my namesake, the Nobel laureate Seamus Heaney, reminds me:

She goes back in and gets out the black lead
And emery paper, this nineteen-forties mother,
All business round her stove ...

Faber and Faber

Being a coalman was no easy job then – and it's still not easy. It involves humphing hundredweight sacks up closes and steep stairs and round the backs of big houses to the bunkers and cellars, where the coal was housed. And kept under lock and key. Jacksons kept their lorries up Harrison's pend in West Bridgend and had their coal delivered by train to a siding at Dalreoch Station. Thompsons had their yard opposite the main gate of Denny's shipyard in the Dumbarton South railway station in Glasgow Road. The Store – Dumbarton Equitable Co-operative Society – had large brown and gold liveried lorries which toured the town and countryside around Dumbarton and the Vale. Perhaps there's a Valeman or woman out there who can tell us who it was delivered coal in the villages from Balloch to Jamestown and Renton and up Loch Lomondside to Luss and Arden and Gartocharn? Robin Spy was the coalman in Helensburgh. Who can forget toasting their toes – and a slice or two of Scottish plain bread, or perhaps a delicious, black-crusted outsider – on a fork at the living room fire? And do you recall the rather unpleasant 'fire tartan' which women who spent too long in a chair by the fireside acquired around their shins? Coal cost money, of course, and not everyone could afford as much as they would like to have, so they had to back up the fire with dross, briquettes and logs from the likes of Paddy Reid's yard at the corner of George Street and Levenhaugh Street in Dennystown. Newspapers and sticks were used to light the fire. The Lennox Herald, which was variously known (affectionately, of course) as The Two Minutes' Silence or The Jawbox, - because everything goes into it - was printed on poor quality newsprint which didn't catch light easily. This led to the jocular jibe locally that the Lennox wasn't even good enough to light the fire with.

Neighbours kept a watchful eye on the people in their street who were getting coal from the coalman and those who were not. Much of the coal was on credit and those who didn't get a delivery usually hadn't 'paid their tick' and were on the coalman's blacklist. Rather than freeze though, resourceful people would then take an old pram or a wooden barrow made of an orange box with pram wheels and trundle it out to the Gasworks at Castlegreen Street in Dumbarton East to salvage charcoal from the gas making process there. When I went to visit friends in Connemara in the West of Ireland, one of the joys of the holiday was those gatherings round the old turf fire. Turf was the name given to peat there and the people never allowed the fire to go out because it was used for boiling the kettle, cooking and baking soda bread. There were no cookers then. Even when people moved out of their thatched cottages to newly-built houses, they took the fire with them. The red hot turf was carried carefully with tongs or on shovels to the hearth of the new house. I once went out to the mountain with my donkey to cut turf on the bog, and these lines from another Heaney poem, Digging, recall that day:

My grandfather cut more turf in a day
Than any other man on Toner's bog.
Once I carried him milk in a bottle
Corked sloppily with paper. He straightened up
To drink it, then fell to right away
Published by Faber and Faber

Who realised you could capture such nostalgia in December, 2016? That you could have your very own peat or turf fire this festive season in your own home? Provided you are on the right side of the Health and Safety laws, you can have peat or coal or logs delivered to your door in West Dunbartonshire. Alan Clark from E H Noble and Son of Linwood in Renfrewshire will transport it across the Erskine Bridge for you for just £5.50 a bag (it may be dearer now). He delivers regularly round the towns and villages from Old Kilpatrick to Arrochar and his telephone number is: 01505-335749. Should you want your turf to be a little bit of Ireland then you can order it on-line. McAndrew's Turf Store. In the village of Belleek where Fermanagh meets Donegal is a unique rural enterprise called McAndrew's Store. The store has developed a range of products that are sold on-line at www.mcandrewstore.com and delivered direct to the customer via courier. McAndrew's Store sells turf, peat briquettes and can even package turf in a hessian sack, which can then be personalised. Turf can even be matched with whiskey, Guinness and even tea for quirky Christmas gift solutions. Back here in Scotland, Alan Clark gets his peat from the Northern Peat & Moss Company, which was founded in 1905 and has remained a family owned and operated company ever since. They own over 1000 acres of peat lands in Aberdeenshire, but only 300 acres are actively worked with the rest given over entirely to nature. For the uninitiated peat is a dark fibrous material, created when decomposition fails to keep pace with organic matter. In order for this to happen, conditions must be wet, acidic and cool. Peat is a significant fuel source in countries such as Ireland and Finland, where it is harvested on an industrial scale. It has low atmospheric emissions and is clean and easy to handle. From 20p per kg, it is also one of the cheapest fuel products on the market today compared with coal (50p per kg), hardwood (39p per kg) and softwood (28p per kg). That means you will have a few more bawbees in your sporran to buy your Ne'erday bottle, which will also have had the benefits of acquaintanceship with peat, which is produced for the malt whisky industry. Throw another sod on the fire then …

A warm fire in the grate is especially comforting around Christmas and New Year. New Year was the main holiday and time of celebration in Scotland until about 30 years ago when Christmas took over. Christmas Day wasn't even a holiday at all then for shipyard and factory workers. People had to get up and go to work as usual in places like Denny's in Dumbarton and the Torpedo Factory in Alexandria. But in the strange way things turn out, it wasn't because Scotland became more Christian that Christmas was brought into sharper focus. It was precisely the opposite. As the country became more affluent after the Second World War, more and more people drifted away from religion. And Scotland moved slowly but inexorably along the path to becoming a secular society. New Year is, of course, also known as Hogmanay. It signifies the last day of a year and at the same time, the celebrations of New Year. The celebrations start on December 31 evening and last until the daybreak of January 1, are known here as Ne'erday. A number of customs are associated with Hogmanay. Some of the most popular New Year traditions are, 'First Footing', 'the Bells', and 'redding'. 'The

Bells' is one of the primary New Year customs in Scotland and the first New Year stroke or chime is called The Bells. People used to gather round the town clock in the High Street, Jock McQueen's Clock in the Newtown and at the Fountain in Alexandria to sing 'Auld Lang Syne' together while holding hands.

After 'the Bells', people visit the homes of their family and friends. Neighbours gifted a dram from their whisky bottle to each other as the New Year spirit caught hold. The whisky was placed by the fireplace or on a handy shelf and was opened at midnight when people wished each other a Happy New Year with Hogmanay toasts. As that redoubtable Glasgow comedy duo of Francie and Josie might say: 'Orra best, orra time!' First Footing is usually observed at midnight, which used to be long after the pubs closed. Now licensed premises stay open through the bells and people dance the night away. In the old custom, people tried to become the first person to knock at a friend or neighbour's door and give him or her a customary gift such as salt, shortbread, whisky, coal or black bun. It was considered the fate-deciding factor for the New Year if your first foot was tall, dark and handsome. Folk no longer these days give salt, of course, and the whisky has been elbowed aside by a glass of Prosecco or even champagne. All these gifts were presented to the family and friends in order to bring good luck and keep away evil spirits. People calling in unexpectedly often ended up in 'a wee perty' with lots of food and drink on offer. And the TV got switched off as people entertained themselves rather than watch the cringe-making offerings from Edinburgh and elsewhere.

One tradition has almost gone entirely and that is the business of redding. It once was one of the most important New Year traditions to prepare for the New Year by cleaning your house from top to bottom. The men used to clear out to the pub while the women got on with the clear up in the house and the food preparation. But in these emancipated times women no longer allow themselves to be put upon – and the celebrating is nowadays a joint venture. Although Masterchef has introduced more and more men to the kitchen, it is the older women who have the recipes for the best 'clooty dumpling,' which used to have silver sixpences in it that the children would have great delight in discovering. It was said that a clean and tidy home could welcome the good spirits of the New Year in the best possible way. Special attention was given to the fireplaces, but coal is no longer king here and central heating and gas and electric fires have taken over. Peat or turf – as alluded to earlier – is making a comeback in the festive season and the aroma from it provides a perfume of nostalgia for those who can accommodate it in their homes. There are a number of things, which the Scottish families do to bring good luck. According to tradition, people used to think that debts brought bad luck, so they cleared all their debts before New Year Eve.

Nowadays I suppose that would mean having a bonfire of the credit cards, but this is something that is unlikely to happen in this age of buying goods on the 'never, never'. In the old days people placed Rowan trees at the entrances to their houses. They also placed a piece of mistletoe in the house, which was thought to bring good health for the family. Hazel and yew were reputed to bring magical power and protection respectively. Juniper was burnt in the house and all the doors and windows were kept opened during the process. It was said that burning juniper could bring a fresh air into a house. In some homes, pieces of holly were placed inside the house in order to keep away the evil spirits. So, let's hope your home keeps free of evil spirits for the next 12 months. All the best and here's to your health, wealth and happiness. A Guid New Year tae yin an' a' and many may ye hae.

Stocking up on turf to keep the home fires burning.

We three chefs from Oxhill are – Marie Digby, Bernie Heaney and Josephine Leahy get ready for the festivities.

These little Shepherd boys were getting a little anxious waiting for their Christmas dinner while taking part in the festive season service at St Patrick's in Dumbarton.
Pictures by Bill Heaney

Chapter 23

THE CONDUCTOR

Miss Jean Graham

Music teacher and choir mistress extraordinaire the late Jean Graham took her final bow to cheers and encores at a packed concert at Renton Trinity Parish Church. Hitting the high notes for one last time were Jean's 'girls', the Dalvait Singers, who have brought their wonderful music to concerts in community halls and churches across the West Dunbartonshire for the past 40 years. They have also helped to raise large sums of money for charity and been ambassadors for Scotland, earning plaudits and prizes and lifting the laurels along the way of their crotchet and quaver strewn path. Jean Graham was 81 at that time and in remarkable form and, a bit like author Muriel Spark's Miss Jean Brodie, had shown tremendous dedication and loyalty to the musical education of her 'girls', the generations of young ladies who have formed her choirs. Their singing under Jean's direction has gave huge pleasure to the thousands of people who listened to the

Dalvaits over four decades. Children who, during a remarkable 50 years of Jean teaching music in primary and secondary schools, loved Miss Graham and received huge encouragement from her. Jean, whose service to the community was recognised when she was awarded the MBE by HM the Queen, told me: 'When I began teaching, not many of the boys appeared to be interested in music and probably thought it all a bit high falutin'. But I got them interested by talking about football. I won their attention by discussing the results of teams from Arsenal to Alloa and local teams and that was what grabbed their attention. I absolutely love football – and, of course, I love music and I cherished my pupils and won most of them round.' The Dalvaits were formed in 1972 when Jean's family were members of Upper Bridge Street Church of Scotland in Alexandria, and it was as there that Jean's first choir, Upper Bridge Street Junior Choir, was formed in the 1950s. Within a few years the name was changed to the Loch Lomond Junior Singers. In the late 60s Jean had been encouraged to further her own career by moving to London and The Loch Lomond Singers were disbanded, but due to family responsibilities Jean decided to give up the opportunity. At this time Jean was teaching music and training choirs in local primary schools in the Vale of Leven and Dumbarton. Mentored by Miss Mary Hogg, then Music Adviser for Dunbartonshire County Council, Jean completed her teaching degree and was appointed to teach at Notre Dame High School in Dumbarton. In due course she became Principal Teacher of Music at the old convent school overlooking the River Clyde at Clerkhill, where she worked hand in hand with her colleague and friend, the late Anna Cameron. Some of the former members of the Loch Lomond Singers had kept in contact and began to meet in each other's homes and from this core group the Dalvait Singers were born in 1972. Over the years, senior pupils from Notre Dame and other sources joined The Dalvaits and, to the present time, many of the former Loch Lomond Singers and ex- pupils remain as part of the choir. Jean had outstanding success with all UK and abroad winning major Ladies and Open competitions and also on radio and television, including Songs of Praise. The Dalvait Singers, named after the modest Balloch street where Jean lived, continued this success and enjoyed recognition both locally and nationally with Jean at the helm and Anna as the irreplaceable accompanist. They took prizes at prestigious events, the Southport Music Festival, Inverclyde and Renfrew Music Festival, the Saltire Scots Songs competition, the Freckleton Music Festival, the Glasgow Music Festival and the Cork International Music Festival. Choir practices were held over the years in Vale of Leven Academy and then in the West Kirk in Dumbarton, moving on to the Carmelite Convent in Kirktonhill, where Jean's 80th birthday celebration took place last year, and now the new Carmel at Clerkhill. Jean said: 'I will always be grateful to the Carmelite Sisters who have for many years have provided us with accommodation for practices and indeed have become close friends.' She added that Dalvait highlights over the years included a 1983 civic reception from Dumbarton District Council, a Silver Jubilee Concert in 1997 and the fact that some truly international stars took part in a number of their annual concerts. They included Anne Lorne Gillies, Collette Ruddy, John Heddle Nash jnr., Covent Garden and Scottish Opera singer David Ward from Dumbarton and organist Nigel Ogden. Dalvait member Margo Wilson, a former teacher at Knoxland PS in Dumbarton, said: 'Jean loved to encourage young musicians and they were provided with a platform at annual concerts. When Jean became involved in adjudication she handed over festival participation to our depute conductor, Patricia Duffy, who also led us to success in festivals in the last few years. Jean has left control of the choir to Patricia and Maureen Rogers, of Our Lady and St Patrick's High School, both of whom are excellent musicians and conductors in their own right, and both of whom were pupils of Jean's at Notre Dame High School.'

Jean Graham, Anna Cameron, Patricia Duffy, Susan Jo Hanna, Hazel McLaughlin and Carol McLean, of the irreplaceable Dalvait Singers.

Packed audiences were guaranteed for the Dalvait Singers (above and below). *Pictures by Bill Heaney*

The Dalvait Singers performing at a charity concert for children in Zimbabwe at St Patrick's Church in Dumbarton.

The Dalvait Singers with Jean Graham and Anna Cameron.

Maureen Rodger, left, and the Dalvait Singers performing in Dumbarton.

Chapter 24

THE CREDIT UNION

Dumbarton Credit Union chairman Pat Tonner pictured with Kate Hosie, the assistant manager, and founder member Tom O'Neill outside their new premises at 147 High Street, Dumbarton.
Picture by Bill Heaney

A remarkable £22 million has been loaned to the 7000 members of Dumbarton Credit Union since the organisation was formed in 1990. Large numbers of local people were struggling to obtain loans from banks and other financial institutions at that time. It was even difficult to open a bank account which is essential for people to receive benefits or do almost any kind of business. The CU was founded by a small group of like minded activists, including the Justice and Peace groups from local churches, who wished to provide a positive alternative to high interest loan companies and loan sharks. It has now become a focal point for good and ethical banking facilities within the town and operates from new premises at 147 High Street,

Dumbarton. The membership has grown from just 27 members in 1990 to currently over 7000 adults and about 1500 junior account holders following a campaign in the schools to persuade young people to manage their money. Those junior members who had accounts opened for them as toddlers and children have been able to transfer their accounts to adult membership and most have continued to save and as adults borrow from the credit union. The services provided by Dumbarton Credit Union are varied and include savings, loans, free insurance and death benefits and have recently become available to internet users, with access available to all members. The website is *www.dumbartoncreditunion.org.* Dumbarton man Pat Tonner, chairman of the Credit Union, is delighted with their success and proud of the work done by so many volunteers under his leadership. He said: 'We are especially pleased that the community has placed their trust in us to look after their hard-earned savings and that they come to us to borrow money when they need it. We provide a safe home for their savings and a sympathetic ear for ordinary working people and that is very important in these times of cutbacks and economic austerity. It is especially important to celebrate the excellent work that our credit union carries out over 25 successful years during which we have only once failed to make a profit. Ours is a not for profit organisation owned by all the members and we are looking to the future with a view to increasing the products and services we provide. Our members come to us at those important times in their life when they require extra money to see them through – times like births, deaths and marriages. We are also here to help them fund Christmas and holiday expenses and with money to assist them when they are moving house, buying furniture and decorating.'

The Credit Union stepped in when customers of the workplace 'ménage' organisation Farepak encountered serious problems during the banking crisis. Pat Tonner said: 'Setting up the Credit Union wasn't easy but we persevered and after a while, with the help of the late Rose Dorman and spirited others, we managed it. We are grateful to all those volunteers, some of whom continue to be volunteers today, and also to our staff who are there to make our members feel welcome and comfortable when they doing business here. 'Our watchword here is trust. Our members trust us with their savings and we trust them to repay what they borrow from the Union. That way we all benefit. We have had a steady growth of members over the years and we are now getting into second and third generations of members. The C U is an ethical banking alternative. Apart from favourable loans interest rates of 12.7% apr – that is just 6p in the pound per year - and a dividend on savings, currently 1.5% for adults and 4.0% for juniors we provide life insurance on savings and loan balances. Since 1990 almost £22 million has been loaned to members. We have an adult membership of slightly over 7000 plus 1500 juniors. A Super Savers scheme is operating in a number of local schools and West Dunbartonshire Council have helped to encourage this by offering £10 to every pupil joining scheme.' The CU is run by an annually elected Board of Directors. Pat Tonner added: 'We would hope to continue with well managed growth of membership and while in no way diminishing the personal touch which is a big feature of our operation, this growth would hopefully be accompanied by use of technology such as phone apps and so on.'

This photograph of office bearers was taken in Riverside Parish Church Hall on June 7, 1990, at the formal opening of Dumbarton Credit Union. Standing left to right. Deirdre Lynch, Tom O'Neill, Pat Tonner, Eileen Lally, Anna Trainer, Sister Anne Jane O'Rourke, Margaret Orr, Sarah Davis, Helen McGillen, Sally Connolly, Jock Findlay and Eamonn Cullen. Seated: Siobhan Kerr, Sandra Scott, Anindya Majumdar, Gregor Gordon, Barbara Croft, Carol McCafferty and Helen Devlin. Missing due to work commitments is Tommy Trainer who was also involved in a previous attempt to set up credit union in the West End.

Chapter 25

THE SAILOR

Arthur McWatt celebrates with Jackie Baillie MSP

Dumbarton war veteran Arthur McWatt received the surprise of a very long lifetime when the Consul General of the Russian Federation in Edinburgh turned up at his 90th birthday party in Cardross Golf Club. Consul General Andrey Pritsepov arrived to present Arthur with the Ushakov medal for bravely taking part in the Arctic Convoys near the end of the Second World War. The Ushakov medal is awarded to sailors who have displayed courage in the course of defending Russia or its interests. Winston Churchill said the Arctic convoys' missions through the North Sea in winter were 'the worst Journey on earth'. Under constant threat of attack by German U-boats and aircraft, the convoys also had to deal with severe cold, storms, and ice floes. By May 1945, the Arctic route had claimed 104 merchant and 16 military vessels and thousands of Allied seamen lost their lives. Arthur was the first person in Scotland to receive the medal for serving on the Denny-built destroyer *HMS Walker*, while escorting merchant ships between the UK and the Soviet Union. Just 18 at the time, Able Seaman McWatt said his ship was 'leaking like a sieve' when, along with the destroyers *HMS Beagle* and *HMS Boadicea*, and four Flower-class corvettes, *HMS Walker* took part in that dangerous duty. Although the convoy, carrying vital arms and food supplies to northern Russia, endured German air and submarine attacks during its passage, it suffered no losses among its ships and arrived safely at the Kola Inlet on February 28, 1944. Two months later, *HMS Walker* joined the same vessels as close escort for the returning convoy, carrying from Russia reciprocal supplies of timber, coal, fur and magnesium, when it was attacked by German submarines. It arrived safely at Loch Ewe in Scotland, on March 10. The convoy escort ships were constantly threatened as they went about their business, which included escorting the merchant ship *Nea Hellas* on a voyage to collect ships and personnel from various Soviet Arctic ports. At one point, *HMS Walker* took on board 13 United States Navy enlisted men and brought them back to the UK. Again they experienced freezing conditions and two days of terrifying German submarine torpedo attacks.

The UK Foreign Office initially did not allow Russia to honour veterans like Arthur as it broke the rules on foreign medals. At his home in Geils Avenue, Dumbarton, surrounded by birthday cards and flowers to mark his 90th birthday, Arthur said: 'I certainly didn't feel like a hero. I was just a teenager at the time, too young even to qualify for a tot of rum. I just did what I had to do and that was that. The conditions were atrocious and our ship, which was built here in Dumbarton, leaked like a sieve. We were up to our knees and sometimes up to our waists in freezing water.' He said the medal presentation was a great surprise to him – 'I knew nothing about it. I didn't even know it was going to happen.' Arthur was born in Burma where his father worked as part of a team from Denny's shipyard building the Irrawaddy fleet. He returned to Dumbarton as a teenager and went to Dumbarton Academy for two years before taking up a post at the old Employment

Exchange in College Street. 'It was there that I signed up for service in the Royal Navy,' he said. Arthur, who married Cardross farmer's daughter, the late Margaret McKinstry, at Cardross Parish Church in July, 1952, worked as a civil servant until his retirement. He is the proud father of Brian, David and Marie and devoted grandfather of Joanne, Martin, Tina, Kevan, David, Scott, Paul, Catherine, Andrew and Adam. He is well known and respected throughout Dunbartonshire and beyond as a keen golfer and has been a member at Cardross Golf Club since 1948. 'My grandpa is an absolute legend,' said grandson Scott. Civic Dumbarton also turned up at the golf club, festooned with Russian Federation flags, and Jackie Baillie MSP and Deputy Provost John Miller congratulated Arthur.

In addition to the Ushakov medal, Arthur has also been presented with a splendid pocket flask emblazoned with the Russian eagle. He is also the proud possessor of the Arctic Star which the British Government created in 2012 following a long campaign for the convoy veterans to be recognised.

HMS Walker, Denny-built and 'leaked like a sieve'.

Arthur McWatt, pictured on his 90th birthday.

Chapter 26

THE GREATS

James Reston, brought up in Alexandria and Renton.

Dunbartonshire people are everywhere. Some of them are, or were, people of extraordinary talent, achievements and influence in the history of the world.

We have had authors such as AJ Cronin, Tobias Smollett and John Quigley, who wrote King's Royal about whisky and tobacco barons. Many of these people once lived in turreted, sandstone mansions along the banks of Loch Lomond and the Gareloch, where they sailed their luxury yachts. Others, like Tom Gallacher, who wrote The Apprentice and Mr Joyce Is Leaving Paris, a completely different sort of book about Dubliner James Joyce, the author of Ulysses, had a more modest upbringing. Gallacher also acted in and produced plays for the Dumbarton People's Theatre, which put on its popular productions in

The Tin Hall in Glasgow Road and later in the Denny Civic Theatre. Then there is Agnes Owens, the Haldane housewife who wrote A Working Mother and For the Love of Willie. Maurice Lindsay, the poet from Milton Hill, wrote many poems including a memorable one about children feeding swans on the Leven.

The fridge was invented by James Harrison, who had connections with Renton, and television was the brainchild of John Logie Baird, of Helensburgh, where architect Charles Rennie Macintosh's iconic Hill House stands. It is said that King Robert the Bruce and St Patrick were born in these parts. There is no doubt, when you include the history of the great ships built on Clydeside and the textile industry which burgeoned along the banks of the River Leven, that we have a rich and colourful past.

Add to that the Bonnie Banks, Ben Lomond and Conic Hill plus the Cobbler and the mountains along the route to Glencoe and we have riches beyond the dreams of avarice. Dumbarton Academy FP Lord Steel of Aikwood, whose father was the minister at Bridgend Parish Church, became the first Presiding Officer of the Scottish Parliament. Stars of stage and screen include Deborah Kerr, from Helensburgh, who with Yule Bryner starred in *The King and I* and James Copeland, from Dumbarton, who was in *Braveheart* with Mel Gibson. Then there were the journalists, many of whom worked for the *Lennox Herald* and went on to great success.

Film star Deborah Kerr (left) and author Agnes Owens

The most famous journalist of all was James 'Scotty' Reston, who was brought up in Renton, Alexandria and Clydebank, where he was born. The Restons emigrated in the Hungry Thirties and Scotty rose through the ranks of reporters and sub editors to become editor of the world's most famous newspaper, the *New York Times*. I wrote about him when he was given an honorary doctorate from the University of Glasgow and I reviewed his autobiography, *Deadline*.

Reston's name has come up yet again in a new book, the *Letters of John F Kennedy*. There are some fascinating insights into Kennedy's life and work in this volume of personal correspondence. Arthur Slesinger Jr., wrote in 1960 to the then aspiring President Kennedy about the views of the Restons, Scotty and his wife, Sally. He said he had spoken to them after Reston was critical in his column of a speech Kennedy made about religion and politics. Reston had wondered whether America was ready to elect its first Catholic president and to what extent the religion card would be played.

Schlesinger said the effect of the column was to give the Catholic-bloc issue 'an importance out of all proportion to its place in the speech'. And that, in doing this, he 'failed badly to do justice to what seemed to me in the main an exceptionally clear and courageous statement'. The Restons were said to be well disposed towards Kennedy 'but still unsatisfied by your treatment of the religious problem'. Their main concern was that they felt Kennedy by implication in his speech made out that 'bigotry is essentially a Protestant monopoly'. From then on Kennedy denounced bigotry in all its forms and made it clear it was not a Protestant failing, but something that Catholics too were guilty of. Kennedy's words then hold good today -- 'I don't want a single Catholic vote for me for the reason I am a Catholic any more than a single Protestant to vote against me for that reason.'

James Reston's obituary, which appears later in this book, and is from the New York Times, states: 'First as a reporter and then, beginning in 1953, as a columnist, Mr. Reston was perhaps the most influential journalist of his generation. In Washington, where he was based, and also in other capitals around the world, he had unrivalled access to the high and the mighty. Yet he retained a wry, self-deprecating personality, free of bombast, and always sought to reduce political complexity to plain language.'

* *The Letters of John F Kennedy, edited by Martin W. Sanders is published by Bloomsbury, price £20.*

Renton – the view from Carman Hill towards Dumbarton.

Chapter 27

THE BOATMAN

Edward Sweeney (left) and brother, John, aboard one of the family's line of luxury cruisers on Loch Lomond.

Edward Sweeney, one of the longest serving and best known luxury cruise boatmen on Loch Lomond, sadly died of cancer at his home in Balloch, West Dunbartonshire, in July 2015 aged just 53. A wonderful guide to the Bonnie Banks and colourful story-teller known to tens of thousands of people who visit the loch each year, Ed, a marine engineer, was part of the family which operates Sweeney's Cruises which has operated boats on Loch Lomond since the 1880s. Ed was literally immersed in the business from the age of three when, while playing near the boatyard he fell into the River Leven and had to be rescued by his father, John, after a friend, Emilio Giannini, raised the alarm. When his father got to him to pull him out Ed was clinging for dear life to the edge of a pontoon with his head under the water. Emilio's parents owned an Italian café at nearby Balloch Bridge and after that incident the two boys became friends for life. "It has never been forgotten that Mio saved Ed's life that day," his brother, John, told friends. Over the next half century, Ed was seldom far from Loch Lomond and in that time he came to know every inch and fathom of the famed 24-mile loch, which is the largest inland stretch of water in Great Britain.

He was an expert on the loch's 22 islands and 27 islets and could name the wildlife on each of them from the red-necked wallabies and capercailzie on Inchconnachan to the magnificent ospreys which nest in the woods in Inchcailloch. Ed often pointed out to visitors the Highland Boundary Fault which runs south-west through the islands and informed them of the stunning views to be had of this from Ben Lomond and Conic Hill. Inevitably there were always smiles among the passengers when Ed steered his boat close – but never too close – to the naturist colony on Inchmurrin, the loch's largest island. Ed was a fountain of knowledge about Loch

Lomond, its hugely varied wildlife, its wealth of history, including the adventures of cattle rustler Rob Roy MacGregor, the folklore and the legend:

Waves without win'
Fish without fin
Floating islands

The Cobbler at Arrochar and Tarbet Hotel one of the views Eddie showed thousands of visitors. *Picture by Bill Heaney*

After about 20 years, Ed bowed to technology and gave up doing commentaries for visitors from behind the wheel. Neil Oliver, the archaeologist, historian, broadcaster and writer who has become widely known as the presenter of BBC television's series 'A History of Scotland' and 'Coast' took over on tape. Ed also knew where the best music was to be found in the lochside village; which pubs had the best beer and whiskies, and where visitors could find a bed for the night and the best fish suppers. His nephew, John Sweeney, told the large congregation at Ed's funeral Mass, which was celebrated by Father Jim Lawlor at St Kessog's Church in Balloch, that it was seriously reckoned that Ed had spent more hours on Loch Lomond than anyone else alive - "maybe even more than anyone ever. The family take great comfort in the fact that so much of Ed's life was spent in such a beautiful part of the world."

Ed was born in the family home in Cardross Road, Dumbarton, in 1962. He was the youngest child of Mary and John Sweeney, an engineer, and brother to Jimmy, John and Noreen. The Sweeneys lived in Dumbarton until Ed was three when they moved to Balloch after his grandparents took over the boatyard. Nearly all of Ed's life was spent around the boats and he had a fund of stories about all the characters and personalities who lived and worked around the river and Loch Lomond for years. He was one himself.

He went to school at St Mary's in Alexandria and St Patrick's High School in Dumbarton before serving his apprenticeship at the marine engineering firm, Mitchell Outboard Services in Glasgow. All the while he was helping out driving boats on Loch Lomond at the weekend, a job which he eventually started to do full-time. Ed was a talented water and snow skier and he enjoyed scuba diving. A familiar face in Balloch's pubs, Ed made no secret of the fact that once upon a time he might have been partial to a pint of lager but one day he suddenly quit cigarettes and alcohol and took to drinking diet Irn Bru. Ever a creature of habit, Ed, who never married, could still be found in the pub most nights. He enjoyed holidays in Florida, Spain and Cyprus, where he would hire a motorbike, cruise around the island and go water-skiing and scuba diving. Ed loved driving the fleet of luxury cruise boats on the Loch and took great pride in the success of the business and in his brother, John, who built it up into a major force in Scottish tourism.

One of the earliest ships in the Sweeney fleet was, Skylark IX, one of the "little ships" which took part in D-Day and which they modernised and made a more comfortable vessel to cruise in before it was sold. For many years John Sweeney gave Skylark IX's services free, to Dunkirk Veterans once a year, for their reunion on Loch Lomond and Ed was part of the team who looked after them. Ed Sweeney, whose funeral took place to Vale of Leven Cemetery, is survived by his mother, Mary, and his siblings, Jimmy, John and Noreen and their children.

The Sweeneys receive a visit from John McFall, then MP for West Dunbartonshire. Left to right are Ed and John Sweeney, Lord McFall of Alcluith and Jay Green.
Picture by Bill Heaney

Chapter 28

THE GUILD

Reunion for St Michael's BG in the church hall in 1982 (Bill is 3rd from right). *Picture by Brian Averell*

Like many young Brucehill men, it was one of the biggest and happiest days of my life when I came of age to join the Boy's Guild in the West End. It's a long time ago now – more than 50 years - so the photographs on this page will bring back happy memories of St Michael's Boys' Guild camps in Ireland. These holidays for pupils of St Patrick's High School cost a total of £7 per young person for their boat ticket and two weeks living in fresh air and fallow fields in bell tents in places like Buncrana in Co Donegal, Greystones, Bray and Wicklow town in Co Wicklow. Seventy or 80 boys travelled overnight on board the Burns Laird Line's *Scottish Coast* from Broomielaw to Dublin. The highlight of the first part of the journey was to sail past Dumbarton Rock and then Brucehill where friends and family would stand and wave at the top of the cliff at Firthview. Some tearful mothers there even waved sheets off the bed out of the window and shouted a fond farewell to their sons heading off for their annual adventure.

Not infrequently the boat journey took between 14 to 22 hours when the weather was rough. And it could be really choppy out on the Irish Sea beyond Ailsa Craig, otherwise known as Paddy's Milestane. The lads travelled steerage, usually reserved for cattle, carrying their kitbags and a paillasses for bedding plus their own knives, forks and spoons. It was a case of bring your own cup and saucer and a bun – and it really was fun. Half a crown a day most of them had for pocket money. It was spread between playing the juke box, buying ice cream and sweeties and bottles of 'ginger' and going to the 'pictures'. The most popular record on the juke box at the Anchor Café in Greystones - and Deirdre's in the main street in Wicklow – at that time was Del Shannon's 'My Little Runaway'. Having just had a look at Shannon singing that song on *YouTube*, I can exclusively reveal that it has been played a remarkable 5,403,803 times. The big Buncrana picture, which has lots of familiar local faces in it with their chaplain, Father Donal Burke, right there in the centre, will bring back memories for many people. Take a close look at it and see who you can pick out.

Horse riding in Wicklow – Ian 'Wiggie' McFall is given a lesson.

Tommy Gardiner (standing), Davie Rainey, Donnie Wilson and Tom Macdonnell.

St Michael's BG at one of the first camps in Buncrana, Co Donegal

Among the volunteers adult helpers are, extreme left in row two, John 'Snowy' Currie. The two men on the extreme right are Eddie Sweeney and Dick McCallion, the camp medical man. Faces to look out for include Gerry Holloran, Graham Sweeney, Eddie Devlin, John Kelly, Chris McKay, George Philpott, Hughie Scullion, John 'Whistler' McFall, Jim Donnelly, Willie Diamond, Tom 'Skip' Walsh, Eddie Sweeney junior, Tony Donaldson and Peter Currie. We're certain you will know even more of these faces. Those Fair Isle pullovers are bang in fashion these days and cost a small fortune. The Wicklow picture was taken at a camp on the banks of the Murrough River around 1957. I have some of the names including Ian 'Wiggy' McFall, who learnt horse riding in Wicklow. Some of John Sweeney, John Kelly, Frank Kelly, Frank Beattie, Joe Bell, Jimmy Carr, Danny Walker, and the late Mrs Annie McKay, who lived to celebrate her 102nd birthday. Brucehill man Jimmy Moran, who played in Vale of Leven Juniors Scottish Cup winning team 60 years ago in 1953, Elizabeth Carr, Felix Devlin, Johnny 'Drummer' Reilly and Paddy Reilly are in the picture. These photographs were passed on to me by Annie McKay's son, Archie McKay, who now lives in Canada. And the on-site camp photographs were taken in Greystones. The photograph of the 1982 reunion of the Boys' Guild in St Michael's Church Hall has lots of familiar faces.

John Sweeney, John Kelly, Frank Kelly, Frank Beattie, Joe Bell, Jimmy Carr, Danny Walker, and the late Mrs Annie McKay, who lived to celebrate her 102nd birthday. Brucehill man Jimmy Moran, who played in Vale of Leven Juniors Scottish Cup winning team in 1953, Elizabeth Carr, Felix Devlin, Johnny 'Drummer' Reilly and Paddy Reilly are in this picture taken in Wicklow on the banks of the Murrough.

That's Joe Bell and John McLaughlin drumming up and Tom Currie, Frank Beattie and Felix Devlin on the binoculars.

St Michael's BG under 15s (left to right) back row Neil McCallion, John McCann, Seamus McCallion, John Diamond, David Rainey, Brian McGoldrick, Eddie Sweeney (coach) and Bill Heaney. Front Brian Palfrey, Frank Law, Jack Sweeney, Donnie Wilson and Gerry Brennan.

Picture by Peter Leddy, Dunbartonshire News

Denmark-based John Reilly, David Rainey, Jim Broadley, Evan Williams, the former Celtic goalkeeper, John 'Toora' Quigley, Jimmy Neeson and Pat McHugh.

Jack McGinn, Michael Currie, Kevin Clancy, Eddie McKinley, Father John McLaren, Malky Stewart, Alex Hanna, Felix McGrogan, Joe Doherty. Front – Jimmy Cairney, Donal Currie, Fred Sharp, George Stewart and Arthur Williams.

(bottom of previous page) St Michael's team from Dumbarton in 1961. Back row, left to right, Pat Currie, Tommy Casey (whose wife, Avril, sent this picture from Canada where they now live), Matt McTaggart, John Toora Quigley, Hugh Deeney, Pat Boyle and Harry Gow. Front row are Tam McEwan, Tommy McFall, Joe Currie, Columb McKinley, Tommy McMullen and Adam Robinson.

Guild members go swimming in Greystones.

Chapter 29

THE COLLEGE

Trashed by vandals before the renovation scheme started to save St Peter's College, Cardross. Pictures by Bill Heaney

I have always thought of the hills above Cardross as a holy place. Perhaps that has been because from childhood I associated the village with churches and seminaries and ministers and priests. I knew quite a few of the seminarians at St Peter's College and played football with and against some of them. For supposedly holy men, they had a reputation for being pretty brutal on the pitch and never shy about putting the boot into the opposition. I often wondered if they ever confessed to diving or going in over the ball. There were a number of the students – and their lecturers – who were very good golfers. And why wouldn't they be when they only had to hop over the fence and they were on the undulating fairways and manicured greens of Cardross Golf Club?

From my early days as a newspaper reporter I knew the Rev Andrew Scobie, the late minister of Cardross Parish Church. I used to cover the meetings of the Dumbarton Presbytery of the Church of Scotland and I recall Andrew, as a minister newly called by the congregation to Cardross, bravely standing up to speak out against nuclear weapons. Why 'bravely' you may ask? Well, one of the Kirk Session at Cardross was also one of the fathers and brethren of the Presbytery and he was at the meeting. He was none other than Admiral Sir Angus Cunninghame Graham, of Ardoch, Her Majesty's Lord Lieutenant of Dunbartonshire. Sir Angus had also served in the Royal

Navy at the Battle of Jutland in 1916 and on the Arctic Convoys during the Second World and was a formidable military figure. This did not deter the youthful, not so wet behind the ears Andrew Scobie from challenging him on the question of possession of Polaris missiles, which were soon to be stored in Glen Douglas and sent out on submarines from Faslane. I must say I admired the minister's courage which was frowned upon by many of the elders and ministers present. Ban the Bomb wasn't something the establishment embraced warmly at that time. It was quite a battle between Andrew and Sir Angus and quite a story for the local and national press at the time.

But back to the churches and St Peter's College, which is an enigma not easily explained or understood. So many people think of the seminary, which was built close by Kilmahew House, as an unsightly pile of concrete and glass which despoils the countryside above the Clyde. However, for others, it is a masterpiece of modernist architecture towards which the Heritage Lottery Fund has been persuaded to donate substantial funds to rescue it. Various schemes have been explored by the owners, the Archdiocese of Glasgow, to find an alternative use for the building. These include establishing a luxury spa hotel with swimming pools and gardens and access to the golf course. One bold plan after another fell through to the great consternation and dismay of a number of Archbishops, including Cardinal Tom Winning and Archbishop Mario Conti, and the building became a derelict ruin.

Monsignor Charles Burns (left) concelebrates Mass with Archbishop Emeritus Mario Conti and St Mahew's parish priest, Father Dominic Doogan.

There were numerous visitations by councillors to see what could be done and on one of them Provost Billy Petrie was badly hurt when he fell through the floor into a pit. The Church could not simply bulldoze the college it since it was an A-listed building, and the saga went on. St Peter's was designed by Gillespie, Kidd and Coia and built in 1966 – I was present at the 'topping out' ceremony - as a training college for priests. However, clerical recruitment dried up and it has not been used since the 1980s.

NVA, an arts organisation and charity based in Glasgow, was founded in 1992 and its name is an acronym of nacionale vitae activa, a Latin term meaning 'the right to influence public affairs'. The company is best known for its dramatic, large-scale environmental artworks in Scottish natural landscapes. Despite the National Lottery cash however it needs to raise another £7.5m in funding to finish the project. NVA aims to partially restore parts of the seminary, including the chapel, and maintain the rest of the site as a modern ruin, which can be visited. Angus Farquhar, creative director of NVA, said: 'The seminary building is held in high regard throughout the world. It has now been given the chance of a second life after 25 years of decline. St Peter's Seminary is a masterpiece of Scottish modern architecture but after decades of neglect its condition is perilous'.

The World Monuments Fund, which works to preserve endangered cultural landmarks, added St Peter's College to its register in June 2007. Colin McLean, head of the Heritage Lottery Fund in Scotland, said: 'We hope that at some time in the future people will be able to explore, learn from and enjoy the layers of history and heritage that lie within this unique building and the estate surrounding it.' Culture secretary Fiona Hyslop has described St Peter's as 'one of Scotland's most important modern 20th century buildings'. This project would at last see the buildings and their wonderful landscape setting conserved and enhanced for the benefit of the community, she said.

St Peter's College at Cardross, Dunbartonshire.

Since then the college has hosted Hinterland - 10 sound and light shows and the NVA has been raising money to make the remnants of St Peter's safe for music and theatre. NVA creative director Angus Farquhar said the staging of the Hinterland programme was a significant milestone.

He said: 'Almost 50 years on from the day the seminary opened, we are witnessing the first positive steps towards a new purpose, one that accepts loss and ruination as part of the site's history creating an evolving arts programme for local people, all of Scotland and visitors attracted to this iconic site from around the world.'

He added that Hinterland had offered everyone a chance to visit the St Peter's at a key moment in its evolution and was one of the must-see arts events of 2016 'leading on to the delivery of an important new creative and heritage resource for progressive public art in Scotland and beyond'.

The inside of the ruin was transformed for the Hinterland programme, but obviously not completely. St Peter's was deconsecrated in 1980 and soon became a playground for vandals and graffiti artists. Even as the interior was slowly degraded by fire and rain, students of architecture continued to come from around the world to view the vaulted ceilings and floating staircases of its creators, Andy MacMillan and Isi Metzstein. Formal recognition followed and the seminary was Category A listed by Historic Scotland in 1992. The World Monuments Fund, which works to preserve endangered cultural landmarks, added St Peter's College to its register in June 2007 and experts believe it is now on the brink of becoming a quite new type of visitor and a national cultural attraction.

'The impressive spaces and dramatic allure of its contrasting concrete geometries will be a remarkable setting for public art, music and theatre,' the NVA believe.

From the crumbling seminary then you can make your way across the Carman hills in the direction of Helensburgh, past the remains of another college run by the Xavarian Fathers, and find tiny St Mahew's chapel in Cardross, the smallest Catholic Church in the Archdiocese of Glasgow. Monsignor Charles Burns, a former student at St Peter's when it was based in Kilmahew House, joined fellow students in 1951 on a project to save St Mahew's when they volunteered to restore it.

Monsignor Burns is now based in Rome where he is a canon of St Peter's Basilica, the first Scot ever to hold this prestigious appointment in the Vatican. An 81-year-old historian and archivist, he first went to Rome as a seminarian at the Scots College back in the early 1950s. After doctoral studies in church history at the Gregorian University, he ended up spending 35 years as the chief archivist at the Vatican's Secret Archives. Because of his vast knowledge of the popes and the Vatican, the Pontifical Ecclesiastical Academy hired him in 1987 to lecture to the 'future' Church on papal diplomacy. He officially retired in 2002, but in 2003, the British Embassy to the Holy See invited him to be its ecclesiastical adviser.

Monsignor Charles Burns pictured with a family of parishioners at St Mahew's in Cardross. *Picture by Bill Heaney*

Monsignor Charlie was back in Cardross on Tuesday morning of August 17, 2010, he and Archbishop Mario Conti, an old friend from his student days concelebrated Mass there with the parish priest, Father Dominic Doogan He said afterwards that he and Archbishop Conti had shared a common interest in history and heraldry and in gardens and gardening and the Arts. He had a special affinity with St Mahew's because he and his fellow students had worked hard manually to clear and restore the little chapel, which dates back to 1370, and bring it back into use in 1955. It is one of the smallest and oldest chapels in Scotland and only Pluscarden Abbey in Morayshire can claim to have been in use longer. St Mahew's had fallen into serious disrepair and near dereliction until after the Second World War. However, in 1948, the chapel once again became the property of the Archdiocese. This was after Monsignor Burns and some of the seminarians and staff enthusiastically lobbied the then archbishop, Archbishop Campbell, to purchase it and bring it back into use. Monsignor Burns said: 'The restoration work began when the Cardross seminarians were encouraged to look into the history of St Mahew's. We believed then that it was well worth it – and it was.'

Monsignor Charlie Burns helped to restore St Mahew's chapel in Cardross.

Chapter 30

THE FACTORY

Singer's famous clock.

Those were the days when nearly everyone had a job that paid well. The Sixties was a wonderful period when local people worked hard and played hard. It the era of Rock 'n' Roll, the Beatles and the Rolling Stones and, for the woolly jumper brigade, Val Doonican. Dancing was the name of the game at weekends – and on high days and holidays. And a 'works dance' was really special, something everyone looked forward to. The photograph with this article of workers from Singer's in Clydebank at their annual 'knees up' around 1967/68 was posted on social media by Councillor George Black. And it brought back memories for many of the people from right across West Dunbartonshire who worked in the sprawling factory north of Kilbowie Road. Many thousands of people – a remarkable number – were employed on putting those famous sewing machines together. *A Stitch in Time* – a history of the Singer factory - was one of the first exhibitions which West Dunbartonshire Council launched in the refurbished Town Hall Museum about ten years ago. Former employees – many of them from Clydebank, Dumbarton, Vale of Leven and Helensburgh - who put the world famous sewing machines together, went along for the trip down memory lane. The exhibition brought back many happy memories for people – and sad ones too of old colleagues and friends from the factory who have since passed on. Singer was first established in 1885 at Kilbowie, which only later became Clydebank, and grew to become the largest factory in the world. In 1867, Singer set up a factory near Queen Street Station in Glasgow. This factory assembled sewing machines from parts shipped from Singer factories in America to supply the UK and European markets. As demand grew world-wide, Singer relocated to Bridgeton and eventually to Clydebank, which had excellent transport links via road, rail and river and an abundant skilled labour resource thanks mainly to the existing shipbuilding industry in the area. The factory building was completed in 1885 and had the capacity to manufacture 8000 sewing machines a week, employed 3500 people and manufactured sewing machines that were sent around the globe. Singer's gave Clydebank its most famous landmark - the 200ft clock tower stood over the central wing and had the reputation of being the largest four faced clock in the world. Each face weighed five tons and it took four men fifteen minutes twice a week to keep it wound.

Having a wonderful night out – workers from Singer in 1967.
Picture courtesy George Black

As demand continued to grow so did the factory. In the early 1900s a new power station was built to supply the factory with electricity, a cabinet factory, store and sawmill were also added to the site. This expansion necessitated the relocation of Kilbowie train station in 1907. The new station was named Singer Station, one of only a few stations to take its name from a local industry in the UK. In 1913 production peaked at the factory and space was again becoming an issue. Several more extensions and new buildings were added that year; the last phase of major building works at the site. At its production peak in 1913 the factory had grown to occupy a site of over 100 acres, more than double the initial area of land purchased in 1881, manufactured over 80% of the company's product and, in 1913, shipped 1,301,851 sewing machines from its factory doors around the world with help from its 14,000 employees. The onset of the Great War brought the beginning of a general decline in demand for sewing machines in the 1920's and the Great Depression of the 1930s meant production rates at the Clydebank factory never again reached the highs of 1913. In 1913, the Singer Recreation Hall and Grounds were formally opened. Sporting clubs, horticultural societies and music groups were some of the many activities provided for employees. During the Second World War, Singer continued to manufacture domestic and industrial sewing machines but at a greatly reduced rate. The Clydebank factory was awarded its first war contract for the production of tools used in the manufacture of aircraft and focused on the manufacture of munitions, aircraft parts and equipment for the war effort. On the nights of the Clydebank Blitz, the factory was bombed and suffered extensive damage. No loss of life was recorded at the factory, but 39 Singer workers died in the town. Less than six weeks after the Blitz full production had resumed despite the loss of 390,000 square feet of the factory. Singer's had its own company of the Home Guard, several of whom were involved in the action on the evenings of the Blitz. Among them was Platoon Commander Alexander Ballantyne of the 2nd Dunbartonshire Battalion, whose actions during the nights of the 13th and 14th March 1941 won him the George Medal. In the post war years the rebuilding of the destroyed areas of the factory and the training of staff in normal production techniques was slow and steady but never again reached the peak of 1913. Between 1961 and 1964 the Clydebank factory underwent a £4 million modernization programme which saw the Clydebank factory cease the production of cast iron machines and focus on the production of aluminium machines for western markets. As part of this modernisation programme the famous Singer Clock was demolished in 1963. With modernisation of the factory, managerial reorganisation and increasing competition in the sewing machine market in the post war period there was a steady fall in orders. This impacted on employment at the Clydebank factory. Employee figures dropped from over 15,000 in 1960 to just over 6,000 on 1972. Changing fashion also impacted on sewing machine sales which had a direct effect on employment at Clydebank. As the preference moved from treadle or cabinet enclosed machine to portable, light weight machines the Woodwork Division closed in 1966 with the loss of 1,200 jobs. As a result of increased competition and with a history of 180 years of sewing machine manufacture, it was announced on the 12th October 1979 that 'with the deepest regret' the Clydebank factory would close. It was a sad day for Dunbartonshire when Singer's finally closed.

Singer employees attend an exhibition about the Clydebank factory. *Picture by Bill Heaney*

Chapter 31

THE NAVAL BASE

Commander Peter Fickling and the Clyde Naval Base.

The Base. Some people have always called it that, but it is officially HM Naval Base Clyde. Before that it was as HMS Neptune, home of the Third Submarine Squadron, and before that again HMS Maidstone was the submarine mother ship there. Maidstone was at the heart of one of the biggest stories I ever worked on as a reporter. I was just 20 and covering Dunbartonshire for a national news agency when I was told that Commander Peter Fickling, 42, who lived in Helensburgh with his wife and five sons, had gone missing. His clothes were said to have been left on the shore in a bundle at Rhu Spit, near the Royal Northern Yacht Club.

A Royal Navy submarine being escorted up the Gareloch to Faslane.
Picture by Bill Heaney

Colleagues said he left HMS Maidstone at Faslane at 11pm on Wednesday, February 10, 1965, and had not been seen since. To this day, Commander Fickling's disappearance has been steeped in mystery. It has been compared over the years to the vanishing of John Stonehouse, the MP who attempted to fake his own drowning when he was reported missing, presumed drowned, off the coast of Miami. But the Navyman's disappearance was certainly not a copycat of Stonehouse since that incident did not happen until November, 1974. Fickling's light grey and red Volkswagen Caravette, registration number 2936 BH, was found far out on Rhu Spit, pointing inland, and his cap and wrist watch were inside. It was the era of James Bond spy thrillers and there was widespread speculation that Fickling may either have been taken by the Russians – or that he had defected to them. Reports of sightings of him on trains and boats and planes flooded in from all over Europe and every time a body was found around Loch Lomondside or in the nearby mountains reports that it might be him continued to make all the front pages. His light grey and red camper van, registration number 2936 BH, was found far out on Rhu Spit, pointing inland, and his cap and wrist watch were inside.

Although a massive search of the area was made by naval and police personnel, and part of the Gareloch was dragged, but there was no sign of the popular officer. One theory, repeated by my colleague Donald Fullarton in the Helensburgh Heritage website, was that Fickling must have gone to check the navigation lights on the Spit. And that he had fallen into the fast flowing tide at the Narrows, and — although he was a strong swimmer — been swept away to his death. Questions were raised about his disappearance in the House of Commons, but the whole episode remains a mystery to this day.

The history of HMS Maidstone, which was built by local tradesmen at John Brown's shipyard in Clydebank and launched in October 1937, is itself colourful. Her job was to support the increasing numbers of submarines, especially on distant stations, such as the Mediterranean and the Pacific Far East. And her equipment included a foundry, coppersmiths, plumbers and carpenters shops, heavy and light machine shops, electrical and torpedo repair shops and plants for charging submarine batteries. She was designed to look after nine operational submarines, supplying over 100 torpedoes and a similar number of mines. Besides large workshops, there were repair facilities for all material in the attached submarines and extensive diving and salvage equipment was carried. There were steam laundries, a cinema, hospital, chapel, two canteens, a bakery, barber's shop, and a fully equipped operating theatre and dental surgery. She operated in Gibraltar and Algiers Harbour, the main Allied base in the Mediterranean, before being assigned to the Eastern Fleet. And in September, 1944, Maidstone and the 8th Submarine Flotilla were transferred from Ceylon to Fremantle in Western Australia to operate in the Pacific.

In late 1945 Maidstone left Fremantle, and *en route* to the UK, docked in the Shelburne dry dock at Simonstown, South Africa. While on passage, she was diverted to Makassar to pick up 400 British naval prisoners of war from HMS Exeter, HMS Encounter and HMS Stronghold, and in November she arrived at Portsmouth.

In 1946, Maidstone became mother ship to the 2nd and 7th Submarine Flotillas. The 2nd Flotilla comprised operational boats, the latter a trials and training squadron. Maidstone had a semi-permanent mooring off Monkey Island at Portland but often put to sea with her brood of submarines. Five years later, in 1951 Maidstone called briefly at Corunna to land a sick crew man. This was not classified an official visit, although it was the first time a British warship had entered a Spanish harbour since the end of the Spanish Civil War. In 1953 she took part in the Fleet Review to celebrate the coronation of Queen Elizabeth II.

Press ganged by the Navy at the opening of the Base at Faslane – left to right – Bill Heaney, *Lennox Herald*, **Gerry Fitzgerald,** *Fitzgerald Owens News Agency*, **John Esplin, Greenock freelance, Donald Fullarton,** *Helensburgh Advertiser,* **Commodore Peter G LaNeice, Angela Sandeman Munro,** *Helensburgh and Gareloch Times*, **Alex Aitken,** *The Scotsman* **and Terry Duncan,** *Scottish Daily Express. Pictures courtesy of the Royal Navy and Helensburgh Heritage.*

On 16 June, 1955, the submarine HMS Sidon sank in Portland harbour alongside Maidstone 20 minutes after an explosion in the forward torpedo compartment. A rescue party from Maidstone saved a number of the Sidon's crew, but 13 died. A week later, the submarine was raised and the accident was found to be caused by the high-test peroxide fuel in a torpedo. Surgeon Lieutenant Charles Rhodes was posthumously awarded the Albert Medal for his part in the rescue. In 1956, Maidstone was Flagship of the Commander-in-Chief, Home Fleet. In September 1957, the Russians protested when Maidstone accompanied the training aircraft carrier HMS Ocean on a visit to

Helsinki. In 1959 Maidstone received an extensive refit to accommodate nuclear submarines and the 2nd Flotilla was then moved to Devonport. It was around 1961 that Maidstone sailed to Faslane, where she was the depot ship to the 3rd and 10th Submarine Squadrons. In 1965 she undertook a trip to Liverpool, and she visited the same port one year later. She also undertook a trip to Rothesay during this period and then in 1967 she sailed to Rosyth Dockyard to undertake preparations to 'mothball' her.

In October 1969, however, Maidstone was refitted and re-commissioned as accommodation for 2,000 troops and sent to Belfast where she arrived under tow to serve as barracks for the increased security forces in the area. In 1971, she was used as a prison ship to hold internees without trial, including Gerry Adams, the alleged Provisional IRA terrorist, who is today a Sinn Fein MP in the Republic of Ireland. The holding area itself was at the stern and consisted of two bunkhouses, one up, one down, and two mess rooms. The accommodation for the prison governor and his staff - previously the captain's cabin – was on a deck used twice a day for prisoners to exercise and was surrounded by 10-foot-high barbed wire. Maidstone was moored in Belfast harbour 20 feet from the land and the entrance to the jetty was guarded by sand-bagged Army emplacements.

However, there was huge embarrassment for the Government when seven Provisional IRA members escaped on 17 January, 1972. The men swam close to 300 yards through icy water and evaded army and police guards, later holding a press conference before the world's media. Sadly, on 23 May, 1978, Maidstone was broken up for scrap at the Thomas Ward shipbreaking yard at Inverkeithing in Fife.

Chapter 32

THE BISHOP

Richard Holloway, who was brought up in the Vale of Leven.

Richard Holloway's memoir is the remarkable story of a local boy who left a cramped 'cottage' in working class Random Street, Alexandria, to become a student priest. And then rose to the giddy heights of bishop in the Scottish Episcopal Church, causing colossal controversy and consternation along the way. The 82-year-old churchman will not be surprised that in the Vale of Leven, where he was brought up, few people will be shocked that he has revealed serious doubts about the existence of God. For the bishop has a long and colourful track record for making headlines on that score. Eyebrows will be raised however from Balloch to Burnbrae when word gets out that the prelate's new book touches on the fact that there was more than heavy petting going on in the double divans in the dimly lit recesses of the old Hall cinema at the foot of Bank Street. And that paedophilia, a 21st century phenomenon for many, is nothing new in West Dunbartonshire or indeed elsewhere in the world.

In his memoir, *Leaving Alexandria*, the bishop recalls how, when he was a movie mad youngster in the Fifties, he was pestered by a man in the stalls of the Rialto picture house in College Street, Dumbarton. Holloway's compelling account of his journey through life has zipped up the best-seller charts. But this book is not all about the old Vale and its inhabitants in the latter half of last century. Although it does contain some wonderful recollections and anecdotes that local people will relish. It is a big book about big issues and, needless to say, in true Holloway fashion, it is not without controversy. It majors on religion and it is topical too given the bitter row that has raged – and goes on raging yet - between Scotland's churches and gay lobby groups over same sex marriage.

The author raises a host of sensitive subjects such as why all Christians cannot receive Communion in the same church at the same time; why divorced people cannot be married in church and why some churches continue to refuse to ordain women. There will be a great deal of angst and 'tutt-tutting' amongst churchgoers at many of Holloway's observations. He has called for a re-evaluation of the Churches' moral teaching on sex, particularly in its attitude to gay and lesbian people. And he sees no reason why the Churches cannot craft suitable liturgies for same sex unions – 'different but modelled on heterosexual marriage'. No way does the man the tabloids once called 'The Barmy Bishop' think, for example, that the Pope is infallible – or that you should believe everything you read in the Bible. He has questioned the Virgin birth and gone public on the fact that he claims to understand the 'promiscuous genes' that drive men to promiscuity. Holloway excoriates clergy for rattling around in manses and chapel houses far too large for their needs without giving any thought to allocating temporary space in them to poor, homeless and mentally ill people. This is what he did himself, despite being married with three children, when he was in Edinburgh. He had a large board screwed on to the top of the family dining table so that it could accommodate more people and homeless people often stayed the night – or longer.

He believes priests and ministers should roll up their sleeves, get out into the community and mix with lonesome, down and out, dirty and diseased people, providing them with food and shelter. Holloway isn't much given to excessive spectacle when it comes to church services either. He once persuaded a group of Anglican bishops to make a show of throwing their ornate mitres into the Thames after a conference at Lambeth Palace. The clergy are scolded for wearing elaborate, colourful vestments, expensive rings and pectoral crosses, 'flouncing around' on the altar in 'long pink dresses' and behaving like actors on a stage during excessively long liturgical services.

The book cover and St Mungo's Episcopal Church in Alexandria.

Holloway's journey begins in Glasgow, where he was born, and moved to Random Street in Alexandria after his father, wee Arthur, finds work at last in the 'Croft', the United Turkey Red factory on the banks of the River Leven. Until then Arthur had trudged the streets as part of the hungry army of Scottish men looking for work in the Great Depression of the 1930s. Once the job was landed, Holloway's mother, Mary, pestered the local factor – there were few council houses then - into allocating them a 'cottage' – complete with outside lavatory – in Random Street in the heart of the Vale. He went to the local academy on the edge of Christie Park and joined the choir of St Mungo's Episcopal Church at the Burnbrae end of Main Street.

Holloway recalls a happy but poor childhood and remembers fondly high days and holidays and Hogmanays in the bosom of his family. Theirs was a happy home and there were Saturday night sing songs when his father brought home a 'cairry oot' from the local pub, probably Mattha Thomson's in Random Street. His father, who never went to church on Sunday and gambled instead on the bogie line at Jamestown, smuggled out bolt ends of brightly dyed cloth from his workplace at the Croft. His modus operandum was the same as that of many other workers and he concealed it from the gatemen by wrapping it around his body and putting on his overcoat to cover up the bump. This colourful material helped to brighten up many Vale homes as it was turned into curtains and cushion covers and dresses the women wore to the dancing. Holloway loved long walks up Carman Hill above Renton with his mother and sisters, dreaming as he looked north to Loch Lomond and the snow-covered Ben.

The Random Street tenement where Richard Holloway was brought up. *Picture by courtesy of West Dunbartonshire Council.*

Then, at the age of 14, the priest at St Mungo's got him a placement at Kelham Hall in Nottinghamshire, an Anglican seminary where working class boys were trained for the priesthood. His mother bought him a new suit from Burton's in Dumbarton High Street, measured for it no doubt by my father-in-law, John Scullion - and they took a workers' bus together from the Fountain to Waterloo Street, where she saw him off to his new life. Holiday times he loved and Holloway always came back to Scotland where he worked on Admiral Mackenzie's farm at Caldarvan, near Gartocharn, and at Muirhead's Farm at Millburn to earn some pocket money.

After spending a few happy years at Kelham Hall, and before being ordained a priest, he was sent to Africa to work as a bishop's secretary. Typically, he arranged for the bishop's son to come to Scotland to be educated. Older folk in the Vale will remember that boy, Bernard Kojo Laing, who went on to graduate from Glasgow University, coming to join them as a pupil at the old Academy. Bernard – he was nicknamed Ebenezer - lived with Holloway's parents at their new council house in Elmbank Drive, Bonhill, before he left Alexandria to lodge with the bishop in a flat in a decaying tenement in the Gorbals.

By that time Holloway, who drove a motor bike with only one brake, had been ordained and was working as a curate in an Anglican parish in Pollokshields. Involved in this type of work at the time were the Rev Geoff Shaw, a Church of Scotland minister – Geoff was later to become Convener of Strathclyde Regional Council - who later became Holloway's best man, and Lilias Graham, the grand-daughter of the Duke of Montrose, whose family owns extensive lands on Loch Lomondside. He finished his priestly life when he stood down in 2000 after a term as Bishop of Edinburgh and Primus of the Scottish Episcopal Church. But his journey has taken him not just to Africa and America, where he had a parish in Boston at the height of the AIDS epidemic, but across the world. He is the author of 25 books and a regular broadcaster and commentator on the Arts and Culture for BBC Scotland. He has been a Professor of Divinity in London and chairman of the Scottish Arts Council as well as founder and chair of Sistema Scotland, the charity that seeks to change the lives of children through music.

Richard Holloway no longer believes in religion and he is done with praying, although he thinks it would be a greatly pleasurable surprise if God were to prove him wrong. This memoir has been described by author Alexander McCall Smith as 'a compelling account of a journey through life, told with great frankness', and it is that and more. It's a wonderful book, but it's not for the faint-hearted. It has, for local people, the added attraction of nostalgia which is contained in the many references to the Vale of Leven and Dumbarton which crop up throughout its 358 pages.

* ***Leaving Alexandria, A Memoir of Faith and Doubt*** *by Richard Holloway, is published by Canongate and is available on Amazon and in all good bookshops, price £17.99.*

Beautiful Vale - Alexandria and Loch Lomond from the air.

Chapter 33

THE FASHION

They seek him here, they seek him there,
His clothes are loud, but never square.
It will make or break him so he's got to buy the best,
'Cause he's a dedicated follower of fashion.

Dedicated Follower of Fashion was a hit song for the Kinks' which most of you with a ticket to travel Down Memory Lane will remember. I came across it again while I was looking through some old photographs for this page. It didn't just come to me though. It jumped out at me. Now there's a smart looking fellow, I thought to myself. It is in fact a Mr McCallum taking his grandchildren for a stroll along West Clyde Street in Helensburgh round about 1954, which is exactly 62 years ago. And it appears on Helensburgh Memories, a comparatively new website which has attracted 900 members in a few short weeks. Nothing sells like nostalgia, according to Robert Ryan, who moderates the site. Debonair Mr McCallum was snapped by a street photographer outside the bank on the corner opposite Helensburgh Pier near Woolworths. It was the bunnet that first caught my eye – and then the pocket handkerchief. I have just purchased an eight-piece tweed cap from a mail order company that cost me just £11.My old one was stolen from the locker room of a never to be mentioned golf club. These caps – they are never called hats around here - are all the rage now that *Peaky Blinders* is drawing in big audiences on television. But it was not just the bunnet and the hankie but the Fair Isle jumper, the Harris Tweed jacket, the open neck shirt and the slacks (they used to call them flannels) that caused me to pause. This remarkably is the 'uniform' of the fashion conscious, relatively well-off mature man of the early 21st century.

To wear that outfit these days would cost a fair few bob. The jacket would come in at anything from £250 to £400, the trousers £50, the shirt £35 and the Fair Isle jumper maybe £100-£150 with it costing anything from £60 to £110 for the shoes. Go into a good, but now departed, menswear shop like the late, lamented Stewarts of Helensburgh or Bobby Cawley's trend-setting Craig's International Menswear in Alexandria, or Edwards in Dumbarton High Street, which was bought over by the late Sir Hugh Fraser and eponymously named Sir Hugh's, and you would be lucky to retreat with a seriously damaged plastic bank card. The total cost for this very smart outfit would be in the region of £500. Sadly, all of these shops have disappeared from our local shopping streets and squares. Everyone goes casual these days and the fashion shops have gone the way of Central SMT's double decker buses. It's all denims and T-shirts and trainers and baseball boots now. People dress down instead of dressing up as we used to do before going to work or even to what used to be important, formal events. Ties are out the window and when people do wear them they are very quick to remove them at the first opportunity. Fashion was always a big thing around here.

The old Regal Cinema, owned by Miss Bilsland, in Church Street, Dumbarton.

There were three big tailor shops in the High Street – Burtons, Claude Alexander and John Collier, the 50 Shilling Tailor. When the 'Swinging Sixties arrived they brought with them an end to much of the austerity that had attached itself to the dull 15 years of the nation's recovery from the Second World War. Fashion was in for men and they snapped up made to measure suits and coats. Italian suits took over from the Teddy Boys' drapes, semi drapes, string ties, skin tight, drainpipe trousers and blue suede shoes. Those guys had wanted to look like Elvis Presley as he appeared in Jailhouse Rock. That look was toned down a bit by the arrival on the pop scene of Cliff Richard, whom parents thought a bit more respectable and less raunchy than Elvis.

But it was the Frank Sinatra look that prevailed for the more mature individuals who wore Italian suits, smart shirts and ties and even a pork pie hat from time to time. The suits were mainly three-button jackets with narrow lapels and trousers with 14 inch bottoms. The shoes were winkle pickers. This gear was covered up when it was raining – and when wasn't it raining? – with a smart beige overcoat with the collar turned up. The raincoat was ideal for walking a girl home from the

Rialto or the Picture House, the Regal, La Scala, Roxy, Strand, Tower or whichever cinema you had chosen if you came from Dumbarton, Helensburgh, Renton or the Vale. Only the rich, the very well-heeled, travelled up to Glasgow on the train to the big movie houses in Renfield and Sauchiehall Street to catch the first viewing of the new releases. For some reason everything went to Glasgow first and the reels were then taken by van to all the outlying cinemas in the suburbs. I know this because, having missed the last bus or train, I often hitched a lift in this van from Glasgow to Dumbarton. It took an interminable time to get home because it had to stop at every cinema along the way through Partick and Hillhead and Clydebank.

They've got your number – your Store number, and they are wearing nice little fashion numbers from the 1960s. Lads about town wished they had their telephone numbers. These smartly dressed young women all worked at the Dumbarton Equitable Co-operative Society store and this was them on holiday together in the Isle of Man. They are Elizabeth Riddell, Nancy Willet, Anne Lyden, Margaret Elliott, Rose Maley, Annette Smith and Jackie Neeson. What happened in the Isle of Man stays in the Isle of Man.

Chapter 34

THE APACHES

The Apaches reshuffled: The full line-up in 1963 was (back row) Jim Mullen, Tommy Burke and Charlie Daly with Jim Molloy and Phil Pattison at the front

Inevitably, the death in New Zealand of Valeman Jim Mullen, who was lead guitarist with the Apaches rock group in Dunbartonshire in the 'Sixties, has caused lots of people of a certain vintage to recall the band and some of their contemporaries at that time. Everywhere I go – from getting my haircut in John McCann's on Bridge Street to shopping at the supermarkets in St James' - there are people who ask me, in the Dumbarton vernacular, of course, do I 'mind' this one and that one connected with 'the dancing' at that time. Well, I do. It was when people used to go out for the night on a Saturday, not sit at home with a bottle of wine and a curry and watch *Strictly Come Dancing* (or Spanish football?) on television. The *Lennox Herald* published a picture of Jim Mullen with his Apache pals alongside Amanda Graham's obituary shortly after his death. Since then I have managed to come up with another one which includes a different drummer, Dumbarton man Jim Molloy who, like Jim Mullen, also emigrated to New Zealand. Jim Molloy and I were close friends on the Helensburgh café scene, where we frequented the King's Café and Dino's Radio Cafe, which was where Jackie Stewart and his then wife to be, Helen McNeill, hung out, drank Coke and played the juke box.

We were all innocents abroad. There was no substance abuse then. We had never heard of Charlie, and a favourite question for naïve teenagers at that time was: 'Does your Mammy know you're oot?' With Stewart and his motor mad crowd around the place, cars were a big thing, and they were certainly a major 'pulling' factor when it came to the girls. That was when I teamed up with Jim Molloy and Tom Mitchell, another Dumbarton teenager who was also in the motor trade. Tom's old red convertible Morris 7 caught the eye as we sped down the road through Cardross and Colgrain most week nights to the esplanade cafes and, on a Saturday night, to the dancing. And it wasn't just the traffic cops – were there traffic cops in those days – who spotted us making our way sedately from Dumbarton to Helensburgh. That was life as we knew it until Jim Molloy hit the big time and became otherwise engaged with The Apaches, who were packing them in at every venue they played in. The photograph shows Jim (bottom left) with Tommy and the Apaches, as they became known and the personnel changed around a bit and Johnny Cannon got fed up with all the travelling and late nights. The full line-up in 1963 was (back row) Jim Mullen, Tommy Burke and Charlie Daly with Jim Molloy and Phil Pattison at the front.

All these questions about bands and which ones you liked best, and which ones you went to see, or danced to, when you were a teenager took me to a website people of that era will love to look back on. It's rockingscots.co.uk. Rockingscots is a website dedicated to Scottish beat groups and rock bands of the Sixties and Seventies. the time when the guys wore three-button Italian mohair suits with drain-pipe trousers and 14-inch bottoms, made to measure and five bob a week on the never,

never from Burton's in the High Street. Sky blue shirts with button down collars and pencil slim ties were all the go and we all thought we were the cat's pyjamas. And so these recollections have gone on with some of my old journalist pals joining in on Facebook. Former *Herald* war reporter Ian Bruce remembered the Chris McClure Section – 'He used to have a standing gig at a hotel in Newarthill on a Sunday night. I also saw Lulu perform at Bellshill YM before she was Lulu. On another famous night, I saw Alan Price being thrown out of Motherwell United Services Club because he turned up completely out of it for his show.' I said Lulu used to come up to the Scottish Daily Express office where I worked in Albion Street to see Gordon Reed who was the showbiz editor and Molly Kelly of the women's features section. She lived just along the road in Dennistoun and she was at that time starting out as Lulu and the Luvvers. All the copy boys used to line up to have a look at her. I recalled too once having hired Marmalade when they were Dean Ford and the Gaylords for the astronomical sum of £17 to play all night at a dance in the Ardencaple Hotel in Helensburgh. It was a sell-out. Ian Bruce said his *Herald* colleague John Easton – some of you may remember he was their expert on Clyde steamers - was a stage-hand at Rothesay Winter Gardens and saw and met most of the big acts when they were on tour.

He added: 'He always rated Emile Ford and the Checkmates and said Emile was a generous guy who'd take all the stage-hands for a drink after the shows to thank them for their hard work.' Easton, widely known as The Skipper, used to marvel at Andy Stewart, whose fondness for a dram made him sometimes rather unsteady on his feet on his way up to the stage, where he would suddenly be transformed – 'He would then go on automatic pilot and wow the audience.' As we tried to outdo each other, I recalled having seen Adam Faith at the Alhambra and Cliff Richard when he came to the Rialto with Billy Grainger – of Teensville fame - in Dumbarton when Summer Holiday was on the go. Then there was Gene Pitney at Duck Bay Marina, the Rolling Stones at Greens Playhouse and Alex Harvey at the Lennoxbank Hotel in Balloch. Since it's their 50th anniversary, let's finish with a story about the Rolling Stones. The Herald municipal correspondent John MacCalman has a great tale to tell about the Stones when they turned up for a gig in Hamilton – 'It had been horribly overbooked and the result was a riot.'

Photographer Stewart Cunningham remembered: 'After the Hamilton gig, the Stones had all their gear nicked from the van and the next night's sell-out gig at the Odeon in Sauchiehall Street was threatened with cancellation. The then owner of McCormack's music shop heard about their plight and told them to help themselves to instruments. There is a great photo of a very young, Mick, Keith, Bill, Charlie and Brian in existence with the said instruments hanging on the wall there. This was just a few years before my time, I'm afraid and I was sorry to hear about the closure of the shop.'

The Apaches just before the rock group broke up.

Chapter 35

THE BLITZ

The blitzed ruin of old Cardross Parish Church. *Picture by Bill Heaney*

I have been handed a scoop - a first-hand account of that dramatic and terrible night of The Clydeside Blitz in March, 1941. Mrs Jeanette Scobie, wife of the late Rev Andrew Scobie, who was minister of Cardross Parish Church for 45 years and who died in 2010 aged 75, has passed on to me previously unpublished correspondence which came into the hands of her husband. It was a letter from an Air Raid Patrol man, Mr Shanks, of Westonlee Terrace in Bonhill Road, Dumbarton, who was on duty in the village that fateful night.

First though, I must to say something about Mr Scobie, a minister who gave long and distinguished service to the Church of Scotland at a time when, unlike today, ministers were plentiful. Andrew was proud to describe himself as the last kirk minister who could not be forced to retire. His fellow minister, the Rev Johnston McKay, said Mr Scobie belonged to a former age -- 'not in the sense of being out of date or touch but both his preparation for and style of ministry have been overtaken by far less academic training and much less formality in church life. 'I doubt if any minister will ever again serve 45 years in the same parish.'

He added: 'Always impeccably dressed and wearing a pectoral cross, he would never have dreamed of being casually clothed for parochial duties or General Assembly. Unlike many today, he had a view of the parish ministry as requiring him to be available whenever he was needed.' His friend and presbytery colleague, the Rev David Munro, said: 'Andrew was a very keen parish minister. His congregation knew that they could contact him any hour of the day because he was totally committed to the ministry.'

The correspondence from Mr Shanks about the Blitz is contained in two accounts, one of which he sent to his daughter and son-in-law, Frank and Jean, who lived in Liverpool and who offered to put the Shanks family up after their own house in Cardross was razed to the ground. He wrote: 'Very many thanks for your very welcome letter which I was exceedingly pleased to receive and I am delighted to learn that you are both so well and quite happy. Isn't the coming home a wonderful thing. And I think I should know after all the experience I have had. I note that you speak of Frank being transferred to another vessel and the possibility of shorter voyages, which if it materialises, will be a decided and much more pleasanter change and more congenial to you both. You will observe the change of address this week. Ella and I have moved into Westonlee this morning. Grandpaw is staying on with Aunt Nellie. They have built a fine new shelter in the garden and think it will be more convenient for them should the Jerries make up their minds to pay us another visit. Not that we have any desire to go through the same again but of course one never knows.'

Mr Shanks then added: 'I know your city (Liverpool) has had its share or perhaps more than its share, not to mention your own particular district. As for myself, I am carrying on or at least trying to carry on as usual but it does indeed seem strange that the home we took so much pride in, is no more. However, this is, I suppose, the fortune or should I say, misfortune of war and I have only to look around me and see, many more who have been less fortunate than me and thank God I have still got my life. I appreciate to the full, the consideration that both Frank and you have shown and for the sincere and open-hearted offer you have extended to me – to reside in your home. I have been thinking this over and I feel in leaving here I would be guilty of deserting Alex who, poor boy, has lost everything, not only in clothes but in home comforts – and only newly engaged too. Then I also know, you will be taking up your new appointment when Frank rejoins his ship and that would mean you being on duty all day and so in order not to upset your arrangements, I think I will (with Grandpaw's permission) stay put, until the war is finished and I see Alex settled down, just as your dear mother and I had the pleasure of seeing Frank and you happily settled, almost three years ago. When this war will finish no one knows – but we all have the faith we will be on the winning side, however short or long it may be.'

The Muirholm Hotel in Main Road, Cardross, which narrowly escaped being bombed by the Luftwaffe. Picture by Bill Heaney

What did you do in the war, Daddy?

This is a question often asked in jest. However, there was nothing funny about the war for the people here who had to suffer it. In Cardross, 60 families lost their homes and the parish church in Main Street was destroyed. The following is a first-hand account of that night in 1941 when bombs fell on the village. It is from an Air Raid Patrol man, Mr Shanks, who fought the blaze which destroyed the parish church and damaged the manse. And whose own home was bombed by the Luftwaffe while he fought the blaze in the church and manse alongside the minister, the Rev T.D. Stewart Brown, his wife and a volunteer evacuee. It is contained in a letter from the survivor that was passed on to the Rev Andrew Scobie, who was the Church of Scotland minister in the village for 45 years.

'In my last letter I said there was a history attached to my experience during the Blitz we had here. I was on duty all night and what a night it was. Two incendiaries came through the roof of the Manse. The Minister and an evacuee put the one out in the loft, while I put one out in the roof of the passage between the kitchen and back room. I had to stand upon a pair of steps and as I could not get the skylight window open I had to lift a 60lb sandbag right above my head and crash it through the glass. Talk about perspiration. It was simply oozing out in gallons. Then the electric light failed just as I was groping for the stirrup-pump. When I managed to get hold of the hose I had to feel for the nozzle end. Eventually I shoved my hand with the nozzle out the broken window and started spraying the bomb, the minister's wife down below was working the pump like a hero! As soon as the spray doused the bomb, the molten metal commenced to fly about and it was some job, dodging the molten fragments. All this time the steps I was standing on were swaying backwards and forwards and I had to prop myself up against the wall to save myself being precipitated. After ten minutes of hard work we finally had the fire under control while the minister and his helpmate upstairs were equally successful with the blaze inside the loft. I was at the telephone, when the church was set alight and what a blaze!!

'Then one of the Jerries came down low and dropped an H.E ten feet from the wall facing the river side. What a thud! The whole manse shook, down came the ceilings, in came the windows and shutters. I dropped on my face against a wall in the lobby. I thought my last hour had come and yet I had the feeling I would get out of it safe. I was covered over with plaster and soot and as I picked myself up and shook myself like a terrier dog out of the water I can still hear myself saying, 'You're O.K. Shanks carry on'. Instinctively I gripped the phone but no reply, the telephone wires had been smashed and we were isolated with no means of communication. Incidentally I had a phone message earlier on, stating there was an incendiary on the roof of Lenaville (Mr Shanks' own house in Station Road). And later when I phoned back, I was informed it was okay and the fire was under control. That was all

I knew and the severing of the telephone connection cut us off from all further news.

'After I found the telephone to be out of action the next best thing to do was to find out about Mrs Brown (the minister's wife), the two children and the maid whom I knew were in the front dining room and naturally I wondered were they killed, were they injured or had they escaped unscathed and as I groped my way in the darkness over gas mask boxes and skin suits and broken plaster and debris on the floor. I could not hear a sound or even a moan as I struggled into the room which was brilliantly lighted by the glare of the burning church outside. I noticed all the windows, window frames, shutters and so on had been blown in and broken glass was lying everywhere. Even the room door had been lifted from its hinges and was lying across the dining room table which had been placed, not in the centre of the room, but against one of the side walls for safety. I shouted out 'Are you alright' and lo and behold four figures struggled out from below the table where they had been lying on a mattress and beyond being badly shaken, were, 'glory be' unhurt. The children were whimpering but what an escape. That table saved them alright littered as it was with fragments of glass, broken frames and on the top of it lay the big heavy school room door. Then Miss Chrystal of Bloomhill and a Mr Mitchell arrived on the scene. They had braved the dangers of falling bombs and took Mrs Brown, the two children and the maid up to Miss Chrystal's house which had fortunately escaped damage. At this moment Mr Brown arrived. He had been in the Church porch when the H.E. exploded and for five minutes he said he remembered nothing. And then what do you think we did? Out we went 'him and I' into the churchyard. By this time the flames were reaching from 100 to 150 feet into the sky. Then down would come some of the strutted roof beams, then a clatter of slates, then up would go showers of sparks and dense volumes of smoke and fire. The pews were burning out and flames were dancing out in forks everywhere. We had to get two firemen to burst open the vestry door and in Mr Brown and I went and trailed out a large wardrobe containing the robes, hymn books and valuable papers. When I tell you that this piece of furniture measured about 5 feet x 4 feet x 2 feet broad and was made of solid oak you will have an idea of the job we had, more especially as the roof of the vestry was alight and the flames from the church were just missing us by inches. Then as we laid the wardrobe on its back on the graves outside, back into the vestry we went and broke open the locker and saved all the communion cups and silver, collection plates, forms and church chairs. The last thing I came out with was a statue about 12 inches high of John the Baptist. All the time the flames inside the church were crackling away, then the pillars, those solid iron pillars, supporting the gallery fell outward, and down came the gallery in flames and with it the beautiful organ reduced to scrap the pipes twisted and bent beyond recognition. Even the War Memorial marble plate, erected to those who died in 1914-18 was cracked and damaged, the lead letters comprising their names all molten and running like silver streams down the beautiful polished marble face. 'No wonder Mr Brown and I shook hands and no wonder he said 'Mr Shanks don't you think we should get down on our knees and pray that our lives have been saved?'

'And the irony of it all was the fact that my own house was being burned to the ground and I did not know. After we had done all we could humanly do at the church, we both got into Mr Brown's car and proceeded in the darkness out to Ardoch. Up the Lea Brae we met Mr Cunningham Graham [Admiral Sir Angus Cunningham Graham] and the district warden Mr McSporran and learned from them that part of the village had escaped unscathed. Then back we went to the village and as we arrived at the Golf Club House, which was blazing like an inferno, there were firemen, lengths of hose lying all over the road and an ambulance and an urgent request from those in charge of it for someone to obtain a doctor or at least someone able to give the patient an injection. Mr Brown immediately set off to bring Miss Chrystal who by the way is a qualified nurse.

'I got out the car and proceeded home. At Station Road I saw a huge blaze and the outline of Mrs Plowdon's house silhouetted against the flames. I said to myself 'if that is not my house I'll eat my hat'. As I came nearer there it was, dear old Lenaville, the upper storey well alight and sparks and flames belching out smoke in ever increasing intensity.

My first thought was, where was my sister? Quite a number of people were standing on the road gazing awe-stricken at the scene. I was then told she and Mrs Michie and the girls were in the shelter across the road. I stumbled in and there they were, white faced, shocked and badly shaken but otherwise unhurt. It was then I learned that when the Fire Brigade arrived they had been sitting on the couch in the kitchen and were ordered to proceed to the shelter at once. Ella had time to grab my attaché case with my valuable papers and two small suitcases containing a change of clothing and get out as quickly as possible. The firemen were afraid the blaze would attract the bombers and that these planes might drop their heavy stuff into the flames and that of course would have been the finish. After ascertaining they were alright, I went over to the house. The main stairway was burning away fiercely and the flames were coming out the front door and parts of the ceiling in the hall were dropping down with a clatter which gave off millions of sparks. As I looked in I saw the hat stand. Upon it was my good soft felt hat, my light grey overcoat and my waterproof. I said to myself 'So to it' and believe me in I went, keeping close to the wall, grabbed these articles which were so hot I thought they would burst into flame before I got out. Fortunately I did get out and most wonderful of all, without either a scratch or burn.

'The Fire Brigade at the house were running out lengths of hose to the little burn at the Geilston end of the village. You see the H.E. bomb had shattered the water mains and this failure of water supply was the cause of disaster to Mr Vallance's house and mine. Mrs Michie and family were indeed guardian angels to us at this stage. Then to complete the picture Mr McIntyre and I were asked to warn all the residents in Church Avenue and the little village at the shore. A landmine was discovered at the sawmill on the shore and was liable to explode any minute. This was successfully accomplished. As all our telephone connections had been blown to smithereens what do you thing Mr Brown did? He proceeded to Helensburgh at 4,30a.m.to put in his report. It was pitch dark at the time and he stood the risk of running into or over any unexploded bomb that may have been lying on the road. However, he managed to get through safely and might I say luckily. Mrs Michie and the girls made breakfast for Ella and me but I could hardly taste it. My nose ears, and throat seemed to be full of lime, soot and dust but I can assure you we were very grateful indeed and will never forget her kindness to us. This is my experience of the blitz and none too good a one as you will see. I did not want to write to you in detail, it all seemed to me to breathe of a kind of hero-worship and yet on the other hand I feel you would be interested to know. At this moment when I can view all the incidents impartially, I have set them down as briefly as possible. It seems like a story in a novel save that it actually occurred.'

The letter is signed 'Daddy'.

Arthur Jones and James Adie and the old Cardross clubhouse that fell victim to the Blitz.

One man caught up in the Blitz in Cardross that night was James Adie, who was born in the village in 1924, where his grandfather was the chauffeur to a member of the famous Denny shipbuilding family at Cardross Park, *writes Arthur F. Jones.* Jim's father was a sea-going engineer, while his mother was the well-respected clubmistress at Cardross Golf Club. Jim was born in the old clubhouse and, as a teenager, had the horrific war-time experience of seeing it burned to the ground during the Cardross blitz. He had to rescue his mother, who was reluctant to leave her charge and her home despite incendiary bombs raining down. Jim always spoke with compassion for all the victims of that terrible period, which added emotional depth to his life-long love of the village of Cardross, its people and its history. He served an engineering apprenticeship with Denny's and hankered after a life at sea, like his father. He joined the merchant navy in 1945 and studied in Glasgow for his sea-going certificates, eventually gaining his chief's ticket. He spent many years sailing the seven seas with the famous City Line, of which he always spoke with pride and affection. After a period as chief engineer on some of the Clyde steamers until 1970, he became the on-site engineer at the Brock Baths at Dumbarton, then manager. He used to joke that they had given him this job because, unlike other possible candidates, he would be able to fix the boilers if something went wrong. Engineering inspection work with the Scottish Development Agency then took him all over Scotland and the friendships he made with colleagues outlasted the agency itself.

A spell as a researcher with the Denny Tank Museum in Dumbarton followed before he ended his working life as caretaker of Dumbarton Library. He retired in 1989. Jim was a member of Cardross Golf Club for 74 years and joint author of the centenary history of the club in 1996.

For more than 60 years he was a member of Dumbarton Kilwinning Lodge, in which he held the office of Almoner. He was, in later years, an enthusiastic member of the Dumbarton Burns Club. He researched details about Dumbarton men in the Irrawaddy Flotilla Company (Burma), and wrote historical accounts of Cardross Park estate and the Cardross blitz. Jim, who died in Scarborough six years ago, collected old photographs and provided interesting and valuable information to the local history section at Dumbarton Library. Right into his eighties he was busy compiling a photographic record of old Cardross. His knowledge of individual people past and present in Cardross and Dumbarton was astounding.

* *Arthur F. Jones was librarian in charge of the public libraries in Dumbarton and Alexandria and is author of* ***Cardross: The village in days gone by***

A race between a limo and the Luftwaffe

A Dumbarton woman had a narrow escape that night of the Blitz. Rose Cleary was the daughter of Paddy Cleary, the well known undertaker and hirer of limousines in Strathleven Place. Rose, who later became Mrs Rose Carey and lived in Round Riding Road, was the first woman in Dumbarton to pass her driving test. Her brothers, Charlie, James and Willie also worked in the motor hire business but that night Rose was given the task of driving a priest from St Patrick's in Dumbarton to St Joseph's in Helensburgh. She was driving down the Lea Brae towards Cardross when she heard a

Luftwaffe plane flying low overhead. The plane started to follow the path of the limousine she was driving when the pilot homed in on her headlights. Rose immediately shut off the lights of the car, pulled off the road and waited in the darkness until the plane had gone and it was safe to complete her journey.

The old kirk at Cardross village before it was bombed by the Luftwaffe.

How Dumbarton coped with the Blitz

Jock McQueen's Clock on the Co-op building in Glasgow Road, which was destroyed.

Clydebank was the town worst hit by the Blitz, and much has been written about that by the local writers' group and journalist John MacLeod in his book, River of Fire. Towns and villages further down the river did not escape the Luftwaffe bombs though and had it not been for pre-war preparation the loss of life and destruction of homes, churches and important public buildings would have been much greater.

Before the Munich Agreement was signed in September, 1938, trenches were being dug in Levengrove Park, Dumbarton – this happened in public parks throughout Britain – and gas masks were being distributed. It was some time after the start of the Second World War in 1939 however that the first bombs fell on Dumbarton. Householders were ordered to black out their windows at night and cars and bicycles were permitted only dimmed lamps and headlights. Air Raid Precautions (ARP) wardens patrolled the street at night to ensure the regulations were observed. Air-raid shelters, which were called Anderson shelters, were erected in the parks and open spaces, in schools and factories, and warning signs were sounded from time to time to call people to practice drill with gas respirators. The closes of tenements were strutted and baffle walls, which could be awkward obstacles to negotiate in the blackout. Parents were encouraged to evacuate their children to safe country areas, where some remained for the duration of the war, although most returned after the first few months which were comparatively free of air raid warnings.

Dr Ian MacPhail, the Dumbarton historian, has recorded that in the Leven Shipyard, owned by Denny's, and the Blackburn Aircraft Factory in Newtown overtime became regular for the first time since the First World War. For those who were not called up, local defence companies were organised which in time became known as the Home Guard. In addition to the ordinary British service personnel, Dumbarton had for most of the war a Norwegian Royal Navy Unit stationed at Helenslee House in Kirktonhill – it later became part of Keil School – and from time to time Polish and French soldiers, exiled from their homelands, were also based there. Some of the Poles, unable or unwilling to return to their home country, which had been given over to Communist rule after the war, stayed on in Dumbarton as did some of the East Germans from prisoner of war camps in places like Drymen, where Rudolf Hess, deputy Führer to Adolf Hitler, was held. Hess had flown to Scotland and landed in a field in Eaglesham, Renfrewshire, in an attempt to negotiate peace. He was taken prisoner and held with other POWs in Drymen. Eventually, he was was convicted of crimes against peace and sentenced to life imprisonment but committed suicide.

German raiders swooped over Dumbarton regularly between March and May of 1941, and in all 17 lives were lost and around 100 houses destroyed. On March 13 and 14, under a full moon, Clydebank and Partick bore the brunt of those raids, but on the night of May 5 considerable damage was caused in Dumbarton by high explosive bombs and incendiaries. Fortunately, according to Dr MacPhail, the quick action of the ATRP wardens and fire-fighting units prevented the spread of many fires but the Catholic school near Dumbarton Central Station and the Scottish People's Theatre, a wood and iron structure at Dumbarton Common, were burned to the ground. A parachute mine and incendiary bombs destroyed houses at the end of Levengrove Terrace and Veir Terrace. One woman was killed in that incident. High explosive bombs wrecked two tenements in the Newtown, one in Glasgow Road, where the majority of the casualties were badly injured and one woman was killed. In Wallace Street it is believed the strutted closes saved all but one child and the following morning a delayed action bomb destroyed the Co-operative Society building and Jock McQueen's clock. Many of the large sandstone executive houses in Kirktonhill received direct hits and a woman ambulance driver was killed in Dixon Drive. On the other side of town, at Stirling Road opposite Dumbarton Cemetery, a fortunately unoccupied bungalow was razed to the ground. Windows in houses and shops all over the town were shattered and ceilings brought down by the blasts. Up in the Long Crags behind Maryland Farm more than 90 bombs were dropped on decoy targets prepared and manned by the Royal Air Force. A series of sites on the Kilpatrick Hills had been arranged to simulate the lights of the shipyards and docks on Clydeside. This clever ploy by the RAF, who were stationed in MTBs at Sandpoint beneath Dumbarton Rock, resulted in the shipyards receiving little or no attention from the Luftwaffe and saved many lives in Dumbarton and Clydebank.

The management and staff at the Blackburn Aircraft Factory in Dumbarton in 1945.

They were known as the Aluminiums – Blackburn-built bungalows and some of the community who lived in them at Castlehill in Dumbarton.

Munitions workers who were employed on building the aircraft at the Blackburn factory include my mother, Mary Heaney, Tilly Neeson Allison, Jessie Cooley Gillies and Nan Smith Roberts.

Dr MacPhail, in a publication for the old Dumbarton Town Council, states that one of the consequences of the ending of the war in 1945 was a drastic reduction in the manufacture of aircraft and another was "a pent-up demand" for new housing because none had been built for more than five years. As a result, the Blackburn aircraft factory went over to the production of aluminium houses, which were intended for temporary use until the housing shortage was remedied. Two of the streets in Castlehill where these first houses were erected were called Blackburn Crescent and Sunderland Avenue, after the flying boats which had been built by the aircraft company. Later the company continued with the manufacture of pre-fabricated houses, but the conventional, standard types of houses, which were often cheaper, were preferred and by 1960 the Blackburn factory was being run down and eventually it closed.

Castlehill prefab mothers and grandmothers pictured celebrating the Coronation in 1953.

Chapter 36

THE NAVVIES

A squad of navvies working on the West Highland railway.

When I was much younger, I read the stories of Patrick MacGill, the navvy poet from Donegal in the West of Ireland. MacGill's stories were riveting and ranged from *The Rat Pit to Children of the Dead End, Glenmornan,* the *Great Push* and *Moleskin Joe.* These were the real life stories of tattie howkers and navvies, Islanders and Highlanders and Irish men and women who immigrated to Scotland to escape the austerity of their dirt poor crofts and farming communities. These hardy people built the West Highland Railway line and laboured on hydro electric schemes and aluminium strip mills from Kinlochleven to Loch Sloy to Lochaber. Like Patrick MacGill I had been employed as a navvy for a few short weeks at Glen Douglas during a cold, wet and windy summer in the Sixties and then, again like him, as a reporter on the *Daily Express.*

The work at Glen Douglas building storage bunkers for nuclear weapons was hard, too hard for a skinny teenager like me, but I travelled each day from Dumbarton with the rest of the team in one of Howard's fleet of green buses. And I slept, covered in mud and completely exhausted, all the way home after doing back breaking 12-hour shifts armed with a round mouth shovel and a jack hammer. I have never worked so hard in my life. Little wonder then that I found MacGill's books fascinating, especially where I could recognise many of the places and identify with the characters in them. We lived in different eras though, through times that were similar but not the same, and my own experiences, although tough enough in themselves, were not nearly as harsh or cruel as that army of 5,000 navvies had to endure.

The West Highland Railway Line from Craigendoran to Oban, Fort William and Mallaig is one of the world's most scenic train journeys. It is up there with Riding the Iron Rooster through China or taking the Rocky Mountain Loop from New York to Montreal in Canada. However, like the creation of most beautiful things, the route of the West Highland Railway was extremely dangerous. Certainly it was perilous for the 37 navvies who died – and scores more who were injured or crippled – during its construction on the Arrochar-Tarbet-Ardlui stretch of the line. This is where the Arrochar Alps, the Cobbler and Ben Lomond stare down from on high and Loch Lomondside meets Loch Longside. Thirty seven dead, you may ask? That is a staggering statistic which I came across while researching an article on the line as it is today, now one of the top ten most popular railway excursions in the world. The Arrochar, Ardlui and Tarbet Heritage website carries the story of those 37 navvies who died at the end of the 19th century. And the story too of how Cardross man Billy Thomson and his wife, Peggy, campaigned for the erection of a memorial to these brave men now buried near the Ballyhennan Cemetery. Construction of this line started in 1887 and was completed in 1895 and there is a list of those who lost their lives there between 1890 and 1894. Their ages ranged between 18 and 70 and not only did they die in construction accidents but they were struck down by diseases, including smallpox, which ravaged the roughly constructed navvy camps alongside the newly-laid tracks. The Heritage website tells us construction started in 1887 but there were no fatalities in this area until 1890.

A locomotive at work on the construction of the West Highland Line.

The railway was opened in August 1894 - the longest stretch of railway opened in a single day at 100 miles. The main camps for the railway workers were located at Helensburgh, Arrochar, Ardlui and Crianlarich. There was also a camp at Creaganardain viaduct on Loch Lomondside called Hunter's Huts. Each camp had medical facilities for the workers manned by nurses provided by the railway. The Church of Scotland ministers of that area also set up libraries for the workers, and there was one of these in the manse at Arrochar Parish Church. These were designed to keep off the booze men like MacGill's magnificent Moleskin Joe and Carroty Dan and other colourfully named characters in *Children of the Dead End*. The workers, who were a mix of Highlanders, Irishmen, Poles and Lithuanians, didn't mix very much with the local communities. Large numbers of the Irish navvies didn't stay around long due to the remoteness of the terrain and the harshness of the conditions. They made enough for their fare down to England where there was more social life.

Helensburgh was the first camp as it was next to the railway and the Firth of Clyde and a short trip from Greenock, where the Irish and Island ferries berthed. Arrochar was the next one as there was a road and railway. On the Loch Lomond side, workers could come up the railway to Balloch then onward by steamer to Ardlui, where construction equipment and materials were brought up by barge. The five camps, in which the accommodation was canvas covered wooden huts with open stoves for cooking, had around 5,000 men billeted in them at any one time. Stores were also provided within the camps for the workers to purchase provisions. The wages were 21 shillings (a week) for Ardlui and North and 15 shillings for South of Ardlui. One navvy, Kenneth Munro, aged 37 from Alness, was murdered up the lochside in Ardlui. Naturally, local people wanted to benefit from the new line and they asked for a siding at Craggan in Glen Douglas. They raised a petition to this effect, stating that the nearest stations at Arrochar and Whistlefield would provide them with little benefit.

A memorial to those men who lost their lives during the construction in this area is in place at the Ballyhennan Cemetery. This was erected in 1994 on the centenary of the opening of the railway. Left to right in the picture are Cardross couple Billy and Peggy Thomson, Arrochar woman Margaret Rose and Nick Johnson from the Clyde Naval Base.

The Scottish Record Office stated at the time that the farming community expected to benefit from the railway – and they did when the siding at Glen Douglas, which served both Loch Lomondside and Loch Longside, was built in 1895. There is something dark about this whole story though.

It is believed that the navvies who died while building the railway were buried outside the walls of Ballyhennan cemetery because either the cemetery was full or it was 'in some way down to the various persuasions of the men'. This was official speak to indicate that they were Catholic and not welcome in the Protestant graveyard. Excuses for this having happened include the fact that the church was planning to extend the cemetery walls to incorporate the mass grave, but this never did happen in the grounds there, which belong to the local lairds, the Colquhouns of Luss. Even in death then people in those times were separated for reasons of religion as well as race and gender. Prejudices failed to keep them apart altogether in life, however and some of the railwaymen probably went to the dances in the Arrochar village hall as no women were allowed in the railway camps.

The working conditions on the West Highland Line were in a word appalling with little or no shelter. There were very few mechanical tools save steam shovels and the navvies would have been wet to the bone for much of the time. They operated a system of hot bedding and slept in the clothes they stood up in, gambling away their wages in card games which often ended in serious fights during the little time they had off from working. Power blasting was used and this was carried out by the 'powder monkeys' who risked their lives daily. There was no Health and Safety legislation then. The first train on the line left Fort William at the back of 6 o'clock in the morning. The drivers worked one long 12-hour shift from Fort William to Craigendoran and then back to Fort William. The railway changed the way of life in many villages and was the first such large construction to have this affect on these small communities. Just a year after the official opening of the line, in 1895, the worst snow storm of the century struck the area and the West Highland line had to be closed. It is reported that two engines were stuck in a snow drift at Glen Douglas and the snow was so deep it went up to the chimney of one of them.

Train drivers and other workmen on the West Highland Line. When it snowed then, it really snowed. Railways officials inspect a locomotive buried in snow up to its chimney in Glen Douglas.

Rannoch station, like many stations, including Craigendoran and Arrochar, had a post office and bookstall, where newspapers were available. Some had tearooms. All were built to look like Swiss chalets and were what railwaymen call 'island stations' – they sat between the north and southbound tracks. Most of the mail then came in via the train, and fish from the ports in Oban and elsewhere was exported from there to Glasgow. Arrochar became strategically important and all the Canadian and American troops that were training in Inverary were brought there by rail to connect with buses which took them over the Rest and Be Thankful to their destination. Later tour trains, including The Northern Belle, came up from King's Cross in London to Balloch, where passengers took the steamer to Ardlui and transferred there to the West Highland Line. The famous 'deer stalker express' which carried the gentry, judges and politicians from London to go shooting at St. James' Hunting Lodge and other estates stopped at Arrochar. Today the West Highland Line and the stations along the way are a dropping off point for climbers and route to a back packers' paradise.

* *Thanks to the Arrochar, Tarbet and Ardlui Heritage Group for information and photographs. http://www.arrocharheritage.com Children of the Dead End and other Patrick MacGill books are published by Caliban Books.*

Pictures by courtesy of Scotrail and Colin McNab

Scenery along the line today and a newsagent's shop at Arrochar and Tarbet station, which was used by American and Canadian troops during the Second World War.

Chapter 37

THE COURTS

The Dumbarton Courts building in Church Street, where more lenient sentences are handed down in the 21st century.

Are you chaps warm enough? That was the question put by the Duke of Edinburgh to the Provost and Bailies of Dumbarton one very hot June day during a royal visit to the town. Prince Philip would have been in his prime at that time, a few years after his marriage to the Queen. He was joking, of course, with the local dignitaries who were lined up to meet Her Majesty in the grounds of the Municipal Buildings. It was those ermine trimmed ceremonial robes and heavy gold chains that drew the prince's comments. I would imagine the robes have been carefully folded and locked away in a drawer in the Provost's Room almost ever since, although one is never quite sure how much importance new local government regimes attach to our heritage and patrimony. Perhaps they will be wheeled out again when the new West Dunbartonshire Council offices open at the old Burgh Hall in Church Street, but I doubt it. The robes and chains go back to the days when Provosts and Bailies were a power in the land. The maintenance of law and order, in the absence of any police, was the responsibility of the bailies and councillors, who could and did invoke the help of other prominent citizens to deal with offenders. Since this was such a small community at that time, a policeman was hardly required, but there was a town's officer or lockman or hangman, who undertook the unpleasant tasks of hanging or flogging criminals. Dr Ian MacPhail tells us the gallows stood behind where the Burgh Hall is today, on the site of the ancient gasworks. The punishment for minor offences was generally by fines, for which someone had to act as cautioner or security. Drunkenness was punished by so many hours sitting in the stocks; 'flyting' or slanderous gossip by standing at the jogs or jougs with an iron collar placed around the offender's throat and attached by a chain to the wall of the tollbooth. Public flogging or whipping through the streets was sometimes ordered. In 1659, Alastair MacAlpine suffered this punishment for stealing herring, and in the previous year Catherine Smith was similarly punished for 'getting a bairn with a soldier'. Petty theft was sometimes punished by branding and one Isabella Cunningham who was caught red-handed in 1629 with stolen articles was found to be already branded twice and after trial was ordered to be branded again and whipped. The most gruesome punishment was reserved for witches, who were first strangled and then burned. There were however only a few such cases ion Dumbarton. In the 17th century punishment of crime seems to us today to border on inhumanity, but the maintenance of law and order was sometimes mingled with kindness. The Burgh accounts show that the bailies were far more generous than the present day Chancellor George Osborne when it came to welfare payments. There was a touch of Osborne though about the way cripples, as disabled people were then referred to, were treated. They are said to have received 'short shrift' lest they should become a burden to the town. Indeed, such was the concern amongst the bailies about disabled people that men were paid to for putting them 'aff the toun'. Twelve shillings was the going rate for people who were prepared to carry out this task with their horse and cart. Sometimes though it appeared that the authorities allowed themselves to be rather easily imposed upon, as in the case of 'a poor distressed Irishman who was robbed by Spaniards in the south of Ireland,' and had a printed pass to prove it. They were not so easily taken in however when John MacKerral, a Highlander who pretended to be dumb and produced forged testimonials, was sent through to Edinburgh for trial. Witches were hunted down and in 1628, Janet Boyd, wife of Dumbarton man Robert Neill, confessed to the provost, bailies and minister of Dumbarton that she had entered into a contract with the devil. She had been tortured of course before confessing that she had received his mark, had renounced her baptism and had 'carnal dealings' with him – 'and that she had laid sundry diseases on different people by the powers granted to her by the devil'. Later in the same year, Janet Donald, wife of Humphrey Colquhoun, and two other local women were lodged in the tollbooth and charged with witchcraft. At that time it was thought that the possession of 'the Devil's mark' on the skin, a spot insensitive to pain, was proof that a person was a witch or a warlock. For some men it was a full-time occupation pricking the skin of witches with needles at a time when witch-hunting was rampant. After almost a year in the tollbooth, Janet Donald was taken out to be strangled with a rope and then burned at the stake. When another witch, Bessie Bargillie, was burnt in 1644, seven loads of peats, five loads of coal and two barrels of tar were used for the fire. There was just one case of a warlock when a man called John MacWilliam, a slater to trade, was convicted of witchcraft and bigamy and was strangled and burnt. The bailies have today been replaced by Justices of the Peace who sit in the Dumbarton Courts building in Church Street and who dispense, thankfully and much more humanely, far more lenient sentences than were handed down then when the new West Dunbartonshire Council offices open at the old Burgh Hall in Church Street, but I doubt it. The robes and chains go back to the days when Provosts and Bailies were a power in the land. The maintenance of law and order, in the absence of any police, was the responsibility of the bailies and councillors, who could and did invoke the help of other prominent citizens to deal with offenders. Since this was such a small community at that time, a policeman was hardly required, but there was a town's officer or lockman or hangman, who undertook the unpleasant tasks of hanging or flogging criminals. The gallows stood behind where the Burgh Hall is today, on the site of the ancient gasworks. The punishment for minor offences was generally by fines, for which someone had to act as cautioner or security.

Provost Ian MacDuff and the bailies and councillors of Dumbarton around 1972 when the town celebrated the 750th anniversary of the granting of the royal charter by King Alexander II. They are (back row, l to r) J Elliott Hill, Peter McCann, Alastair Tuach, Willie Hemphill, Jack Hannah, Ian Leitch, Jim Miller, Isobel MacLeod and Alex McLean. Front row – Patrick O'Neill, James Bain, Lachlan MacKinnon, Provost Ian MacDuff, William Adam, Brian Crowther and Ian Bell.

Drunkenness was punished by so many hours sitting in the stocks; 'flyting' or slanderous gossip by standing at the jogs or jougs with an iron collar placed around the offender's throat and attached by a chain to the wall of the tollbooth. Public flogging or whipping through the streets was sometimes ordered. In 1659, Alastair MacAlpine suffered this punishment for stealing herring, and in the previous year Catherine Smith was similarly punished for 'getting a bairn with a soldier'. Petty theft was sometimes punished by branding and one Isabella Cunningham who was caught red-handed in 1629 with stolen articles was found to be already branded twice and after trial was ordered to be branded again and whipped. The most gruesome punishment was reserved for witches, who were first strangled and then burned. There were however only a few such cases ion Dumbarton. In the 17th century punishment of crime seems to us today to border on inhumanity, but the maintenance of law and order was sometimes mingled with kindness. The Burgh accounts show that the bailies were far more generous than the present day Chancellor George Osborne when it came to welfare payments. There was a touch of Osborne though about the way cripples, as disabled people were then referred to, were treated. They are said to have received 'short shrift' lest they should become a burden to the town. Indeed, such was the concern amongst the bailies about disabled people that men were paid to for putting them 'aff the toun'. Twelve shillings was the going rate for people who were prepared to carry out this task with their horse and cart. Sometimes though it appeared that the authorities allowed themselves to be rather easily imposed upon, as in the case of 'a poor distressed Irishman who was robbed by Spaniards in the south of Ireland,' and had a printed pass to prove it. They were not so easily taken in however when John MacKerral, a Highlander who pretended to be dumb and produced forged testimonials, was sent through to Edinburgh for trial. Witches were hunted down and in 1628, Janet Boyd, wife of Dumbarton man Robert Neill, confessed to the provost, bailies and minister of Dumbarton that she had entered into a contract with the devil. She had been tortured of course before confessing that she had received his mark, had renounced her baptism and had 'carnal dealings' with him – 'and that she had laid sundry diseases on different people by the powers granted to her by the devil'. Later in the same year, Janet Donald, wife of Humphrey Colquhoun, and two other local women were lodged in the tollbooth and charged with witchcraft. At that time it was thought that the possession of 'the Devil's mark' on the skin, a spot insensitive to pain, was proof that a person was a witch or a warlock. For some men it was a full-time occupation pricking the skin of witches with needles at a time when witch-hunting was rampant. After almost a year in the tollbooth, Janet Donald was taken out to be strangled with a rope and then burned at the stake. When another witch, Bessie Bargillie, was burnt in 1644, seven loads of peats, five loads of coal and two barrels of tar were used for the fire. There was just one case of a warlock when a man called John MacWilliam, a slater to trade, was convicted of witchcraft and bigamy and was strangled and burnt. The bailies have today been replaced by Justices of the Peace who sit in the Dumbarton Courts building in Church Street and who dispense, thankfully and much more humanely, far more lenient sentences than were handed down then.

Dumbarton Jail in McLean Place, where people accused of witchcraft, were detained before being strangled and burned to death in the public square outside the courts.
Below is the Municipal Buildings, where the police station and court was housed.

Chapter 38

THE POLICE

Detective Chief Inspector Angus McLeod Murder squad officer

Born: Isle of Lewis, October 23, 1927
Died: Paisley, September 21, 2013

Detective Chief Inspector Angus MacLeod, who was involved in 31 Scottish murder cases in Strathclyde, all of which were solved bar one, died at the Royal Alexandra Hospital in Paisley, aged 86. He was born on the MacLeod family croft and brought up in the village of Swordale on the Isle of Lewis, where his first language was Gaelic. He learned only faltering English at Knock School, which he left to go to work as a ploughman at the age of 13. Angus was the second oldest of six children born to Catherine and Alexander MacLeod. He was a popular young man in Point where, with his horse called Jimmy, he tilled the fields of every family in the small crofting community. He took the boat to the mainland and joined Dumbarton Burgh Police Force on the 19th of March, 1949. Angus was the last officer to be recruited by that small force before it was disbanded and integrated into Dunbartonshire Constabulary, which later became part of Strathclyde Police. The beat allocated to him by Chief Constable Bert Gunn was Dumbarton High Street and the working class communities of Brucehill and West Bridgend. Big Angus, as he was widely known, developed his English on the beat, making himself hugely popular in the community where people loved his friendly ways and his lilting Gaelic accent. The children especially liked him for the fact that he chased them for playing football in the street or stealing apples from gardens in nearby posh Kirktonhill but never seemed to be able to catch any of them.

The recalcitrants and criminals in the West End were wary of him however because he seemed to have a sixth sense when it came to finding out who had been involved in a fist fight or carried out the latest housebreaking, robbed a gas meter or stole someone's purse. Angus was transferred to Dunbartonshire CID in 1960 after his potential as a detective was spotted by Chief Constable William Kerr, who had himself been a member of Royal Protection Squad. MacLeod moved swiftly through the ranks of detectives and worked under some notable police officers including Kerr himself and later Acting Chief Constable Sir David McNee, who became Chief Constable of Strathclyde and Commissioner of the Metropolitan Police. Sir David had stepped in after Chief Constable Kerr, one of the detectives in the Stone of Destiny case, was seriously hurt in a helicopter accident in the grounds of the police HQ at Crosslet, Dumbarton. One of the first murder cases MacLeod was involved in was as a young constable in the notorious Dumbarton Surgery Murder on his beat in West Bridgend. It began when a young apprentice aged only 14 walked into a police station and told the officers he had been coaxed into a disused shop by a fat man with a scar on his face who offered him ten shillings to help lift a fireplace grating. The stranger produced a gun and tried to tie him to a chair and gag him, but the youngster escaped and ran home to his father who took him to the police. Detectives were sceptical at first until they found paint in the empty shop used to black out the windows and a chair similar to that the victim had told them about.

The shop owner said the premises had been rented to a 'Mr Green' whose description matched that given by the boy, but despite extensive inquiries in July 1962 the trail to 'Mr Green' went cold. Then a few weeks later Fred Dowden, aged 15, vanished from his home in Dumbarton. A massive hunt drew a blank. Police who scoured the town with tracker dogs failed to find Fred. Reports stated the inquiry was going nowhere until the then PC Angus MacLeod – 'an eagle-eyed police constable' - noticed someone had used paint to black out the windows of Dr Alexander Forrester's old surgery at 66 West Bridgend.

Remembering his briefing to be on the lookout for anything that might bear a similarity to the earlier incident, MacLeod peered inside and saw a horrific sight that turned his stomach. Tied to a chair was the body of the young victim who had been asphyxiated, his face and mouth covered with sticking tape. The surgery had been rented to a man with a scar calling himself 'Mr Black'. Then police discovered a 'Mr Blue' had rented another empty building in Govan, Glasgow, a few weeks earlier. Inside were rolls of sticky tape. The killer was obviously planning to snatch another victim. But who was the murderer?

Police eventually arrested Philip Givens, 35, who pleaded guilty at the High Court in Glasgow in March 1963 to abduction and murder and was sent to the State Hospital at Carstairs. Another high profile murder Detective Inspector MacLeod was involved in was the case of Dumbarton sex killer Robert Gemmill, a gardener who was raised in the town and who was recognised as a psychopath from the age of 16. Yet Gemmill, who had spent 14 years in mental hospitals and previously attacked four young women, was freed from Carstairs before he murdered the daughter of a Nottingham millionaire. Lynda Jane Walters was stabbed to death in the grounds of luxury Stonefield Castle Hotel near Tarbert, Argyll, while she was holidaying in Scotland with parents.

MacLeod discovered that the gardener and handyman was a notorious sexual sadist who attacked women and had been held for eight years in maximum security in the State Hospital. Gemmill was originally accused of murdering Lynda-Jayne but, the Crown agreed to reduce the charge to culpable homicide and Lord Kincraig sentenced him Gemmill to be detained indefinitely. The murder mystery DCI MacLeod and his Strathclyde colleagues failed to solve is still on the books of newly-formed Police Scotland. Although Angus often said privately that although he was convinced he knew who had killed photographer 'Wee Eddie' Cotogno who lived in Valeview Terrace, Bellsmyre, Dumbarton, in July 1979, the criminal might never be brought to justice due to lack of evidence. The body of Cotogno, 63, was discovered in his burning flat but scene of crime experts quickly established that Cotogno had not died as a result of smoke inhalation or flames. Firemen had been on the scene so quickly there was little damage and they even saved thousands of sexually explicit photographs strewn around his body. DCI MacLeod retired from Strathclyde Police in 1980 with distinction after 31 years in the force. He was married to Mairi, a nursing sister, who died from cancer in December, 1988, aged just 45. The couple married in 1970 and they are survived by their daughter, Lorna, and son, Angus, and seven grandchildren. Angus was a long-time member of Dumbarton Rotary Club after he retired from the police and Mairi joined the Inner Wheel Club. Angus was latterly cared for, through a long illness, at an eventide home in Dumbarton. He has been buried at the Aignish cemetery on Lewis, near his beloved home village of Swordale, where the policeman started out his working life as a ploughman.

The old Dumbarton Police Office and JP Court was housed in the Municipal Buildings.

Chapter 39

THE MODERATOR

The Very Rev Dr Sir John Cairns

A good friend of mine was knighted by the Queen - and deservedly so. Now it's not often a columnist on a local newspaper can say that. John Cairns is now Sir John Cairns, but the former minister of Riverside Parish Church in the High Street won't be using his newly-acquired title on a day to day basis. Adding Sir to the Very Rev Dr John Cairns would not have been easy for John - nor will it be for many delighted Dumbartonians. They are the ones who will be sending congratulations to Sir John and Lady Elizabeth at the Bell House in Dunbar, East Lothian, where they are now living in blissful retirement. Lady Elizabeth was, of course, Dr Liz Cairns, a popular GP at Dumbarton Medical Centre in the Artizan.

She worked there and was much loved by her patients during all the years her husband was 'stationed' in Dumbarton. Their sons, Ben, Dan and William, all former pupils of Keil School in Kirktonhill, are rightly proud – as are their wives and John and Liz's grandchildren. I have known the Cairns Clan since they arrived at the Riverside Manse in Dixon Drive from Langholm in the Scottish Borders many years ago. John, the late Dr Ray McNamee and I often played golf together at the Carrick on Loch Lomond, Cardross and Gullane, East Lothian. With our respective spouses, Liz, Alison and Bernie, we have holidayed together at home and abroad. And we have always enjoyed ourselves, with the unassuming minister never dropping names or titles or letting people know he was once Moderator of the General Assembly of the Church of Scotland – or for that matter Chaplain to the Queen. The last time I saw John was when he was on his feet at the General Assembly in Edinburgh telling the world in his own inimitable but understated manner that the 21st century was a time for ecumenical and attitudinal change. He used Dumbarton, which he loves, as an example saying the Churches Together movement in the town had been responsible for breaking down long-standing prejudices and barriers which had been associated with religious discrimination and sectarianism for many years. He said too that Church of Scotland congregations should be allowed to call gay ministers to their pulpits provided that was the will of their own kirk session. The Kirk is crying out for people to study for the ministry at the present time, just as the Catholic Church in Scotland is looking to recruit new blood for the priesthood. They will find that good people like Sir John, the Very Rev Dr Cairns, will be extremely difficult to replace. He has an impressive CV: John Ballantyne Cairns KCVO was born in 1942 and is a retired minister of the Church of Scotland. Following a career as a solicitor, he studied theology and was ordained in 1974. His first charge was as minister at the parishes of Langholm, Ewes and Westerkirk. He then became minister at Riverside Parish Church, Dumbarton (1985-2001). Later he served as minister of Aberlady and Gullane Parish Churches, East Lothian, until retiring in 2008. In retirement, he served as part-time locum minister at St Columba's Church, London. His formal title, following the end of his Moderatorial year, is the Very Reverend Dr John

The Chapel Royal, from left: Rev Ian Paterson; Very Rev Dr John Cairns; Rev Alistair Bennett; Rt Rev Dr Angus Morrison; Very Rev John Chalmers; Rev Prof David Fergusson; Very Rev Prof Iain Torrance, Dean of the Order of the Thistle and Dean of the Chapel Royal; Very Rev Dr James Harkness; Rev Neil Gardner; Very Rev Dr Finlay Macdonald; Very Rev Dr Lorna Hood; Very Rev Dr James Simpson; Rev Charles Robertson and the Rev Dr Norman Drummond.

Cairns. He was Moderator of the General Assembly of the Church of Scotland in 1999-2000 and was appointed Chaplain to the Queen in 1997. He became Dean of the Chapel Royal in Scotland in 2006 and has held convenerships of several General Assembly boards and committees. The General Assembly over which he moderated was uniquely held in the Edinburgh International Conference Centre. This was to allow the Scottish Parliament to meet in the Church's Assembly Hall. This fulsome tribute was paid to Sir John in 2004 when he was presented with an Honorary Doctorate of Laws at his alma mater, Bristol University: Madame Pro-Vice-Chancellor, it is a quirk of history that Her Majesty the Queen, as she progresses north to Balmoral for her summer vacation, starts her journey as the temporal head of the Church of England, a church that is both

Catholic and reformed; and that when she crosses the border into Scotland she becomes a member of the Church of Scotland, a church wholly reformed, Presbyterian and free. Today we honour The Very Reverend John Ballantyne Cairns, who as a past Moderator of the General Assembly of the Church of Scotland crosses the border to return to England, the country of his birth and to the University in which he gained his degree in Law. In his self-deprecating manner he claims to have been less than assiduous as a student, and his inadequacy in the eyes of his fellow Scots is that he is only an English lawyer. After a brief period in legal practice he responded to a perceived vocation to the ordained ministry in the Church of Scotland. His has been primarily a parish ministry in Elgin in the Borders, in Dumbarton, on the Clyde and now in Gullane on the Firth of Forth. His ministry has been characterized by working with and for the local community and not just his congregations. This wide perspective and inclusivity will be seen as a hallmark of his vocation as a minister of the Church of Scotland. The Church of Scotland's governing system is Presbyterian, which claims that no one person or group within the Church has more influence, perhaps power, than any other. It is organized by a system of courts at local, district and national levels. It highest court is the General Assembly

Another Moderator and Assembly Clerk, the Very Rev John Chalmers, formerly of Trinity Church in Renton with the Rev Eleanor McMahon, who was at Riverside, Dumbarton, for a time and the Very Rev Lorna Hood pictured in Edinburgh.

of the Church of Scotland which meets annually in Edinburgh and has the authority to make laws to determine how the Church of Scotland operates. In 1999 John Cairns was nominated and elected Moderator of the General Assembly for one year. It is not without significance that in that year the Scottish Parliament was reconvened for the first time since 1707. Moderators have little or no power, but have a platform in which to exercise considerable influence. During his time as a minister John Cairns has made a significant contribution to the life of the Church and people of Scotland. He was instrumental in reforming the Church's ministry. Ministers with a virtual freehold can be and are independently-minded, making them difficult to lead and even more difficult to support. Theirs is often a lonely, isolated and work driven life, which leads at times to depression and burn out. It is said that John Cairns virtually single-handedly introduced a programme of continuing ministerial education, planned study leave and the provision of health advisers. Such innovations included, for the first time, a recognition of the demands made on women ministers, who often combine the roles of wife, mother and full-time minister. Alongside this work, as chairman of the Church's Judicial Commission he was instrumental in bringing clarity, openness and the highest standards of human rights to those the Church chose to discipline. Such a contribution has meant that the Church as a whole understands the pressures on its ministry and the ministers and their families can feel justly supported. It is said of John Cairns that, 'He is a robust and compassionate man, who has never been afraid to name incompetence, but then to assist those in need.' As the Convener of the Committee on Chaplains to Her Majesty's Forces, John Cairns brought his ecumenical zeal to bear to ensure that the chaplains from numerous church traditions in the Army, the Royal Navy and Royal Air Force worked together. This pattern of inclusivity has marked his ministry, wherever he has served. Good relationships with other churches and faith communities have not always been the patterns of Scottish life. Indeed relationships have been in the past bitter, and division endemic. Such sectarian divides have their public face in the 'Old Firm' matches between Celtic and Rangers. Yet John Cairns' commitment to inclusivity has always been to the fore. The notion of building an inclusive society is not without its difficulties.

John Cairns showed support for women in the ministry

End of the line - Dr John Cairns with Bernie Heaney, Drs Alison and Ray McNamee, and Dr Liz Cairns, who was a well-loved GP in Dumbarton, at Parsons Green in London. *Picture by Bill Heaney*

The place of women in public ministry has not always been wholly supported by members of congregations, yet John Cairns has actively supported their place in the mission and ministry of the Church. Perhaps his most contentious commitment to an inclusive society came during his year as Moderator of the General Assembly, when the Scottish Parliament proposed to repeal Section 28, as it was known in England, of the Local Government Act 1988, which forbade the promotion of homosexuality by local authorities. John Cairns argued that the Act was discriminatory and contrary to human rights. The debate was fierce, but it was John Cairns' courageous public stance as Moderator of the General Assembly, that this was a bad law which was unworthy of Scotland, that gave the fledgling Scottish Parliament the confidence to repeal Section 28 in June 2000. John Cairns has supported two charities, Glasgow the Caring City, which provides material aid to those suffering in war zones, and perhaps more importantly the African Children's Choir, which educates children in areas of conflict or those who suffer from the ravages of HIV/Aids. His first- hand knowledge of the rebel areas of the Sudan, Kenya and Uganda, where the Lord's Resistance Army has continued its insurgency for 17 years, abducting children to serve as soldiers, has given this cause an authentic immediacy. For many these needs are known only too well, but often passed by because we do not know how to help. John Cairns' public support has encouraged others to express their concern in action. John Cairns is a courageous man whose ministry has been characterized by a continuing desire to build inclusive communities, to stand against discrimination and to care actively for some of the most disadvantaged children on this earth. The Very Reverend John Ballantyne Cairns as eminently worthy of the degree of Doctor of Laws *honoris causa.*

The Armed Services representatives in the black and white corridor at the General Assembly of the Church of Scotland in Edinburgh. *Picture by Bill Heaney*

Chapter 40

THE LUSITANIA

The sinking of the Clyde-built Lusitania off Kinsale on the West of Ireland.

Dumbarton woman Elizabeth McCorkindale and her two children were amongst the 1201 passengers drowned at sea when the Clyde-built RMS Lusitania was torpedoed by a German U-boat 100 years ago on May 7, 1915. Just days away from the centenary of the disaster, the owner of the John Brown-built Cunarder accused the Irish Government of abandoning the graveyard of the wreck to pirates and treasure hunters. The ship was en route from New York to Liverpool and sank in the Atlantic, 11 miles off the Old Head of Kinsale in County Cork during the First World War. Amongst the 1,201 lives lost in the disaster were Mrs Elizabeth McCorkindale, 33, Duncan McCorkindale, three, and his infant sister, Mary, whose deaths are commemorated on the Ritchie family gravestone in Dumbarton

Cemetery. None of the victims is buried in that leafy corner of God's Acre at Dumbarton however, and it is likely that their bodies were never recovered, but they could be among more than 100 victims whose bodies were brought ashore and who are buried in Ireland in a mass grave. Meanwhile, Gregg Bemis, an 87-year-old US entrepreneur, has described as 'spiteful' the strict conditions imposed on his lifelong quest to save valuable and historically important artefacts and priceless paintings from the Clyde-built liner. Genealogist Ann Graham, who lives in Bonhill Road, Dumbarton, has been investigating the Dumbarton connection to one of the biggest maritime disasters of last century. She said: 'My mother has always known there was a gravestone in Dumbarton Cemetery which mentioned victims of the Lusitania. She remembers seeing it when she was a child and it stuck in her mind. She went to the cemetery a few weeks ago and noted the details and that the family name was Ritchie. I did some research but could find no Elizabeth Ritchie among the Lusitania passengers, but I deduced that she was married given that she had two young children. So, I logged on to the Scotland's People website, paid my money and did a search of the marriages from 1990 onwards. And lo and behold I found her marriage at the Tullichewan Hotel in Balloch on Loch Lomondside in 1907. William's first wife, Janet, is mentioned on the headstone as having died in 1874, so I realised that she could not have been Elizabeth's mother. I did some more digging in the Census, Births, Marriages and Deaths records and turned up most of the information I was after. After that, it was just a matter of fitting all the pieces of information together, rather like a jigsaw. As I have been an amateur genealogist for over 30 years, it was knowing where to look for the information that was the key to the whole thing.' Mystery still surrounds the sinking of the Lusitania. The liner's new owner Mr Bemis has spent decades trying to confirm a theory that the ship's sinking - 18 minutes compared to two hours and 40 minutes for the Titanic - was hastened by a second explosion caused by a secret cache of munitions destined for Britain's war effort. 'The Irish Government officials are so glib and innocent sounding like they walk on water, but they add all these restrictions on and throw them at me so they interfere and impede,' he told the *Irish Independent*. One of the conditions ordered Mr Bemis to indemnify the Irish state against any incidents or injury if he organizes a dive into the wreck.

The people of Ireland are being deprived of an opportunity to share in a very historic event and to share in the income to be derived from this - a substantial tourist attraction could be developed that will go on for years,' he claimed. The businessman from New Mexico bought the wreck in the 1960s and now claims diving on the site could leave him open to claims from descendants of the dead for the desecration of graves. As the centenary of the sinking approached, Mr Bemis sought permission to recover the double-faced bridge telegraph, which is visible 300 feet down and potentially records the last instruction from Captain William Thomas Turner to the engine room after the torpedo strike.

Boston Evening Globe

Evening Edition 1¢

EVENING EDITION—7:30 O'CLOCK—LATEST

LUSITANIA SUNK

Not Known How Many Passengers Saved

TORPEDOED BY GERMANS, REMAINED AFLOAT 12 HOURS

TORPEDOED OFF THE IRISH COAST

Left New York Last Saturday With 1253 Passengers

ULTIMATUM TO CHINA

Japan's Cabinet Issues an Official Statement

UNITED STATES MAKES INQUIRY

Captain William Turner and the headline story about the sinking.

It may confirm another theory that an order for full steam ahead may have hastened the Lusitania's demise as water rushed in where it was holed. Other items being sought are the triple chime steam whistle, known as the voice of the ship, which marked the ill-fated departure from New York, the captain's cabin safe and silver spoons made to celebrate the war career of Lord Kitchener. In a statement, Irish Government officials said: 'The conditions attached to Mr Bemis' licence are no more onerous than is absolutely necessary to protect a wreck of this global significance. It is also the final resting place of over 1,000 individuals who lost their lives during the tragic event of May 1915 and therefore deserves due respect as the grave site of those unfortunate passengers.' Of 18,000 wrecks lying in seas around Ireland, the Lusitania is the only one with a ministerial order declaring it of cultural and historical significance. It was placed amid claims that art collector Sir Hugh Lane brought valuable paintings on board including works by Rubens. 'The order has a purpose for the state. It also provides me with the supposed opportunity to do my research without being inhibited by a bunch coming and pirating stuff from the ship,' Mr Bemis said. 'Piracy is obviously something of a concern as are treasure hunters, and it's something that can happen. Ireland and Britain have an equal interest in not having that happen. We have no idea how much of that has gone on.' Eoin McGarry, who has dived on the wreck more than anyone else, fears some of the artefacts have already been taken illegally. 'We've been banging our heads off the wall for years and not getting anywhere with the officials. It's now the right time for the wider audience to hear about this,' he said. RMS Lusitania was the jewel in the Cunard crown and the fastest ship on the Atlantic having taken the Blue Riband in 1907. Mr Bemis, who travelled to Ireland for the centenary, spent 50 years trying to find how the ship sank so quickly, but he rejects recent research which found no evidence of a secret munitions cargo. He said: 'I'm trying to find out what caused the second explosion properly. It's my property. I bought it. I invested in it. Is it wrong for me to want to recover it? I don't think that's being arrogant, I think that's being responsible.' Ann Graham, who works at the Army Cadet office in Latta Street, Dumbarton, said: 'The information I have been able to gather about this Dumbarton connection so far is that William Ritchie was a baker born in Alexandria. In 1866 he married Janet Blair, who died in 1874, leaving him with a son, William. Mr Ritchie lived at 129 High Street, Dumbarton, and in 1881, he married his shop-girl Mary Carrick with whom he had another nine children. The oldest of these was Elizabeth Ritchie, who was a schoolteacher and lived at 1 Veir Terrace, Dumbarton, when she married Daniel McCorkindale, a machinist at Singer in Clydebank, in 1907 which, ironically, is the year the Lusitania was launched in Clydebank. The couple had a son, Duncan, who was born in Clydebank in 1908 and they left Scotland for America in 1911, sailing to New York where they were to join Daniel's cousin, Daniel Glen, in Staten Island. They somehow ended up in Chromo, Colorado, where they had a daughter, Mary, born in 1914.' Mrs Elizabeth McCorkindale, 33, Duncan McCorkindale, aged three, and Mary McCorkindale, infant, are named on the Lusitania passenger list. All were registered lost when the ship was torpedoed. Ann added: 'I have no idea where Daniel was at this point, but he was with his wife on the passenger list of another ship, the Cameronian a few years earlier, and he went on to re-marry in 1917. He died in Auchinleck in Ayrshire in 1949. Coincidentally the Cameronian was torpedoed and sunk 50 miles North, North West of Alexandria in Egypt in June 1917. Elizabeth's half-brother William, (the son of William and Janet), became a solicitor in Dumbarton, with offices at 74 Church Street and a home in Oxhill Road. When he died suddenly on his way to work in 1945, the business was carried on by his son, John. In the trade directory for 1928, William Ritchie has three shops in Dumbarton, two in the High Street and one in West Bridgend.'

The names of the Lusitania victims in Dumbarton Cemetery.

William was a well-known member and former Dean of the Faculty of Procurators and had been in business for almost half a century. Just before his death, he attained his jubilee in the eldership of the High

Church in Dumbarton. The Lusitania lived and died in the shadow of the Belfast-built Titanic, which also met a cruel fate in the icy waters of the Atlantic. The Titanic died a 'natural' death in that it was an iceberg which took the great vessel to the bottom of the sea, while the Lusitania was taken out by man. The story of how the Lusitania was holed by a single torpedo fired from a German U-boat is detailed in a new book by Erik Larson – 'Dead Wake'. More information about the Dumbarton connection came to me however when a Lennox Herald reader, Isabella Kerr, wrote to me from her home in Dunblane, Perthshire, to explain how the McCorkindale family was linked with the people who were drowned. Known in Vale of Leven, where she was brought up, as Ishbel Kerr, she left her home at Gaitskell Avenue in Alexandria, and went to Dunblane to live with her daughter after she was widowed in 2004. Ishbel, who spent most of her life between Renton and Alexandria, says Daniel McCorkindale, whose wife, Elizabeth Ritchie, and their two children, Duncan and Mary, were drowned, were her relatives. Daniel's father, Duncan McCorkindale, married Helen McLaren (Shepherd) and made their home in Carman Cottage on Carman Hill in Renton. Their children, Isabella, Annie, Helen, Sarah, Duncan and Daniel were all born there. When Daniel married Elizabeth Ritchie the couple decided to go to America to farm and had two children there, Duncan and Mary. Elizabeth was very homesick and set out in the Lusitania to come back with the two children leaving her husband behind to wind things up in the US. 'Unfortunately Elizabeth and the children were on the ill-fated Lusitania,' she said. Daniel came back eventually and was married again to a woman called Nan. They had a son, Alan, who was in the Royal Navy and who eventually married in Australia and made his home there. Their daughter, Margaret, was a nurse and married a miner from Auchinleck in Ayrshire and the couple made their home there while Daniel and Nan lived in Glasgow Street in Ardrossan and Saltcoats. Ishbel told me: 'Isabella McCorkindale, my grandmother, married William Martin who had a grocer's shop in Renton and they had three children, Helen, Christina and William. Helen, my mother, married David McIntosh from Jamestown and Christina married George Sneddon from Alexandria. William never married as he had spina bifida.' An indication of how far flung families were at that time is that Daniel Glen, whom the Lusitania survivor,

Daniel McCorkindale, had first joined in Staten Island when he went to America had a sister, Jessie, who married William Ritchie, who was a baker in Renton. That William Ritchie opened a baker's shop in Dumbarton High Street where he lived above the shop. Eventually, when he retired, William and his family went to live above the Co-op shop in Greenhead Road, Silverton, Dumbarton. When he died his widow and daughter, Mary, stayed on in Silverton and eventually had built for them a bungalow in Clydeshore Road opposite Levengrove Park. Mary later lived in the new flats at Crosslet Road, Silverton, but died there six years ago. Ishbel said: 'I have a cousin, Walter, who is in Newfoundland, and another cousin, Aileen, who is in Hamilton, Ontario. We are spread out across the world.'

Genealogist Anne Graham pictured at the Lusitania disaster victims' grave in Dumbarton. *Picture by Bill Heaney.*

The Lusitania under construction at John Brown's shipyard.

Mystery surrounds the sinking of a great ship and what caused the final, fatal damage

Few tales in history are more haunting, more tangled with investigatory mazes or more fraught with toxic secrets than that of the final voyage of the Lusitania. The four-funneled, 787-foot Clydebank-built superliner, on a run from New York to Liverpool, encountered a German submarine, the U-20, about 11 miles off the south west coast of Ireland. The U-boat's captain, Walther Schwieger, was pleased to discover that the passenger steamer had no naval escort. Following his government's new policy of unrestricted warfare, Schwinger fired a single torpedo into her hull. Less than half a minute later, a second explosion shuddered from somewhere deep within the bowels of the vessel, and she listed precariously to starboard. The Lusitania sank in just 18 minutes. Nearly 1,200 people, including 128 Americans, died with it. Mrs McCorkindale and her two children's names appear on the casualty list beside the millionaire Alfred Vanderbilt, the Broadway impresario Charles Frohman and the noted art collector Hugh Lane – a gallery in Parnell Square, Dublin, is named after him - who was thought to be carrying sealed lead tubes containing paintings by Rembrandt and Monet. Outrage followed and the sinking turned American opinion against the Germans — and became a rallying cry when America finally entered the war in 1917. As we steered slowly towards the centenary of the sinking, it was clear that unsettling questions have clung like limpets to the Lusitania case, contributing to a persistent hunch that the ship had somehow been allowed to sail into a trap. Or that there was a diplomatic cover-up and why the British Admiralty failed to provide a military escort for the Lusitania. The main questions still to be answered are: what was the cause of that catastrophic second explosion? Why was a British cruiser sent to rescue the Lusitania's dying victims suddenly called back to port? What about Winston Churchill, who was then First Lord of the Admiralty, who left Britain for France just days before the sinking? What did he know, and when did he know it? Shortly before the disaster, Churchill had written in a confidential letter that it was 'most important to attract neutral shipping to our shores, in the hopes especially of embroiling the United States with Germany'. Afterwards, he is alleged to have all but celebrated the sinking as a great Allied victory, saying, 'The poor babies who perished in the ocean struck a blow at German power more deadly than could have been achieved by the sacrifice of a hundred thousand fighting men.' Initially the authorities tried to pin the blame for the sinking on Commander William Thomas Turner, the ship's captain, but he was cleared after a public inquiry in Liverpool. The nagging question of the second explosion is one of many Lusitania riddles that persist to this day, and that is the subject of a new book, *Dead Wake* by Erik Larson. What makes the story of that particular U-boat's ceaseless predations so much more discomfiting is that the British Admiralty apparently had a very good idea of the submarine's whereabouts in the days leading up to the sinking — and yet did nothing. 'It was a curious moment in the history of naval warfare,' Larson writes. 'Room 40 knew a U-boat was heading south to Liverpool — knew the boat's history; knew that it was now somewhere in the North Atlantic under orders to sink troop transports and any other British vessel it encountered; and knew as well that the submarine was armed with enough shells and torpedoes to sink a dozen ships. It was like knowing that a particular killer was loose on the streets of London, armed with a particular weapon, and certain to strike in a particular neighborhood within the next few days, the only unknown being exactly when.' In an interview, Larson once said: 'It is my goal to create a historical experience with my books. My dream, my ideal, is that someone picks up a book of mine, starts reading it, and just lets themselves sink into the past and then read the thing straight through, and emerge at the end feeling as though they've lived in another world entirely.' Larson seems puzzlingly incurious about the second explosion — which remains the single greatest mystery of the Lusitania's rapid sinking, and the ultimate cause of the terrible carnage in which a local mother and her two young children lost their lives.

Lusitania ready to launch at John Brown's, Clydebank.

Chapter 41

THE ENTERTAINER

Bobby Cawley

Robert Burns Cawley, Hotelier and businessman
Born January 25, 1934, died January 14, 1999

If ever a local boy made good, it was Bobby Cawley. He was an entertainer on stage and off it. He starred with the Osdon Merrymakers and various other theatre groups, raising hundreds of pounds for charity – when £100 was a lot of money – and graduated through retail to the hotel business. His legacy is the thriving Cawley Hotel chain, which encompasses the world famous Duck Bay Hotel and Marina on the Bonnie Banks of Loch Lomond. The fundamental elements in Bobby Cawley's life revolved round four main tenets

- hard work, attention to detail, shrewd marketing skill, and, most importantly, family values, wrote Helensburgh-based solicitor John Gilmour in a fitting tribute in the Glasgow Herald. Born in Alexandria and educated at Levenvale Primary and Vale of Leven Academy. Bobby's first job was as the delivery boy at the Co-operative Society. Thereafter, he moved to Edwards Outfitters, Dumbarton, where he developed his unique style of salesmanship that was to stand him in good stead in later life. He purchased Craigs of Alexandria in 1963 and, in typically ''Bransonesque" fashion, renamed it Craigs International Menswear. Six other similar shops were to be opened and successfully operated until Bobby, astutely sensing the wind of change in retailing, resolved to redirect his considerable energy in the burgeoning leisure industry. His first venture into the licensed trade was at Cawley's Bar & Diner in Jamestown, where it was soon apparent that, as ''Mine Host", he was a natural. Bobby had long harboured the hope that one day he would own Duck Bay Hotel and Marina on Loch Lomond. The premises had been for sale without attracting a serious bidder, but Bobby, realising the great potential of the site, successfully offered for the premises at the opportune time. After considerable rebuilding and total refurbishment, Bobby's dream was fulfilled when, in late 1985, the new hotel and nightclub was opened by Sir Hugh Fraser amid huge publicity. Sir Hugh 'shot himself' that night when the starting pistol he fired to open the proceedings and scorched his forehead. Fortunately he was not badly hurt, but it was a great picture for the photographers and the images filled the newspapers.PR and marketing skills helped Bobby steer the new venture from strength to strength, realising the potential he always knew was there. Leaving aside hotels such as Gleneagles and its ilk, it is arguable that Duck Bay is Scotland's best-known licensed premises, a testament to the man who made it happen. Bobby's entrepreneurial yearnings were far from satisfied so in 1990 he acquired the run-down Village Hotel in Gartocharn on the east side of the loch, which he renamed The Hungry Monk and transformed into a thriving hotel and restaurant with a loyal clientele from far and near. His success led to well-merited accolades for his business acumen and the high standards of service and food. In December 1998, he received a prestigious Lifetime Achievement Award from William Petrie, chairman of the Loch Lomond and Trossachs Tourist Board.

Duck Bay Hotel and Marina on Loch Lomondside from the air. Picture by Bill Heaney.

Duck Bay Marina opened with a bang when a starting pistol back-fired into the face of Sir Hugh Fraser, seen here with the gun in hand. Highland Games athlete Jay Scott of Inchmurrin throws up his hands in horror as others cover their ears.
Picture by John Wysocki, of Fitzgerald Owens News Agency, Dumbarton.

By this time Bobby knew he was afflicted by terminal cancer and, characteristically, he decided, with full family backing, to purchase another celebrated hostelry in the West of Scotland which the family to over months later in October, 1999. Even during his last few days at the St Margaret of Scotland Hospice, Clydebank, Bobby spent hours planning for the new venture, right down to the design of the wallpaper; all this for a hotel he knew he would never operate. His wife, Margaret, daughter, Margo, and sons, Russell and Alan, have pledged to make the new venture a lasting monument of Bobby's business sagacity and unique style. Having association with Dumbarton People's Theatre, The Green Room Club, and the Osdon Merrymakers, Bobby was a great personality and no mean entertainer himself. His rendition of Hello Dolly, inevitably a special request at charity dances, was the stuff of legends. His kindness to charities and other deserving causes was never trumpeted but always appreciated. When news of Bobby's passing broke, among the many personal callers to offer condolences to the family was John McFall MP, now Lord Alcluith, whose words proved a suitable epitaph: "Bobby Cawley made a real contribution to the future of Loch Lomond. He will be greatly missed."

Boats and bens on lovely Loch Lomond. *Picture by Bill Heaney.*

Chapter 42

THE HORRORS OF WAR

Bill Heaney pictured by Eddie McMurray with Valeman James Aitken in the town Square at Ypres in Belgium, John Healey, from Helensburgh, who was killed in the First World War and Dumbarton man Michael Lyden, who fought with the Connacht Rangers.

Green Fields of France: You must have a story about the First World War, or maybe even a photograph of one of your forebears who took part in it. Sometimes, in books or documentaries about that era, the hostilities from 1914-18 are referred to as the Great War. But it was far from 'great' for those who took part in it, so many thousands upon thousands of whom were brutally slaughtered. These brave heroes were later referred to as lions led by donkeys, young men such as Willy McBride, whose memorial ballad – also called The Green Fields of France - our folk singers still recall in music and song 100 years after the event. Many of you will know and love this song, which was a great favourite in those halcyon days when there were folk clubs like the one run by Drew Moyes in the Dumbuck Hotel and the SNP Hall in Wallace Street.

In those early 1960s days, singers of the stature of the late, lamented Luke Kelly would come to Dumbarton, sing my favourite Raglan Road and stir our Celtic blood. A couple of pints and a few drams helped to heighten the patriotism, of course, and the audience, shock horror, were allowed to smoke and drink during the sessions. While the audience joined in with the choruses, performers the likes of Hamish Imlach and Josh MacRae took part in the drinking and smoking, which sadly saw him into his grave long before his time.

Green Fields of France

Oh how do you do, young Willy McBride
Do you mind if I sit here down by your graveside
And rest for a while in the warm summer sun
I've been walking all day, and I'm nearly done
And I see by your gravestone you were only nineteen
When you joined the great fallen in 1916
Well I hope you died quick
And I hope you died clean
Or Willy McBride, was is it slow and obscene?

Did they beat the drums slowly
Did they play the fife lowly
Did they sound the death march as they lowered you down
Did the band play the last post and chorus
Did the pipes play the flowers of the forest

Written by Eric Bogle

I recall two large brown pennies on the mantelpiece of our house in Napier Crescent commemorating the death in that war of my grandmother's brother, John Healey, of Hanover Street, Helensburgh.

She dusted and polished them slowly and lovingly along with all her fireside brasses, and she shed the occasional tear over them. In the mid 'Nineties I travelled to Ypres and the Somme with James Aitken, a veteran from Renton, who was at the time well on his way to his 100th birthday which he saw out at Erskine Hospital. It was a time of huge poignancy, something I will never forget.

Jimmy was wonderful company as we visited the battlefields and beautifully cared for cemeteries 'where the red poppies danced'. He sang *The Lord's My Shepherd* under the Mennen Gate, where the Ypres fire brigade assembles each evening to play *The Last Post* in tribute to the fallen of the First World War.

And, again, in Ypres Town Hall, in the war museum that is now part of it, he sang *The Cameron Men* for the mothers and children who had come to visit it and who couldn't believe that they had met in person an actual survivor of the conflict so graphically depicted before them. James Aitken's stories on that long journey through France and Belgium – we were guests of the builder, Eddie McMurray - had me completely enthralled. There are now only a few survivors of that horrible war still with us, but we owe them so much, so very, very much.

A group of Dumbarton Servicemen who took part in the First World War. *Photograph by courtesy of Anne Cunningham, Toronto*

Many of the articles I have been writing on the Dumbarton of yesteryear have brought back memories – some of them unfortunately poignant, most, thankfully, happy – of the town during much of last century. The e-mails that pop into my in-box are invariably interesting as are the photographs that accompany them, and they come from all over the world. They say journalism is the first draft of history and if that is true then people will look here in the *Lennox Herald* and other journals in years to come to find out the way we were. Some of the most interesting film footage we have seen about the Coronation has featured not just the Queen herself but ordinary folk. It showed how they lived, what they ate, the clothes they wore, the films they watched, the sport they played, how they danced and sang and where they did their courting. And sadly too these films recalled how families found themselves caught up in two terrible world wars.

The anniversary of the First World War is just around the corner at the time of writing and people are looking out memorabilia and recalling the men and women who have gone before. Anne Cunningham, who lives in Canada, found the old photograph on this page amongst family heirlooms while she and her husband, Jimmy, were redecorating their home. It is of a group of young men from Dumbarton who were leaving for the Dardanelles. The fighting in the Dardanelles was done mainly by the Royal Navy with substantial support from the French and contributions from Russia and Australia. They failed initially to overcome the Ottoman defences and an invasion of the Gallipoli peninsula was launched. Throughout the campaign, attempts were made by submarines to pass through the Dardanelles and disrupt Ottoman Empire shipping in the Sea of Marmara. Anne doesn't know any names of these local sailors, apart from those of her father, Philip Curran, who is right in the centre eating a sandwich, and two others, one of them whose name is Neeson and the other one Hainey. She said: 'It's a shame I didn't get more information before, but my dad died in 1964. I remember reporters from the Sunday papers back in the early Sixties coming to our house to ask if my father would tell his story but he said No because he believed there were too many bad memories for too many families still living in Dumbarton.'

The Currans lived at 25 High Street and news came there that Philip who served in Gallipoli was missing presumed dead. He returned home unexpectedly and was walking up the close to the house when the door opened and his 22-year-old brother Michael's coffin was brought out to be buried. His parents, John and Annie, were overcome by a mixture of joy and grief because they believed their two sons had died in action. Despite this trauma, Philip returned to his unit and his parents suffered further shock when they learned that his ship, HMS Itchen, was torpedoed in the North Sea on 6 July, 1917, by the German U-boat SM UC-44. Fortunately, Philip survived that. Anne tells me her parents married in 1937 and lived at 61 College Street, across the road from the Rialto cinema and next door to the cobbler's shop. She was one of seven children, one of whom died aged just two, and they lived up the same Vennel close as the family of former Celtic goalkeeper Evan Williams. The Gracies, the Sneddons, Maddens, McIvors, Dochertys, Elliots and Glovers also lived there. Anne's father was hospitalised in 1945 with tuberculosis and he spent 18 months in a sanatorium in Kingussie. The Currans moved to Overburn Crescent in 1950 and then to Whiteford Crescent in 1957 and Anne who was a pupil at Wee St Pat's in McLean Place before moving up to Notre Dame at Clerkhill in 1960. She worked in Co-op and then Westclox and also in the canteen at J&B's Strathleven Bond. She is married to an Old Kilpatrick man, Jimmy Cunningham, and they have two daughters. Over the next few months the names Dardanelles and Gallipoli were to come up again and again in documentaries about the First World War. If young people ask you what relevance these battles and these faraway lands have to do with Dumbarton, you can tell them that some of our forebears fought and died there. Anne said: 'Our family was a bit unusual in that my father was twenty years older than my mother, so my youngest brother must have been one of the few people alive that had first hand stories of the First World War.'

Veterans Day Committee (left to right) George Sharp, Canon Gerry Conroy, of St Patrick's Church, Colonel Bobby Steele, of Erskine Hospital and the Rev Robert Watt, of Riverside Parish Church. *Picture by Bill Heaney*

Pipers Colin Lawrie (right) and Iain MacPhee pipe Lord McFall and Colonel Bobby Steele from St Augustine's Church in Dumbarton after the Veterans Day service.
Pictures by Bill Heaney

Colin Lawrie, Piper o' Dumbarton, and a pipe band playing at Levengrove Park.

The piper who composed for the bagpipes The Battle of the Somme was the uncle of Dumbarton piper Colin Lawrie. William Lawrie - Gaelic, Uilleam Labhruidh/Laobhrach (1881–1916) was born into a slate quarrying family in Ballachulish, Argyll, and was the son of Hugh Lawrie, (Eòghann Thomais Uilleam) who gave him his first lessons on the Highland bagpipes. He is remembered as a composer for the bagpipes although only about twenty of his tunes survive. His most celebrated compositions include The Pap of Glencoe, The Battle of the Somme and Inverary Castle. In 1914 he became Pipe Major of the 8th Argyllshire Battalion of the Argyll and Sutherland Highlanders and served with them in France from 1915 to 1916 when he became ill as a result of trench conditions. He was invalided to England where he died in the Third Southern General Hospital in Oxford, leaving behind his wife and three children. A 'marbhrann' (Gaelic lament) was written upon his death by the Islay bard Duncan Johnston (Donnchadh MacIain) who was a close personal friend. His bagpipes are now on display in The Argyll and Sutherland Highlanders Regimental Museum in Stirling Castle.

Proud veterans parade in Dumbarton

Dignitaries at a Veterans' Day parade in Dumbarton are left to right former Provost Billy Petrie, Bailie Ian Bell and his wife, Ruth, and Denis Kearns from Duntocher.

Frank 'Batch' Hannaway (right) at the Veterans' Day parade.

A happy group of Veterans at the parade in Dumbarton.

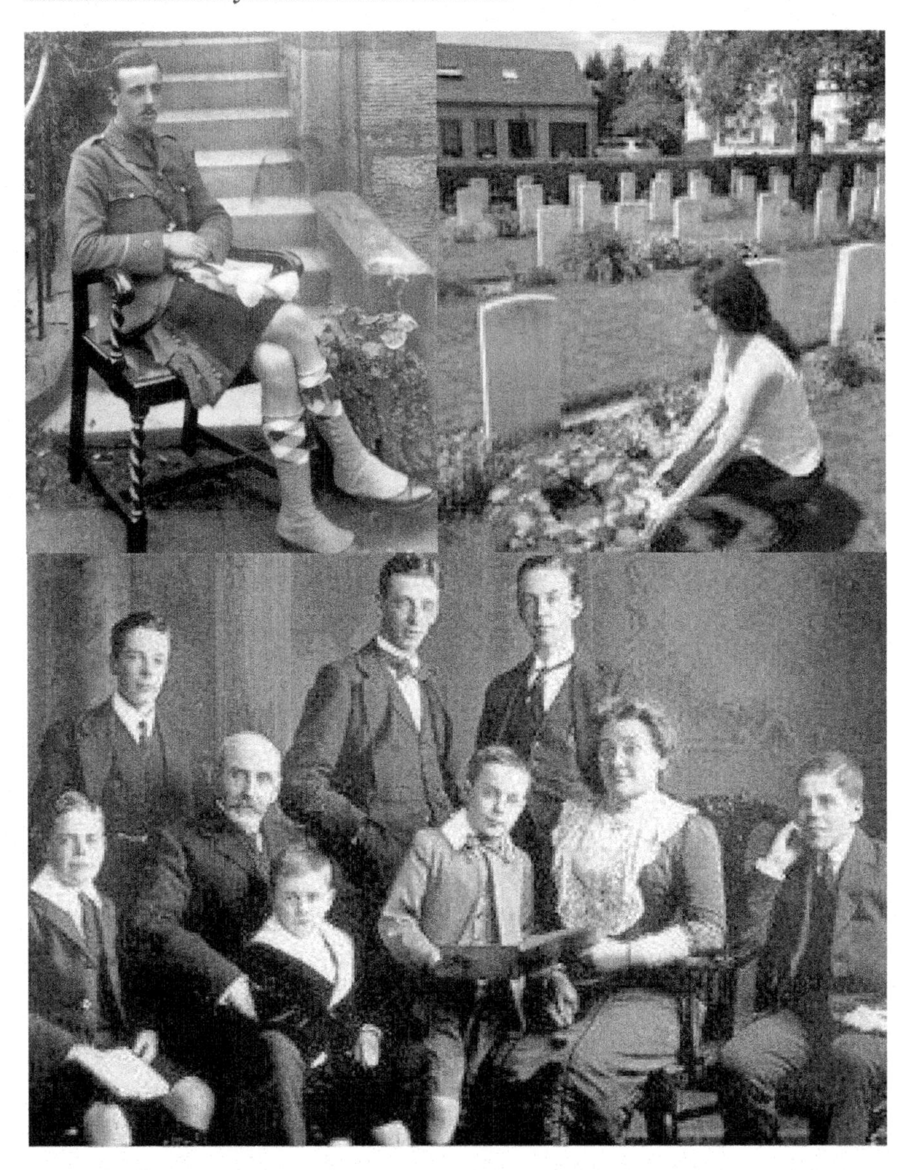

Clockwise: Second Lieutenant Bobbie Humble of the Argyll and Sutherland Highlanders; Noreen Humble lays a wreath on her uncle's grave in Belgium and the Humble family pictured at their home, Bellfield in West Bridgend, Dumbarton.

Dumbarton piper Iain MacPhee leads the Veterans Remembrance Day parade down the High Street. *Picture by Bill Heaney*

Remembrance Sunday is just around the corner. Here in Dumbarton, to the great credit of our community, it's not something we forget – or are prepared to forget. People turn out in large numbers at cenotaphs from Rosneath to Renton to remember the fallen of all the wars and conflicts that have afflicted us during the past 100 years. They wear their poppies with pride and donate generously to charities such as Erskine Hospital, where elderly and infirm Ex-Service personnel are so wonderfully looked after. For one local family, the Humbles, of Bellfield in West Bridgend, Dumbarton, this is a very special year since it is the centenary of Bobbie Humble's death at the Battle of Ypres in Belgium. Roy Humble, a consultant anaesthetist who, with his wife Betty, is now living in retirement in Canada, tells me he managed to track down through the Commonwealth War Graves Commission the place where Bobbie is buried.

He said: 'I had always planned to visit and place a wreath on Bobbie Humble's grave in 2015, the centenary year of his death in Belgium, but in the event my wife Betty's health prevented this. However, the visit was made by our eldest daughter, Noreen, while attending a conference in Germany in late June, two months ahead of the exact 100 years this past September. Like so many local soldiers, Bobbie Humble was in the Argyll and Sutherland Highlanders, a fresh-faced young Second Lieutenant. Roy was determined to ensure that Bobbie's death was not forgotten and was delighted when Noreen said she and her husband, Keith, would on June 28 – the day of Roy's 85th birthday – visit Brandhoek Military Cemetery in West-Vlaanderen, Belgium, 6.5 km from the town centre of Ypres, to lay a wreath at the grave of Bobbie Humble.

Brandhoek was the location of field ambulances for most of the war. It was at a relatively safe distance from the range of German artillery and was also situated on the main road and the railway line from Ypres to Poperinge. For this reason it was a good position for medical units to receive wounded soldiers from the front lines, treat them where possible and send them by road or by rail to Poperinge. From there they could be evacuated by rail to the base hospitals in France, such as Boulogne on the French coast. At the cemetery itself, Noreen read an inscription noting that those buried there were 602 British, 63 Canadians, four Australians and two Germans. All were said to have died in the Second and Third Battle of Ypres, but this is not entirely accurate. The Second Battle at Ypres took place in April/May of 1915 and stands out as the first occasion on which the Germans used chlorine gas. The Third Battle was two years later, but the front line remained around Ypres long after the second battle and Bobbie's descriptions, contained in the letters referred to below, are a reminder that there was constant reconnaissance, hard labour, fighting and danger between the big pushes.

Roy Humble has Bobbie's last letters home to his parents, six in total, the first dated 30 July, the last 5 September, just two days before he was killed. All are addressed to his father except the third, which is to his mother. In all of the letters, Bobbie asks for certain things to be sent out from home, such as tinned fruits, chocolate, candles, tobacco, cigarettes and newspapers. These are to share with his fellow-soldiers.

He also asks for practical items such as boots, a compass with a luminous dial, and most poignantly in the last letter, a warm lining for his jacket to cope with the coming winter. He sends his thanks for the letters and parcels he receives which arrive speedily and regularly and he sends home too news about other soldiers his family would have known.

On 30 July, 1915, Bobbie wrote: 'I sent you a postcard on Tuesday saying that we were just leaving Rouen to join our battalion. Well tonight we arrived at our headquarters. Where that is, of course, I am not allowed to say. We had a very dreary journey coming up the line but it was quite interesting. The battalion is some way back from the first line but we can hear the big guns quite distinctly.'

On 5 August, 1915, Bobbie sent another letter: 'For the last week we have been sending a party up in the direction of the firing line where they are laying a cable and today I was away with another officer and 50 men re-paving a road that had got rather cut up. We were digging drains to draw the water from the road properly and intend to level it up. I had a new experience and was sent up with a fatigue party of about 30 men to do some digging at a place about two and a half miles from the firing line. We were digging about 400 or 500 yards in front of one of our 4.7ins batteries which was reminding the Germans of its presence now and again and of course the shells were going right over our heads. So for a time things were quite exciting for those of us who had never been so near to big guns before However, we got quite used to it and got home here safely again in the evening.

I mentioned at the beginning of my letter that we were moving tomorrow. We are going to a place ten miles further up the line and will probably be living in dug outs. It is rather more in the danger zone than we are here. We are to be what is called a pioneer battalion and will be employed mainly I suspect in building dugouts along the canal for winter quarters. It will be all night work and sleeping through the day. As I said there will be some danger but not a great deal …

'Tell mother that the bananas sent out were fairly well bashed when they got here. I have just been reading in Friday's Herald which came in to-day a denial by the Secretary for War that the pink forms have anything to do at all with compulsory service. I quite agree with you in that I think compulsory service will not be brought in now. The

Government have dilly dallied with it too long. I have just been reading a series of letters in which the writer who appears to be a regular officer says one or two very strong things about the slackers.

'The boys out here do not want men sent out now who have waited till they have been compelled to join and I believe that is quite a general feeling. I know I myself would have hated being sent out here instead of coming out of my own free will. I don't in the least regret I did join and am now out among it. There are a lot of inconveniences to be put up with about which one cannot write but still I think there is an education in it all which those who don't join will be sorry afterwards they missed.'

Bobbie added: 'You were asking what opinion I had formed of the French people. Well on a whole I found them very nice, though at one place where we had to spend a night after we left Rouen, we found them rather curt and distant and could hardly get a room to sleep in. However, with that exception we have found them all right. The Belgians are very nice though but there are a big number of spies among them.'

On 5 September, 1915 – two days before his death – Bobbie wrote: 'I myself was up in the front line last week though, along with another officer. We were sent up for instruction purposes and were there for 48 hours. As we were there for instruction we just did what the other officers of the companies had to do. I was over the parapet and out in No Man's Land on both the nights. I was there seeing to some wire entanglements and listening posts. One felt rather strange the first time one got over the parapet of the trenches and got out into the open and felt the bullets whizzing about but you soon got used to it all. In front of the line held by the company I was with, the German line was only about 40 yards away at one part and not more than 250 yards at any other.

I made a small sketch of the position just for practice and for this I had to use a periscope pretty often. With it I could see the Germans moving about opposite - in fact the beggars tried to smash up the periscope two or three time. They gave us a pretty hot times both evenings with bombs, shells and so on (this sort of display of theirs is called by our men the Evening Hate). I was greatly struck with the cheery spirit of the men in spite of the conditions and the prospect of having to spend another winter out here. There were no slackers I can tell you.'

At this point Bobbie Humble told his parents: 'I wouldn't mind another tin of chocolate in the next parcel and don't forget candles.' He also asked his mother for a warm lining for his Burberry coat to see him through the winter. But Bobbie Humble never saw that lining or that chocolate or those candles. The light of his life was cruelly extinguished by a German bullet before that parcel arrived from Dumbarton.

Veterans all at the service in St Augustine's Scottish Episcopal Church in Dumbarton High Street.

Chapter 43

BONNIE JEAN

Jean and Billy Petrie at the Papal Mass in Glasgow. Picture by Bill Heaney.

Jean Petrie, who died in May, 2014, aged 86, was one of Helensburgh's best known women and her sad loss is felt by the many people who knew her right across Scotland. Jean will be remembered by everyone who met her, and there were thousands, as a gentlewoman of great grace and dignity, and by her family as 'a five star mum'. Jean was the devoted wife and constant support of Billy Petrie, former Provost of Argyll and Bute Council and Freeman of Argyll and Bute. She was his great support through the 45 years he gave of his life to public service on councils ranging from the old Dunbartonshire County Council to Strathclyde Region to Dumbarton District Council and on a host of their bodies throughout Scotland. He held more provostships and convenerships than any other local government politician ever. Born in Auchinleck, Ayrshire, Jean came to Helensburgh as a two week old baby and grew up in the town with her parents and her younger brother, John. As a young girl attending Hermitage Primary School she found herself sitting near a lad called Billy and the two became friends unaware that they were destined to spend their lives together. Jean was a keen swimmer and was involved in the town swimming club as well as in many church and youth organisations and when she graduated from the Commercial College in Glasgow her first job was as secretary at Helensburgh Police office, which was then in Sinclair Street.

One of Jean's great joys was the adventure of travel, and she travelled extensively throughout her life, but her first venture into international travel was when she moved to New York, crossing the Atlantic on board the Queen Mary, to work for the Paisley company JP Coates and she spent 18 months in the Big Apple before coming home to Helensburgh. A job with a Glasgow firm of solicitors meant a daily commute to the city, a journey she often made in the company of her old school friend Billy, who was, by that time, back from National service in the RAF and working for the National Coal Board. The friendship developed over time and the couple were married in St Columba Church almost 59 years ago. Because Jean lived at that time in a flat opposite the church a red carpet was stretched across Sinclair Street and the traffic stopped to allow her to walk to the church where her groom was waiting. Her colleagues at the police office ensured that the bride got across the road safely. The newlyweds had their honeymoon in Barcelona. Jean was a devoted mum to Elizabeth, Billy and Barbara and rejoiced in becoming a grandmother in time to Alan, Sheryl, April, Lynsey, Nicola and Fraser and then great-grandmother to Lewis. Her children remember her as a 'five star mum'. Jean threw herself with huge enthusiasm and energy into Billy's public life and was always at his side providing her own brand of gentle grace to every event she attended.

She will be remembered by thousands for her gift of words, always knowing the right thing to say whatever the occasion. Happy to remain, however, in the background, Jean was not one for making speeches, but she was all in favour of taking action where she felt it was needed and it was Jean who was the power behind the establishment of senior citizens lunch clubs in Helensburgh, Rhu, Garelochhead, Rosneath and Cove and Kilcreggan. She canvassed tirelessly for Billy in every election and was also closely involved in a group that provided holidays in Spain for elderly people. She was the inspiration behind the establishment of the now famous New Year Swim at Rhu Marina and attended herself every year to lend a hand. The Swim has now raised well over £11,000 for the RNLI as well as many thousands of pounds more for other charities supported by the swimmers. Jean enjoyed many special occasions at Billy's side including being a guest on the Royal Yacht Britannia when the ship visited the Gareloch. She considered it a great privilege to have met Her Majesty the Queen and many other members of the Royal Family and attended a number of Royal Garden Parties at the Palace of Holyrood House in Edinburgh. Her happiest memories of such events were a visit to Buckingham Palace as an invited guest and as a guest at the Mass when Pope Benedict visited Glasgow. Mrs Petrie died at the Royal Alexandra Hospital in Paisley a month after taking ill suddenly during a Sunday morning service at Luss Parish Church on Loch Lomondside, where her husband is an elder. Jean will always be remembered for her unassuming personality, her warm and gentle nature and her wonderful smile and she will be missed by more people than she herself would ever have believed. She is survived by her husband, Billy, daughter Elizabeth and son, Billy. A second daughter, Barbara, died suddenly two years ago. Her funeral service, conducted by the Rev George Vidits and Canon George Bradburn, of St Gildas RC Church, Rosneath, took place in St Andrew's Church of Scotland in Colquhoun Square, Helensburgh, followed by committal at Cardross Crematorium.

Bill Heaney and Fiona Howard

Chapter 44

THE GLORY DAYS

Craig M Jeffrey and Bill Heaney reporting from the Erskine Bridge in 1970.

There is an old saying that one should look back but never go back. Half a century in this business is a long time by any stretch of the imagination, and this year will be my 55th in newspapers. That's how long it is since I walked into Beaverbrook's black palace in Albion Street, Glasgow, to take up a post as a copy boy on the old *Scottish Daily Express*. Those were happy days in the newspaper industry with the *Express* and the *Daily Record* fighting it out to be top dogs and the *Scotsman* and *Herald* flourishing in the quality market. The circulation of the *Express* was knocking on 700,000 and, on high days and holidays and big story days, it was much, much higher than that. No expense was spared in producing the best newspapers for the *Express*, which had six editions at that time and a correspondent in every city, town, village and hamlet in the country. *Express* reporters were king -- top professionals like Bill Allsop, David Scott, Phil Mackie, Ian Sharp, Andrew McCallum, Jimmy Ballantyne, Jack Webster, Magnus Magnusson, Wilson Russell (Stashy Dan) and the Bullet, Stuart McCartney. News editors Jack Coupar and Ian Brown (the Bomber) sent them out, each with star photographers – Tommy Fitzpatrick, Gordon Forbes, Jack Middleton, Robin Gray, Peter McVean, Ron Vavasour and Ray Beltrami to name a few – in chauffeur-driven limos to cover every story from Shetlands to the Solway Firth. No story was too small and certainly none too big for the *Express* to send out a formidable team on. Herograms from the editor, Ian McColl and his deputy, Clive Sandground, were posted on the third floor editorial department praising the journalists who had scooped the Record, which they did often. I was extremely lucky to be raised to the dizzy heights of a very junior reporter on the *Express* before those good and happy times rolled away. The reporters' expenses, which were looked on as a legitimately claimed part of their salary, had queues forming to pick up full-to-bursting pay packets at the cashier's department on a Tuesday afternoon.

And so it was until Beaverbrook pulled the plug in 1974, and redundancy notices were issued to the hundreds of journalists and print workers who produced the *Scottish Daily Express* and *Evening Citizen*.

By that time I was editing the Lennox Herald in Dumbarton and when Scottish and Universal Newspapers started a subbing pool, I was able to throw a lifeline to some of my old colleagues and give them jobs. Little did I know at the time that the subbing pool, which was to produce pages for about six weekly papers, was the thin end of the wedge. This was the catalyst for a remorseless round of staff and expenditure cuts and technology changes that took us into those dark place newspapers now find themselves in. The technology changes were supposed to herald an era of undreamed of success. Pagination soared and advertising poured in. The old circulation department became the marketing department and, worst of all, the accounts department burgeoned from being a place employing just a few people to the busiest office in the building. Accountants were now king. Cuts were heaped upon cuts as the old case rooms and stereo departments closed and printing, like the sub-editing pools, was centralised. Riches beyond the dreams of avarice were harvested as banks of tele-ads people arrived and advertising reps increased in large numbers. Investment managers were able to persuade their clients to pay millions of pounds for shares in what had been merely modest publications.

It was then the directors and accountants had to seek out substantial returns for their clients' investments, and so the cuts were made to bite deeper and deeper with the axe falling mainly on editorial departments. The shareholders got greedy, as they do, and the suits pushed up their charges for advertising. Councils and commercial clients were squeezed until the pips squeaked. Salaries soared for the managements and the shareholders' cashed in … and then, at the start of the 'Nineties, the internet arrived.

Beginning of the end of newspapers

For newspapers this heralded the beginning of the end of the press as we knew and loved it. Some circulations slumped by 50 per cent and more and the advertising centimetre count plummeted as councils, the government and commercial interests took their business to the much more realistically priced internet. The editorial cuts started with the centralised subbing pools and the slashing of reporters' expenses. It then stretched to offices being closed and more and more journalists working from home. This is not a new thing though. I remember Willie Inglis of the Dunoon Observer having a hot metal linotype machine in his bedroom. And the tea cups rattling on the kitchen table at Craig M Jeffrey's house next door to the print works in Helensburgh when the old Cossar flatbed press, which printed the local Advertiser and Reporter, rumbled into action on Thursday nights. Few people in the industry today will have heard of a flat-bed press or know what a type scale was or ems and 'nuts' were, or what Pitman's shorthand is, or how many characters there are in a 48 point Times bold caps and lower case heading across three columns. Times they are a changing as they always have. It's time to look forward, not back, and make the best use of the digital tools we now have at our disposal.

Bill Heaney interviews Bono (U2) and Cameron House manager, Cameron Dallas.

Bill with Clint Eastwood at Cameron House.

Bill with Irish author Edna O'Brien at the Edinburgh Book Festival.

Bill Heaney interviewing Prime Minister Tony Blair.
Picture by Brian Averell

Staff night out at the Lennox Herald in Dumbarton (left to right) are Bill Heaney, Sheena MacKinnon, Tina Kemp, Amanda Graham, Michelle McMenemy, Willie Cochrane, Grace Walker. Brian Averell and Brian Clayton.
Picture by Graeme at Chimes in Jamestown

Murdo MacLeod with the Lennox Herald editorial and advertising staff (left to right) Liz Jones, Hazel Reilly, Morag Graham, Lynn Cochrane, Fiona McLaren, Aileen Stevenson, Archie Fleming, Annette McCann and Bill Heaney. *Pictures by Brian Averell.*

Farewell presentation from the staff at the Lennox Herald, including deputy editor Grace Walker, Mhairi Halliday, Amanda Graham, Fiona McAlpine, Sheona Duff, Fiona McLaren, Margaret McDonald, Sandra McPherson, Tina Kemp, Sheena MacKinnon, Liz Jones, Willie Cochrane, Brian Clayton and Hazel Reilly.

Mr Lennox meets Mr Lennox - Bill with Lisbon Lion Bobby Lennox and with Maire O'Halloran of The Clifden Bookshop at the launch of his recent book 'How are things in Connemara?'

Ally McCoist, Bill Heaney and Murdo MacLeod. *Picture by Brian Averell*

Embedded with the Argylls in the jungles of Kenya.

Close up and rather uncomfortable with cheetahs
and elephants and other the wildlife in Africa.

Headgear to suit every occasion, even a meeting with Daniel,
Masai warrior at Hell's Gate National Park in Kenya.
Pictures courtesy the Argyll and Sutherland Highlanders.

Bill Heaney with poet Seamus Heaney (right)
and Irish Taoiseach Bertie Ahern.

A reception for 'Famous' Seamus Heaney at the Irish Consulate in Edinburgh hosted by now Irish ambassador to the UK Dan Mulhall and his wife, Greta. Also in the picture are poet Hayden Murphy, Scottish Minister Roseanna Cunningham, journalist Ruth Wishart and John Archer of the Scottish Film Council.
Picture by Bill Heaney.

Chapter 45

THE JUDGE

Daniel Lynch JP

Dan Lynch and I were good friends. I have missed him since he died nearly five years ago. I write obituaries from time and I wrote this one for Dan for his favourite newspaper, the *Donegal Democrat*. I also wrote obituaries for Dan in *The Scotsman* and *Glasgow Herald*, but this is the one I think he would like to see included in this book of memories and recollections. It was as follows: Retired Scottish District Court judge Daniel Lynch, who has strong connections with Co Donegal, died at his home in Dumbarton on Clydeside, on Christmas Day, aged 88. Mr Justice Lynch was widely known in Rathmullan, where his forebears came from, and in Dungloe and Kincasslagh, which he visited often and where he occasionally served the weekday Mass at St Mary's Church celebrated by his old friend, Father Eddie Kelly. Father Kelly, who is retired, has a house in Kincasslagh and covers services when he is in the area on holiday for the local parish priest, Father Pat Ward. He often invites friends and family from Scotland to stay with him in Kincasslagh and Mr Justice Lynch was one of that happy holidaying group. The judge visited Co Donegal two or three times a year, summer and winter. He was widely known as just Dan and was a popular figure with local people.

A keen angler, he often dropped into Iggy's bar in Kincasslagh and Beedi's in Dungloe for a dram and discussion about fishing and antique rods and reels and old books in which he was interested. He was a real veteran of the Irish in Scotland and prominent authors and journalists like Tim Pat Coogan and John Cooney consulted him about books they were writing on that subject. Dan was widely read. He loved poetry and was an accomplished artist, who painted mainly landscapes and seascapes in water colours.

Some of his favourite paintings were of places in Co Donegal, Mayo and Connemara, where he was also a well-known and welcome visitor.

The distinguished Scottish author and artist Alasdair Gray painted a portrait of Dan with whom he occasionally socialised in the Staff Club at Glasgow University. Dan was educated at St Patrick's High School, Dumbarton, and started his working life as a marine engineering apprentice in the Clyde shipyards, but lost his left arm in an accident while operating an unguarded piece of machinery. After his recovery and rehabilitation, he qualified as an engineering draughtsman, furthered his education at Strathclyde University and later became a lecturer in the Lennox Technical College in Dumbarton.

These were happy years and Dan would reminisce about the traditional staff room with the coal fire, the big comfortable easy chairs and teaching young engineers and shipbuilders during the halcyon days of full employment. He transferred to Clydebank College and quickly rose to prominence in a number of capacities including trade union activist, senior lecturer in engineering, organiser of social events and a thorn in the management's flesh with his ongoing desire to improve all things for staff and students. According to a fellow lecturer, he was widely acknowledged as being the 'cleverest and most astute man in the college'. Dan was always extremely helpful and supportive of nervous, inexperienced new young lecturer/teachers and became a mentor to many of them.

Dan Lynch and Bill Heaney on a visit to an equestrian centre in the hills above Helensburgh

He guided thousands of students into successful careers and received testimonies from many of them in later years. He was a real educationalist in the full meaning of the word, instructor, mentor and guru rolled into one. College staff who could not solve mathematical/physics/engineering examination problems would beat a path to Dan's door for advice – and a solution was always forthcoming. If he couldn't solve the problem the question was wrong (this turned out to be the case on a number of occasions). He took an interest in disabled people and invented a number of devices to assist them in getting about their homes and with their leisure activities. Dan took an active interest in trade unionism, politics, religion and the law and was made a Justice of the Peace, sitting on the Bench of the busy District Courts of Dumbarton. He was recognised nationally as one of the finest and fairest judges in the country and he lectured to recruits to the Bench of the Scottish District Courts until his retirement at the age of 75.

Dan Lynch JP (left) was a leading light in the Home from Home charity with Tim Rhead, Peter Foster, Tommy Lusk and friends in Dumbarton. *Picture by Bill Heaney*

He was made a Fellow of the Institution of Engineers before he retired from his college work at 64 years of age to look after his wife, Elizabeth, mother of their five children, when she was terminally ill with cancer. Dan was devastated when Liz died, but he kept going and went on to enjoy 25 years of 'retirement'. He was a past chairman of Dumbarton Constituency Labour Party; a Justice of the Peace; a director of a number of charities, including the St Vincent De Paul Society and Home from Home, which furnishes poor people's houses, and a prominent activist in Dumbarton Churches Together.

The fact that he had just one arm didn't hold him back when it came to sport. Dan was a keen tennis and table tennis player as a young man and he went cycling and camping. He travelled widely by push bike throughout the UK, Ireland and France. He loved long train journeys and his favourite was the scenic West Highland Line from Glasgow to Oban and Mallaig. A lifelong member of the Loch Lomond Angling Improvement Association, he was also a season ticket holder at Dumbarton Football Club. Although he was 'Dumbarton daft' and seldom missed a match, home or away, Dan also had a fondness for Celtic and he took a keen interest in their results. He may also have been a shareholder in the club since he attended their annual general meetings, but he never said so. He did talk about fishing though – a lot. One of his angling friends, Dick Dickson, another retired JP and college lecturer who now does the angling column for the Lennox Herald, said: 'Fishing days spent with Dan were more than just outings. Drum ups with his old primus stove on the riverbank; drams of his home made sloe gin; his Keith Floyd style of cooking (and the food was good); his recounting of wonderful stories; making friends with every angler he met; showing young boys how to fish and so on, he was a remarkable person. A day's fishing in Dan's company was always an adventure.

'To watch him playing a salmon to a standstill then balancing it finely on the toe of his wader and flipping it skilfully in one movement on to the bank behind him was a truly amazing sight to behold. This feat demanded remarkable skill, technique, timing and balance. He had developed this down to a fine art in order to overcome his disability caused by that shipyard accident as a youth – nothing could prevent him from angling. He could cast a lovely fly line with his one arm rolling technique.' Friends and colleagues will remember Dan Lynch as a clever, generous man with a quick wit and serious intellect, who always had time and a kind word for the less fortunate in society. He was a leading member of the St Vincent De Paul Society (SVDP). Dan was a wise counsel to many, a fair judge in the courts, a skilled and clever engineer and teacher and loving husband, father and grandparent. The large turnout at his funeral in St Michael's Church in Cardross Road, Dumbarton, and final committal at Dumbarton Cemetery was testimony to the esteem in which Dan was held across the Dunbartonshire community.

District justice Dan Lynch enjoys a pint while on holiday with Father Eddie Kelly, Bill Heaney and the late Hughie Boyle, angling expert, in Beedi's bar in Dungloe, Co Donegal.
Picture by Rodger Scullion

Chapter 46

THE PHILANTHROPIST

Sir Hugh Fraser

My interest in the past takes me down many highways and by-ways. One of the most rewarding and poignant places to visit in any town or village is the graveyard. And so it was when I travelled up the Lochside to Gartocharn on other business and decided to call in at Kilmaronock Cemetery in the grounds of the tiny parish church there. It is a lovely part of the world with rolling fields, belts of mature trees, rivers and steeply rising purple mountains. And, of course, there is Loch Lomond itself, the world renowned Bonnie Banks with its misty islands, Ben Lomond and Conic Hill. One grave at Kilmaronock caught my eye immediately – the last resting place of the Fraser family, which is situated amid the neatly-trimmed shrubbery to the left when you come through the cemetery gates. A modest headstone, bearing the family crest, informs you that Lord Fraser of Allander, rests here alongside his wife, Lady Kathleen, and son, Sir Hugh, who died, aged just 50 in May, 1987. Had he lived, Sir Hugh would now be 79 and coming up to his eightieth birthday. Contrary to what some people thought of him – both in the media and locally – Sir Hugh was neither a failure nor a fool. In local parlance he was no mug. He was in fact a great, good, likeable and philanthropic man who made a real and significant difference to the lives of so many ordinary people. Sir Hugh demonstrated this in 1966, after his father's death, when he was elected chairman of House of Fraser and of Scottish and Universal Investments and appointed to the board of Harrods in Knightsbridge and a host of famous Scottish businesses. Sir Hugh renounced his father's peerage but was unable to disclaim the baronetcy and made friends not in the stockbroker set amongst the rich and privileged but of talented and good companions. These included Duck Bay Marina owner Bobby Cawley, music teacher Jack Pickup and the friends and directors of Dumbarton Football Club, which he saved from certain extinction. He was also a welcome much loved Christmas gift for his parents when he was born on December 18, 1936, in Bearsden, the only son and younger child of Hugh Fraser, 1st Baron Fraser of Allander, the chairman and managing director of the House of Fraser, and Kathleen Hutcheon, née Lewis, daughter of Sir Andrew Jopp Williams Lewis, shipbuilder and lord provost of Aberdeen.

Sir Hugh was educated at St Mary's School, Melrose, and Kelvinside Academy., which he left at 16 to go into the family business, joining it on his 17th birthday. He worked closely with his father, who made him a director at the age of 21 and gave him overall responsibility for the stores in Scotland, to prepare him for the time when he would take over the whole business. Sir Hugh married Patricia Mary Bowie, radiographer, and daughter of John Bowie, dyer and cleaner, of Milngavie, the Bowies of Castlebank. The couple had three daughters but the marriage ended in divorce in 1971, and in 1973 Fraser married an international showjumper, Gartocharn woman Aileen Margaret Ross, daughter of George Paterson Ross. The second Lady Fraser sadly died in a microlight aircraft accident. Far from being feckless, Sir Hugh was something of a genius in the retail business. He converted the original Fraser store in Glasgow into a high-class fashion shop for well-to-do young women, and began to introduce boutiques into other stores and set up the Young World chain of children's fashion shops.

Sir Hugh embarked on a policy of expansion and modernisation, introducing a more youthful style into existing stores and – in the face of competition from supermarket chains which began to sell clothing - he pursued a policy of trading up, aiming to make the House of Fraser the best store in every large town in Britain. Between 1966 and 1973, sales doubled to over £200 million, and profits doubled to over £10 million. Sir Hugh was chosen as the Young Business Man of the Year in 1973, acknowledging how he had restructured and expanded the family business, and the new and exciting style he had brought in to the stores. The failure of the merger with Boots proved the turning point in Sir Hugh's career. The years after 1974 were difficult. He gave up the chairmanship of Harrods but continued to buy department stores. However, Sir Hugh became increasingly addicted to gambling and a stock exchange inquiry in 1976 revealed that he had been selling House of Fraser shares to finance his gambling. In 1976, he was fined £600 under the Companies Act for the misclassification of a loan, and for improper share dealings.

Winners of the Scottish Press Awards with Sir Hugh Fraser and Lord MacKay of Clashfern in 1985. They include Anne Dalrymple, third from left in front row, who with me won the Weekly Newspaper Journalist of the Year award that year.

In January 1981, following the involvement of Lonrho in the fortunes of the House of Fraser, Sir Hugh lost the support of the directors and was removed as chairman. He subsequently resigned from the chairmanship of Harrods, which he had just resumed. After that, Sir Hugh spent most of his time in Scotland. He built up a chain of menswear shops, which he started by buying Edward's stores in Dumbarton and Alexandria, and held a number of directorships, mainly in Scotland, as well as the chairmanship of Dumbarton Football Club. Alex Wright, who was then the general manager of the Boghead club, said Sons could not have survived without him. He also worked hard on behalf of the Hugh Fraser Foundation, the charitable trust set up by his father, to give substantial amounts of money to medical research in Scotland. A huge tranche of money was gifted to Yorkhill Children's Hospital, where Professor Gavin Arneil said the health service should name a department of the hospital after him. Through the trust he bought the island of Iona for the National Trust of Scotland as a memorial to his father, and he gave his Mugdock estate in Milngavie to form the Mugdock Country Park. It is not widely known that Sir Hugh joined the Scottish National Party in 1974, and served for a time on the Scottish Development Council. In 1985, he was awarded an honorary doctorate by the University of Stirling. Not long before he died on 5 May, 1987, I called in at one of his Sir shops at the Fountain in Alexandria to buy a shirt. Sir Hugh served me himself and asked me if I would like to join him that afternoon in the directors' box at Boghead for the Dumbarton match. Regrettably I couldn't make it that day as I was heading off on holiday and it was while I was away that I heard of his death, which made front page headlines across the UK. I had much to be thankful to him for since he employed me as his editor at the Lennox Herald in which he took a keen interest. Dumbarton woman Anne Dalrymple and I won the Weekly Journalist of the Year title in the Scottish Press Awards, which Sir Hugh founded to encourage young journalists and create better newspapers.

He would be delighted to know those awards are still running and the *Lennox Herald* is still going strong. He would be disappointed though to know that the award for weekly newspaper journalist of the year has been discontinued by the Scottish Newspaper Proprietors Association who now organise the competition.

Kilmaronock Parish Church on Loch Lomondside, where the churchyard contains the Fraser family grave.

Chapter 47

THE CONSERVATIONIST

Jock Scott-Park

Organic farmer, conservationist, nutritionist and piper
Born in Rutherglen, Lanarkshire, on July 21, 1930
Died at Royal Alexandra Hospital, Paisley, on February 17, 2015

Old Etonian Jock Scott-Park, who was a farmer at Gartocharn on Loch Lomondside and a ground breaking nutritionist, conservationist and piper, was 84 when he died in 2015. The son of Glasgow-based consultant radiologist Stanley Douglas Scott-Park and Meta Hargrave Wilson, he was born in Rutherglen. Scott-Park was educated at The Glasgow Academy and Hurst Grange School for Boys in Stirling before going on to Eton College. He read agriculture at

St John's College Cambridge, and it was during these years that he met many people who were to become life-long friends. It was also at this time that he discovered many interests which he pursued throughout his life. Rowing was his greatest passion and he was introduced to it at Eton. He was instrumental in inspiring many others to take up the sport and as a result received a commendation from his House Master. When he went up to Cambridge he rowed for the Lady Margaret Boat Club (LMBC) in their second boat which was an tremendous achievement, given that all of the first boat were Blues and rowed for Cambridge and England in the Tokyo Olympic Games. In those days, the LMBC had no less than 13 boats. In 1950, Scott-Park rowed at Henley in the Lady's Plate and, in 1951, he rowed in the Marlow Eight and achieved second place. In that same year, he also rowed in the 'B' Four but had the misfortune to hit a punt and so lost to Leander. In the 1951 Lent races, Scott-Park rowed for the Lady Margaret Boat Club's first boat, where they started as Head of River but finished fourth. His Cambridge friends described him as 'an outstanding oarsman'.

While at Eton he had become Captain of Sailing and it was there too that he first met Raymond Johnstone, head of the Glasgow investment company, Murray Johnstone, who later became a neighbour at Gartocharn and chairman of the Forestry Commission. This was after an incident when Johnstone had 'abandoned ship' just before a weir. Johnstone was told to report to the captain of sailing. He described Scott-Park as very tolerant - given that nothing larger than a matchstick remained of the boat. Sailing was a lifelong interest for Scott-Park, who loved the peace of sailing with the sound of water lapping on the hull. However, he rather despised noisy speed boats until recent summers when he enjoyed entertaining friends on speed boat trips around Loch Lomond with his grandson, Chris, at the helm. The family have a photograph of Scott-Park in his deckchair with his cool shades on - at the helm of their work boat, heading for the pub on the island of Inchmurrin. As a young man, he spent many summer holidays with his parents sailing up the West Coast and would have his pipes at the ready as they entered or left an anchorage. Scott-Park was a keen piper and, as Pipe Major, he once led the Cambridge University pipe band on an Armistice Day parade. At Eton, practising his pipes in the House was not always popular and his tutor eventually banished him to the

Arches Bridge, which was about half a mile away from the college. Scott-Park piped for the Reel & Strathspey Society at Cambridge and was also part of a Highland Dance demonstration team, performing the sword dance and Highland fling. For many years he piped with the Glasgow Highland Club and The Royal Scottish Pipers. It gave him great pleasure to play at a ceilidh in Gartocharn with his son, David, and his two grandsons, Chris and Mark. It was fitting that the pipes David played at the funeral were the ones his father had at Cambridge. Scott-Park was always proud to do things on a tight budget and when he and two companions from Cambridge wanted to tour Europe, it was decided they should travel by bicycle and camp in a small tent. His two companions had Raleigh three-speed bikes, but Scott-Park's was his mother's pre-war 'sit up and beg' type - so he had no gears to assist him despite the fact they were averaging between 70 and 90 miles a day. Their route took them across northern France into Switzerland and to Lake Como, Milan and Nice and this was all done for the princely sum of £25 a head. Scott-Park was often seen out on his grandfather's Penny Farthing bicycle. In the tribute given by him at the funeral service, conducted by the Rev Liz O'Ryan, in St Mungo's Scottish Episcopal Church in Alexandria, Dunbartonshire, his son, David, told the congregation about this. He said there was the time when the late Tom Weir, the television personality who was a neighbour in Gartocharn, brought down to the farm a couple of his mountaineering pals who were introduced the Penny Farthing. They just happened to be the New Zealander Edmund Hillary, and the Nepalese Sherpa Tenzing Norgay, who became the first to reach the summit of Mount Everest. 'I think they feared more for their lives on this machine than on any mountain,' said David. Hill walking, camping, cycling and boating were all part of the Scott-Park lifestyle and, with his wife, Myrtle, they went on cycling holidays into their eighties. When camping became too much for them they yielded to the temptation of B&Bs. Latterly, when his balance deteriorated and he was unable to ride a bicycle, Scott-Park researched and bought a tricycle. Skiing was another of his passions which he continued into his seventies with regular trips to Andorra. Just when the family thought he that he had hung up his skis, he was spotted testing them – despite being in recovery from a fractured hip - on a snow covered field at Portnellan. Scott-Park spent 63 years at

Portnellan Farm, where he met Myrtle, who came to ask him if he had a piece of land where she could graze her horse. Jock secured not just a wife but a lifelong partner and farm secretary all at once. They were married in 1956. Portnellan had been a mixed farm in 1952 with a bit of everything - cereals, cows, pigs, sheep and hens. Scott-Park was always keen to move ahead of the times and Portnellan was one of the first farms on Loch Lomondside to move from hay to silage, a wise move in the West of Scotland. Twenty years later, he decided that the future of Portnellan lay in dairying and a milking parlour, cubicles and slurry store were constructed and the family continued dairying until five years ago. Scott-Park had a longstanding interest in diet and nutrition and completed a paper on the subject a few days prior to his death. His interest in diet and nutrition influenced the way Scott-Park farmed. Ammonium nitrate fertiliser was replaced with calcium nitrate and pesticides and herbicides ceased to be used. By this stage Portnellan was well on the way to being organic and went on to become certified as organic in 2001. Scott-Park was never afraid to voice his views when it came to diet and nutrition and was a staunch supporter of the McCarrison Society and its work promoting a healthy diet. David Scott-Park said: 'It is only now that nutrition has really entered mainstream European politics.'

More recently, Scott-Park took an interest in the renovation of the Old Farmhouse at Portnellan and considered the project had been completed so well that he decided he would like to move in. It was a little ironic that on the day it was officially opened for the first guests, he was taken by ambulance to hospital in Paisley. Scott-Park will be missed by many on Loch Lomondside and beyond. He contributed a great deal in so many ways to his various communities and his wise counsel was always valued. He was involved in the Gartocharn Community Council for 40 years and was its chairman for nearly 30 years. Farming was his life, however, and, amidst other roles, he sat on the Legal & Technical Committee of NFU Scotland. Other work in the community included The Loch Lomond and Trossachs National Park, of which he was a board member; the Health Promotion Group of the Glasgow and Clyde Health Board and St Mungo's Church, where he was vestry member. His coffin was piped from St Mungo's and later to his graveside in Vale of Leven Cemetery by his son, David Scott-Park, and grandsons, Chris Scott-Park and Mark Bushby. Scott-Park, who was predeceased by his wife Myrtle and son Mark, is survived by his son, David and daughter, Elizabeth Bushby, and their spouses, Freda Scott-Park and Charles Bushby and by his grandchildren.

Jock Scott-Park was a farmer first and foremost.

Chapter 48

THE VENNEL

Alex Scott and Saul Docherty behind the bar in McCafferty's Railway Tavern with John McAllister on the right. *Picture by Peter Leddy*

It is probably the most talked about street in Dumbarton. When people get together here at home or abroad, it's not long before College Street enters the conversation. The Vennel, as it was widely known, was a huddle of crumbling, teeming tenements and small cottages jammed together up pends and closes in the centre of town. Single ends and two rooms and kitchens were stuffed with large families many of whom kept lodgers to make ends meet. The kitchen sink was known as the 'jawbox'. There was no running hot water -- and sometimes no water at all. There was a coal fire and a fireplace, which had to be black leaded and there were beds set in to the wall. The kettle often stood on the hob or the teapot was left to stew on a peep of gas on the tiny cooker. A lavatory shared with three other large families was located on the 'stairheid' landing and there was no bath. There were fleas in the beds which were caught by taking a wet bar of carbolic soap and crushing it down on them as they leapt across the sheets. Most people worked in the shipyards when there was work to be had although they could be paid off at the drop of a riveter's hammer. There was grinding poverty which was alleviated only by occasional nights at 'the pictures' and the Rialto in College Street was one of four 'picture houses' in Dumbarton. They were never known as cinemas. The others were the Picture House in High Street, the La Scala in Glasgow Road and the Regal, which was up a pend Church Street. Miss Bisland, who owned the Regal where the balcony was only a couple of steps above the stalls, took jam jars in lieu of admission money. I recall seeing *The Robe* there with Victor Mature. It was in cinemascope – and Technicolor too. However, the best days were Saturdays at the ABC Minors in the Rialto in College Street. Remember the old song?

We are the boys and girls well known as Minors of the ABC
And every Saturday we line up to see the films we love and shout aloud with glee ...

The films I loved best were the Westerns with cowboys – Tom Mix, Roy Rogers and his faithful Palomino steed Trigger and Hopalong Cassidy to name but three. There was Flash Gordon too, of course, and Ming the Unmerciful, who was quite terrifying. Laurel and Hardy, Charlie Chaplin, Bob Hope, Bing Crosby, Clark Gable, Jeff Chandler, Alan Ladd, Dean Martin and Jerry Lewis, Shirley Temple, Greta Garbo, and John Oswald's favourite, Alice Fay, were big stars. John, who worked in Dewrance and was an accomplished pianist, was in the Osdon Merrymakers with the likes of Bobby Cawley, Chick Gordon Tom Gallacher, later ran the Vintage Film Club in the Concord Centre at the Denny Civic Theatre for local film buffs. The Vennel itself had many characters including John McAllister who played the coconuts (they made a sound like a horse clip clopping along) behind the big screen in the silent movie days in the Rialto. Then there was Tommy McIntyre and the Black and White Minstrels who sang at the old school hall in Church Street. College Park Street had Minnie Steel's famous sweetie shop and there was the Corner Shop at the Church Street end with the wayside pulpit outside it.

McCafferty's Railway Tavern in College Street in the Sixties.

The Council rent office was there, opposite the Municipal Buildings, as was Dr Jimmy Goldie's surgery. Then in College Street, opposite the Central Station, was the Employment Exchange, an imposing grey sandstone tenement building where out of work people queued to inquire about jobs and collect their 'burroo money'. The Lennox Technical College dominated the corner of College Street and College Park Street and was the place where the likes of Dan Lynch, Jack Evans and Neilly McQueen taught hundreds of aspiring marine engineers and others the subjects they would need to pass to take them into jobs at Denny's, John Brown's and the yards of the Upper Clyde. Bill Buchanan ran the Careers' Office in that building through which there was a close which took you into Dumbarton Bowling Club, locally known as the Big Green. Across the street was Dumbarton Post Office which had a number of famous postmasters including Pat White and John T Helm and famous postmen like Jackie Sword. There was Thomson's the baker shop, the Market Garage from which cattle being taken to market would occasionally escape and – occasionally have to be shot by police marksmen – and Jeannie McFall's newsagent's and holy shop, which was effectively the college tuck shop. Next door to McFall's was John Mullen's record shop where all the Sixties hits were sold from a vast selection from the Beatles to the Rolling Stones to Bach and Beethoven, stocked for the likes of champion bowler Ernie Johnson, a classical music lover who collected every record ever made by David Ward, the boy from Brucehill, who sang Wotan in Wagner's Ring Cycle at Covent Garden. Alex Douglas and his son, Jackie, had a barber's shop near there and then there was the Masonic Hall about which, for obvious reasons, I can tell you very little. There was the fish and chip shop run by Paul Tamburini and Helen King and Bobby Allen's sweetshop across the road where the people queuing to get into the Rialto bought their cigarettes and sweeties. A place I can tell you about though is the Railway Tavern, a favourite watering hole frequented by politicians, businessmen and journalists.

The public bar crowd in McCafferty's Railway Tavern – Joe Muldoon, Bud O'Neill, Jimmy McIntyre, Joe Gilmartin, John McAllister, Ronnie Shaw, Mr Robinson, Bobby McDermott, Junior Deigman and Joe McHugh. Note the Bible John wanted poster on the wall, and the coal fire burning in the grate.
Picture by Hector Cameron

Hugh McCafferty owned the pub, formerly known as Kirk's, and his wife, Margaret, an immaculately dressed, beautifully coiffured and kind-hearted woman known to one and all (out of her earshot, of course) as The Duchess, presided in the Tavern Lounge, one step up from the public bar. The stories about McCafferty's, which later moved up the road to the Employment Exchange which, as one wag had it, was where the customers all started out anyway, are legion. Someone should write an entire book about the pub and its baristas who included John 'Bud' O'Neill, Saul Docherty and Alex Scott, along with the owners' sons, architect Gerard and artist Robert, who served behind the bar from time to time. Mary McKinley and Jackie MacDonald looked after the lounge. Another barber's shop, Peter McCann's, previously owned by Alex Murphy, was next door to the pub and before betting was legal there was a 'shuffle betting' or illegal bookie's shop nearby. Want to bet you can't remember the names of all the pends in College Street? Answers on an e mail with any old photographs please to heaneymedia@btinternet.com

The queue outside the Rialto in College Street on a Saturday morning in 1957. Look closely and you'll see former Vale of Leven footballer John McCourt and his brother, Peter, in the group to the left of the picture. *Picture by Peter Leddy.*

College Park Street looking towards the Post Office and a policeman at the junction of the Vennel and High Street, otherwise known as Dumbarton Cross.

Nicholas and Mary Russell, who owned a general store in College Street, and Jim Mulkerrin, who played football for Scotland.

My grandparents wedding day, William and Elizabeth Healey Heaney, with John Ward and Charlotte Heaney, their best man and bridesmaid, parents of Pat Ward, who played for Hibernian and Leicester City. They were all 'Vennel folk'.

The old Post Office and telephone exchange in College Street with Mullen's record shop and McFall's shop on the left of the photograph.

Legendary Strathleven Juveniles, most of whom came from the Vennel, with the Maryhill Challenge Cup, the James Bell Trophy, the Cameron Cup and the League Championship. Back row (left to right) are Danny McDonnell, manager, Finnegan, Doherty, Quinn, Montgomery, McCallum, Donachy with trainers Bernie McKay and Frank Kelly. Front row are Earley, Heaney, Queen, Mulkerrin and O'Neill. Jim Mulkerrin played for Scotland, Hibernian and Accrington Stanley and John Heaney played for Dumbarton and Bury.

One of the teams from St Patrick's Primary School, McLean Place, Dumbarton, with Peter Goldie, a future Celtic player, in the front row, second from right.

Janitor John Boxer McFall was manager of this Wee St Pat's team which includes back row (left to right) Jim McKay, Jim Cullen, James McCallion, Chic Lilly, Pat King, Ronnie Shaw. Front – Tommy Holleran, Stevie Murray, of Celtic, Aberdeen and Dundee, James, Johnny and Joe McGroarty.

Chapter 49

THE BOXER

Richard Gallacher

Richard Gallacher, who boxed for Great Britain against the Golden Gloves champion of the USA at Wembley's Empire Pool and was afterwards named 'the uncrowned flyweight champion of the world,' died in Dumbarton 2013, aged 88. A member of a large and successful sporting family, he was one of five children, the second eldest of four boys and a girl, born to Clydeside shipyard riveter Jim Gallacher and his wife, Martha. He was brought up in the village of Renton, a close knit community whose main workplaces were silk-dyeing factories and bleach fields on the banks of the River Leven. Renton or 'the Renton' as it is widely known, was famous for its footballers and became legendary throughout the country as the cradle of Scottish football. That was when teams from the neighbouring towns of Vale of Leven and Dumbarton were amongst the best in Scotland, and Renton FC itself was world famous. They are remembered as one of the first clubs to have laid claim to the title Champions of the World when in 1888, as Scottish Cup holders, they challenged and beat the FA Cup holders West Bromwich Albion. The village also produced James Kelly, one of the founders of Celtic Football Club, Alex Jackson, who played for Arsenal and Scotland and was one of the Wembley Wizards, John 'Solly' O'Hare, who won two European Cup medals with Brian Clough's Nottingham Forest and 12 caps for Scotland, and John Ryan, who became captain of Tottenham Hotspur. It was expected that Richard would follow the path of the men who had gone before and take up soccer. He did so for a time and showed promise, but unlike his brothers, Hugh and Jim, who were twins and became professional footballers in Scotland and England, he traded in his football boots for boxing gloves. His eldest brother, Willie, was a well-known Scottish international marathon and cross country runner. Born into hard times in 1925 at a time of widespread unemployment, Richard was educated at North Street School in Alexandria and later at nearby St Mary's Primary School and then St Patrick's High School, Dumbarton. He was a bright pupil who went on to become a marine engineering apprentice at Babcock and Wilcox in Dumbarton and a time-served journeyman in John Brown's shipyard in Clydebank. He had played in juvenile soccer with Alexandria's Argyle Select and it was next door to their training centre in a tenement room in the town's Main Street that Vale of Leven Boxing Club met. Its founders, Alan Jardine and Jim Brown, invited him and a few of his pals in to watch and then box and he was a member there until he was 17 when he enrolled in jujitsu classes and more boxing training just to keep fit. He was just seven stones in weight at the time and was spotted by a Clydebank bookmaker, Harry Woods, who had an interest in boxing and considered he had the potential – and the proper physique - to make the grade at flyweight. Woods recommended Gallacher, who by this time had been nicknamed Skeets after the handsome Hollywood film actor of that era, to his brother, Danny Woods, and persuaded him to train him. Boxing gymnasiums were dank, dark and dirty places in those Second World War days prior to the Clydebank Blitz, but

Gallacher's talent and southpaw stance were unusual and eye-catching and shone through the gloom at the John Brown Welfare club. Benny Lynch, the most famous Scottish boxer of all time, who toured around the gyms and spit and sawdust pubs of the West of Scotland with his mentors and hangers on, took a shine to the wee lad from Renton. Skeets' son, Richard, has a memorable story about the relationship between his father and Benny Lynch, who came into the gym one night unannounced. He says Skeets, who had initially been trained by his own father, had never worn the correct bandaging on his hands or been gloved up properly while he was training.

Skeets Gallacher and Benny Lynch, who admired the young Renton pugilist.

When Lynch, who was the world professional fly-weight champion, appeared he asked him about this and Skeets said he had a couple of old bandages which he had used when he cut his hand at work. Lynch then gloved him up himself – 'the first night my father actually boxed Benny Lynch put the bandages and gloves on him. From then on the champion was always in and around my father's corner when he went into the ring.' Lynch's words to Skeets that night were: 'a word of advice son, always remember there is no point in fighting three rounds when you can finish the fight in one, good luck to you.' Skeets went on to win 34 consecutive amateur contests and in doing so became Scottish and British champion. Defeats of French and American rivals later saw him crowned unofficial flyweight champion of the world. Gallacher was also considered to be a good singer and in addition to the boxing circuit he played the music halls with a group called the Rae brothers. This involved doing impersonations of the ink spots at prestigious venues including the usher hall in Edinburgh, the Caird Hall in Dundee and the Metropole in Glasgow. His sister, Mary, was also a singer and sang with a dance band while his brother, Hugh, who played for Dumbarton, Clyde and Queen of the South, was Britain's highest scorer with 47 goals in one season. Jim, Hugh's twin, played for Hamilton Academicals and was a gifted half-back with Rotherham and Gillingham and the eldest brother, Willie, was an international athlete. It was little wonder then that when the Gallagher children turned up at their parents' home for dinner on a Sunday that the street outside was crowded with children seeking autographs. Skeets fought for Scotland against Ireland in Dublin and for Britain against France in Paris and London, where he also showed that he could be a peace maker by settling a row over the insignia on the vest the boxers had to wear. Some of the Scots in the team were unhappy that the English rose was on their vests and wanted the Union flag there, but the team managers said there was no time to make new vests and Skeets persuaded his fellow countrymen to settle for the rose. Britain won by five bouts to three and Gallagher was lauded in the press – 'the 19-year-old shipyard worker's meteoric rise in amateur boxing in this country seems destined to eclipse in brilliance the records of such famous fighting scots as benny lynch and Jackie Paterson.' The pinnacle of Skeets' amateur career came in 1946 when he was the only scot chosen to represent Britain in a team which included the legendary Freddie Mills against the use's golden gloves champions and he was immediately offered a professional contract by Jackie Paterson. Gallacher declined the offer and went on to beat the American flyweight champion John

Arduino who told him after a close contest during which both fighters were knocked down: 'by winning tonight I hear this makes you world champion.' When he returned home the following evening he found Renton *en fete* with flags and bunting everywhere, a dance band playing and villagers dancing in Cordale Crescent, the street where he lived. He was hoisted shoulder high and carried through the streets accompanied by Renton pipe band which had also turned out for the occasion. It was later that evening that Gallacher was finally persuaded to turn professional. That was the wrong decision and he suffered a serious eye wound in a clash of heads during a fight in Dundee. This sent his professional career into a downward spiral and he ended his days fighting in mismatched contests in boxing booths in the North of England and as a sparring partner for famous boxers, including Dado Marino and Rinty Monaghan. Gallacher met and married his wife, Annie Dunn, in November, 1948, and they had two children, Richard and John James, who died in infancy. Although he lost his last job in industry when the singer factory closed in Clydebank in 1982, Skeets was a well-respected figure in the community. He involved himself in keep fit classes and local boxing clubs and was honoured with a civic reception for his community work by Dumbarton district council. Richard Skeets Gallagher, who is survived by his brother, Willie, son, Richard and daughter in law Shona, died in Dalreoch old people's home in Dumbarton. His funeral Mass, conducted by Father Charles McElwee, took place at Our Lady and St Mark's Church, Alexandria, and the final committal thereafter in Vale of Leven cemetery. Skeets had been unwell for some years and sadly most of his scrap books and other memorabilia were destroyed in a fire at his home in Vale of Leven, but his many trophies were saved and are treasured by his son and his wife.

These youngsters from St Martin's Primary School in Renton in 1966 had a lot to live up to and plenty of heroes, including Richard Gallacher and his brothers, all of whom distinguished themselves at sport. *Picture courtesy Thomas Tek Kelly.*

Chapter 50

THE RAILWAY

A steam locomotive on the West Highland Line.
Picture courtesy Scotrail and Colin Nairn

The West Highland Line, which runs through Dumbarton, Cardross and Craigendoran, has a wonderful Gaelic name - *Rathad Iarainn nan Eilean*, which means the Iron Road to the Isles. I have written about it many times, but travelled on it only once, 50 years ago when the first custom-built observation carriage was introduced. It was an unforgettable journey on which I was accompanied by Craig M Jeffrey, a colleague from Helensburgh. We took our places in the glass-roofed, beautifully upholstered compartment beside important, bowler-hatted officials of British Railways and their smartly-dressed WAGS. We dined on Scottish seafood and drank fine wines and island malts and took part in a seemingly interminable party through some of the most beautiful scenery in the world. It was a wonderful experience and I don't think we could have been better looked after had we been on the Orient Express. Louis Theroux eat your heart out.

The world's best known travel writer, Theroux did the West Highland odyssey once and his account of it includes and interview with well known Dumbarton man, Lewars Davidson. He described Lewars as the image of Pope John XXIII which Lewars, had he lived to read it, might have been truly discomfited by since he was zealously Wee Free and not particularly fond of popes. My friends Lewars and his brother, John, who saw themselves as self-appointed public watchdogs who kept their gimlet eyes on the work of the local councils, travelled often on the West Highland Line. The Davidson brothers would deliver little parcels of books for the signalman at Rannoch Moor and these were off-loaded with the mail and other items via an ingenious hoop system without the train ever stopping.

Enthusiasm for the West Highland Line is infectious and it has many supporters including Cardross man Billy Thomson, who has built a complete model of it in a shed in garden. Billy and his wife, Peggy, were the prime movers in having a memorial erected to the 37 navvies, many of them from Donegal, who lost their lives during the construction of the railway in the Arrochar, Tarbet, and Ardlui section. Modestly Billy points to the others who helped to raise the money to have the gravestone and plaque at Ballyhennan Cemetery during the railway's centenary celebrations in 1995.

Cardross railway enthusiast Billy Thomson in his garden shed where he has built a model of Helensburgh Station and the West Highland Line. *Picture by Bill Heaney*

The line was built 120 years ago to serve the farming and fishing communities in the West Highlands from Arrochar and Tarbet and Ardlui north to the ports of Mallaig and Oban. It has been voted the top rail journey in the world, ahead of the iconic Trans-Siberian line in Russia and the Cuzco to Machu Picchu line in Peru. The Scotrail website has since reported that the line was voted the most scenic for the second year running. Passenger services are three daily returns between Glasgow Queen Street and Mallaig/Oban, and one nightly, except Saturdays, Caledonian Sleeper service between London Euston and Fort William. During the summer season from May until October a steam locomotive-hauled daily return service between Fort William and Mallaig known as 'The Jacobite' is operated by West Coast Railways. There is usually one train a day, which can be caught at Dumbarton or Helensburgh Upper, but this is increased to two trains from June until the end of August.

Onward ferry connections operated by Caledonian MacBrayne are available from Mallaig to the Isle of Skye, to the small isles of Rùm, Eigg, Muck, and Canna, and to Inverie on the Knoydart peninsula. From Oban ferries sail to the islands of Lismore, Colonsay, Coll, Tiree, Mull, Barra and South Uist. The West Highland Line is one of two railway lines which access the remote and mountainous west coast, the other being the Kyle of Lochalsh Line which connects Inverness with Kyle of Lochalsh. The line is the westernmost railway line in Great Britain. At least in part, the West Highland Line and the West Highland Railway are one and the same. For motorists attempting to travel up the A82 along Loch Lomondside to Crianlarich or over the Rest and Be Thankful to Oban, the line has been a godsend. The achingly long improvement works at Pulpit Rock are now almost at an end and the short-by-pass road at Crianlarich has taken another of the bottle-necks out of the road journey. The fact that the train can take significantly longer – sometimes – is down to the fact that there is a tremendous amount of make up time in the schedule. Critics blame the poor scheduling of stopping trains in front of the West Highland on the North Clyde line and the fact that 15 minutes are allowed in the timetable to divide or attach portions of trains at Crianlarich. There is too the fact that the line is single track almost throughout, and trains must wait at stations with crossing loops for opposite direction trains to pass. Over much of the Rannoch Moor section the speed limit is 60 mph for the Sprinter and 70 mph on the approach to Rannoch station.

The Caledonian Sleeper on the other hand only does 40 mph maximum, slowing down for a number of bridges on the route due to the heavy weight of the Class 67 locomotive which hauls the train. From Glasgow to Dumbarton, the route is shared with the North Clyde Line before branching northward at Craigendoran Junction towards Garelochhead, the section where the West Highland Line itself is generally accepted to begin. It gives high-level views of the Gareloch and Loch Long before emerging alongside the north westerly shores of Loch Lomond, then climbs up to Glen Falloch. Significant points on the journey include Crianlarich, an important Highland junction of both road and rail, and Tyndrum of the gold mines, the smallest place in Scotland, and the northernmost place in Britain, with two railway stations. After Bridge of Orchy, the line climbs onto Rannoch Moor, past the former crossing point at Gorton Crossing to Rannoch station. In winter, the moor is often covered with snow, and deer may be seen running away from the approaching train. The station at Corrour is one of the most remote stations in Britain and is not accessible by any public road. It was one of the stations used by the 'deer stalker special' which carried the rich and famous from London to Scotland on shooting holidays. This is the summit of the line at 410 m (1347 ft) above sea level.

Carrying on northwards, the line descends above the shores of Loch Treig and through the narrow Monessie Gorge. The the final stop before Fort William is Spean Bridge. The section between Fort William and Mallaig passes over the much filmed and much photographed Glenfinnan Viaduct and continues through Arisaig with its views of the Small Isles of Rùm, Eigg, Muck and Canna, and the white sands of Morar before coming to Mallaig itself. The branch to Oban diverges at Crianlarich, and runs through Glen Lochy to Dalmally and through the Pass of Brander to reach salt water at Taynuilt and Connel Ferry before a final climb over a hill to Oban.

The final leg of the Road to the Isles is embarked upon by Calmac ferry from Oban, seen here passing St Columba's Cathedral on the Esplanade. *Picture by Bill Heaney*

Railway buffs should know that, with the exception of the route between Glasgow Queen Street and Helensburgh Upper, and the short section between Fort William Junction and Fort William station, the railway is signalled using the Radio Electronic Token Block, controlled from the signal box at Banavie station. Notable features on the West Highland Railway include the Horse Shoe Curve, between Upper Tyndrum and Bridge of Orchy; the Cruach Rock snow shed, between Rannoch and Corrour; Glenfinnan viaduct, between Locheilside and Glenfinnan; the Pass of Brander stone signals, between Dalmally and Taynuilt and Arisaig, the furthest west railway station in Great Britain. The West Highland Line was originally seen as a railway for toffs to go touring or hunting, shooting and fishing on the moors, mountains and rivers.

John McGregor, in his book celebrating the 120th anniversary of the line, says that special trips for visitors included all-day passage of the Caledonian Canal from Banavie to Inverness. The North British company were keenly aware that many summer travellers on the canal were 'first class and cabin' as against 'third class and steerage'. A mass market began to develop in the years just before the First World War.

McGregor states: 'The fashionable Highland season, August-October, meant not just across the Border first class return traffic but to-ing and fro-ing by rail within Scotland as house parties moved about; moreover accompanying servants, indoor and outdoor luggage and other equipment generated additional revenue at third-class rates.' He adds: 'As elsewhere in the Highlands, horse and carriage business – traditionally a year-round standby which expanded markedly in summer and autumn – began to decline when the well-to-do discovered that the convenience of motoring might outweigh its hazards.' One of the victims of this was the Shandon Hydropathic Hotel, near Helensburgh, which closed when patronage fell away as fashions changed. Caught up in the redundancies which followed this was my own great grandfather, Patrick Healey, who was the head groom and chief gardener at the Hydro. And so history is made and everything changes ....

* *The West Highland Railway by John McGregor is published by Amberley and available from all good bookshops or on-line from Amazon. Thanks for additional information and photographs to Scotrail.*

Dan Lynch JP looks out at the spectacular Glenfinnan Viaduct and (right) the old Shandon Hydro Hotel on Garelochside.

Picture by Deidre McGowan.

Maid of the Loch at Lomond Shores in Balloch.

Chapter 51

THE MAID OF THE LOCH

The way we were – the Maid of the Loch heading for Luss Pier.

The Maid of the Loch is a wonderful looking ship. She has kept her figure despite being 62 years old, which today is the new 40. Her photograph appears in postcards and publicity material which are sent all over the world advertising the Bonnie Banks as place to visit. This has put the old paddler at the centre of a successful tourist attraction campaign for Visit Scotland and the Loch Lomond and Trossachs National Park. The problem with the Maid of the Loch is that she is an empty vessel. She has no engine and no boiler to produce the steam to turn her very pretty paddles. The Maid was withdrawn from service in August 1981 when it was generally agreed she was not fit for purpose. Her dated appearance meant few people wished to waltz around the loch's islands in her rapidly deteriorating bars and passenger lounges. Abandoned and neglected, she became an old Maid and her age really began to take its toll. Discerning visitors turned their attention to the younger vessels at Balloch and Tarbert which provided better accommodation, nicer bars and lounges. The old Maid had been in service for 29 years and had gone out of fashion. Jazz band cruises and other entertainments on weekend evenings lost their popularity.

The paddler had become little more than a floating public bar – and not a very nice one at that - which left whisky bottles and beer cans in her wake. These had been surreptitiously smuggled aboard by passengers who wanted to avoid the inflated CalMac drinks prices. Occasionally there was the odd body too, someone with too much drink taken who had fallen overboard and had to be rescued. Don't get me wrong, the Maid had its moments like the day the Queen, the Duke of Edinburgh and Princess Anne went aboard for a sail. It was the day before the Erskine Bridge was officially opened by Princess Anne, a glorious summer day on the loch. It was the kind of day when some people think they have died and gone to heaven. I should know because I was there as a guest of the government and sat down to lunch with the Queen and Prince Philip. There had been earlier royal visits to Lomond. The first of the modern royal visits to Loch Lomond was in August 1849 as Queen Victoria and Prince Albert were making their way to Balmoral, which they did not as yet own, for a summer holiday.

The journey to Scotland was preceded by an official visit to Ireland where the royal couple made official visits to Cork, Dublin and Belfast, travelling between these cities on the Royal Yacht. Ireland has now been more or less written out of Queen Victoria's biographies. For many years though, in the early part of her reign, Victoria had a great affinity with Ireland and although she holidayed at Balmoral from 1848 onwards and Albert bought the estate in 1852, it was possible after her visit to Killarney in 1861 that she might have added a holiday home there. However, a combination of the deteriorating political situation in Ireland and Prince Albert's death a few months after her 1861 visit meant that nothing came of any possible Irish home. It is true that if you want to make God laugh, tell him what your plans are. Even Queen Victoria is unlikely to have considered that her wishes would not be fulfilled as she planned, or that her dear Albert would not be with her in old age. Little did I think then that just ten years after my own glorious day out with the royals, I would be suggesting that the Maid of the Loch should be towed out into the middle of Loch Lomond and unceremoniously scuttled. An enraged steam navigation enthusiast wrote a Letter to the Editor of a national newspaper stating the only way she would agree to that happening was if I was securely tied to the mast at the time. My wished for sinking never happened of course, and the Maid remained happed up in green tarpaulins and looking forlorn at her berth at Balloch Pier. The Maid was given a companion for a time, a lady in waiting, whose tenure too was brief and unsuccessful.

And so it was that the Maid was left to rust in the loch's front parlour, opposite Lomond Shores. In 1992, Dumbarton District Council bought the Maid and restoration work started. Initially it amounted giving the ship a coat of paint, which critics said was the equivalent of putting lipstick on a corpse. In 1995, the Council supported a group of local enthusiasts led by a council official, John Beveridge, to set up a charitable organisation, the Loch Lomond Steamship Company.

Its intention was to take over ownership of the Maid and carry on restoration. The Maid however became a money pit into which a great deal of public money was questionably invested. There were daft contributions during a debate about her future from members in the council chamber, including one that suggested the Maid project would provide work for the skilled craftsmen who had been paid off when Denny's closed in 1963. That closure was 30 years previously and the craftsmen would have been well into retirement if not actually dead.

Instead of producing steam for the boiler though, the Maid produced cups of tea and coffee, sandwiches and iced buns. She had metamorphosed from pretty maid to modest waitress in 2000 and has been operating a café bar and static function suite. Meanwhile, for the past 16 years, this has been without as much as blast on her steam whistle. The enthusiasts did complete the restoration, repair and refurbishment of the slipway adjacent to the pier at Balloch, although the trains stopped calling there years before. It has been impossible to take the Maid to a dry dock for repairs to the hull because there is no link to the sea and a slipway. A steam-operated cable-hauled cradle was built, mainly with charity money and public finance. Remarkably this slipway had fallen into disrepair by the 1990s and eventually a Heritage Lottery Fund grant was awarded to restore it. This enabled the paddle steamer to be lifted out of the water in June, 2006. The Maid of the Loch does not as much as limp along into the 21st century. It is open to the public every day from Easter to October, and at weekends only in winter months. An indication of its popularity and viability is that the café closes each night at 5pm. The ship has a new livery of red, white and black, the funnel now red with a black top and the Maid looks splendid from Lomond Shores.

More and more money is being poured into her and the repairs and servicing the finance has been donated for stagger along at a very slow pace. Perhaps it is time to say goodbye to those earnestly held aspirations? And to ditch the dreams of the enthusiasts, whose dearest wish is to see the steam operation in the ship restored. In my view, a sailing again Maid is a pipe dream that will never be fulfilled. If it were possible to put the Maid of the Loch back into service, it would have happened years ago. By all means, keep the ship at Lomond Shores as an icon for the Bonnie Banks, but the time may be right for consideration to be given to calling a halt to the charity fund-raising and public grants. Maybe it's time the Maid called it a day. Even pleasant old ladies have to realise their life is coming to an end. It's time to move on.

Loch Lomond is known the world over for its beauty and the song – By Yon Bonnie Banks. One of the small ferries taking cyclists from Balmaha. *Picture by Bill Heaney*

Chapter 52

THE FLAGS

Clockwise: The Saltire, the Irish tricolor, The European flag and the Union Flag.

Fly the flag, they used to say. And sing up! Nowadays there's usually a health warning attached to that statement: Do so at your own risk of ending up in jail. The controversy over football and sports columnists Graham Speirs and Angela Haggerty's sacking by the Herald brought back memories, mostly bad ones, of assignments I was given as a young news reporter to cover stories involving Celtic and Rangers. One of the first of these was when I was a staff reporter in Ayrshire for the Scottish Daily Express. I was sent to Rugby Park, Kilmarnock, after Celtic supporters shinned up a flagpole behind one of the goals and stole the League Championship flag which, remarkably, Kilmarnock had won for the first and only time in their history in

1965, under the management of the ex-Rangers winger, Willie Waddell. My assignment was difficult since the incident happened near the end of an evening floodlit match and the large crowd was streaming out of the stadium as I got there. But I had a stroke of good fortune – or at least I thought I had. Willie Waddell had, despite his managerial success, quit Kilmarnock to become a sportswriter with the Express and he was covering the match. He would have seen everything that had happened from his seat in the press box and would be helpful. Or so I thought. I battled my way through the departing crowd to the main stand, dodged the doorman and made my way up the stairs to the boardroom, where Waddell and the club directors were having a post-match refreshment with Kilmarnock's new manager, Malky McDonald. Malky was personable as football managers go, and I got a few quotes from him. However, as the 'suits' began to tune in to our conversation, he became agitated and asked what permission I had to be there. He then said I should leave – immediately. I pointed out that I was Waddell's Express colleague from the news desk and suggested that if there were any developments (I don't think the flag had been recovered by then) he could maybe let him know. I then told Waddell who I was and added that that the editor, Ian McColl, had asked me to team up with him on the story. Waddell simply growled into his whisky and looked at me as though I was something that he had accidentally trod on. He did nothing to prevent me being ushered out of the boardroom. And he added absolutely nothing to the news report I sent from a telephone box at the end of the street. I never did hear from my 'colleague' again. So far as Jock Stein is concerned, I remember being sent to Prestwick Airport in 1968, with photographer Ronnie Vavasour, to cover Celtic's homecoming from a tour of the United States. Ronnie got great pictures of the players being hugged and kissed by their wives and girlfriends. I recall Tommy Gemmell being particularly helpful and that I noted down a few innocuous quotes to make a story. Suddenly, Stein appeared on the scene scowling and asking us what we thought we were doing. So, I thought I had better ask him a question about football, which wasn't really my remit. There was to be an international match against Portugal on the Saturday and the morning papers and radio had reported that Celtic's Steve Chalmers and John Clark, who had been chosen to play in that game, were doubtful through injury. Would they be fit to play, I asked. Stein snapped: 'Of course they'll be effing fit. The reports are rubbish.' The assembled clique of sportswriters, who had filed this 'story' from the States, laughed out loud at me for being so naïve as to believe that one of their reports might be true. They had all gone native, fans with typewriters. Jock Stein was enraged with another story I did about him after the European Cup Final in 1967. Celtic were at that time notoriously tight-fisted. It was the era of 'the biscuit tin' in which they were alleged to keep all their money. It became clear that the Lisbon Lions were unhappy with the bonus money they received from the club for their historic win. Stein wasn't backing them in their talks about this with club chairman Sir Robert Kelly and the Express had been tipped off that this was because he himself had been 'well looked after' by the club. I was asked to make inquiries. I found out that Sir Robert was an executive of the Eagle Star insurance company which had offices in St Vincent Street in Glasgow. And that members of the company's staff were said to be talking quietly - but publicly - about a deal Sir Robert was said to have done for Stein. The story went that Stein was to receive what was known as a 'top hat' insurance policy. This would mature a few years down the line and give the manager a tidy sum to see him into a comfortable retirement. This was Stein's Lisbon bonus, or so the word on the street had it. When this was put to Celtic, they were furious, not just with the people who had leaked the information but with the Express itself for even contemplating publishing it. The Express would be banned from Celtic Park if one word of it appeared in the paper, I was told. Stein would be upset and wouldn't talk to the paper again ever. A short time later, the Express news editor, Ian Brown, told me the story had been spiked because neither the newspaper nor the club wanted to upset Stein. A few years later Celtic, so protective of their manager at that time, eased him out of his post. And to Stein's great chagrin - and the huge dismay of the club's fans - offered him a job in the Celtic Pools office. Naturally he used a gambling metaphor when he told them to go and raffle themselves and headed off to Leeds United. Stein was still around though in October, 1968, when Rangers played Dundalk, a team from the Republic of Ireland, at Ibrox Park. I was sent to the St Enoch Hotel in Glasgow, where Dundalk were staying, with a question for the club chairman, Vincent McKee. It was this: Would he be asking Rangers to observe the normal courtesies in these European matches, one of which was that the host club should fly the flag of the visiting nation? Vincent was very personable. We had a chat over a drink. He said he hadn't thought of it, but he would ask Rangers to do it. A few hours later he said they intended to meet his request. They had borrowed an Irish tricolour from Jock Stein at Celtic and it was being sent over to Ibrox. I got off my mark with my photographer, Tommy Fitzpatrick. We would have to get some kind of picture. This was history in the making. It would be the first time ever that the Irish flag had been flown at a Scottish football ground other than Celtic Park. And that ground was Ibrox! We reached the stadium just as a black taxi cab drew up. The driver stepped out with a large brown paper parcel which he took inside. An elderly man with spectacles, a cloth cap and dungarees met the driver in the foyer. It was the Rangers' groundsman, Jock Shaw, and he took the possession of the flag. I asked him – nicely – if we could get a picture of him running the tricolour up the flagpole, but we were soon interrupted. Willie Allison, a *Sunday Mail* sportswriter who had been recruited by Rangers as one of the first staff PR persons in Scottish football – shouted from the top of the marble staircase telling us to stop. He then came down and ordered us off the premises. The F-word came into it again and I have ever since been able to boast that I was ordered off at Ibrox. When I reported into the *Express* office that we had failed in our mission, the news editor said other members of staff had been on the telephone to Allison. Since I was going off shift, they would now take over the story. This was probably what had alerted the PR man to the fact that I would be out there soon to doorstep him. Next morning as I recall there was a short, front page piece in the paper saying that the flag had not been flown. When I looked for that edition in the National Library of Scotland in Edinburgh year it wasn't there. But I have since found out what happened from Vincent McKee. He told me the club had reached a deal with Rangers that if Dundalk did not insist that the Irish flag be flown over Ibrox, then Rangers would not insist that the Union Jack should be flown over Oriel Park in Dundalk. While the Troubles in the North didn't start until August 1969, tensions at the time were running very high, so it made a lot of sense not flying the tricolour at Ibrox or the Union Jack at Oriel Park, according to Vincent. 'I don't think either flag would have been appreciated by both sets of home supporters,' he told me. For the record, Rangers beat Dundalk 6-1 at Ibrox with Sir Alexander Ferguson scoring two of the goals. The Dundalk leg score was 0-3. Who knows what would have happened had the Irish tricolour been flown over Ibrox? Meanwhile, closer to home, flags have been in the headlines again because some people neglect and abuse them. Flag stories are meat and drink to newspapers. They get the readers animated, bristling with indignation or shaking the heads in dismay. They send the green ink brigade – and the blue ink crowd too - rushing off to write letters to their MP and to the editor of their local newspaper. They jam the telephone lines of programmes like the Morning Rant on Radio Scotland. One of the best happened here when the late Ferdie Thurgood climbed high on to the roof of the Victoria Halls in Helensburgh and replaced the Red Flag, put there by the old Dumbarton District Council -- with a large pair of knickers. Ferdie was a local Customs and Excise officer who kept an eye on the Scotch whisky operations at local distilleries and bonded warehouses in Dumbarton. He was also the chairman of the RNLI based at Rhu Marina. And the Red Flag did not signify his views or the political views of most of the people of well-heeled, Conservative-voting Helensburgh. The bloomers he attached to the flagpole were a clear indication of what he thought about socialism being foisted on them from afar. It led to a referendum and Helensburgh's decision to throw its lot in with Argyll and Bute. In my experience all flags are trouble. Remember the outcry when Alex Salmond unfurled the Saltire when Andy Murray won at Wimbledon? It was claimed to be a political gesture, and of course it was. All flags and flag waving are political.

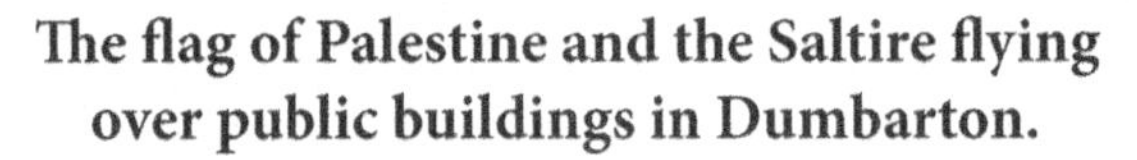

The flag of Palestine and the Saltire flying over public buildings in Dumbarton.

Why it is illegal to neglect to maltreat or our national flags

I neglected my usual jobs of making sure the town clock was at the right time and the tide was coming and going as it should at the Quay by taking a special interest in the flags that are flown around the town. The Saltire, the Scottish flag with the St Andrew's cross emblazoned on it in blue and white, is the most prominent. It is there almost all the time, flying proudly from Dumbarton Municipal Buildings and over the Dumbarton Courts building in Church Street. The Union Flag does not get much of a look-in, but it can be seen from time to time, flying from the Castle or the Masonic Hall in Church Street. We seldom if ever see the European flag in these parts and I believe not many people here would recognise it if they did see it. Other flags which fly here are the flag of West Dunbartonshire Council, which includes an image of St Patrick to indicate that he was born in Old Kilpatrick, and the Irish tricolour, the Lion Rampant and even the Papal flag. There used to be a number of flagpoles in prominent places in the town. Some of these were ship's masts and at least two of them came from the Americas Cup-winning yachts, the Shamrock series, built for Sir Thomas Lipton, the grocery millionaire, at Denny's shipyard. One of these was in the grounds of St Patrick's Church and was looked after by the late Willie McCallum, a rigger who was an expert on all things to do with flags and flagpoles. The other was in Levengrove Park, and there was a third at the eponymous Flagpole at the junction of Brucehill Road and Cardross Road. The Royal Standard of the United Kingdom is the flag used by Elizabeth II in her capacity as Sovereign and it flies from Dumbarton Castle whenever she visits Dunbartonshire. It is flown when the Queen is in residence in one of the royal palaces and on her car during official journeys. It may be flown on any building, official or private, during a visit by the Queen. The Royal Standard was flown aboard the Clyde-built royal yacht Britannia when it was in service and the Queen was on board. In 1934, King George V permitted his subjects in Scotland to display the ancient Royal Standard of Scotland, the Lion Rampant, as part of his silver jubilee. Today, it flies above Holyrood Palace and Balmoral Castle when the Queen is not in residence. Unlike the Union Flag, the Royal Standard is never flown at half-mast, even after the demise of the Crown, as there is always a sovereign on the throne. There was a row about that when the standard was not flown over Buckingham Palace following the death of Princess Diana, but the least said about that …

The flag of West Dunbartonshire Council.

The Lion Rampant differs from the Saltire in that its correct use is restricted by an Act of the Parliament of Scotland to only a few Great Officers of State who officially represent the Sovereign in Scotland. The earliest recorded use of the Lion Rampant as a royal emblem in Scotland was by Alexander II in 1222. It was used by the King of Scots until the Union of the Crowns in 1603, when James VI acceded to the thrones of the Kingdom of England and Kingdom of Ireland. Since 1603, it has been incorporated into both the royal arms and royal banners of successive Scottish then British monarchs in order to symbolise Scotland. Although now officially restricted to use by representatives of the Sovereign and at royal residences, the Royal Banner continues to be one of Scotland's most recognisable symbols. Since the 17th of March is St Patrick's Day, we can expect to see the odd Irish tricolour flying around Dunbartonshire, where many people have family links with Ireland. Supporters, including Scotland fans, who take the Irish tricolour and the Union flag and the Lion rampant to wave at sporting events – they include racing at Cheltenham and Davis Cup tennis and rugby - may be unaware that they are often insulting these flags. There are special rules for using national flags. The main rule is that no other flag or pennant should be flown above it. Care must also be taken not to let the flag touch the ground or be dropped or abused, even unintentionally. The rules also say that a national flag should also never be defaced by placing slogans, logos, lettering or pictures of any kind on it, for example at sporting events or for political purposes.

They emphasise that the national flag should be replaced if it has become worn or frayed, as it is no longer fit for display in a respectful manner. I hope West Dunbartonshire Council officials are listening. How often do we see tattered flags hanging on grimly in the wind above the Municipal Buildings and other buildings? Football supporters too should pay attention to these rules. Paddy's Pub in Auchenshuggle or Billy's Bar in Bridgeton should NOT be emblazoned on these national flags, which should be treated with respect. It is often stated that the Union Flag should only be described as the Union Jack when flown in the bows of a warship, but this is a relatively recent idea. From early in its life the Admiralty frequently referred to the flag as the Union Jack, whatever its use, and in 1902 an Admiralty circular said either name could be used officially. Such use was given Parliamentary approval in 1908 when it was stated that 'the Union Jack should be regarded as the National flag'. Meanwhile – fly the flag by all means … but be careful out there and treat your flags with the respect they merit.

Chapter 53

THE FLOTILLA

Some of the men who worked in the Pattern Shop at Denny's in Dumbarton in 1936.

The town of Dumbarton, the Leven shipyard in the shadow of the Rock and the many hundreds of local people who worked there last century, have a long-standing connection with Burma and the Burmese people. As have the Findlays, whose family home is at Boturich on the banks of Loch Lomond near Balloch, and who were rich teak merchants in Asia in the 19th century. With shipbuilder Peter Denny, whose imposing statue stands today in the gardens of the Municipal Buildings in the town's College Park Street, the Findlays were founders of the Irrawaddy Flotilla Company in Burma, which is now called Mayanmar. The company, with more than 600 shallow draught vessels in its fleet, became the biggest river transport company in the world and brought riches and prosperity to the warm, wet country that became known as the rice bowl of Asia.

Generations of local shipyard workers took the road to Mandalay. They worked on these ships alongside indigenous Burmese people and Chittagong Indians and travelled frequently from Dumbarton to Burma to secure and cement their reputations as experts in marine engineering. The steamers of the Irrawaddy Flotilla came in various shapes and sizes. Amongst the biggest were the grand Main Line paddle steamers like the Mindoon built by Denny's in 1885 and 310ft in length. The fleet was designed and built by local men in the Leven shipyard and dismantled by them before being shipped out to Mandalay, the old name for Burma, and reconstructed on site there. Indians from Chittagong crewed the vessels, while the officers and masters were primarily of Scottish descent, many of them from Dunbartonshire and the West of Scotland. One of the characters in local author A. J. Cronin's famous novel, Hatter's Castle, set in the fictional town of Levenford, is the son of a High Street business owner who is banished to Burma to seek out his fortune and to work on the construction of the Irrawaddy fleet. According to internet website sources, the Irrawaddy Flotilla Company (IFC), which was Glasgow based, was run by a character called Paddy Henderson, a name that was still well known on the River Clyde up to the 1950s. It began services on the Irrawaddy Delta with four steamers and three attached barges, which were known as cargo flats. In 1868 King Mindon, the monarch of Mandalay, allowed services to the upper reaches of the river delta, and by 1869 a service started to Bhamo.

The style of steamer built, which was also put into use as a riverboat in New Orleans in the USA, was distinctive. Generally it had no bridge, the captain conning his ship from a position towards the bow on the main (lower) deck where the wheel was sited. The extended veranda above the captain's head was reserved to give the best views of the river scenery to the first class passengers taking tea on deck. The smaller sternwheelers included the 100ft long Hata, which was also built at Denny's in 1887 for the Chindwin River services. Navigating the Irrawaddy River, which is today the scene of such horror, devastation and death, amongst shifting sandbanks and through the occasional whirlpool, was always hazardous. A number of steamers, like the Rangoon, came to grief. The ship became stranded and broke her back in 1873 only a year after her arrival fresh from her builders, R. Duncan of Glasgow, whose work augmented Denny's prodigious output. Her engines were by Rankin and Blackmore, who were to provide the engines three quarters of a century later for the PS Waverley, which sailed the Firth of Clyde and the Kyles of Bute from its base at Craigendoran Pier in Helensburgh and is today Britain's last seagoing paddle steamer.

The world's last seagoing paddle steamer, PS Waverley, leaving Helensburgh. *Pictures by Bill Heaney*

The larger steamers carried European, particularly British and most particularly Scottish captains, chief and second officers, chief, second, third and fourth engineers with the rest of the crew made up from various local and other Asian nationalities. The smallest steamers would have had a European captain and chief engineer with Chittagonians on deck and tending the engine. In 1885, before the third Anglo-Burman War, Britain commandeered the Irrawaddy fleet. It is recorded that a 3km line of vessels stretched below the upper and lower Myanmar border at Minhla. Some of the vessels, measuring 93m long with a 12m beam, a deck capacity of 3,000 passengers and cargo weighing 500 tons, took upper Myanmar in 1886. The Irrawaddy Flotilla Company became 'the greatest river fleet on earth' and by 1930, there were 602 vessels carrying nine million people. The Burma operation, T D Findlay and Son Ltd, East India Merchants, was set up in 1839, being founded by and named after the late Robert Findlay's great-grandfather. 'It was a private family company, the smallest of the five British teak firms in Burma,' explains Robert, who today is a prominent environmental campaigner on Loch Lomondside, 'but when it was nationalised in 1948, it was Britain's oldest existing trading connection with Burma. The company felled trees in the Shan States and the Pegu Yomas, after ringing them to dry out on stump for a few years. To ensure future supplies, for every tree felled, five saplings were planted. A couple of hundred contractors' elephants then dragged the logs to the nearest floating stream to await the rains which would carry them to the main river. Here they were turned into rafts large enough to carry a whole family downstream to a railhead or to the base in Moulmein where the logs were sawn into saleable products, latterly including fine tongue-and-groove parquet flooring.' The story of the Findlay family's fortunes and misfortunes is told by Robert himself on the Burke's Peerage and Gentry's internet website. He wrote: 'T D Findlay's finest achievement was the creation of the Irrawaddy Flotilla, a fleet of over 600 shallow draught ships. The ships were specifically designed to navigate the Irrawaddy and they became the lifeblood of the nation's prosperity, ensuring trade up and down the great rivers, and aiding Burma's transformation into the rice-bowl of Asia.' This exotic industry was to come to an abrupt end when the Japanese invaded Burma in November 1941. The company scuttled its flotilla to prevent it falling into the hands of the Japanese. The Scottish manager, John Morton, ordered the entire fleet to be destroyed, the thin steel hulls sunk by dynamite or machine gunned.

Robert Findlay said: 'This action brought Burmese trade and transport to a standstill. The flotilla had been the greatest-ever fleet for river transport in the world. The teak business paid off its employees and dispensed with the elephants in 1945. Following the liberation of Burma by the 14th Army, the family endeavoured to build up the Burma business once again only to see it nationalised by the new, independent Burmese government in 1948.' That year, the Irrawaddy Flotilla Company became the Government Inland Water Transport Board. Their vessels still sport the black and white funnel of the former Irrawaddy Flotilla Company, but the Denny days are just a memory now.

Denny-built ships and shipping under construction in Burma.

Denny's built this similar low draught paddler, the Delta Queen, which became a casino ship on the Mississippi River in the United States.

Chapter 54

THE POKEY HAT

The Pokey Hat in Oban, always a favourite treat after a sail in unpredictable Scottish summer weather. *Pictures by Bill Heaney*

We have not had the weather for it recently, but ice cream and 'ginger' were the favourites on hot summer days. Pokey hats were top of the pops with the children and big people liked a wafer, single or double, which had two scoops of ice cream. Well-heeled folk had a double nugget with raspberry. This was otherwise known as a McCallum, because it had a splash of *Tally Blood* poured over it. Tally Blood is the name of the novel written by Marcella Evaristi about the immigrant Italian community in the West of Scotland. The 'Tallies' were the immigrants who succeeded here through sheer hard work and an ability to make the most superb ice cream. And they knew their way around a fish supper, single fish or a wee bag of chips. People like the Porcianis, Biagis, Cascis, Palombos, Cocozzas, Veracchias, Valentis, Togneris, Rossis, Moscardinis and Tamburinis made their way round the housing schemes in brightly coloured vans, gaudily decorated with their names. They blew their horns and later introduced chimes, playing popular tunes to attract children and dement their parents. 'Mammy, can I get a pokey hat,' was the cry that went up amongst children out playing the street. The children who couldn't afford a pokey hat begged their friends for a share or a 'slug' of their 'ginger'. You have to laugh at this exchange of pleasantries: 'Geez a slug o' yer ginger, Jimmy.' Followed by, if you were lucky, 'Awright well, but nae floaters.'

The Gallone family opened a famous café in Main Street, Alexandria, in which the décor had never been changed since the day it opened. The wood panelling and aspidistras and private booths were still there when it closed a few years ago. The Gianini family had a huge café and juke box near Balloch Bridge, where hundreds of teenagers gathered looking for 'talent' on a Sunday afternoon. In Helensburgh, Eric Rossi's King's Café was the place to go and then there was Dino's Radio Café and the Augusta Lodge. How many people met their wives or husbands in an ice cream shop or Italian cafe? I know I did. Best known, of course, of these young romantics were the champion racing driver, Sir Jackie Stewart, and his wife, Helen McNeill, who met in Dino's to the sound of Sixties music on the juke box. There were many families who made ice cream in West Dunbartonshire. Young children queued eagerly with their pennies and ha'pennies for the mouth-watering creations. The cone was king, the pokey hat won it. Nowadays grandparents themselves, their children and their children's children still buy ice cream from those same families.

Today we dine out on Italian cuisine in the many fabulous restaurants these families have opened over the years. The ice cream business was almost banned at one time on health grounds, and it had nothing to do with obesity or expanding waistlines. The pokey hat's invention probably saved the ice cream industry because cones and wafers and nougats and oyster shells and snowballs replaced the 'licking glasses' in which ice cream was first sold by vendors. In the 1890s there were grave health concerns over the use of the 'licking glass'. An ice cream vendor would serve a customer a scoop of ice cream in a glass, wash it, and then use it again for the next customer. Because a number of glasses were not scrupulously washed and dried properly, the environmental health people threatened to ban the sale of ice cream altogether. The Valvona company's edible cone, saved the modern day industry. These are probably the same Valvonas, of Valvona and Crolla fame, who have a franchise these days at Lomond Shores in Balloch, and who are one of the best known restaurant and delicatessen families in Scotland.

During the Second World War, the ice cream industry in general suffered a complete ban, due to rationing, and the consequences of internment. This led to the closure of many family businesses - ice cream factories, milk bars, and street vending. Most people were dismayed at their Italian friends and neighbours being interned. Italian immigrants got a terrible time at one point. One of the greatest tragedies came when hundreds of those interned in British jails were deported to Canada. I came across some shocking details of this on a visit to Edinburgh, which has a large Italian community. It was just a tiny clipping from an old newspaper. Question of the Week, it said: 'Was it necessary to risk a good ship like the Arandora Star to transporting enemy aliens to a place of safety? Wouldn't some old tub have done as well?' I was shocked, because I knew that the Arandora Star had been sunk in the Atlantic with the loss of many lives. I knew too that a memorial to the survivors had been erected in 2011 at St Andrew's Cathedral in Clyde Street, Glasgow. I peered hard at the yellowing piece of newsprint in the Scottish National Portrait Gallery. It was a letter from the police in Edinburgh to Mrs F. Valente, of 45 Duke Street, Leith.

It was an order from the Chief Constable to get out of town and a warning that if Italian aliens did not comply they would be arrested. It is a small world and I knew that Italians had been treated very badly at that time and that immigrant families had suffered greatly. The wartime austerity was made so much harsher for them by the fact that their breadwinners were snatched from their midst, imprisoned in camps or transported overseas. Guido Porciani had told me once about an incident when his father was being arrested and taken away from his fish and chip shop in College Street, Dumbarton. He said that my wife's Irish grandmother had emerged from her shop nearby and brandished an umbrella at the police, upbraiding them for arresting a good, innocent family man, who was her friend and neighbour.

When I looked into this story further I discovered the Arandora Star was on her way to Canada during the second year of the war with 1,560 Italian prisoners of war, mostly shop owners, barbers, market salesmen. They had been arrested because they were considered a threat once Italy had allied with Germany. The ship was also carrying 400 troops to guard the prisoners and some heavy machine guns for

The Arandora Star, the immigrant ship on which Italians lost their lives. There is a memorial to the victims in St Andrew's Cathedral, Clyde Street, Glasgow.

protection. When the Arandora Star was torpedoed by a German U-boat on its third day at sea the Italians began clambering into the lifeboats to save themselves from drowning. However, many of the lifeboats sunk 400 miles off Ireland and 682 people perished including 200 soldiers. The surviving Italians were shipped back to Liverpool, where they were transported to prison camps in Australia. Three weeks after the sinking one of the lifeboats was picked up by Mickey O'Donnell and a crew of fishermen from Owey, a small island off the coast of Donegal in Ireland. That island is just a mile away from the house where I had been on holiday a few weeks before. You could see it from the garden.

Research revealed that the lifeboat completely waterlogged because the hull was shot through with bullet holes and on the deck there were handfuls of empty bullet shells. The fishermen found evidence that its occupants had tried to prevent her sinking by putting pieces of cloth into the bullet holes. The newspaper clipping and letter which first led me to investigate this matter were part of the Migration Stories: Valentina Bonizza exhibition at the National Portrait Gallery in Edinburgh. Italian-born artist Valentina has lived in Scotland for ten years. Using photography and other objects like the clipping and letter she has created what she calls an 'image document' exploring migrant experiences from 1940 to today. She said her work focuses on the transformational experience of migration -- a transitory and fluid existence which challenges one's sense of place and meaning. It raises many questions about citizenship and belonging, something that Italian and other immigrant families across Scotland know much about.

After the Second World War, the ice cream industry experienced a boom in sales, as people were released from austerity and returned to buying so-called 'luxury' items. As sons returned from the Front, and fathers were released from internment, the old Italian family businesses began to re-establish themselves. Many brought in the latest ice-cream technology, bought new premises, and re-invested in equipment from manufacturers, including Edoni in Scotland. Multi-coloured vans replaced pony carts and push carts, and long gone were the shouts of the ice cream vendors. My own favourite ice cream person was the lovely, olive skinned Julie Gallone from the Vale of Leven. All the children loved Julie, who was ahead of her time in that she not only served the ice cream and 'ginger' at the counter, but drove the van as well. The competition amongst the ice cream families was fierce, but it was memorable. Modern ice cream shops are popping up all over the place and the business is going through a remarkable resurgence. It's no longer vanilla and Tally blood that's the favourite now though. All kinds of colours and flavours are available. Who doesn't love a pokey hat?

Pokey hats are fabulous at my own favourite ice cream shop when I'm on a family outing in Oban. *Picture by Bill Heaney*

Chapter 55

THE PLAYWRIGHT

Tom Gallacher

Tom Gallacher rose from draughtsman and amateur actor to journalist and then a playwright whose work was produced across Europe and in America, *writes Donald Fullarton*. Tom, who was born in Alexandria on February 16 1932, was the third son and one of five children of Edward and Rose Gallacher, who moved from the Vale of Leven to Linn Walk in the village when he was one. He always regarded Garelochhead as his home, and he died there in October 2001 at the age of 69. His first job was framing pictures at the Macneur & Bryden Ltd. shop in East Princes Street, and also making deliveries on a bicycle. He then trained as a draughtsman and worked at Denny's Shipyard in Dumbarton, but decided on a career change and served as a reporter for the *Helensburgh Advertiser* until he was 31. He also wrote a series of articles for the *County Reporter* about old Dumbarton and the Vale of Leven which was later published as a collection under the title 'Hunting Shadows'.

Years later the BBC produced two half-hour programmes made up of these articles read by an actor from Dumbarton, Robert Trotter. During this period he gained his early theatrical experience as an amateur actor and producer with Dumbarton People's Theatre and Helensburgh Theatre Arts Club. It convinced him that he wanted to be a playwright. He gave up his reporting career in 1965, then spent two years working as a draughtsman before moving to a similar job in Montreal, Canada. He then decided to take the plunge into full-time writing and settled in London, where he lived for four years. During that period, several of his plays were performed in London theatres, notably '*Mr Joyce is leaving Paris*', '*Bright Scene Fading*' *at the Royal Court*, and '*The Only Street*' at the Kings Head Theatre. Of these the most successful was his play about James Joyce, which created a sensation amongst Irishmen at their Dublin Festival and was also presented in Canada and Italy, filmed by a London company, and broadcast on radio and TV. Other works such as '*Our Kindness to Five Persons*', '*Revival*', '*Schellenbrack*' and '*Personal Effects*' were staged in Glasgow, Dublin and Pitlochry. He also translated or adapted '*Deacon Brodie*' from Henley & Stevenson, '*An Enemy of the People*' and '*A Doll's House*' from Ibsen, '*The Father*' from Strindberg, and '*Cyrano de Bergerac*' from Rostand. In 1975 he decided to return home to Garelochhead. He said at the time: 'It seems to me that the climate of theatre in Scotland is such that it has a new sense of enthusiasm and urgency. 'This is partly due to the Scottish Society of Playwrights, of which I was a founder member, who in the last 18 months have done a great deal to advance the benefits and possibilities for Scottish playwrights. 'It is also due to the Scottish Arts Council, who have taken a very enterprising attitude to new writing in Scotland. The theatres too — perhaps the most difficult area in the past — are now eager to present new plays by Scottish writers or writers living in Scotland. In fact the whole atmosphere has changed radically in the past two years. Theatre in Scotland seems on the brink of taking a big leap forwards. I want to be part of it, and share the excitement of it.' He certainly was, and he moved in exalted drama circles as more of his plays were produced in Glasgow, Edinburgh, Perth, Pitlochry, Dundee, St Andrews and Montrose. He had spells as writer in residence both at Pitlochry Festival Theatre and, briefly, at Edinburgh's Royal Lyceum Theatre, although most of his later work was prose fiction.

Tom gave a lot of credit for his success to his parents. 'I think a lot of it comes from my father, who had a great sense of theatre and a great love of drama,' he said. 'From my mother I got this particular precision of language which many people have commented upon. She instilled into me the value and precise meaning of the spoken word.' In his later years Tom Gallacher resumed contributing to local newspapers, at various times writing comment columns in the two Dumbarton weeklies, the *Lennox Herald* and the by then renamed *Dumbarton and Vale of Leven Reporter*.

Conference time – Bill, Bernie and Bryan Heaney with Donald and Phyllis Fullarton. *Picture by Brian Averell.*

Chapter 56

POPE OF THE CLYDE

Monsignor Kelly with Frs Richard O'Callaghan, John McCready and John Bradley in the gardens at Strathleven Place.

The Right Rev. Monsignor Hugh Provost Kelly Protonotary Apostolic was born in London, 19th November, 1864, educated at St Aloysius College, Glasgow, and the College of Propaganda, Rome, *writes Thomas O'Donnell* about the man who shaped Catholicism in Dumbarton, especially in regard to education. The Monsignor, who became known as the Pope of the Clyde, was ordained to the priesthood by Monsignor Lenti in the Oratory of St Marcellus on Holy Saturday, 1889, and stationed, came to St Patrick's

Dumbarton, in 1901, where he remained for 50 years. In 1923, he was appointed a Canon of the Cathedral Chapter and a Domestic Prelate of His Holiness in 1926. Provost of the Cathedral Chapter in 1938, he celebrated the Golden Jubilee of his priesthood the following year and was honoured by the people with a generous presentation. It was in keeping with his character that this was given to the Archbishop for the needs of the new parish of St Michael's, Dumbarton, which was established in 1946. He played a leading part in establishing the Diocesan Seminary at Cardross and was created a Protonotary Apostolic by His Holiness Pope Pius XII in 1948. Following the Solemn Consecration of St Patrick's on 27th April, 1950, he retired in May to live in County Down, where he died at Newry on 26th January 1953, and was buried in Rostrevor. Such are the 'bare-bones' of the priest who was to become in that much abused phrase 'a legend in his own lifetime'. As with all legends, one has to separate the wheat from the chaff in an attempt to strike a proper balance, but it is well-nigh impossible for those of us lucky enough to have been brought up under his aegis to render an impartial and objective judgement. 'If you wish to see his memorial, look around you'. This was said of Sir Christopher Wren in London and it is just as apt in the case of Monsignor Kelly in the Dumbarton area. His achievements were in both senses of the word - monumental - the beautiful modern church, the mortuary chapel with its Pieta, the tower with its carillon of bells, the statuary with its catholic appeal, the Community of Notre Dame Sisters and the First Secondary School for Girls, St Patrick's High School and last but by no means least, the Carmelite Monastery and its powerhouse of prayer. Most parish priests would be well pleased to achieve any one of these projects in their lifetime's work. He was determined that his people should not remain 'hewers of wood and drawers of water' and he encouraged their education in every way possible. Education was of paramount importance, and only through well-trained Catholic teachers well versed in their religion, lay the hope for the future of the Catholic people. During a prize-giving address in 1928 he said: 'The business of education is to train the heart as well as the mind, for a trained mind without a trained heart, is something to be feared. There would be something seriously wanting if the minds and hearts of children were not directed to their eternal destiny as well as to their temporal destiny'. Those who are ecumenically minded today may be gratified to know that the Monsignor expressed these sentiments when he was invited to preside at the prize-giving ceremony of Dumbarton Academy in the Burgh Hall. His advice then was given to an audience which approved of Religious Education being given in schools, and in view of the present educational climate with regard to the teaching of religion, it is worthwhile repeating and enshrining in all schools, colleges and universities.

St Patrick's High School primary and secondary staff around 1960 with headmaster William B Monaghan.

The necessity of the religious ingredient in any meaningful education was to be frequently repeated in his public speeches and written articles: ``The most formidable enemy we have to contend with is ignorance of the teaching of the Church and the worst form of ignorance is half-knowledge. The really ignorant man is not he who merely lacks knowledge but he who falsely believes that he knows'.

Again: 'From our schools there must come the type of person who not uncharitable in his outlook but who, being strong and unshaken in his religious principles, will enforce respect for himself and for his Church. Further, he must be prepared to join in the ordinary social life of his neighbours and to show them that he also claims a pride in the great achievements of the Scottish nation. In education we must find our strength no less than in religion. In a common culture we must find a meeting place with our non-Catholic friends whom we must convince that we have no wish to dominate and no further inclination to be dominated. We must develop continuously and with vigour our educational system, co-operating closely with those in control of the public system but not being led by threat or argument to merge our system in theirs'. Co-operation 'Yes', Integration 'No'. He did not of course, confine himself to theory in educational matters it was his job to provide the tools.

At the official opening of St Patrick's High School in June, 1927, he began his address by saying: 'I think it eminently fitting that I should have been chosen to move the votes of thanks. I am a member of three different bodies all rolled into one. I can speak on behalf of the Diocesan Board of Management, on behalf of the Education Authority and I can speak on behalf of the Catholics of Dumbarton. And if I may add, I can speak as the one who dreamed the dream'. The Monsignor must have been the most practical visionary of all time as Provost Garrick, speaking on the same occasion, remarked that ``the Town Council had earmarked this particular plot of land for house-building but someone more astute stepped in and walked off with it from below their noses'. The contribution made by the late Monsignor towards fulfilling this dream of providing a truly Catholic education in Dunbartonshire cannot be exaggerated or over emphasised. The multitude of former pupils of Patrick's High and of Notre Dame who are at the moment adorning the various professions and religious orders, owe their education and its attendant opportunities mainly to his inspiration.

Monsignor Kelly welcomes the Sister of Notre Dame to Clerkhill in Dumbarton.

Stairway to heaven? The Carmelite Sisters whom Monsignor Kelly brought to Dumbarton. *Photograph by Bill Heaney.*

It was entirely as the result of his efforts that Dunbartonshire made better provision for the secondary education of its Catholic children than any other city or county in Scotland, and it was no coincidence that the number of vocations to the priesthood and the various female religious orders remained amazingly high in the Dumbarton area compared with others during the half-century of his administration. Of course, he had able lieutenants in the twin fields of Religion and Education. In Sister Augustine and Mr T. F. Mulgrew he had the right people, in the right place, at the right time - and a glance at the names of his assistant priests during his period speaks for itself. Many of the priests who served their apprenticeships in St Patrick's under his guidance were soon to distinguish themselves in their own right not only in the Archdiocese but much further afield. The years he spent in the College of Propaganda inflamed him with a burning zeal for the work of the foreign missions, a zeal which later found expression in his great work for the Association of the Propagation of the Faith and in his encouragement of vocations to the various Missionary Societies among the people committed to his care. The success of his efforts in this field may be apparent to older parishioners if they reflect for a few moments and consider the number of people in the area, known to them personally, who have volunteered for this mission of spreading the Good News in other lands. At a time of excessive drinking, he built up a flourishing League of the Cross which did so much to inculcate habits of temperance and sobriety. He was immediately aware of the need for culture and refinement and he relied on the women of the parish to exercise this influence, hence the invitation to the Sisters of Notre Dame and the opening of the new Secondary School for Girls in 1912 which was marked by a triumphal procession through the town. In a public speech some years later he was to remark: 'I have tried to give you a sense of your own dignity. I have tried to make you respect yourselves.

"Twenty-five years ago I made my first appearance and spoke to you for the first time from the altar of the old church, and those of you who were there remember that I was a very poor specimen of humanity on that occasion. To think that the Archbishop would send to this great and important parish of Dumbarton such a poor, miserable wretch as appeared before them that morning was something too awful to think of and the sooner His Grace was informed that Fr. Kelly would never do, the better! I was the most useless tool that God could have sent to take Dumbarton out of the mud and I think I have taken it out of the mud - with God's help.'

Monsignor Kelly (left) with a football team from St Patrick's in 1908. *Photograph by courtesy of Ellen Heaney Springer in Canada.*

Chapter 57

THE BOSS

Craig M Jeffery

Craig M Jeffrey was my hero in newspapers. I looked up to him from the day I first met him, which was when he interviewed me for a junior reporter's job, which I didn't get, on the *Helensburgh Advertiser*. Craig enjoyed the fact that he bore a resemblance to Alan Whicker, of *Whicker's World*, and strove to be every bit as flamboyant as Whicker, who was a giant of television in the 1960s. Craig was from a very different background though. He had been brought up in Paisley's deprived Ferguslie Park council housing estate, where poverty and a high crime rate went hand in hand. He once told me that he and his pals used to throw stones at passing engines on the nearby railway line in the hope that the drivers and stokers would throw coal back for the fire. I worked for Craig eventually though as a freelance when our Dumbarton-based Fitzgerald Owens national newspaper agreed to supply all the copy and pictures for Craig's new venture in the 1960s, the *County Reporter*. Only a man of true courage and determination, such as Craig, would have taken on the mammoth task of challenging the *Lennox Herald* which had been the dominant weekly newspaper in Dumbarton for a century at that time.

Advertiser team (left to right) are Gordon Terris, advertising manager; Bill Heaney, Reporter editor; Craig M Jeffrey, Murdo MacPherson and sub editor Jimmy Allen.

Picture by Helensburgh Heritage Trust.

When he went around the newsagents in Dumbarton and Vale of Leven, he received little or no encouragement. Tommy Kerr, who owned one of the biggest and busiest shops in Glasgow Road told him, he would be better off putting the money he proposed to invest into a briefcase and throwing it off Dumbarton Bridge into the River Leven. Typically CMJ was not put off. *The Reporter* became so popular that it needed its own full-time staff dedicated to it and Craig chose me to be editor. I was the youngest newspaper editor in Scotland at the time at the age of just 21. He taught me all I needed to know as a hot metal editor. My colleagues operating in Helensburgh at that time were Tom Gallacher, Jimmy Allen and Donald Fullarton, one of the best journalists in the country, who became not just editor of the *Helensburgh Advertiser* but secretary of the Guild of Newspaper Editors in Scotland. It is now the Society of Editors. Donald has the *Advertiser* story down to a T, so there was no better man to tell it here, and he kindly agreed to do that. I have told you something of the *Reporter* story, but Donald, who keeps his hand in putting together excellent pages for the *Helensburgh Heritage* website and taking photographs of all the Dumbarton FC games, home and away. The *Helensburgh Advertiser* was launched by Craig M. Jeffrey and his brother Ronnie in 1957, and the paid-for weekly became .one of Scotland's mostly highly respected local papers, although there are people today who would say that it is now only a shadow of its former self. Few people have made a greater impact on the life of Helensburgh and district in the past half century than Craig — a talented writer, a consummate salesman, a man of real character with a tremendous sense of humour, a 100 miles an hour man to those who knew him or worked for him. His brother, Ronnie, while not so flamboyant, was the production man who made sure everything happened when it should. From the first issue on August 30 1957 until the business was sold to Express Newspapers on September 3 1985, Craig made a significant contribution to the area and to the local newspaper industry in Scotland. The Paisley 'Buddie', who was twice to become president of the Scottish Newspaper Publishers Association, served his apprenticeship as a linotype operator with the *Paisley Daily Express*, where he also first came to grips with writing through compiling cricket reports to the exacting standards set by the paper's editor. He left after eight years to become a freelance journalist. Soon after he met Margaret Slater, who was to become his wife, and before long he abandoned the precarious life of the freelance to settle for the regular income of linotype operator for the then Glasgow *Evening Citizen*. Three years later, in June 1956, when the young couple were about to buy a home, Craig decided instead to buy a small letterpress printing business at 4 Colquhoun Street, Helensburgh. For a year he handset small commercial printing jobs until he amassed enough money to buy an old second-hand linotype machine from the *Scotsman* in Edinburgh. Helensburgh already had a weekly newspaper, the long established *Helensburgh and Gareloch Times.* Privately-owned by Macneur & Bryden Ltd., the stationers, printers and gift shop opposite the railway station in East Princes Street, it was a respected but conservative publication, and Craig began to dream of taking it on with his own paper. In January 1957 he had been joined by his younger brother Ronnie, a time-served compositor, after he was demobbed from the Scots Guards. Printing work was increasing, and they took on a young local lad, Howard McWilliam. Soon they bought a flatbed printing press and a second linotype machine to augment the equipment for the hot metal process from the *Scotsman*, and on May 24, 1957, the first *Helensburgh Advertiser* appeared. It was not a newspaper — it was a one-page coloured wallsheet, containing the steamer and bus timetables and paid advertising, which was published weekly and appeared on the walls of shops and businesses. After 15 weeks enough regular advertising had been generated to justify launching a four-page, five-column broadsheet newspaper, and the first issue went on sale on Friday August 30. Some 1,500 copies were printed and sold. Soon after their first journalist employee, very talented feature writer Betty Wood, joined and began a highly popular weekly column. Betty was the mother of Lynn Faulds Wood, the award-winning consumer affairs reporter on BBC television's *Watchdog* programme. The bright, breezy and humorous *Advertiser* — reported, subbed and typeset by Craig, printed by Ronnie and hand-folded by both with the help of Howard — had arrived in douce Helensburgh, and battle was joined with the Times. Craig said the small bold humorous paragraphs scattered throughout the paper were worth all the sensational page-leads in the world. A story was only a story when it had the remarkability factor, when people would say to each other 'did you see that' in the *Advertiser* or the *Reporter.* Soon a staff reporter was needed, and Graham Williams, another Paisley man, joined the firm. It was a competition which lasted till the mid-seventies, when the *Times* was turned into a free newspaper and then closed by Scottish and Universal Newspapers, who had acquired it from Macneur & Bryden. Within a few weeks of the *Advertiser's* launch the circulation had reached 3,000, compared with the 4,500 of the *Times,* and it was some eight years before the Times was overtaken. The secret was punchy, fearless and fun editorial, backed by campaigns such as to gain admission for the press to meetings of the Town Council of the time. Remarkably, aged only two and designed with a ragbag of old typefaces, the paper was highly commended in the sixth annual United Kingdom Newspaper Design Awards, the first of many awards to be won by the paper and its staff over the years.

On Friday August 4 1961 Craig was in Glasgow when he suddenly thought that he should return to the town. As he drove past Cardross Crematorium he saw a pall of smoke in the air over Helensburgh town centre . . . the Colquhoun Street printshop was on fire. Firemen saved the building, but the roof was lost and all the printing machinery was in a foot of water. Friends and other local firms rallied round, everyone rolled up their sleeves, and by Monday they were back in business with the machines working, but over ten tons of paper lost. The following year Craig and Ronnie moved the business to a former coalyard at 7-9 East King Street, and a new printing press was installed. Next year the paper went tabloid and reached 12 pages for the first time, and in 1964 they launched a sister weekly, the Dumbarton *County Reporter* (later to become the Dumbarton and Vale of Leven Reporter). As Craig (pictured with the chain of office of president of the Scottish Newspaper Publishers Association) was fond of saying, like Topsy the company, which now included a significant commercial printing operation, just growed to the point where it had 60 employees and was the area's biggest private employer. There were, of course, difficulties, not least when almost all the local advertisers pulled out because the paper ran an advertisement for a one-day sale in the Victoria Hall. The bright content of the paper appealed to local people, although in the early days many would not admit it — gardeners were sent to buy the paper, or it was discreetly placed inside the *Glasgow Herald.* Craig and Ronnie were undismayed, so long as they bought it and advertised in it. Summing up the early years, Craig wrote in typical flamboyant style in the 21st birthday edition in 1978: 'It can be fairly said that there was a time when the editorial team at the *Advertiser* were at risk. The paper came out once a week, but never weakly. From a policy of honest, straightforward reporting uninfluenced by money or muscle came the inevitable threats. Yes, we were burgled. But we sat knowingly in the dark with sceptical police officers and four intruders fell through a skylight into our arms. Yes, we were threatened by influential Helensburghians. But we ran reports of their court cases like everyone else's and in the end finally reaped their respect. Yes, we were confronted by physical violence. But we managed to avoid injury, printed the expose and made our locality a better place. Yes, we were offered bribes. But we steadfastly refused, did our job and rested well with a clear conscience. Yes, we were subjected to a form of blackmail by advertisers. But we stood firm against unreasonable demands, kept the paper free to publish and be damned, lost a bit of money as a result, winning in the end a reputation for straight reporting.' Once the business moved to East King Street, and although he gave up the editorship to Donald Fullarton after 12 years, Craig could not get away from his work — he and his wife moved into the adjoining house, Eastburn, and from 1966 when a new rotary press was installed, as soon as it was switched on the vibration could be felt in the sitting room floor. Craig's few outside interests were dominated by Helensburgh Rotary Club and the SNPA. He was a founder member of the rotary club, of which Ronnie too was a member, and later president and honorary member, and he was particularly associated with the very successful Helensburgh 80 and Helensburgh 90 exhibitions, run by the club in the Victoria Hall. Later in life he took up golf. When the four shareholders felt in 1985 that the time had come to sell the business, Craig deliberately sought out a buyer who would continue to develop the titles, ultimately choosing to sell to Express Newspapers, whose Scottish chairman Sir David McNee was an old friend. Sir David was at one time Chief Constable of Strathclyde and Commissioner of the Metropolitan Police in London. Three months after the completion, Express Newspapers were in turn bought by United Newspapers, and the *Advertiser* and Reporter became part of United Provincial Newspapers. Craig served as a non-executive director for a year, and his brother Ronnie was appointed managing director. In due course both left the firm, with Craig retiring and Ronnie and his late wife, Tillie, buying and running for some years the Helensburgh Fine Arts Gallery on West Clyde Street. In 1991, UPN sold their Scottish interests to the Clyde and Forth Press Group, owned by Iain and Deirdre Romanes, and the *Advertiser* returned to Scottish private family ownership. Under UPN the business moved to a shop and custom-built office premises at 15 Colquhoun Square, embracing new and ever-improving technology. Later, as part of the Clyde and Forth Press Group, and benefiting from massive investment in computer and network hardware and software, the *Advertiser* continued to produce award-winning journalists and photographers. However, like all newspapers, it has lost a large number of readers of its print edition to its own regularly updated website, a concept which would never have been thought of in 1957. It now has a sister radio station, Your Radio, The group photograph was taken outside the East King Street premises the day the paper was sold to Express Newspapers.

This photograph was taken outside the East King Street premises the day the *Helensburgh Advertiser* and *County Reporter* paper was sold to Express Newspapers. It shows (from left) Helensburgh man Ronnie Fowler of Express Newspapers, an Express executive, Craig Jeffrey, Sir David McNee, *Advertiser* chief cashier Mrs Freda Aram from Garelochhead, another Express executive, Ronnie Jeffrey, and managing editor Donald Fullarton

Chapter 58

THE GOLFER

Champion golfer Charlie Green

Born: 2 August, 1932, in Dumbarton.
Died: 28 January, 2013, in Cardross, aged 80

The word 'legend' may be much overused the modern sporting arena, but it is entirely appropriate in describing the late Charlie Green, who devoted his golfing career to the amateur game and enjoyed a level of success that is unlikely to be matched. In fact, no-one will probably come close, such was Green's prodigality, both in his 'regular' career then in the senior ranks, *writes Martin Dempster of The Scotsman*. One notable exception apart – he failed to win the Amateur Championship, the blue ribbon event in the unpaid ranks – every single trophy worth its salt in amateur golf has the name 'CW Green' inscribed on it at least once and, in most cases, it appears frequently. The Scottish Amateur Championship, for instance, fell to Green three times – 1970, 1982 and 1983 – while he was a finalist in the Scottish Golf Union's flagship event on two other occasions. In the last of those triumphs, Green beat Dunbar's John Huggan, 27 years his junior, by one hole in their 36-hole title showdown at Gullane. 'Charlie had retired from playing competitive golf when he won his last two Scottish Amateur Championships,' said Glencorse's George Macgregor, the man Green had beaten, again on the final green, at Carnoustie 12 months earlier, having opened his account in the event by holing a 6ft putt at the last to beat Hugh Stuart at Royal Aberdeen. Green also chalked up two Scottish Stroke-Play Championship successes – 1975 and 1984 – and was runner-up in that event twice as well while other notable triumphs with a card and pencil in his hand came in the Lytham Trophy (1970 and 1974), Tennant Cup (1968, 1970 and 1975), Craigmillar Park Open (1971, 1972 and 1977), Edward Trophy (1968, 1973, 1974 and 1975) and Cameron Corbett Vase (1968).In his beloved Dunbartonshire – his home club was Dumbarton though he played most of his golf at Cardross, where he lived close to the 18th – Green won the country stroke-play and match-play championship five times each while he was also a three-time West of Scotland Open champion. At no stage in his career was Green, a long-time salesman for whisky company Allied Distillers in Dumbarton, tempted into turning professional. Even though he gave a good account of himself on one of the biggest stages in the game when winning the Silver Medal as leading amateur behind Arnold Palmer in the 1962 Open Championship, he was content to play the game for fun and, of course, the voucher which he picked up with unerring regularity when club Opens were popular. 'Charlie was a licence to print money in those days as he would win £100 vouchers almost every weekend,' recalled Cliff Jones, who, in his days as an assistant professional at Cardross, cherished the regular Friday afternoon games he enjoyed with Green. 'Charlie was unbeatable back then and it certainly wasn't just down to luck or anything like that,' added Jones, now the club professional at Glencorse and who shared Green's passion for the Sons, Dumbarton Football Club. He was a regular at Boghead Park on a Saturday with his Golf Club pals Andy Neil, John Miller and Johnny Broadley, father of the sportswriter, Ian. 'He was the first guy I came across with a work ethic – he'd come down to the club and practice for hours.' In addition to all the individual success that hard work brought – in his 50s he won the Senior Open Amateur Championship six times and the Scottish Seniors Championship on five occasions – Green also enjoyed an incredible career in team golf. With 63 appearances under his belt, he was Scotland's most-capped player, enjoying six outright triumphs and three shared successes in the Home Internationals, an event he played in 18 times in a row (19 if you include the 1979 contest that only involved Scotland and England, due to an outbreak of foot and mouth in Ireland). In Great Britain & Ireland colours, he made five appearances in the Walker Cup, an event he also had the honour of participating in twice as captain. On the second occasion – at Pine Valley, New Jersey, in 1985 – his side included a certain Colin Montgomerie, who also played under Green in two Eisenhower Trophy teams (1984 and 1986). Prior to that, Green had also held the Scottish captaincy, finishing in that role in 1983, the year he was awarded an OBE for his services to golf. Three years ago, Green travelled through to Edinburgh to attend the last day of the Craigmillar Park Open, an event for which he had a great affinity. Standing at the back of the 18th green before doing the honours at the prize-giving, he admitted to feeling a sense of incredulity at seeing Kilmacolm's Matthew Clark post a winning aggregate of 20-under-par to follow in his own spike marks on the capital course. Fittingly, Clark is a career amateur, just as Green was, but, in general, that environment and the attitudes of those in it has changed enormously from the days when Green, the aforementioned Stuart and Macgregor, Alan Brodie, Ian Hutcheon, Gordon Cosh, Sandy Saddler and Sandy Pirie were all totally committed to the unpaid ranks. Not that Green seemed to mind, having gleaned nothing but pleasure from a remarkable career. 'I was 16 when I started the game,' he recalled in an interview last year, soon after he had been diagnosed with cancer. 'My dad was a member at Dumbarton and he introduced me to it. It was swimming and football I was keen on at the time, but they quickly got dropped. It was an instant love affair with golf, I was dead keen. It's been a good game to me. I had some very good times and the good times seemed to last a long time.' The impact Green had on Scottish amateur golf will last forever, his string of successes recorded in black-and-white likely to provoke gapes of astonishment from future generations as they flick through record books. Dean Robertson, a former Scottish Amateur champion who went on to become a European Tour winner, came from a different generation to Green but, in paying tribute to him, he summed up his stature in the Scottish game. 'If he and DB [the late D Barclay Howard] get together in an after-life, what a partnership that will be,' said Robertson. Charlie Green is survived by his wife, Dorothy, and daughter, Debbie.

Dumbarton to the spikes on his golf shoes – Charlie Green, in short trousers, is on the extreme right in this old picture with neighbours and friends in Park Avenue, Newtown, just a three iron from his beloved Boghead, home of Dumbarton Football Club.

Chapter 59

THE CHIEF EXECUTIVE

Gilbert Lawrie of Dumbarton Football Club.

Born: Vale of Leven, July 4, 1960
Died: Houston, Renfrewshire, January 21, 2016

Gilbert Lawrie, chief executive of Dumbarton Football Club and chartered surveyor, has died at his home in Houston, Renfrewshire, aged 55. A rotund, outgoing man who often wore a 'bunnet' to his team's matches, Gilbert was a football fan from childhood. He then graduated from the terracing at Boghead Park to become a kenspeckle figure in the directors' boxes and boardrooms of Scotland's senior football clubs.

Dumbarton, the Sons of the Rock, were always Gilbert's team and he supported them fervently from his time as a pupil at Dumbarton's Knoxland Primary School, whose black and gold uniform colours were identical to the team's. It could also be said of Gilbert Lawrie that he was the man who saved Sons from extinction at a crisis point in their proud history, which dates back to 1872 when a group of shinty players decided to switch codes after watching a match between Queen's Park and Vale of Leven at Hampden Park in Glasgow. Dumbarton first won the Scottish League in 1891 and celebrated its centenary in 1972, which was around the time when Lawrie left Knoxland and went on to continue his education at Dumbarton Academy.

A bright pupil, who was especially good at Maths, Lawrie complete his education to qualify as a chartered surveyor at Glasgow College of Building and Technology. Lawrie's Seventies school years were amongst the best in Sons' history when they won the Second Division Championship and were for a time in the top division. Meanwhile, he landed a job at Tennent's Wellpark Brewery in the East End of the city where he was mentored by one of the directors, Robert Campbell Ward, who just happened also to be a director of Dumbarton FC. Lawrie went on to be successful in the commercial property business when he moved to Bell Ingram and eventually on to the board at Chestertons Estates. He was the Scottish director in charge of the care and maintenance of prestigious private properties and government buildings in Scotland. Apart from watching football, his leisure time was taken up in Dumbarton Riverside Parish Church where he was a well-known and respected Boys Brigade Officer. After his first marriage, to Lesley, which unfortunately failed to last, Gilbert Lawrie married in 2007 Dumbarton woman Fiona McLaren who, his friends say was 'the true love of his life'. This was a tragically short-lived marriage as Fiona sadly passed away 18 months later around Hogmanay, which thereafter became an annual period of mourning rather than celebration for her husband. Gilbert and Fiona were always welcoming and generous hosts to family and friends and they all enjoyed these social evenings immensely.

Following Fiona's death, Gilbert immersed himself in his work and particularly in Dumbarton FC where he concentrated full-time on his CEO duties. He was instrumental in the present owners of the club, Brabco, purchasing most of the shares and securing the move to a new stadium in the shadow of Dumbarton Rock, where they are today taking part in the Championship League. Right up to the time of his death, Gilbert Lawrie was playing a pivotal role in progressing the aim of Brabco, the DFC majority shareholding consortium, to move the club to a new ground for Sons at Dalmoak, near Renton, Dunbartonshire.

That process is ongoing. His friend David Carson said: 'Gilbert was a quiet but formidable 'backroom' operator and presence at DFC and helped steer the club to safer waters during a few periods of concern and uncertainty.'

Tributes to Gilbert Lawrie have been flooding into his social media site since news of his death broke on Friday morning. Dumbarton fans showed their appreciation of his life and work with a minute's applause before their match with Raith Rovers at Stark's Park on Saturday. Gilbert was a sociable person who liked nothing better than to go out after the match to his local pub in Houston for a few drinks with football friends, who included Alistair McCoy, formerly manager of Rangers. He would later watch the sport on television and listen to music relaxing at home. Occasionally he enjoyed good food and wine with friends at his favourite restaurant, La Parmigiana, in Glasgow. Gilbert was a lifelong fan of The Who with vast knowledge and collection of the band's CDs. He was a fanatical music devotee with huge recording collection across a whole spectrum of genres. He also loved dogs and would walk his across the fields near Houston. Born in Vale of Leven, Gilbert was the only child of Jim Lawrie, a director of Allied Distillers, Dumbarton, and his wife, Jessie, by whom he is survived.

Dumbarton FC's stadium at Dumbarton Rock, which was the brainchild of Gilbert Lawrie. *Picture by Bill Heaney*

Chapter 60

THE PEACE CAMPAIGNER

Margaret Harrison, peace campaigner and poet

Born on May 5, 1918, in Dumbarton
Died on April 15, 2015, in Castle Douglas

Margaret Harrison, who was one of Scotland's best known campaigners against nuclear weapons and helped to found the Faslane Peace Camp, has died aged 96. Margaret was arrested at least 14 times while taking part in demonstrations against the Polaris and Trident missiles and submarines based at Dunoon and Coulport on the Firth of Clyde. She was also taken into custody by the police at the annual Easter demonstration at the Atomic Weapons Research Establishment at Aldermaston in Berkshire, Greenham Common and the United States air base at Molesworth in Cambridgeshire. Her involvement in the peace movement arose naturally from her strong Christian convictions. She always said in her straightforward uncomplicated way that Jesus told us to love one another so killing people must be wrong. This was a belief from which this quiet, dignified woman who brought up a family and wrote poetry in her old age never wavered her whole life. Margaret's beliefs underpinned her desire to see an end to poverty and war in the world. With her husband, Bobby, she was a well kent face at the Clyde Naval Base at Faslane and the US Polaris missile base in the Holy Loch at Dunoon. The Harrisons always went as a family to the Aldermaston marches where in the 1950s and 1960s thousands of banner carrying and placard waving protestors walked 52 miles (83km) between London and Berkshire. This was the high point of the Campaign for Nuclear Disarmament (CND) calendar at Easter. Margaret, who hated the formality of being called Mrs, also attended the annual pensioners' gathering at Greenham Common and was regularly seen showing solidarity with fellow peace activists at RAF Molesworth. This was while facilities were being constructed for the United States Air Force in Europe to support ground-launched cruise missile operations in the early 1980s. It was here Margaret began a lifelong friendship with the internationally renowned peace campaigner Jean Kaye Hutchison, who was deeply involved in the women's peace camps at Greenham Common and Aldermaston. She was thrown out of the House of Commons during a protest there in 1991. Margaret Harrison knew well what it was to be lifted by the police and then spend a night in the cells during demonstrations. About 1962, she decided to not pay the fine and go to jail to highlight the cause for peace. She was however furious when a newspaper paid the fine in order to get a story for their front page – 'especially when they printed a lot of nonsense.' Margaret and Bobby were presented with a crystal bowl by the CND in 1970s for their tireless work for peace which included helping to establish the universally known peace camp at the Faslane gates of the Clyde Naval Base on the Gareloch. They were also awarded the Freedom of Dumbarton for their work for peace along with her sister, Bee, and Church of Scotland minister Arthur McEwan for their work for Amnesty International. Margaret said that one of the most wonderful experiences of her life happened in 1981 when she and her husband took part in a Peace Pilgrimage from Iona to Canterbury. Born in Dumbarton, Margaret was the daughter of John George and Maggie

Burnett of Dalreoch Terrace in Dennystown and later Dumbuie Avenue in Silverton. She had two sisters, Ruth and Lizzie (Bee), to whom she was very close all of their lives. Margaret went to Knoxland Primary School and Dumbarton Academy and spent a happy childhood in the east end of the town. She enjoyed sharing memories of her favourite haunts up the glen at Strowans Well to pick primroses and being chased by the gamekeeper on Lord Overtoun's estate. Her first and only job was as a tracer in Denny's shipyard drawing office where she happily worked for ten years until her marriage to Bobby on June 1, 1945, in St Augustine's Church Scottish Episcopal Church in Dumbarton High Street. She always said that the work was 'a bit tedious' but she enjoyed the company in the office. By her own admission, Margaret was clever but lacking in confidence, which is why she didn't go on to higher education. The Harrisons had two daughters, Ruth and Anne, five grandchildren, Sarah, Rachael, Ewan, Douglas and Callum, and six great grandchildren, James. Patrick, Sean, Lachlan, Loic and Taylor, and Margaret is survived by them. During her time at Denny's Margaret's interests included acting. She was a member of Scottish People's Theatre (SPT) when their Little Theatre at Bankend was destroyed by an enemy bomb in 1941. In a little book of Dumbarton Memories Margaret writes that when she heard of the bomb her first thought was that she had just polished the seats in the auditorium. She joined Dumbarton Peoples' Theatre where she had a lot of fun and where she took part in Romeo and Juliet. Margaret usually arrived at her work on a Saturday morning with her rucksack, ready to go off with her friends or sisters youth hostelling around Loch Lomond and the Trossachs. It was on one of these weekends that Bobby, a Liverpool man who adopted Scotland as his home, came cycling into her life at Monachyle, near Balquidder. Margaret was a life-long member of the Scottish Episcopal Church, firstly St. Augustine's and then St. Mungo's, Alexandria where she moved to support a friend who had become the vicar there. She taught Sunday school for about 40 years or more and during the war, when she was expected to work on Sundays, she just told her boss she had to leave early to teach her Sunday school class. Her family would not have called Margaret Harrison a feminist. She was a woman who was traditional in the raising of her children and never would have left them to go to work.

She did, of course, believe in equality for women but it wasn't directly one of her 'causes'. Her work was to do what she could as a mother and housewife to make the world a better place. Margaret always wanted to write and joined the Alexandria Writing Group, where she was made an honorary member and had a collection of the group's poems dedicated to her when she left Dumbarton aged 95 to go and live with her daughter, Anne, and her husband, Eric Macarthur, in Castle Douglas, Kirkcudbrightshire. Many of her writings reflected her deep desire to see an end to poverty and war. She loved to entertain audiences with funny recitations, some of which she adapted to suit the situation, acting all the parts with different voices and accents. Margaret continued to do this after her move to Castle Douglas, entertaining the other senior citizens at the day care group which she attended twice a week. Throughout her life, Margaret welcomed lonely people into the family, providing hospitality by sharing meals and even holidays, always putting the needs of others before her own. This was something which her husband didn't always find easy. She had a particular compassion for people with mental health problems as she herself had gone through a period of severe depression and knew how debilitating and isolating that could be. She spent many years visiting regularly patients in Gartnavel Hospital in Glasgow. Excepting a few months being wardens of the youth hostel at Kinlochard in the Trossachs, where during a drought they did the washing in Loch Ard, Margaret and Bobby spent the rest of their lives in Dumbarton, where he had a cycle shop and bicycle repair business. She embraced her new life in South West Scotland and enjoyed being part of the family but never forgot her dear friends in Dumbarton and surrounding area. Although only spending two years there, she touched the lives of the many people in Castle Douglas who got to know and love her. In his own autobiography, Bobby said of Margaret that she was' the kind of person who could never deceive anyone even if she tried, and I have never met a kinder, more trusting or unsophisticated person before or since'. This sums up the feelings of her many friends and family who will miss her greatly. The Rev John Ainslie, who is coordinator for the Scottish Campaign for Nuclear Disarmament, said: 'Margaret Harrison was an inspiration for many people of all ages in the peace movement. Along with her husband Bobby, she played a key role in establishing the peace camp at Faslane. Her friendly attitude and resilience encouraged others to join her in the struggle against nuclear weapons. She will be sorely missed by those who strive for nuclear disarmament.' Louise Robertson, from Balloch, a well known member of CND and Woman's Aid, said: 'Margaret was a peace activist, a poet and an inspiration to many. She was always full of hope and optimism and only ever spoke well of people. She devoted her life to peace and she will always be remembered with a smile.' There was a memorial and thanksgiving service for Margaret in St. Mungo's Scottish Episcopal Church, Alexandria, followed by a gathering for reminiscences and refreshments in the church hall afterwards.

Margaret Harrison and friends founded the peace camp at Faslane.

Chapter 61

THE CHAIRMAN

James Lumsden with his dog on the banks of Loch Lomond.

Lawyer and businessman James Lumsden, or Hamish as he was more generally known, who died in March 2013, aged 98, was one of Scotland's best-known lawyers and businessmen. He was born at Arden House, the family home on Loch Lomondside, to James Robert Lumsden, who was later knighted, and Henrietta Macfarlane Lumsden, nee Reid. His grandfather was Sir James Lumsden, a former Lord Provost of Glasgow. James was educated at Cargilfield School, Edinburgh, where he was head boy and from where he won a scholarship to Rugby School. From there he went on to win a further scholarship to Corpus Christi College, Cambridge. Handsome, urbane and hugely intelligent, he studied Classics and Law at Cambridge and secured degrees in both, including a First Class Honours in Law for which he won the Bishop Green Cup in 1936. He completed his studies with an LLB postgraduate degree at the University of Glasgow while also working as a law apprentice with the firm of Mackenzie, Roberton, where his great uncle, Robert Mackenzie of Caldarvan, had been a senior partner until his death in 1936.

During his second year at the University of Glasgow he joined the 74th Heavy Anti-Aircraft regiment as a second lieutenant. His unit was mobilised just days before the declaration of war and thus his three-year apprenticeship with Mackenzie Roberton was deemed to have been completed. His unit was initially deployed to cover the ICI works at Mossend, Lanarkshire, and subsequently at vulnerable and important sites around the Clyde basin, including Rosneath Peninsula and Cardross. He was posted as part of a cadre to train a new AA battery at Oswestry, where he was swiftly promoted to the rank of captain before moving to Wick and from there, within just a few weeks, to brigade major in King's Park, Glasgow. It was while in this post at the headquarters of 42 AA Brigade that he was in charge of the Operations Room during two nights of the Clydebank Blitz in 1941. A year later, he was posted to Edinburgh, where he served as an intelligence officer before being transferred to Southampton to command the AA regiments deployed in that area to cover the Normandy invasion, which took place in June, 1944. He also had to deal with the VI flying bombs aimed at London and it was at that time he was awarded the MBE (Military). He was demobilised on his 31st birthday. In April 1946, he joined the Glasgow law firm Maclay Murray and Spens on secondment from Mackenzie Roberton to gain experience in company and commercial law before returning to Mackenzie Roberton as a partner. However, later that year he was offered a partnership by Maclay Murray that he readily accepted. In January 1947, while on a skiing holiday in Davos, he became engaged to Sheila Cross from Kirkcudbrightshire. They were married in Borgue Parish Church in June, 1947. It was the start of 61 years of a very happy marriage and partnership. They made their home at Bannachra, near Helensburgh, on the Arden Estate and it was there that they raised three sons, James, Ian and Michael who (together with nine grandchildren and one great grandchild) survive them today. Bannachra was their home for 54 of these years until they moved to a smaller house at Craigendoran, near Helensburgh.

Hamish Lumsden had a remarkable career in the law and in business. Having become a partner in the Maclay Murray and Spens in 1947, he stayed with the firm, in which he became the senior partner, until 1982 when he retired aged 67. With his undoubted legal talent and high standards, both moral and ethical, came the privilege of serving in many different areas. He was a member of the Jenkins Committee on Company Law Reform in 1960 as one of two representing Scotland. He was a Fellow of the Law Society of Scotland and a member of the Royal Faculty of Procurators, Glasgow. He served as a director of a variety of companies from about the mid-1950s until he resigned on his 70th birthday, including Scottish Union and National Insurance Company, which was taken over by Norwich Union when he was chairman; Bank of Scotland, the Weir Group, William Baird, Scottish Provident, Murray Johnstone and many others including many of the Investment Trusts managed by Murray Johnstone. He served as chairman of many of them. In 1959 he joined Burmah Oil and rose to chairman and saw that company through some very difficult times. He was chairman of the General Commission of Income Tax for many years, a Deputy Lieutenant of Dunbartonshire since 1966, a member of the Royal Company of Archers since 1963, and the oldest and longest-serving member of Prestwick Golf Club. He was a staunch supporter of the Conservative Party since his Cambridge days. Locally he was a very active member of the Dunbartonshire constituency including various stints as constituency chairman and latterly honorary president. Hamish Lumsden was a popular figure in the community on Loch Lomondside. He was an elder of Luss Parish Church since 1950 and treasurer for about 30 years and also a member of Dumbarton Presbytery of the Church of Scotland. He was the driving force behind the Dunbartonshire County Agricultural Show, where he was an enthusiastic MC on the megaphone and where his wife, Sheila, organised the Scottish Women's Rural Institute stalls filled with beautiful craftwork and delicious home baking. He was also a family man and family and family life were very important to him. He and Sheila were married for 61 years until she pre-deceased him in 2008. Luss Parish Church was filled by family and friends for a thanksgiving service, when his eldest son James paid tribute to his father's life and work.

Luss Parish Church, where James Lumsden was an elder and benefactor to the village kirk, and Arden House, Loch Lomond.
Picture by Bill Heaney.

Chapter 62

THE FARMER

Robert Lennox OBE

Robert J. Lennox, the well-known Loch Lomondside sheep farmer and Kirk elder who gave so much to his community, died in April, 2015, aged 90. He was a farmer, councillor, company director and long-serving Church of Scotland elder whose fund-raising skills helped to save one of Scotland's most famous 'wedding churches' on the Banks of Loch Lomond, will be sadly missed. Robbie was born at Shemore Farm in Luss to Robert and Margaret Lennox and although he was an only child his cousins were more like brothers and sisters to him, in particular Craig Davie. This was fortunate since they were there to help out when Robbie's father died and he was left at the age of just 16 with the huge responsibility of looking after their Shemore and Shantron farms in the scenic hills which overlook the loch. He attended tiny Muirlands Primary School in Arden and Vale of Leven Academy, Alexandria, where again he made good friends and one of them, Frazer Mellor, went on to work on the farm with him for about four years until he got his own farm to manage in Northumberland. He was Robbie's best man at both weddings. On his 17th birthday Robbie drove a lorry full of potatoes to Partick in Glasgow having never sat a driving test due to the war going on and he was in the Home Guard, having lied about his age to join. He was always a progressive, innovative and forward thinking farmer who could 'think outside the box' before that phrase was invented. In the early 1940s before mains electricity came to the area he built a water wheel in a fast flowing river and linked it to a generator to provide electricity to the farm. Robbie started putting the farm accounts on to computer when Amstrad launched their first PC before there were farm account packages available. In October, 1952, he married Ailsa Howie, of Drumfork Farm, Helensburgh, and they had two children, Bobby and Margaret, and five grandchildren, Gill, Allan, Kay, David and Michael and Andrew, who unfortunately died five years ago. There are two great grandchildren, Blair and Ailsa. Ailsa died in 1988 and six years later, on January 25, 1994, Robbie married Marie Duncan, of Old Kilpatrick. He was a farmer first and foremost and on the Saturday before he died he was in the sheep yards helping his son, Bobby and daughter-in-law Anne with sheep. Anne said: 'Robbie was a typical farmer. He never retired.' He never retired either from his post as Session Clerk at Luss Parish Church, the lochside setting where so many celebrities have chosen to be married over a long number of years. As an elder he served the tiny kirk for over 60 years and as Session Clerk he was always at the door greeting parishioners and visitors and he stood beside the minister as the congregation left after the service. He would have served 50 years as Session Clerk in August this year and served as Representative Elder for Luss on Dumbarton Presbytery for over 40 years.

Sheep grazing in the hills above Loch Lomond.

Muirlands School and Luss Parish Church

The Rev Dane Sherrard, who recently retired from Luss, said: 'I remember Robbie and his wife at the Bible Study groups we shared in together every Monday evening for more years than I care to remember. I remember his encouragement as we started our youth programme, rebuilt the Pilgrimage Centre and created the bridge over the Luss Water to the Glebe. It was built by members of the Royal Engineers. I remember the great year of 2010 when we celebrated fifteen hundred years of continuous Christianity by Loch Lomondside, a year-long celebration filled with activities at the centre of which Robbie was always to be found as we welcomed visitors and told the congregation's story. He was a totally remarkable man.' Despite an accident which left him with only one kidney, Robbie was forever travelling and learning about farming. His activities within the Young Farmers led to a scholarship and took him to Africa and New Zealand and Australia as he studied sheep farming around the world. He was held in high regard in farming circles throughout Scotland and became a councillor on the old Dunbartonshire County Council, where he sat on a committee which monitored progress on the building of the Erskine Bridge. Always the church had first call on his time., however, and he and the late Hamish Lumsden, the kirk treasurer who was for a time chairman of Burma Oil, he spear-headed the project to totally refurbish the church. They raised funds estimated at around £1 million from Historic Scotland and the Heritage Lottery Fund and by also setting up a church gift shop to raise money locally. In later years, he would come and take a turn as beadle during the wedding season, ensuring that brides' nerves were calmed and visitors were welcomed. Mr Sheppard said: 'Not only was he the embodiment of the church to many people, but he also stood for all that was good in our village. He was a friend to many, an example of all that is good and honest and true to his community, and the best Session Clerk a minister could ever wish to have.' Robbie had a sailing yacht on Loch Lomond in the 1960s and the family and friends enjoyed trips out to the islands on the loch. He was a well-travelled person having visited countries with the Young Farmers and then his Nuffield Scholarship. This started his interest in travel and went on to visit Brazil, Mexico, China, and then Egypt on honeymoon with Marie and they continued travelling to the Holy Land, Thailand, the Canaries and many more countries. His grandchildren reckon he visited about 40 countries in all and he always had a camera or a video camera to record travel and family events. Robbie who attended West of Scotland Agricultural College in 1946 and was awarded the Bronze Medal was elected a governor of the college in 1964. He was a founder member of Loch Lomond Young Farmers Club in 1944 and chairman of the National Farmers Union in 1977. Robbie was awarded a Nuffield Scholarship in 1963 to study the wool production aspects of sheep farming in Australia, New Zealand and South Africa. He was appointed to the Scottish Agricultural Wages Board on which he served for 26 year and the Agricultural Training Board, the NFU Mutual Insurance Society, where he was the Scottish Director in 1965 and served for 26 years, the Department of Agriculture's Farming Advisory committee and the Home Grown Timber Advisory Committee. Other important posts he held include a directorship of Caledonian Marts (Stirling) Ltd., the Animal Diseases Research Association. and the Scottish Agricultural Arbiters Association. He was a member of Dumbarton County Council for six years prior to regionalisation and as convenor of Roads Committee sat on the Erskine Bridge Joint Sub-Committee. He helped to found the Luss & Arden Community Council and was its chairman for the first 20 years. Robbie also sat on the Secretary of State's Loch Lomond and Trossachs working party, drawing up proposals for a National Park and was a Justice of the Peace on the Bench at Dumbarton. He was awarded the OBE in 1977 and became a Fellow of the Royal Agricultural Society in 1987.

Sheep farmers together – Robert Lennox OBE (right) and his son, Robbie, pictured on the Lomond hills looking after their flock.

Chapter 63

THE AMBASSADOR'S WIFE

Margaret Kearns Meehan

Born: Yoker, Glasgow, March 4, 1923
Died: Helensburgh, Dunbartonshire, March 15, 2015

Margaret Kearns Meehan, who died has peacefully at her home in Helensburgh, was the dedicated and talented wife of Francis J Meehan, a career diplomat who became an ambassador in the United States Foreign Service. She was 92.

Mrs Meehan supported her husband, brought up and arranged the education of their four children and entertained and cooked for diplomats and VIP guests during the 66 years of their long and happy marriage. Margaret had a remarkable and exciting but frequently stressful life during which she lived in 23 different houses and embassies in the United States and Eastern Europe before finally settling in their beautiful home in Helensburgh, overlooking the Firth of Clyde. Her husband was the US ambassador in Czechoslovakia, East Germany and Poland during the Cold War and Mrs Meehan's considerable skills as an organiser and hostess at receptions and dinners was legendary. Mr Meehan said: "She was a terrific organiser and cook. They say that moving house is one of the most stressful things a person can do in their lifetime, but Margaret took it all in her stride as we moved from house to house a remarkable 23 times."

Margaret, who was born in Yoker, was third of eight children of Patrick and Annie Kearns, and was educated at Our Holy Redeemer primary and secondary school in Clydebank. Her siblings included Patrick Kearns who won the Distinguished Flying Medal (DFM) while serving in with the Royal Air Force in India and Burma; the Rev Hugh Kearns, who was Catholic chaplain to the British troops serving in Northern Ireland during the Troubles of the 1970s, and Jim Kearns who was a popular teacher at St Patrick's High School, Dumbarton. Margaret's education was interrupted by the Clydebank Blitz in March, 1941, and the Kearns family were evacuated to Helensburgh. They spent most of the rest of the war billeted under the roof of the Blackie book publishing family in the Charles Rennie Mackintosh-designed The Hill House before moving back to Clydebank.

Her husband, who had also been evacuated after the Blitz, in his case from Dalmuir to Dumbarton, was a regular visitor to the Kearns family home in Helensburgh and Clydebank. Frank and Margaret were part of a happy and talented circle of friends from family, church, school and university, whose shared interests included hill walking, music, football and tennis. Frank had been born in East Orange, New Jersey, in 1924, but had returned home to Clydebank as a small child with his mother who was homesick. He went to St Stephen's PS in Dalmuir and St Patrick's High School in Dumbarton and graduated MA from the University of Glasgow before taking up a sub-editing post on the then *Glasgow Herald*. He later was awarded an LLD (Hon) from Glasgow. Margaret joined the Army (ATS) and worked in communications. She and Frank were courting when he received his call-up papers for the US Army and was sent to Fontainebleau in France to complete his infantry training. Margaret and Frank were married in 1949 in Manhattan, New York, where she had emigrated to work initially as a child minder and become reunited with her husband-to-be. Frank was a talented linguist who spoke fluent German and Russian. He entered the US Foreign Service in 1951 and was a clerk in the American Consulate in Bremen and a junior officer in the Marshall Plan Administration.

Margaret was at Frank's side when he graduated MPA from Harvard in 1957 and rose through the ranks of the US Foreign Service, specialising in Eastern European and Communist affairs. His diplomatic postings included Hungary, where the Meehans were friends of Cardinal József Mindszenty, who for five decades personified uncompromising opposition to fascism and communism in Hungary in support of religious freedom and spent eight years in prison before being freed in the Hungarian Revolution of 1956 and granted political asylum by the United States embassy in Budapest, where he lived for the next 15 years; Moscow in the aftermath of the U2 spy plane incident in 1960; East Germany when spies were being swapped prior to the collapse of the Berlin Wall, and Warsaw, when the Solidarity trade union emerged under Lech Walesa and General Jaruzelski declared martial law.

Margaret met world leaders and plenipotentiaries and travelled with her husband to a number of official engagements, including a meeting with Pope John Paul II in Vatican City. She was a delightful conversationalist and an excellent cook, organising and hosting with her husband dinners and receptions for events such as the July 4 US National Day celebrations. Mrs Meehan was renowned for her sense of humour and left a lasting impression on the many American and foreign diplomats and dignitaries whom she met in the embassies in Prague, Warsaw and Berlin between 1979 and 1989. She loved ballet, music, reading, flowers and sewing and became actively engaged with the interior design of some of the embassies in which her family lived. All the while she was involved in bringing up and overseeing the education of her four children – Anne, Catherine, Frances and Jim. Margaret's life was exciting and exhausting at the same time and the eyes of the world were on Eastern Europe during that decade, but she was always there to give unstinting support to her husband. Mrs Meehan was a marvellous story teller - she had lots to tell stories about

– but she never forgot her roots in Clydebank, which she visited often to be with family and friends during her long and fulfilled lifetime. She loved the shipbuilding town where she had so many friends, having worked there in the telephone exchange, and her father had been the champion of Clydebank Bowling Club in the 1930s and her grandfather a founding member of the club in 1884. Margaret, who some years ago suffered a stroke followed by a long period of illness and incapacity with Alzheimer's, was cared for by her devoted husband and children up to the moment of her death. She is survived by her husband, Frank, their four children, seven grandchildren and four great grandchildren.

Chapter 64

THE VOLUNTEER

Nurse and hospital volunteer
Born in Dumbarton on September 29, 1919
Died in Vale of Leven on April 5, 2015

Rose Peacock Dunnigan, who was an RAF nurse and later a diversional therapist at Vale of Leven Hospital where she volunteered until she was 90, has died aged 95. Diversional therapy was an arts and crafts discipline in Scotland's NHS hospitals before it became a priority to move patients through the wards as quickly as possible to prevent bed blocking. It involved the provision of leisure time pursuits such as sewing and embroidery and participating in social events and days out to the country for patients. Rose was born in Dumbarton and went to school at Knoxland Primary School and Dumbarton Academy. She was one of three children, one of whom was Lawrence Peacock, who became a well known councillor in Old Kilpatrick. During the Second World War, Rose served as a nurse in the RAF with a glider detachment in Norfolk. Margaret Hastings, a superintendent physiotherapist at Vale of Leven Hospital, said: 'Many were the stories she told us about her experiences there. I'm not sure what she did immediately after the war, but she did return to Dumbarton and looked after her mother.' Rose married Bill Dunnigan, an engineer, in 1949 and Ian, their only child, was born a year later. The family lived initially in Haldane before moving to Beaton Road in Balloch when an estate of new houses was in Dalvait. Rose stayed at home looking after Ian and got involved with Bridge Street Church of Scotland in Alexandria where Bill became an elder. She was involved with setting up community facilities in Haldane. She took up employment at the old Henry Brock hospital in Alexandria working as a diversional therapist with continuing care patients around 1965. Rose worked at that time to the direction of the matron, who regularly popped in for a tea and a biscuit with the patients. It was in the Henry Brock days that she started taking patients out on the hospital bus, trips round the Three Lochs with a stop for ice cream in Helensburgh. In 1977 she had great pleasure in moving so the new Care of the Elderly Unit attached to Vale of Leven Hospital and now worked as part of the occupational therapy department. Rose badgered the hospital management to replace their ageing bus, which she achieved in the early 1980s. She also organised outings for Christmas shopping to the Thistle Shopping Centre in Stirling, one of the first covered centres most suitable for disabled access and was always warmly welcomed by the centre staff. Dumbarton People's Theatre and other amateur dramatics groups would send her free tickets for pantomimes and drama productions and after a day's work, Rose would continue working, rope in more volunteers and take continuing care and Day Hospital patients out for fish and chips and an evening at the Denny Civic Theatre. With two continuing care wards with some 60 patients - Mrs D's room was often bursting at the seams as she had women patients sewing, weaving and knitting. How many stools, peg bags and blankets there are in Dunbartonshire originating from Mrs D's room is a matter for conjecture, but there must be hundreds if not thousands. Apart from the patients, Mrs D, as Rose was known to everyone at the hospital, looked after the staff by making sure the kettle was on for a tea break or helping with running repairs. She was a dab hand with a needle and thread and the sewing machine. Reaching 65 in 1984 meant that Rose was forced to retire - not that she ever let anyone know how old she was. She went on a visit to London for her birthday and then returned to Ward 15 on a voluntary basis doing what she had done for the past 20 years as a volunteer. In 1995 she was recognised for her voluntary service with an MBE from the Queen and she continued as a volunteer until 2009. Accompanied by her son Ian, she attended Holyrood for her investiture and in honour of the award the hospital held a reception for patients, staff and friends to offer their congratulations. Rose gradually reduced the number of days she had been volunteering and recognised that after a half century of caring for others, it was time to put herself first. Rose was a regular worshipper at Alexandria Parish Church and supported coffee afternoons and fetes - usually by serving teas and working in the kitchen. Members of the congregation looked after Rose during the final weeks of her life and her niece, Doris, and her husband Philip Jones, who did a reading at her funeral service, were regular visitors. Her funeral service, conducted by the Rev Liz Houston, the minister at Alexandria Parish Church, was followed by final committal at Cardross Crematorium.

Chapter 65

THE VALEMAN

Tom Glen

Journalist and businessman
Born: April 18, 1909
Died: July 16, 2010

Tom Glen, who died at his home in Auchterarder at the age of 101, was a late starter in journalism and photography, but he became one of Scotland's best known freelance newspapermen and later a prominent businessman in the Vale of Leven. His mother died in a tragic accident when he was just three years old, and Glen was brought up by his grandmother at Sandbank, Bonhill, where he attended Jamestown Primary School and later Vale of Leven Academy. Unquestionably a talented scholar, he regretted that he was unable to pursue an academic career. In the harsh economic climate of the times, he was obliged to leave school at the age of 14 and follow his father into the silk dyeing industry at Levenbank Works, where he started out as a message boy. Of his own volition, Glen went to night school to learn business studies and successfully completed all the courses necessary to qualify him as a teacher of shorthand and typing. He achieved a shorthand speed of 140 words a minute, a skill he honed taking notes of the minister's sermon in his local parish church on a Sunday and which he later put to good use as a journalist, reporting courts and council meetings. He taught night school classes in Clydebank and Vale of Leven and even now his family meet former pupils, mostly women, who fondly recall learning their secretarial skills from him. Glen moved to the giant Singer sewing machine factory in Clydebank in 1934, where was employed as a stores clerk. He left as chief clerk in 1945. He was always interested in writing and contributed numerous articles to local and national newspapers and periodicals. His breakthrough into journalism came in 1943 when he took over from the late James Russell, the accredited freelance news correspondent in Vale of Leven and Loch Lomondside for the national and local press.

A lifelong member of the Institute of Journalists, Glen contributed extensively to the *Lennox Herald* as 'Valeman' and was known on every Glasgow news desk as Glen of Alexandria, covering all the major hard news, industrial and sports stories in the area. These included the gradual decline of the silk-dyeing industry, which at its zenith was the area's foremost employer. He also recorded in words and pictures Vale of Leven Juniors' famous victory in the Scottish Junior Cup Final against Annbank United at Hampden Park in 1953. He had become interested in photography about four years previously. As well as taking photographs to accompany his written reports, he branched into commercial and wedding photography. Glen then made a business out of printing films handed into local chemist shops for developing. The availability of colour film made photography a favourite hobby for many people and the business flourished. It operated initially from the garage at his home in Luss Road and then from the back shop of premises he purchased in Main Street, Alexandria. It became clear when the dark room had to be extended into the washhouse that larger premises were required.

Tom Glen founded Scottish Colorfoto Laboratories in 1967. He built a state-of-the-art factory on a new industrial estate at Heather Avenue, Alexandria, which at its peak employed 250 people developing and printing films for chemist shop outlets across Scotland, including all the High Street branches of Boots the Chemist. Always impeccably dressed, articulate and well-mannered, friends and family remember him as a determined and optimistic businessman, who was always looking forward to new challenges. Following his retirement from business, he moved to Perthshire and was a familiar figure in the town of Auchterarder, where he was still driving at the age of 99. He was also still writing right up to the time of his death and, at the age of 101, was coming to terms with cutting edge technology which helped him to record his work.

Glen joined Dumbarton Rotary Club in 1963 and was its president in 1970. He was a Council Member of the Scottish Council of the CBI for ten years from 1971 and was the president of the Association of Photographic Laboratories of Great Britain in 1975. He was predeceased by his wife, Meg, but is survived by his son Noel, a solicitor and Church of Scotland elder, his daughter, Margaret, five grandsons and several great grandchildren. He lived at home alone in Auchterarder and died peacefully there on July 16.

Levenvale – just a small part of the Vale which Tom Glen covered for the Lennox Herald and national newspapers. *Picture by Bill Heaney*

Chapter 66

THE ARTIST

Stewart Campbell, artist and musician.

Born: Dumbarton June 7, 1946
Died: Paisley ton, June 6, 2015

Stewart Campbell, who died after a short illness in hospital in Paisley aged 68, designed the coat of arms of West Dunbartonshire and the corporate identity logo of Strathclyde Region. He was a highly talented artist, graphic designer and musician, who sang and played the guitar and drums with a number of popular bands for more than 50 years in leading music and dance venues. These included King Tut's Wah Wah Hut and Mr Micawber's plus a host of hotels and nightspots, mainly in Glasgow and the West of Scotland. Bands he played for included Red Pepper, Tickled Pink, Tree Beard and, most recently, Georgia Skin.

Stewart was a brilliant and popular student at Dumbarton Academy, where he was the dux medallist. He distinguished himself at Glasgow School of Art, where he graduated with a first in graphic design and won the Haldane Travelling Scholarship and the MacLehose Design Scholarship in 1969. Stewart's first job was with the Weir Group in Glasgow as a graphic designer in their publicity department. He later joined the large and hugely successful Rex Advertising Group as their principal designer, and was an associate director in their central design studio.

Stewart was quiet and reserved but extremely efficient, dedicated and talented when it came to the important matter of producing appealing campaigns on a variety of subjects. He knew the merits of meeting strict deadlines and seldom failed to please with his artwork and designs. These were all original and many of them became part of major public authority and corporate advertising and publicity campaigns. Stewart joined the late Harry Dutch, Head of Public Relations, and his communications team at Strathclyde Regional Council's headquarters in Montrose House, where his colleagues included former Scotsman news editor John McClounan, Jean Reid, John Brown and Jimmy McIntyre. High profile politicians in 1974 when the region was founded included the genial the Rev Geoff Shaw, council convener, and the legendary Councillor Dick Stewart, who led the Labour administration. Stewart Campbell worked closely in consultation with them doing the graphics for newspaper, television, magazine and poster campaigns.

He was the council's graphics and exhibitions officer, corporate graphic designer and senior design officer and his assignments, which were challenging, dealt with everything from education to social work to roads and transport. Top of the list was the re-design, maintenance and development of the authority's corporate identity. He also worked on the design and branding of Strathclyde Transport, which took over the Glasgow buses and underground, which became "the clockwork orange", from the old Corporation.

When the regional council was dissolved, Stewart moved back to his home town of Dumbarton and a post at West Dunbartonshire Council, where he was the senior design officer from 1995 to 2008 when he retired. During his time there he designed West Dunbartonshire's new corporate identity, its coat of arms and its flag, using images of shipbuilding, heavy engineering, a dove of peace, the elephant and castle and St Patrick, the local saint. The new council logo was based on the confluence of the rivers Leven and Clyde, Loch Lomond and the Kilpatrick Hills.

Politicians must often wonder what their staff and other public servants think of them. Stewart, normally so reserved but witty with a dry sense of humour, enlightened them when he wrote a valedictory message on social media. He said: "When I worked for the council I was tasked to draw up the 'coat of arms', although we already had an established corporate identity, which was only to be used on councillors' business stationery - and on nothing else. This was a Labour council who all wanted to be little Lords and Ladies - all of them signing up to the whole idea of the class system in Britain. Now they're starting to use it everywhere. What a bunch of closet Tories!"

Stewart, whose political allegiance was to the SNP, said he was glad to be out of local government – "freedom at last," he said, and welcomed the opportunity to spend more time with his family. His wife Agnes, whose brother, Marius Van Der Werff, designed Scottish Television's Taggart detective series, sadly died in 2005. They were soulmates. Stewart is survived by their three children, Shirley, Stewart and Jamie, and their six grandchildren Laura, Craig, Millie, Glen, Isla and Rona. Stewart's interests outside music and design included literature, sport, photography and researching his family tree. His favourite piece of prose was from Shakespeare's Macbeth:

Tomorrow, and tomorrow, and tomorrow,
Creeps in this petty pace from day to day,
To the last syllable of recorded time;
And all our yesterdays have lighted fools
The way to dusty death. Out, out, brief candle!
Life's but a walking shadow, a poor player,
That struts and frets his hour upon the stage,
And then is heard no more. It is a tale
Told by an idiot, full of sound and fury, Signifying nothing.

He also enjoyed sport. His grandfather's elder brother was John Tait (Jacky) Robertson, who played for Dumbarton and Rangers and Scotland. He was the first ever manager of Chelsea FC., a coach in Europe and later a sports writer for the *Daily Record.* Stewart was proud of the connection with Dumbarton, Rangers and Chelsea and was, predictably, interested in the design of their badges. He said: "At the time, the early 20th century, Chelsea Football Club was formed by Scottish ex-pats living and working in London hence the blue shirts and the lion rampant on the club badge." Stewart Campbell is sadly missed by his many friends in music and local government and by many others for whom he produced artwork for their businesses and corporate logos. His daughter, Shirley, who sang with many of her father's bands, said: "My father was devoted to his work with the council and loved nothing better than taking photographs of the area and researching the history of Dumbarton."

BILL HEANEY

Chapter 67

THE BUS DRIVER

Use both sides, please - a Central SMT bus crossing the Old Bridge at Dumbarton heading for Helensburgh and William McKinley.
Photo courtesy DG MacDonald.

Bus driver and transport inspector
Born: January 3, 1928, in Dumbarton
Died: September 30, 2014

Every town has its characters and bus driver and transport inspector Willie McKinley, who died in October, 2014. was certainly one in Dumbarton. Practically everyone across West Dunbartonshire knew Willie, from the old folk who were his passengers for years on the Central SMT buses to the toddlers who sang happily as they travelled to Brucehill nursery school in his mini-bus. Willie lived through an era after the Second World War when there were very few private cars on the roads and everyone took the bus. Taxis and limousines were usually seen only at weddings and funerals -- and 'bus runs' and mystery tours were a favourite day out for local families. Shipyard and factory workers used the buses to get to work and children went to school on them, some of them still doing their homework along the way.

Buses were where people met and news and gossip was exchanged with neighbours. 'Use both sides, please,' was the cry of the conductresses, who urged people queuing to get on board to use both upstairs and downstairs. One bell signalled all the passengers had boarded safely and it was safe to drive off. Two bells meant the driver should stop at the next halt to let people off. And three bells told the driver he should continue without stopping since the bus was full up. The Thatcher government implemented the Transport Act 1985 on 26 October 1986 and the deregulation of bus services in Scotland came in.

The Act abolished road service licensing and allowed for the introduction of competition on local bus services for the first time since the 1930s. To operate a service all an accredited operator was required to do was provide 56 days' notice to the Traffic Commissioner of their intention to commence, cease or alter operation on a route. Almost immediately existing operators like Central SMT faced competition on their most profitable routes, both from new and existing operators, and other municipal operators seeking to increase revenue. This led to 'Bus Wars' with new operator's cutting fares and operating services which were unsustainable in the long term. An assortment of buses took over from the red double deckers which had taken people to football matches, to church and the dancing and bingo halls and before long many of Scotland's bus services were decimated.

The public turned to the railways and private cars and taxis became popular became increasingly popular, some would say necessary, when housing schemes and out of the way places, deemed unprofitable by the operators, saw services withdrawn. Often there were no services at all in the evenings to places which had been served until midnight and later by the old subsidised bus companies for years. Willie McKinley was based at the now closed Central SMT garage at Gavinburn, Old Kilpatrick, which was the depot for West Dunbartonshire and Clydebank. He was one of a number of well-known drivers and conductresses. The drivers were always men like Willie himself, road safety campaigner Alex Donald, Adam Conn, Ian Blair, Tony McGarvey and Freddie Ramage. Their system of letting their fellow drivers know inspectors were around was to give a thumbs up if the route was clear. A thumbs down was the signal if an inspector was waiting along the route and drivers put their hand across their chest if they had an inspector on board. A small number of drivers became inspectors themselves and saw to it that the buses ran on time, the passengers paid their proper fares – or paid at all - and that everyone conducted themselves properly during the journey. Needless to say there were often fights on board the buses when the public houses and dance halls emptied late at night and Willie McKinley was a man with a reputation for sorting them out. No one with any sense fought on Willie McKinley's bus for they knew he could handle himself and, if the trouble persisted, Willie would drive them straight to the police office. Willie died peacefully, aged 86, at his home at 136 Cardross Road, Dumbarton.

He was a member of a large well-known family. He was born at 7 Risk Street in the old Dumbarton town centre, on January 3, 1928, and went to McLean Place and St Patrick's High School. His parents were Charles and Sarah McKinley and he was one of five children, Colm, who was a coal merchant at Dalreoch, Charles, William himself, Daniel and their sister, Rose. Rose was at one time in charge of a horse-drawn travelling shop for the old Dumbarton Equitable Co-operative Society. The shop which took groceries round the Dumbarton housing schemes stood next to the bus terminus in Napier Crescent, Brucehill, and the horse was put out to graze nearby. Willie, who was a popular young man in the community, married and set up home with his wife, Helensburgh woman Susan Mundie, at 129 High Street, Dumbarton. He was something of as prankster in his youth until one of his jokes went wrong. High Street café owner Michele Cocozza was washing the windows at the Central Café and was called inside to serve a customer. Willie placed a stone in the bucket of water and when Michele came out to continue the work he threw at the window, smashing it to smithereens. Willie's punishment was to push the Cocozza's ice cream barrow round the streets of the West End for a month to make enough money to pay for the damage.

Willie and Susan McKinley had seven children, Charlie, Eddie, Danny, Marie, Sally, Colm and Pat. They moved house to Westcliff in 1953 and have stayed there since. Willie was a great dog lover who could often be seen walking his dog, Nakamura, round the Clydeshore at Havoc. His well-attended Requiem Mass was celebrated by Father John Lyons and took place in St Michael's Church in Cardross Road, Dumbarton, and funeral thereafter to Dumbarton Cemetery. He is survived by his seven children, 14 grandchildren and 14 great grandchildren.

The Edward Street bus, number 86 from Castlehill in Dumbarton to Clydebank.

Chapter 68

THE WINGER

Felix McGrogan and St Patrick's High School, Dumbarton.

Professional footballer
Born October 16, 1942
Died November 18, 2010

Felix McGrogan, who has died after a short illness aged 68, played for Raith Rovers and St Johnstone, and was one of four Dumbarton brothers who played senior football in Scotland and England in the Sixties and Seventies. A flying winger like his father, also Felix, who played for Third Lanark, Dumbarton, Kilmarnock, Falkirk, Dunfermline Athletic, Blackburn Rovers and Brighton and Hove Albion, his career was brought to a sad and sudden halt when he broke his neck while playing for Durban City in South Africa. He returned home to Scotland, where he underwent surgery and received treatment for a year by specialists at Killearn Hospital in Stirlingshire. A consultant eventually told him he would never again be able to play football competitively.

Felix, James, Joe and Hugh McGrogan inherited their father's considerable footballing skills and honed them playing in the streets and on the small, makeshift pitches in and around Dumbarton's Brucehill housing scheme, where the brothers were brought up with their siblings, Kathleen and John. James, the eldest of the brothers, played senior for Dumbarton and at junior level for Vale of Leven, Renfrew and Ashfield. Joe played for Hamilton Academicals and Dumbarton and the youngest brother, Hugh, who played for Oxford City and Carlisle United, was tragically killed in a road accident.

The late Joe Davin, Evan Williams and John O'Hare, who won two European Cup medals with Nottingham Forest. *Picture by Bill Heaney*

All the McGrogans went to St Patrick's High School, Dumbarton, which at one time had its own primary department at Castlehill, where the football pitch, which had a wicked slope and was sparse of grass, was notoriously known as The Rockies. Despite the pitch, the school had a remarkable reputation for producing top class footballers the most famous of whom were John Divers, Evan Williams and Steve Murray, of Celtic, and John O'Hare, of Sunderland and Nottingham Forest, who was capped eight times for Scotland and won two European Championship medals with Brian Clough's Forest team. Murray also captained Dundee and Aberdeen. John Ryden, of Tottenham Hotspur and Dundee, Joe Davin, of Hibernian and Nick Sharkey, of Sunderland also made the senior soccer grade. St Patrick's were much feared by their opponents, including Govan High School in Glasgow, one of whose notable players, Sir Alex Ferguson, the Manchester United manager, said: 'St Patrick's in Dumbarton was the one team we didn't want to be drawn against in any competition.'

Felix McGrogan, a contemporary of Sir Alex, was always considered to be one of St Patrick's finest players. He tasted success at an early age when his primary school squad, with Evan Williams in goal, won the coveted Russell Cup, a fiercely contested competition amongst Dunbartonshire primary schools. McGrogan played for the St Patrick's secondary team at every level, picking up medals and honours along the way. The school matches were played in the morning at that time and Felix often turned out for his beloved St Michael's Boys' Guild team in the afternoon. He also played for star-studded Dumbarton Castle Rovers whose coach, Jimmy Riddell, poached the cream of the soccer crop for his St James's Park-based team from all the local schools and boys' clubs. A former team mate said: 'That was the way of it then. Players weren't coached or mollycoddled the way they are now. They lived for football and would play at the drop of a hat and, of course, the rewards then did not compare in any way to the vast fortunes paid to today's professionals.'

Felix – his name means Lucky - was an outgoing personality who was greatly loved not just for what he could do on the football pitch but for his gregarious behaviour and quick wit off it, particularly on holiday at Boys' Guild annual camps in Ireland and at 'the dancing' where his blond locks and athletic good looks made him a hit with the girls.

Soccer scouts flocked to see McGrogan and he was signed by Pollok Juniors in Glasgow. He wasn't there long before Raith Rovers' manager George Farm, a former Scotland international goalkeeper, stepped in and took him to play at Starks Park in Kirkcaldy. McGrogan did well there and soon caught the eye of Bobby Brown, another former Scotland international, who was managing St Johnstone at that time. The dapper ex-Rangers goalkeeper produced his cheque book and paid a not immodest sum to take McGrogan to Perth to play for St Johnstone, where the winger impressed the fans at Muirton Park. He had itchy feet though and took the chance to sign for the South African club Durban City, enjoying a brief sojourn in the sunshine until he sustained the neck injury which eventually put him out of the game.

When he knew there was no chance of a comeback, McGrogan travelled to Liverpool to look for casual work before returning to Dumbarton, where he worked in the local whisky distillery. He then went to Fife to work in Glenrothes in 1975 and it was there he met and married his wife, Leslie. They had a son, Philip. Football continued to course through his veins though and he soon became attached to a number of youth and junior teams which he coached.

McGrogan later complained of suffering from an old foot injury and then he was diagnosed to have diabetes. When he went to get checked out by doctors, they discovered that he had a tumour in his side, and it was from cancer that he eventually died. Warm tributes to Felix McGrogan, who is survived by his wife, Leslie, and son, Philip, his mother Mary, his brothers James, Joe and John and sister Kathleen, have been sent to a website in his name by many friends, including a number of Dumbarton exiles now living in Canada who were brought up with him, played football and went to school with him. Representatives of Glenrothes Juniors and Raith Rovers and old friends from the close knit world of Scottish football turned up to pay their respects at his Requiem Mass, which was celebrated by Father Gerard Hand at St Mary's Church, Leslie, in Fife. The funeral took place thereafter to St Drostan's Cemetery, Markinch.

pictured with his St Patrick's High School primary department team mates who won the Russell Cup in 1955. In the picture are (beck row, left to right) William B Monaghan, head teacher, Pat Sweeney, John Dougan, Joe McCallion, Evan Williams, Jack Kerr (teacher), George Stewart, Tommy O'Keefe, John Brennan and Joe Watters (teacher). Front row (left to right) – Jim Groden, Jimmy Neeson, Felix McGrogan, Paddy McHugh, Gerry Heaney, John McQuade and Billy Bell.

St Patrick's FPs of the 1960s included Tony Hainey, Joe McIntyre, Junior Deigman, Barney Boyle, Arthur Robinson, Billy Johnstone, Ronnie Shaw, John Goldie, Hugh Robinson. Front row – Jack Neeson, John McQuillan, Tommy Casey, Stevie McGrogan, John Niven, Frank McAteer and George Rainey.

Chapter 69

THE ACTOR

Robert Trotter

Television actor, director and photographer, Robert Trotter, who died in August 2013, aged 83, was a talented actor and director who started out with his home town amateur drama company and went on to become a national television soap opera personality.

Although his stage debut was with Dumbarton People's Theatre in the 'Tin Hall' in the town's Glasgow Road, where he made lifelong friendships, he spent much of his career in much larger theatres and on television, before proving an able photographer in later life. He will be remembered by many for his performance as Mr Obadiah Murdoch in Scottish Television's *Take the High Road*, which was filmed in the scenic village of Luss on Loch Lomondside, but his career was far more committed and extended than this somewhat comic role might suggest. Robert's life as an actor began in the 1950s in the Green Room Club which metamorphosed into Dumbarton People's Theatre, where he was joined by the likes of director Vera McIntyre, actors Jessie Brazier, Janette Barnes, Ronnie Armstrong and Joe Donnelly and Tom Gallacher, the author, playwright and essayist. He recorded a memorable compilation of Gallacher's stories about Dumbarton people and places in his book *Hunting Shadows*. Trotter graduated from the University of Glasgow and completed his National Service as a coder in the Royal Navy before training as a teacher. He taught English at Bellahouston Academy in Glasgow, and in 1965, he became a lecturer in drama at his Glasgow university alma mater and took up residence in the West End of the city. While doing so he found time to act in and direct productions for the prestigious Glasgow University Arts Theatre Group, of which he was a co-founder. His work attracted excellent reviews from discerning Scottish theatre critics such as Christopher Small, and his friend, Eric MacDonald, the Glasgow-born playwright and fiction writer, said this may have encouraged him to devote himself to theatre and radio acting. MacDonald added: 'The latter both here, and in London, allowed him to fulfil his talents, particularly his insightful characterisation, his timing and his honest feeling. The actress Edith Macarthur once summed up his gifts in a single word – 'stunning'.' Moving to London, Robert continued to work for the BBC, and played at the King's Head Theatre Club and the Royal Court, in plays by his old friend, Tom Gallacher, who wrote among many things *The Apprentice* and *Mr Joyce Is Leaving Paris*. He was ever aware of Scottish writers, promoting, directing or playing in their works - including those of Joan Ure, Hector MacMillan, Eric MacDonald and Alasdair Gray. Robert returned from London on being offered the posts of assistant director at Dundee Rep and a directorship at Pitlochry Festival Theatre, where he was happy to direct as a freelance and where he again gave great encouragement to Scottish actors and writers. In 1982, his production of Peter Turrini's Josef and Maria, with Kay Gallie and John Shedden in the leads, was the first play to open the main house of the Tron Theatre in Glasgow. He loved his home town of Dumbarton, its gossip, news and social history and its people, with whom he mixed freely with and was comfortable. He enjoyed entertaining them and listening to their reaction to the work he was involved in. Ever restless and creative, he turned his attention in later life from acting and directing to another intense interest, photography. A trip to New York in the 1990s was one of discovery, and he was to return there again and again, armed with cameras and fascinated by the similarities he found there with the energy and pace of life in Glasgow. This resulted in *Sing the City,* published in 2001 which was a book of his own black and white photographs, a haunting collection that led in turn to an exhibition three years later at the Glasgow School of Art. Sadly, his eyesight was quickly failing him and in recent years many of the projects he hoped to carry out could not be met. Frail at the end, yet still strong in spirit, he died at Gartnavel Hospital in Glasgow. He left much of his work to the Glasgow School of Art Archive and more is to be found within the Scottish National Photography Collection held within the Scottish National Portrait Gallery in Edinburgh. Robert Trotter was a multi-talented man and fiercely proud Scot and all who knew him were delighted by his friendship and grateful for his legacy.

Lovely Luss on Loch Lomondside. *Courtesy of Scottish Tourist Board*

Chapter 70

THE DUKE

The Duke of Montrose

We visit Balmaha from time to time, so let's linger on Loch Lomondside's east shore, where the major landowner is the Duke of Montrose, one of the hereditary peers who sits in the House of Lords. Balmaha is the main port of call for climbers and hill walkers who want a taste of Ben Lomond, Conic Hill and the West Highland Way. It is also the place from which worshippers would on a Sunday row - or even swim! - out to Inchcailloch to attend service on the island in the parish church there. A Christian community on the island, which is today popular with 'twitchers' because ospreys nest there, is linked with St Kentigerna (Kind Lady), who was the mother of St Fillan and sister of St Congan. She was said to have had the ability to perform miracles. She founded a nunnery on Inchcailloch – isle of the nuns or old women – where she died in 733AD.

Four centuries later a Romanesque church was built on the site of St Kentigerna's grave in the grounds of Inchailloch Parish Church. By the 1620s the church was in a dilapidated and crumbling state, but the Buchanan lairds, the major landowners at that time, refused repeated requests to repair it. This resulted in the church being abandoned in 1643 and the parishioners having to attend Buchanan's pre-Reformation church of St Mary's. Eventually the name was changed and St Mary's became Buchanan Parish Church. The present Buchanan Parish Church was built in 1764 and it incorporated some of the masonry from the old Chapel of St Mary. The tombstones were also brought over to the new site in the village of Milton of Buchanan, the burial place of the Dukes of Montrose, who, since 1932, reside locally at Auchmar.

The Loch Lomond island of Inchcailloch, where people once swam to church on Sunday. *Picture by Bill Heaney*

The church suffered a fire in 1938 whereby and ancient 8-sided baptismal font was lost. Buchanan Castle, where the golf club now stands, was a gift from Malcolm II to Anselan, who was supposed to be descended from a son of the King of Ulster. For his services against the Viking Danes he was granted the rolling lands of the Buchanan estate. His descendants later took the name of Buchanan, their chief seat being on Clairnish Island. The Buchanans were later granted the privilege of holding 'courts of life and limb' on their estate by the Earls of Lennox. The proviso for this though was that any executions be carried out on the gallows of Catter, near Drymen, which was one of the chief seats of the Earls of Lennox.

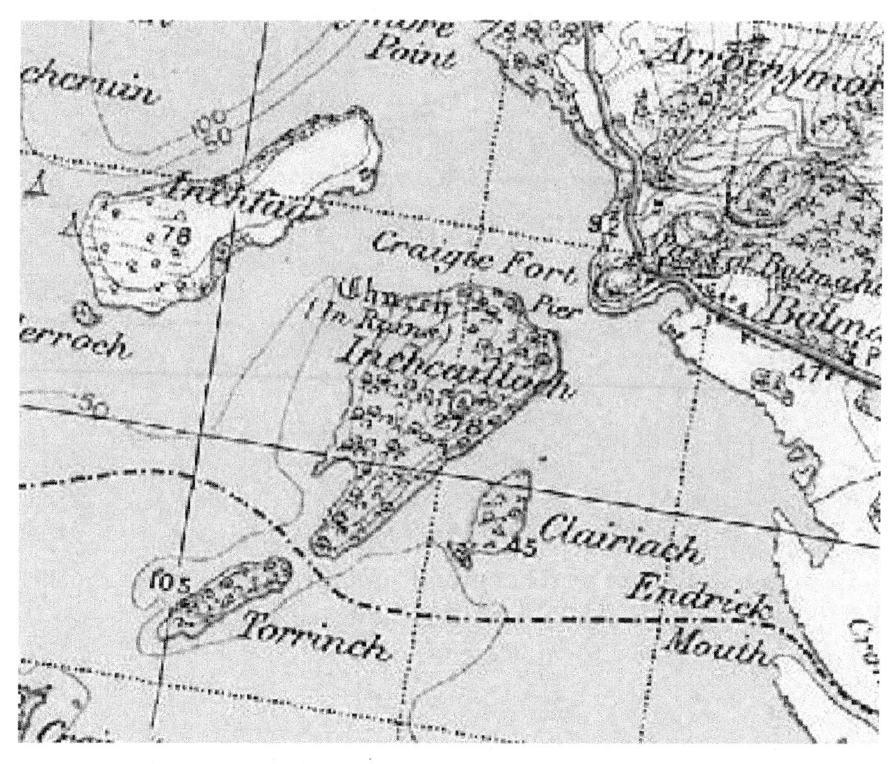

Balmaha map showing Inchcailloch

After 600 years on Loch Lomondside, the Buchanans lost their lands due to the death of the 22nd laird in 1682 without an heir or a written will. The lands were then acquired by the Third Marquis, later Duke of Montrose, and a member of the Graham family, who moved here from Mugdock Castle. The Mugdock estate was later gifted to the National Trust by the late Sir Hugh Fraser, the philanthropist and businessman whose family have long standing connections with Loch Lomondside. A later duke employed the famous gardener Capability Brown to landscape the Buchanan estate with rich woodlands which were harvested and used for the production of vinegar in Balmaha. The old Buchanan House of 1742 was burned down during Christmas 1852, and by 1854 Buchanan Castle, designed by William Burn, was built. The notorious Nazi war criminal, Rudolf Hess, whose plane crashed at Eaglesham on the Kilmarnock Road near Glasgow in 1941, was a 'guest' here for the remainder of the Second World War. But that's another story.

Where peace comes dropping slowly –
Buchanan Parish Church, near Drymen.
Picture by Bill Heaney

Chapter 71

THE BRIGADIER

Brigadier Alastair Pearson

He was a legendary figure within the Parachute Regiment, Alastair Pearson is regarded by many as one of its finest battalion commanders in its history, *writes Harvey Grenville.* By the age of 29 he had commanded two battalions and won five gallantry awards in less than two years through some astonishing feats of arms. He was fiercely dedicated to his soldiers inspiring loyalty and respect in return. The full biography of Alastair Pearson, who died in 1996, aged 80, is recorded in *A Fierce Quality: The Fighting Life of Alastair Pearson DSO & Three Bars, MC*' by Julian James. HRH Prince of Wales commented in the foreword to the book: 'I doubt if any soldier has made a greater contribution to The Parachute Regiment than Alastair Pearson.' After leaving school in 1932 he started as an apprentice at his uncle's bakery in

Glasgow and joined the Territorial Army (6th Highland Light Infantry) as an officer. His unit was mobilised in 1939 and Pearson served twice in France in 1940; latterly as part of the 2nd British Expeditionary Force when his unit was evacuated from Cherbourg. He joined 2nd Para Bn at the formation of No 1 Parachute Brigade in 1941. He was only with them for a week before he was 'requisitioned' by Lt Col Down commanding officer of 1st Para Bn. His initial tenure as 2 i/c of 1st Para Bn was short lived. Following a wild night out in Salisbury he was demoted and replaced as second in command by Major (later Brigadier) James Hill. With the promotion of Lt Col Down (and Major Hill to CO of 1st Para Bn) Alastair Pearson reassumed the role of battalion 2 i/c. In October 1942, 1st Para Bn were deployed as part of Operation Torch, an allied offensive to dislodge axis forces in North Africa. Lt Col Hill was wounded in an attack on enemy forces at Gue Hill in Tunisia; as a consequence Pearson found himself in charge of the battalion at the ripe old age of 27. Pearson was awarded a Military Cross for his role in the fighting of November and December. His citation reads: 'During the night of 23/24 November 1942, when his Commanding Officer was severely wounded, Major Pearson assumed command of his battalion and successfully completed the Operation. He continued to command his unit throughout the subsequent fighting and by his leadership and coolness under fire set an example of the highest degree. On December 11th when the enemy attacked his sector he, under heavy machine gun fire, organised and personally led a most successful counter attack destroying the enemy and capturing a number of prisoners. The conspicuous gallantry shown on this and other occasions has been an inspiration to all.' By January, Hill had discharged himself from hospital (although not fit) with a view to reassuming command of 1st Para Bn. However, he soon realised that Pearson inspired such confidence in his men that they would not accept any other battalion commander. After discussions with Brigade, Pearson remained in post and Hill went back to the UK. At the end of January 1943, Pearson was ordered to seize and hold German fortifications at Djebel Mansour and a secondary objective at Alliliga. Through some bloody close quarter fighting with bayonet the Paras were able to take their objectives. Although dislodged from their secondary objective by a counterattack, the Paras held onto Mansour. It was in situations like this that Pearson's leadership was inspirational;

rallying his men to an effective defence of their newly won position in spite of fierce aerial bombardment and German counterattacks.

It was only after they ran out of ammunition that they were forced to withdraw. The ferocity of this engagement can be measured by the fact that in a space of a few days the battalion suffered around 180 killed, wounded or missing. Pearson was awarded the Distinguished Service Order (DSO). Pearson had an extraordinary instinct for judging the enemy's intentions in battle. One practical illustration occurred after a hard day's fighting in the Bou Arada sector, when he forced his men to dig trenches. To their astonishment at nightfall he ordered them to move off and then ordered them to stop a short way off. Within an hour the Germans had attacked their old trench positions and Pearson organised a counter attack completely decimating the German assault. In March 1943 the battalion were engaged with axis forces at the Battle of Tamera where Pearson won his second DSO: 'For most conspicuous gallantry and devotion to duty at Tamera (Tunisia) on 8th March 1943.

The enemy attacked in considerable force the positions held by this officer's battalion. Completely disregarding his personal safety, when one of his companies had been forced back, he personally led the counter attack and completely restored the situation. In the course of the day his battalion was attacked on three separate occasions. Without hesitation and under intense fire he organised counter attacks and by his brilliant leadership and bravery on all occasions restored the position, killing large numbers of the enemy and forcing some 150 to give themselves up. Attacked again on 10th March he personally led his Battalion HQ staff of clerks and cooks against the enemy who was attacking from the rear of his Battalion HQ. Inspiring all with his great bravery and leadership he completely defeated all efforts of the enemy to penetrate his positions, personally killing many of the enemy and capturing further prisoners. During the night of the 23/24 March he led his Battalion to the attack on a most important feature in the sector, conducting this most difficult operation with such skill that the whole position was soon in our hands with slight losses to ourselves, but with heavy losses to the enemy.' For Operation Husky, the invasion of Sicily, the 1st Parachute Brigade was tasked with securing and holding Primosole Bridge to enable an advance of the 8th Army on Messina. The Paras were taken to their drop zone (DZ) by inexperienced pilots.

Hell on earth - D Day Landings in Normandy in June 1944.

The poor weather and heavy flak resulted in many of the Paras being dropped off target into the sea, with fatal consequences. Pearson himself only made it the drop zone by holding his pilots at gunpoint until they satisfactorily completed their orders. Pearson's men were able to take the bridge, however their vastly depleted numbers severely hampered their ability to maintain a sustained defence. A subsequent attack mounted by the Durham Light Infantry failed, at great cost, to retake the bridge. Pearson attended an orders group where the Brigadier proposed to repeat the attack. Famously Pearson said 'Well if you want to lose another bloody battalion that's the right way to do it'.

He was then presented with the opportunity to suggest his own plan, which he duly did. He then guided the DLI across the river at a fordable point downstream to enable the attack to take place and the bridge was retaken. Pearson was awarded a third DSO for his bravery in Sicily. By now Pearson was suffering badly from the effects of malaria and after two weeks in hospital was sent to convalesce in Sousse. He was posted to a staff job with 6 Airborne Division after he had recovered. The divisional commander, Major General Gale, recognised that they could make better use of Pearson's talents and appointed him as commander of the 8th Battalion, which was in poor shape. The 8th (Midlands) Battalion was formed from the 13th Battalion of the Royal Warwickshire Regiment. Morale was low when Pearson took over as a result of two serious training accidents. He immediately set about replacing unsuitable officers and NCOs. Over several months Pearson's hard work and training, he got the battalion to combat readiness. The battalion jumped at D Day (6 June 1944) on to an area of farmland near to Troarn, not far from Caen. Their objective was to destroy two bridges over the River Dives and disrupt enemy movements. While they were landing at the drop zone, Pearson was shot in the hand by the accidental discharge of a soldier's Sten gun. Although in pain, he did not have this wound treated for 24 hours.

Despite being widely dispersed, elements from the battalion blew up the two bridges. Most of the battalion managed to regroup in the Bois de Bavent and proceeded to harass the Germans over the next few days. While camped in the woods Pearson mounted a daring operation to rescue 14 survivors from a Dakota which had crashed on the night of the D Day drop. They crossed the river in a dinghy commandeered from a crashed glider and left some of the patrol at the river. Pearson and the remainder of his party moved on to the farm where the survivors were being looked after. All of the survivors were injured, some critically, and none of them were capable of walking. Pearson and his men returned to the river crossing pulling the casualties along in a huge farm cart singing 'Roll out the barrel' in loud voices to avoid being shot by the rest of the patrol! During this period the Germans regularly shelled the woods and surrounding area in an attempt to dislodge the 8th Battalion and the 3rd Parachute Brigade. When this failed the Germans launched a massive attack on the 12th of June. Large numbers of Germans started to infiltrate in between battalion positions and following them were 88mm guns firing directly at the British.

The situation was desperate and Pearson personally led a platoon of men to attack one of the 88mm guns. Having killed the crew they then turned the gun on the German infantry and guns. This heroic act was sufficient to turn the tide of the battle and the Germans retreated. The Paras held out for another week from further German attacks until they were finally joined by troops from the Allied beachhead. For the next few weeks a stalemate developed. In August, Pearson and the

8th Battalion led the breakout of the 3rd Parachute Brigade over the Dives. The Brigade continued to press the Germans until they reached the Seine. In early September, after three months of solid fighting, he returned with the rest of 6 AB Div to England. He was subsequently awarded a fourth DSO for his part in the Normandy operations. Pearson got married immediately on his return. However, the recurring malaria aggravated by the dampness in the Normandy marshes had finally taken its toll; he was forced to relinquish his command of the 8th Battalion and took over a reserve battalion in Yorkshire. He declined the opportunity to stay on in the Army after hostilities were concluded. However, shortly after the war he re-joined the TA and from 1947 to 1953 commanded the 15th (Scottish Volunteer) Battalion of the Parachute Regiment in Glasgow. From there he moved to 44 PARA Brigade Headquarters (TA) as Training Colonel and Deputy Commander remaining there until 1963. He was twice Honorary Colonel of 15 PARA. In 1967 he was promoted to Brigadier and became Commandant of the Army Cadet Force in Scotland. He was awarded the Cadet Forces Medal in 1981. His activities in civilian life were just as impressive. After a brief return to the bakery business he and his wife established a farm, Tullochan, on the banks of Loch Lomond at Gartocharn, which they ran for many years. From 1951 to 1990 he held a number of civic posts including Deputy Lord Lieutenant, Lord Lieutenant, Keeper of Dumbarton Castle and Aide de Camp to the Queen. He served on the executive committee of the Erskine Hospital for over forty years, latterly as Vice Chairman. He was awarded an OBE in the early 1950s and made a Companion of the Order of the Bath (CB) in 1958. He was also awarded the Territorial Decoration and three bars for his service to the TA and the Cadet Forces Medal in 1981. This was Pearson the soldier, but what about Pearson the man, the farmer, the neighbour, the husband of Joan and father of Fiona Stuart, founder of the Tullochan Trust, which looks after the interests of young people in Dunbartonshire?

Jack Webster of the Herald caught something of him when he wrote: 'By yon bonnie banks of Loch Lomond, he wanders across his rolling acres with a sheepdog at heel, his gruff, asthmatic voice belying the kindly nature which radiates from a rare and rugged character. Farmer Alastair Pearson has battled long with ill-health but then battles have been the speciality of this extraordinary figure.' Webster portrayed him as a caring family figure with time in his retirement for his grandson, Miles Stuart, who was so fascinated ted by the exploits that the pair visited D-Day landing area – and identified the exact spot where Grandpa's bum hit the ground. Alastair Pearson was persuaded to relate his story to Julian James, a young officer of the Paras. That exercise started in 1983 when Pearson was seriously ill with a stomach complaint. James was advised that an obituary of the legendary Para should be prepared. But the old Red Devil recovered and what should have been a death-notice came out as a book – 15 years down the line. It's a great story in which the foreword was written by the Prince of Wales no less, and never was the royal nod more richly deserved.

The heroism of Britain's soldiers was remarkable as they pushed into France on D Day.

Chapter 72

THE SKIPPER

The packed paddle steamer Waverley leaving Helensburgh for one of her famous jaunts Doon the Watter. *Picture by Bill Heaney.*

The funeral of John 'Skipper' Easton, who was universally and affectionately known as 'The Skipper' because of his decades long crusade to promote the paddle-steamer Waverley, the world's last sea-going ship of her kind, took place in 2015.

John, who was a former *Herald* reporter and assistant night news editor, passed away peacefully at Inverclyde Royal Hospital, Greenock, *writes Ian Bruce*, the long-time defence and geopolitical correspondent of the Glasgow newspaper. Easton's part in the successful fight to save her from the breaker's yard won him praise from conservation enthusiasts. Born in Lanarkshire, John moved to Rothesay at an early age when his father Peter took over as manager of the local Co-operative store. After leaving Rothesay Academy, his father tried to persuade him to apply for a job with the local council. A complete and self-admitted inability to count all the fingers on both hands and reach the same answer twice in a row put paid to that idea and at the age of 15, he instead took gainful employment as a trainee reporter on the Buteman, the island's local paper. While there, he covered the famous occasion when the local Bute island council contemplated declaring unilateral independence from the UK. It began as a joke during a council debate, but quickly grew arms and legs and indeed, wings. As word got out, American journalists and Fleet Street's finest descended on sleepy Rothesay and even *Time* magazine sent a team to cover the story. It also became a time of plenty for the *Buteman* staff, who coined in cash from selling the tale to outlets worldwide before the council finally called a halt to the lucrative charade. Before then, John had supplemented his meagre pay as a junior hack by working weekends as a stage hand at the local Winter Gardens, a venue frequented at the time of Clyde coast holiday hordes by the top variety acts of the day. Andy Stewart, Chic Murray, the Alexander Brothers and comedian Lex McLean, as well as Emile Ford and the Checkmates of *What Do You Wanna Make Those Eyes At Me For*? fame were among the artistes for whom John fetched and carried and occasionally carried on to the stage steps when they turned up over-refreshed or completely tired-and-emotional.

He was also bass guitarist in the *Echoes*, a Rothesay rock band which achieved local fame among the Clyde resorts and boasted Billy McIsaac, later keyboard player with Blur, as one of its members. By the age of 18, he had outgrown the *Buteman* and moved to Hamilton where he joined the local *Advertiser*. To avoid having to travel each day to and from Rothesay, he took up residence with his Uncle Johnny in Wishaw, a move which also led to his inexplicable and lifelong attachment to Heart of Midlothian Football Club. He met Morag, his wife of 45 years, at a party in Rothesay about this time. Romance blossomed and they married in Elderslie, close to her home town of Linwood, in 1970. John then moved to the daily papers and became a *Scotsman* reporter in their Glasgow office in due course before moving to the *Herald* in 1972, where he remained on staff till 2002. While there, he worked as a general news reporter, occasional and pithy feature writer and latterly as an assistant news editor on the night desk. Throughout it all, he took every opportunity to push the cause of the *Waverley*, the only rival his wife Morag ever had for his affections.

Almost uniquely among journalists, John Easton did not have an enemy in the world. His affable personality and dry sense of humour instead made friends of everyone he met. In retirement in Largs, he continued his love of the sea and ships in general by sailing regularly during the Waverley's summer-season and occasionally venturing further afield on cruise liners to France, Spain, Italy and North Africa. The Skipper is missed by his many friends and former colleagues and by the wider 'families' of the Press Bar and the *Waverley* communities. He is survived by his wife, Morag. Fair winds and following seas, old friend.

The PS Waverley passing Dumbarton Rock with Ben Lomond away in the background. *Picture by John Easton.*

Chapter 73

THE MEMBER OF PARLIAMENT

Ian Campbell MP giving his reaction to an election result to Bill Heaney, who was then editor of the Lennox Herald.

Ian Campbell was a politician with a great love of Dumbarton, where he was Provost and Member of Parliament, who was admired and respected for his solid roots in Scottish Labour movement. He died in 2007, in Dumbarton, aged 81, and the large attendance at his funeral service in Riverside Parish Church, where he was an elder, was testament to his popularity in the town and across the wider parliamentary constituency. At national level Ian Campbell was parliamentary private secretary to the Scottish secretary Bruce Millan from 1976-9, a period of industrial and constitutional upheaval. Campbell was far from certain that a Scottish assembly was a good idea, but he loyally toed the party line and backed it in the Commons. After the fall of the Scotland Act, which would have established the assembly, and Jim Callaghan's ill-fated government in 1979, Campbell impressed as a diplomatic chairman of Scottish standing committees and the Scottish grand committee, which began sitting in the old Royal High School building in Edinburgh from 1982. In his 17 years as an MP, five of which found a Labour government in office, Campbell remained a backbencher but never gave any indication that he desired higher status. He was popular in the Labour ranks and a successful secretary of the Scottish group of Labour MPs from 1974-7.

Ian Campbell was born in Dumbarton at the height of the Depression, the second of four children by William and Helen Campbell. Throughout his life he was devoted to the ancient capital of Strathclyde, in his personal and political life. He attended Knoxland Primary School and Dumbarton Academy, where he proved a talented footballer. He left home to study electrical engineering at the then Royal College of Science and Technology, now Strathclyde University, in Glasgow. National Service took him to post-war Germany where he served with the Royal Engineers. In 1950 he married May Millar. It was a strong marriage which produced five children between 1954 and 1965. Campbell worked in the steam test section of the South of Scotland Electricity Board from 1948 and rose steadily within the ranks, but politics was a developing interest.

In 1958 he was elected to Dumbarton Burgh Council. Campbell became provost of Dumbarton, aged only 36, when the Labour group took control of the council. The new administration carried out an ambitious programme of slum clearance, house building and town-centre redevelopment, but early in the first of his three terms as provost, the Denny shipyard, Dumbarton's last major shipyard and one of its major employers, closed. Westminster was the inevitable next step for Campbell.

Tom Steele, the incumbent Labour MP for Dunbartonshire West, decided to stand down at the 1970 general election and Campbell was selected as Labour candidate in his place. He held the seat, in several guises and often narrowly, until retiring in 1987. The 1970s was a heady decade in Scottish and UK politics: industrial strife under Ted Heath's government gave way to constitutional headaches over devolution, in turn, consumed by more industrial unrest as the decade drew to a close. Although Campbell's focus was primarily local, the growing popularity of the SNP nearly cost him his seat in the second general election of 1974. But Campbell held on and took a close interest in the Scotch whisky industry, bottling plants being a major employer in his constituency following the demise of the shipyards, and he was chairman of the all-party Scotch whisky industry group in 1976.

The whisky industry used to be at the very heart of Dumbarton's economy.

An unostentatious MP, he rarely spoke in the Commons and did not seek controversy, although he was a committed anti-abortionist. A religious man who had once thought of becoming a Kirk minister, Campbell was opposed to abortion legislation introduced by David Steel in the late 1960s and, with his friend Jimmy White, the MP for Glasgow Pollok, he did all he could to oppose any further relaxation of the laws, often acting as an informal whip on committees considering such changes. Early in the 1979 parliament, Campbell successfully piloted a private member's bill through the Commons, "to enable Scottish local authorities to provide concessionary travel schemes for mentally handicapped persons". In the run-up to the 1983 general election, he narrowly won a reselection battle within his constituency Labour Party after a left-wing challenge from Vale of Leven man Leo Crawley. That election saw Campbell re-elected for the new Dumbarton constituency, virtually identical to his old seat.

Ian Campbell was a jolly, outgoing person who liked nothing better than to mix and mingle with his constituents. He would meet his friends for an hour of relaxing companionship in the Railway Tavern after completing his surgeries when he returned from Westminster before going off to a local party meeting. He also was a Saturday morning regular in the High Street and was a popular figure with housewives in Dumbarton Co-op where he chatted with them while he and May did their weekly shopping. And then it was off to watch Dumbarton Football Club, who he always had an ambition to for.

He stood down at the 1987 election, succeeded by John McFall, who later became Lord McFall of Alcluith, who had been his election agent. Campbell was content to leave political life behind and increasingly devoted himself to life as a grandfather, while also spending more time as an elder in Riverside Church, Dumbarton. He remained active in the community, most notably as chairman of the school board of Ardlui School for children with special needs, in Helensburgh, where his grand-daughter Michelle was a pupil. Sadly, Michelle died in 2005. Campbell was diagnosed with prostate cancer in 2000. Apart from short hospital stays for treatment, he was cared for at home in The Shanacles, Gartocharn by May, his wife of 57 years, who survives him along with his five children, Willie, Ray, Helen, Sandy and Alison, their spouses and 13 grandchildren.

Riverside Parish Church.

Chapter 74

THE OPERA SINGER

David Ward, famed for Wotan

Born Dumbarton, 3 July 1922.
Died Dunedin, New Zealand, 16 July 1983.

Dumbarton born David Ward was one of the most important Scottish singers of recent decades, with a notable international career, and a vital presence in the early years of Scottish Opera. He had an effortlessly powerful, but attractively soft-grained voice, able to convey strong emotion. Unusually tall, he was easily able to dominate the stage, and was an ideal exponent of the major Wagner and Verdi bass and bass-baritone repertoire. He served in the Royal Navy during the Second World War and then trained at the Royal College of Music with Clive Carey. Much later – around 1962 - he studied his major Wagner roles in Munich with Hans Hotter, who had been the dominant Wotan of his own generation. Ward joined the basses in the Sadler's Wells Opera Chorus in 1952, quickly making an impression and being given his first solo role the following year – the Old Bard in *The Immortal Hour* (Boughton). He created the role of Captain Hardy in Lennox Berkeley's *Nelson* (1954) and remained a principal with the company from 1953 to 1959. Many years later, in 1972, he returned to revive one of his old roles, Bartók's Bluebeard, at the Coliseum.

During the Fifties he sang in Scotland during the annual Sadler's Wells tours, when his roles included Dr Grenvil in *La Traviata* (1957) and Colline in *La Bohème* (1958). During the 1959 tour he sang Zuniga (*Carmen*), Don Fernando (*Fidelio*, conducted by a young Colin Davis), and Monterone in *Rigoletto*. He also returned to Scotland for appearances with amateur companies, including Zaccaria in *Nabucco* (Edinburgh 1957) and Méphistophélès in Faust (Dundee 1958).

His major appearances with Sadler's Wells included the title roles in Bartók's *Duke Bluebeard's Castle* and Wagner's *Flying Dutchman*, and this last gave an indication of how his career would develop. His Covent Garden debut followed in 1959, as Pogner (*Die Meistersinger von Nürnberg*), followed by Fasolt (*Das Rheingold*), Hunding (*Die Walküre*) and Morosus (*The Silent Woman* by Richard Strauss). At the recommendation of Rudolf Kempe he was engaged at the Bayreuth Festival in 1960-2, singing Fasolt, Titurel (*Parsifal*) and Nightwatchman (*Meistersinger*). He then studied the role of Wotan in Munich with Hans Hotter, who had been impressed by his potential. When Covent Garden was directed by Georg Solti, Ward sang major parts regularly. His Wagner roles included Heinrich (*Lohengrin*), Wotan and King Mark. His Verdi repertoire extended to King Philip (*Don Carlos*), Fiesco (*Simon Boccanegra*), Padre Guardiano (*La forza del destino*) and Zaccaria, Other roles with the Royal Opera included Sarastro, Commendatore, Don Basilio, and Rocco, as well as Arkel (Pelléas et Mélisande), Khovansky (*Khovanshchina*), the Grand Inquisitor (*L'Africaine*) and the Pope in *Benvenuto Cellini*, which last he sang with the company on its visit to La Scala in 1976.

He made his first appearance with Scottish Opera in 1964 as the Commendatore (*Don Giovanni*), and returned the following season for Boris Godunov, and in 1966 and 1967 for Wotan in *Die Walküre* and *Das Rheingold* as the company assembled its first *Ring* Cycle.

The Wanderer in *Siegfried* and a complete cycle followed in 1971. In 1973 he added King Mark in *Tristan und Isolde* and repeated Boris Godunov in 1974. His last new roles with the company were Banquo in Macbeth and Pogner in *Die Meistersinger*, both in 1976. He came to the Edinburgh Festival twice as a guest with visiting companies other than Scottish Opera – in 1960 with Glyndebourne (*I Puritani* with Joan Sutherland) and in 1968 with the Hamburg Opera as the Flying Dutchman.

He enjoyed an extensive international career, singing regularly in the USA, Germany and Italy. In 1967 he sang Wotan in five *Ring* cycles in Buenos Aires.

David Ward was born and brought up in Dumbarton and educated at St Patrick's High School, where he was – like many of his peers at that school – and excellent swimmer and water polo player. Ward also played football and it was said he was a hard man to get past. He was from a large, well-educated family who lived in a council flat in Brucehill overlooking the Firth of Clyde and the Renfrewshire Hills. One of his brothers, James, became a priest and was later appointed Vicar General of the Archdiocese of Glasgow and Bishop of Sita.

David Ward did not feature in many studio recordings. He sings Hunding in Erich Leinsdorf's recording of *Die Walküre*, made by Decca in 1961. In 1963 he featured as Monterone in Solti's recording of *Rigoletto*. He is Arkel in the famous Covent Garden recording of *Pelléas et Mélisande* conducted by Pierre Boulez in 1970. There is a live recording of *Parsifal* from Bayreuth in 1960. The conductor is Knappertsbusch and Ward sings the small role of Titurel. The rest of the cast is excellent, including Régine Crespin as Kundry. Glyndebourne has also released a recording of *I Puritani* made in Edinburgh. David Ward is also featured as Friar Lawrence in the recording of Berlioz' dramatic symphony *Romeo et Juliette* with Pierre Monteux conducting the London Symphony Orchestra. It was recorded in Walthamstow Town Hall in 1962 and is presently issued under the Millennium Classics label. There is also a BBC re-issue of a 1963 Proms performance of the Verdi Requiem, with Giulini and the Philharmonia. There were not many pastimes in Dunbartonshire to compete with football, but singing was certainly one of them and David Ward's generation left a marvellous legacy to later generations, which was a great love of it through school choirs and operatic groups. Singing brings people together for pleasure and therapy. It is one of the great ties that binds us a community.

A prize-winning school choir from St Patrick's High School with teachers William B Monaghan, Philip Drake and Jack Pickup. David Ward's nephew, Jim Ward, is seated on the ground fourth from left in the front row.

Dalreoch Primary School with head teacher Mr Sime won the County Shield.

St Patrick's HS primary section showed it wasn't just London's West End where they could make successful musicals.

Wee St Pat's in McLean Place showed they were no slouches either when it came to singing in the 'Sixties.

This happy group were neighbours of David Ward when he was being brought up in Brucehill in Dumbarton. They are from Firthview and Caledonia Terrace.

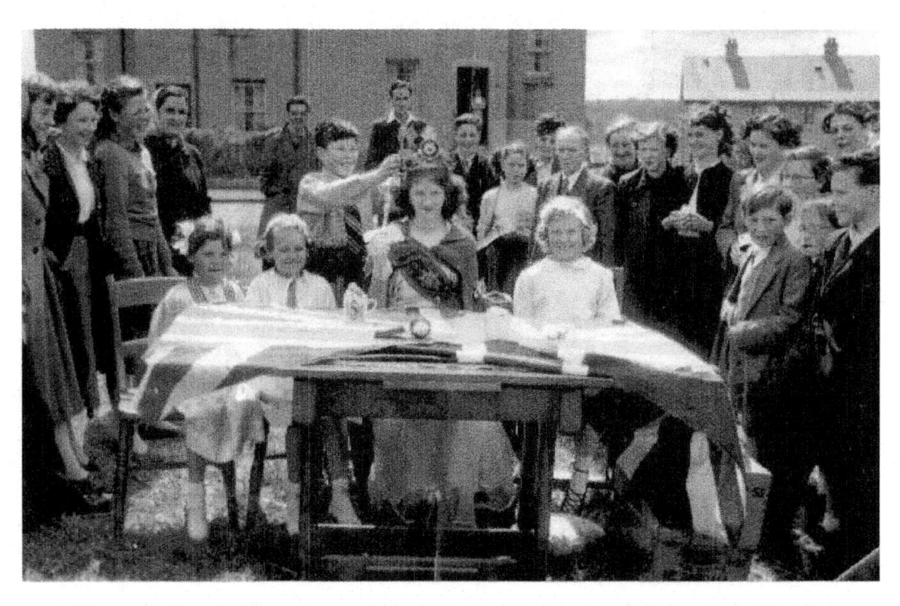

Happy days. The summer princess is crowned in Caledonia Terrace watched by neighbours and friends from the Brucehill neighbourhood. *Pictures by Peter Leddy*

Chapter 75

THE UNDERTAKER

George Lackie Skea
Clydesdale horse breeder, undertaker and Scottish Country Dance band leader

Born: Roscobie, Angus, on September 17, 1923
Died: Cardross, Dunbartonshire, on March 1, 2015

George Lackie Skea, who was a familiar figure in the diverse fields of farming, Scottish Country Dancing, funeral undertaking and buying and breeding Clydesdale horses, died peacefully at his home in Cardross in March, 2015, aged 91. His horses won numerous competitions over many years and were a major attraction at agricultural shows and gala days throughout the country. George's immaculately groomed Clydesdales were also to the fore taking brides to church on their wedding day in a cart decorated with brightly coloured ribbons and gleaming horse brasses.

George was born at Carsebank Farm Cottage, Roscobie, near Forfar in Angus. His parents were Alexander and Mary Skea and he was one of six children, five boys and one girl - Sandy, Jim, Robert, who died in 1922, Nellie and Dave. He spent his formative years attending a small country school, Oathlaw, which he left aged 14. When he was younger George spent many a day in the fields, next to the Glamis Castle home of the Bowes Lyon family, where his father was an apprentice to his grandfather, Robert Fyfe Skea, at Leckaway Smithy at Kinettles. There he would often speak over the fence to Princess Elizabeth and Princess Margaret, whose parents were King George VI and Queen Elizabeth the Queen Mother, a member of the Bowes Lyon family. When he left school George worked first as a message boy for Major Neish at Tannadice Estates. He moved up to become a gardener before becoming the major's driver.

He was a member of the 22nd Angus (Tannadice) scouting troop in 1935 and, in 1940, when Major Neish formed the Home Guard he joined up. Aged just 20, he went to work with horses at Battledykes Farm, where his father was grieve, and in 1945 won the first prize for his ploughing skills at the Roscobie Ploughing Match. He moved to Balquharn Farm in Fern as the foreman and tractorman and stayed there until moving to Cardross. In a life story that evokes Lewis Grassic Gibbons' Sunset Song, George set up and played in his own Scottish Country Dance band, The Four Star Band, which was popular at weddings and dances. It was when he required to recruit an extra accordion player for the band that George met his wife Peggy Timney, a young woman from Clydebank who had been serving with the Land Army. Peggy was one of the Lumber Jills employed on cutting down trees on a farm near Forfar. This was the start of a wonderful friendship and romance and George and Peggy were married at Our Holy Redeemer Church in Clydebank on June 7, 1947. They began married life in Fern, Angus, and their first child, Kathleen, was born there. George, Peggy and Kathleen moved to Cardross in 1950 when George went to work for Morton Cullen at Mollandhu Farm, overlooking the Firth of Clyde. |From there they moved to nearby Moorepark House, where George became head gardener and chauffeur to the two Miss Murrays, Eunice and Sylvia.

During the 1950s and early 1960s George, Peggy and members of their growing family were involved in the village concert party and helped with the annual summer outings from Bloomhill Children's Home. Their band played at many weddings, horticultural and farmer's balls. George became a member of Cardross Bowling Green in 1951 and was club champion in 1976. Club president twice, he was nominated in 1988 to become a Director (Blue Jacket) of the Garelochhead Bowlers Association and in 1995 he became President. George started showing flowers at the Helensburgh Horticultural Society and was on the committee for almost 30 years. He was an accomplished gardener who won a host of trophies for his begonias. He later became a show judge. He was also a member of the British Legion and a Special Constable who in 1958 decided to set up a successful fruit and vegetable shop stocked with home grown produce from his market garden at Lyleston House in the village. In 1962, George and Peggy purchased a milk round in Cardross based at Viewfield Dairy delivering to homes and businesses in the village and to the canteen of the Hiram Walker distillery in Dumbarton. Tragedy struck in September, 1964, when Peggy was injured in a car accident outside Cardross Golf Club, while working on the milk round. She died four days later. After that tragic loss, George was fortunate to have a large group of supportive friends and it was through mutual friendships that George was introduced to Sheila McLean. Sheila, too, knew the heartache of losing a loved one, being widowed in 1964 and left with three young children to bring up on her own. The couple married in 1966 and they and their joint families moved into what became a happy family home. They often travelled back to George's roots in the Forfar area and had many happy holidays with relatives. George started working with Wylie and Lochhead, Funeral Undertakers, during the late 1960s and he learned his trade in that business.

In 1970 George join Bells, the animal feed and veterinary supplies company, and he loved touring the country meeting people in the agricultural industry and visiting the islands of Islay and Jura. He set up on his own in the funeral undertaking business in 1981 in East Princes Street in Helensburgh. The business was sold in 1989 but

George stayed on as a consultant for many years after the sale. George and Sheila were beginning to enjoy their retirement when Sheila became very ill with leukaemia and died in 1991. Just before this they had celebrated their Silver Wedding anniversary with friends and family and renewed their wedding vows in Cardross Parish Church with the late the Rev Andrew Scobie. It was fitting that George was taken to Cardross Crematorium by horse drawn hearse, a remarkable sight, rarely seen in the Helensburgh district. George, who was a well known and loved in the community, is survived by his children Kathleen, Jimmy, Eileen, Sheila and Tommy and his 16 grandchildren and ten great-grandchildren.

The night President Kennedy died

This is a photograph of Cardross Junior Singers – the church choir - taken in 1964. The conductor was Mrs Bilsland and her husband was the pianist and also played the church organ. Leonard Prow, a member of the choir, remembers that night especially. He said: "We were rehearsing that Friday evening when Mr Bilsland arrived and told us President Kennedy had been shot."

Chapter 76

JAMES RESTON

The New York Times

U.S. ATTACKED

HIJACKED JETS DESTROY TWIN TOWERS AND HIT PENTAGON IN DAY OF TERROR

President Vows to Exact Punishment for 'Evil'

A Somber Bush Says Terrorism Cannot Prevail

Awaiting the Aftershocks

James Reston, a Giant of Journalism, Dies at 86
By R. W. APPLE Jr.
Published in the New York Times: December 7, 1995

WASHINGTON, Dec. 6— James Reston, former columnist, Washington correspondent and executive editor of The *New York Times*, died at his home here. He was 86. The cause was cancer, said his son Thomas. First as a reporter and then, beginning in 1953, as a columnist, Mr. Reston was perhaps the most influential journalist of his generation. In Washington, where he was based, and also in other capitals around the world, he had unrivalled access to the high and the mighty. Yet he retained a wry, self-deprecating personality, free of bombast, and always sought to reduce political complexity to plain language. 'What I try to do,' he said, 'is write a letter to a friend who doesn't have time to find out all the goofy things that go on in Washington.'

Interested in China and the Soviet Union as well as the United States, a student of diplomacy as well as domestic politics, he won two Pulitzer Prizes and dozens of other awards. Mr. Reston was forgiving of the frailties of soldiers, statesmen and party hacks -- too forgiving, some of his critics later said, because he was too close to them. But his stern moral standards, rooted in the Victorian values of his youth, never wavered. He remained an idealist in a world of cynics. From his strong-minded mother he inherited a Presbyterian conscience and an abiding sense of duty and responsibility. Work hard, he was taught. Work for large goals that transcend self-interest. Be cooperative. Be modest.

A talent scout of prodigious capacity, Mr. Reston hired and trained many of The Times's best-known journalists, and served as mentor to many more. To each of them, he passed along a lifetime's lessons about craft and country. Mr. Reston's 50-year association with The Times began when he joined its London bureau on Sept. 1, 1939, the day Hitler's armies marched into Poland, igniting World War II. It was a fitting day on which to start his career at the paper, much of which would be spent recording and reflecting upon the aftermath of that fateful day. His nationally syndicated column appeared regularly until 1987, when he became senior columnist. He retired from The Times in 1989, without ceremony, on his 80th birthday. In an interview marking the occasion, he said the two greatest political triumphs in his lifetime had been the common defence system developed by the West after World War II and the improvement in the lot of black people in America since 1960.

Mr. Reston, who was born in Scotland, described the men who met in Philadelphia in 1787 to draft the Constitution as the great heroes in his adopted country's history. The document that they produced, he said, made possible 'the triumph of the moderates' over the next two centuries. A moderate himself, hostile to both fascism and communism, he described journalism's role in their eclipse as 'one of the great pleasures of my life.'

Asked whom he had most admired, he cited Franklin D. Roosevelt as the finest President he had known and Dean Acheson, Secretary of State in the Truman Administration, as 'the key man' who 'came to the fork in the road' and concluded that containing the Soviet Union would require a new alliance. But he chose Jean Monnet, the French visionary who conceived the European Community, as the greatest man he had ever known as well as the person who had most deeply influenced his own thinking. Monnet proved, Mr. Reston often said, that 'if you don't demand credit for things, you can push them through.'

Mr. Reston thought of himself primarily as a reporter, and he often beat his competitors to be the first to write about major news events. His coverage of the Dumbarton Oaks Conference in Washington in 1944, which laid the groundwork for the United Nations, was one of the era's most important exclusives and won him his first Pulitzer, in 1945. Those articles disclosed the substance of secret documents that were then being circulated among delegations from the United States, the Soviet Union, Britain and China on the structure of the proposed international organization.

Mr. Reston won his second Pulitzer in 1957 for distinguished reporting from Washington. The articles cited were written in June 1956 and analysed the effects of President Dwight D. Eisenhower's illness on the functioning of the executive branch. He was also responsible for The Times's publication in 1955 of the documents of the 1945 Yalta Conference. And in 1954 he disclosed that J. Robert Oppenheimer, who had directed the making of the first atomic bomb, had subsequently been denied access to secret documents by the Atomic Energy Commission because of suspicion that he was passing information to the Soviet Union, a charge of which Oppenheimer was later cleared. One exclusive dispatch came by accident. In 1971, as one of the first American reporters allowed into China, Mr. Reston developed appendicitis. His report, filed from his bed in the Anti-Imperialist Hospital in the capital, ran on the front page under the headline 'Now, About My Operation in Peking.'

'My Own Opinions Aren't That Good'

From the 1950's on, Mr. Reston interviewed most of the world's leaders, often producing major news accounts that were scrutinized at the State Department for their every nuance. The interviews often bore the special Reston stamp: He sought to reveal not only the policies and the politics of the people he interviewed, but also their vision of life and their view of history. Mr. Reston, who was called Scotty by virtually everyone who knew him, was 5 feet 8 inches tall and had a round and ruddy face, grey-green eyes, an ever-present pipe and an invariably pleasant manner. He was courteous not only to high-level officials but also to the young people who worked for him. 'He believes in hard work, in thrift, honour your parents, woman's place is in the home, play by the rules and live clean,' his colleague Russell Baker once said.

Mr. Reston was credited by competitors with having more high-level news sources in Washington than almost any other reporter, although some critics felt that he was too kind in print to some of them. The economist John Kenneth Galbraith, reviewing Mr. Reston's The *Artillery of the Press,* a 1967 collection of his talks before the Council on Foreign Relations, suggested that Mr. Reston had learned to his disadvantage 'to treat all people in the manner of a newspaperman who must one day go back and see them again.' But in a 1980 article in The New Republic, Mr. Reston was quoted as saying: 'If you spend your life as a hatchet man -- and there's something to be said for that -- then eventually you find that everybody's out to lunch when you call. You're left with only your own opinion. I wouldn't like that because my own opinions aren't that good.'

James Reston, knocked out evocative descriptions on his typewriter.

Writing his column three times a week, Mr. Reston was a procrastinator, often filing right on deadline, to the dismay of night editors at The Times. A two-finger typist, he regularly wore out typewriters because he banged so hard on the keys, and his desk was a litter of papers, many of which bore tiny black marks where a stream of smouldering matches had landed in the course of a never-ending pipe-lighting ritual. His columns, laced with quotations from Walter Lippmann, H. G. Wells, Matthew Arnold and Churchill, were a combination of high moral tone, detailed reporting, allusions to sports, impish humour and evocative descriptions of seasonal changes along the Potomac. They seldom offered absolute judgments about people or events; he used the word 'maybe' more than most pundits.

His first column, on Oct. 18, 1953, established the Reston style: 'This town is still full of echoes from the days of America's isolation,' he wrote of Washington. 'It has changed in policy and personnel, more than any other world capital in the last generation. No nation has taken on so much or moved so far in such a hurry. Yet the habits of the past, like the bent figures of homeless former senators, still haunt the capital.'

Press and Politics: 'Like Cats and Dogs'

He often returned to certain themes, such as the role of the press. In his column of Oct. 30, 1968, when Spiro T. Agnew, soon to be elected Vice President, was denouncing news organizations, Mr. Reston wrote: 'The candidates and the press are fussing at each other again, and this is the way it should be. They have different jobs, and in many ways they are natural enemies, like cats and dogs. The first job of the candidate is to win, and he usually says what he thinks will help him win. The job of the reporter is to report what happens and decontaminate as much of the political poison as he can. The conflict is obvious.'

In addition to his two Pulitzer Prizes, Mr. Reston was awarded the Presidential Medal of Freedom in 1986 and the Franklin D. Roosevelt Four Freedoms Award in 1991. He received the Overseas Press Club award for interpretation of international news three times, the George Polk Memorial Award for national reporting and the French Legion of Honour, and was named Commander, Order of the British Empire. He also received 28 honorary degrees.

After retiring, he fulfilled a long time promise to his wife, Sally, by writing his memoirs. Titled Deadline, they were published by Random House in 1991. Reviewing the book for The New York Times, Ronald Steel, author of *Walter Lippmann and the American Century*, called Mr. Reston 'the quintessential Washington insider.'

'Officials used him to test out new ideas on the public or to drop leaks for which they did not want to be held accountable,' Mr. Steel wrote. 'Because of his high position at The Times and his personal integrity, he was trusted both by those who provided the news and by those who read it. But what he did so well and so usefully for so long could not be done today. Journalism and the political world have changed too much.'

Born in Scotland into years of poverty.

James Barrett Reston began life about as far from the Washington power centre as one could get. He was born in Clydebank, Scotland, on Nov. 3, 1909, the son of James, a machinist, and Johanna Irving Reston. The Restons migrated to the United States when he was an infant, but Mrs. Reston became ill, and the family returned to Scotland. There followed years of harsh poverty, of life in a brick tenement where young James and his sister slept crosswise at the foot of their parents' bed. In 1920 the family returned to the United States and settled in Dayton, Ohio. His father worked for the Delco Remy Division of General Motors. When his parents were naturalized, young James automatically became an American citizen. In 1932, he graduated from the University of Illinois with an undistinguished academic record. He had majored in journalism, skipping the course in governmental reporting but getting an A in sports writing.

During his high school years he caddied at the Dayton Country Club golf course. His own game became so good that he twice won the Ohio state public links championship and at Illinois was captain of the Big Ten championship golf team in 1932. His father wanted him to become a golf pro. His mother wanted him to be a preacher, which, he was to say later, is really what he became. In the winters during his school days, he hung around *The Dayton Daily News*. 'When the phone rang, I'd pick it up and take down the scores,' he later recalled.

'And from that I just moved into newspapering. I never thought of anything else.'

Another link to the world of newspapers was Governor. James M. Cox, the Ohio publisher and 1920 Democratic Presidential candidate, for whom young Reston had caddied. Mr. Cox gave him his first job after college on one of the Cox newspapers in Ohio, *The Springfield Daily News*, where he earned $10 a week as the sports editor. Later he was hired as traveling secretary and publicity director for the Cincinnati Reds baseball team. In 1934 he moved to New York as a sportswriter for the Associated Press Feature Service.

James Reston and his wife, Sally, and Nikita S. Khrushchev in talks with President John F. Kennedy.

The next year he married Sally Jane Fulton, a former college classmate who had been president of her sorority, an A student and a Phi Beta Kappa in her junior year. Named Sara but always called Sally, she was the daughter of a judge from Sycamore, Ill., a small town near Chicago. Mr. Reston once told a University of Illinois graduating class, 'I should say in passing that I myself married a recklessly beautiful girl whom I first saw on Wright Street wearing a scarlet coat.' 'My Gal Sal,' as he called her in the dedication of 'Sketches in the Sand,' a collection of his columns published in 1967, became his closest confidante, frequent collaborator and steadiest supporter. They had three sons, Richard, James Jr. and Thomas. Mr. Reston's own happy situation made him a champion of marriage, and he was forever asking his young bachelor colleagues when they were going to wed.

In 1937 The Associated Press sent Mr. Reston to London on a rather loose dual assignment: in summer covering sports events, in winter the British Foreign Office. In 1939 he joined The Times and became low man on the totem pole in the London bureau, with a salary of $85 a week. He was so little known on the foreign desk in New York that his first by-line in The Times had his name wrong -- John instead of James. Then came the London blitz. The Times's office for much of the war was on the seventh floor of the Reuters Building on Fleet Street, which offered a view of the dome of St. Paul's Cathedral. He described this view of the battle in his first book, Prelude to Victory. 'Before we got better sense, we used to put the lights off in the Times office every night and watch this effort,' he wrote. 'With uncanny regularity, the German bombers would come over just about 10 minutes after blackout and start dropping incendiary bombs all over this section. About an hour before we could see the flames, we would begin to hear the steady throb of scores of engines along the banks of the Thames; these were the pumps, driving the muddy water from the river up through miles of new hose. A little later the sky would begin to change in colour from midnight blue to a reddish glow, and soon the great dome of the cathedral would stand out in silhouette against the flames of perhaps a dozen raging fires. Night after night we watched this incredible scene, and morning after morning we marvelled at the fact that the fires were somehow put out.'

In December 1940 he was reassigned to Washington, and in 1942 published *Prelude to Victory*, a call to action to the American people that was acclaimed here and abroad. Its theme was pure Reston: Unless Americans put aside personal aims and materialistic thinking and made sacrifices in a crusade for their country, the war would not be won. In late 1942, Elmer Davis, head of the Office of War Information, obtained a leave of absence from The Times for Mr. Reston and sent him to London to set up the agency's effort there. John G. Winant, the

United States Ambassador to Britain, recommended him to Arthur Hays Sulzberger, then president and publisher of The Times, who was looking for an assistant. It was the beginning of Mr. Reston's close friendship with the Sulzberger family.

Mr. Reston returned to Washington and was named national correspondent in 1945. He made his mark with his coverage of Dumbarton Oaks, which illustrated a Reston maxim: Seek out the disgruntled party. His theory was that people who were disenchanted were more likely to talk candidly. In this case, it was the Chinese representatives to the conference who were disenchanted. In his memoirs, Mr. Reston told of having met Chen Yi, one of the Chinese delegates, some years before the war through Iphigene Ochs Sulzberger, wife of The Times's publisher. At Mr. Reston's urging, Chen Yi slipped him the complete texts of the proposals.

Instead of writing one long article, Mr. Reston doled out the information, producing an exclusive a day. The Russians thought Washington had leaked the material; Washington suspected the British, and the F.B.I. started an investigation of Mr. Reston.

In 1948 Mr. Reston became diplomatic correspondent for The Times, and in 1953 he became Washington bureau chief, succeeding Arthur Krock. Mr. Reston continued as bureau chief until 1964, when he voluntarily relinquished the post to concentrate on his column. In 1968 he was summoned to New York by Arthur Ochs Sulzberger, who had become publisher, to succeed Turner Catledge as executive editor, in charge of the entire news operation. The internal politics of the news department had received publicity after an unsuccessful effort by editors in New York to exert more control over the Washington bureau. Mr. Reston's mandate was to re-establish peace. For 13 months he ran the news department while commuting to Washington a few times a week to write his column. It was an almost impossible job. In 1969, knowing that his column was suffering and that he had to choose between it and the editor's post, he gladly chose the column.

Mr. Reston was eminently a Washington man. He loved and understood the capital. Moreover, he had helped shape the Washington bureau. These were his people, and many of them regarded him as a father figure. The New York office, on the other hand, seemed a vast, impersonal beehive, and Mr. Reston never felt totally comfortable there. During these years the Restons lived in a pleasant red brick house on Woodley Road in leafy northwest Washington and spent weekends at their log cabin in Fiery Run, Va. Mr. Reston often used Fiery Run as the dateline on his Thoreau-like columns about the restorative life in the country. In 1968 the Restons purchased The Vineyard Gazette, a 122-year-old weekly on Martha's Vineyard, Mass., where they vacationed in the summer. The paper has remained in the family; their son Richard is editor and publisher, and his wife, Mary Jo, is publisher and general manager.

Mr. Reston played a part in the publication of the Pentagon Papers in 1971 and in two other major news events involving The Times in questions of national security. The others were the Bay of Pigs invasion in 1961 and the Cuban missile crisis of 1962. In the spring of 1961, The Times was preparing to publish an article by Tad Szulc reporting that 5,000 or 6,000 Cuban exiles who had been training in the United States and in Central America for nine months were about to launch an invasion of Cuba to overthrow the regime of Fidel Castro. The article was planned for page 1 on April 7, under a four-column headline. But Orvil Dryfoos, then the publisher, was troubled by the security implications of the report.

On April 6, he and Mr. Catledge, then managing editor, telephoned Mr. Reston, who advised them not to publish the article and cautioned against giving away the proposed timing of the landing as 'imminent.'

The article was published on April 7 under a one-column headline and with no mention of the invasion's date. The Bay of Pigs invasion took place 10 days later and ended in debacle. President John F. Kennedy, who took full responsibility, said that if The Times had published more about the operation, it might have saved the Administration from making such a colossal mistake. 'If I had it to do over, I would do exactly what we did at the time,' Mr. Reston said later. 'It is ridiculous to think that publishing the fact that the invasion was imminent would have avoided this disaster.'

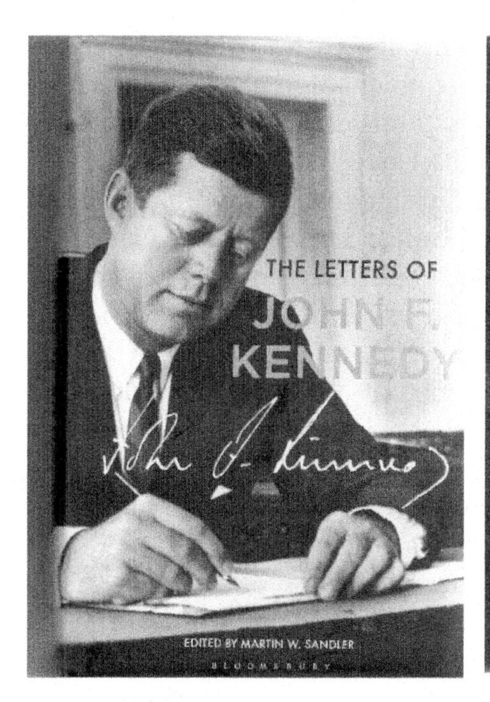

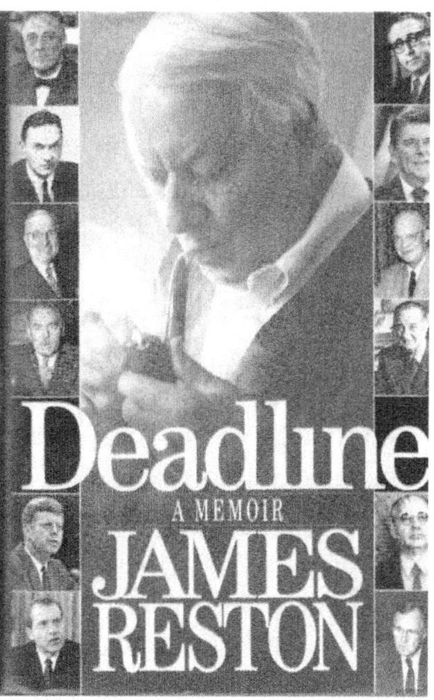

In 1962 Mr. Reston was apparently the only reporter who had found out that the Soviet Union, then under the leadership of Nikita S. Khrushchev, had secreted nuclear missiles in Cuba, only 90 miles from Florida. When Kennedy realized that Mr. Reston had the information, he telephoned him directly. Four years later, Mr. Reston recounted the incident to E. Clifton Daniel, then managing editor of The Times. 'The President told me that he was going on television on Monday evening to report to the American people,' Mr. Reston recalled. 'He said that if we published the news about the missiles, Khrushchev could actually give him an ultimatum before he went on the air. I told the President I would report to my office in New York,' Mr. Reston continued. 'And if my advice was asked, I would recommend that we not publish. It was not my duty to decide.' Kennedy then called Mr. Dryfoos, the publisher, and asked him not to print Mr. Reston's article. Mr. Dryfoos left the matter up to Mr. Reston and his staff, and the article was withheld.

It was a different story, however, in 1971 when The Times obtained and published what became known as the Pentagon Papers, the Government's top-secret documents on the Vietnam War. Seeing this at once as 'the story of the century,' Mr. Reston was one of the editors who felt that the documents should be published because they were history and that therefore no question of national security was involved. One of Mr. Reston's contributions to journalism was the corps of young reporters he discovered and developed. In 1961 he instituted a program of internships for young would-be reporters, modelled on the clerkships at the United States Supreme Court and suggested to him by the late Justice Felix Frankfurter. Each year he would recruit a new college graduate as his clerk and researcher. He paid a price for this program, as time and again the young clerks with lofty journalistic thoughts would mix up his airline reservations or keep the Secretary of State waiting because they had failed to cancel a scheduled appointment.

Linda Greenhouse, who went on to report on the Supreme Court for The Times, recalled that on her first day as a clerk, Mr. Reston asked her to get Ted Sorensen on the phone and suggested she try Paul Weiss in New York. After unsuccessfully calling every Weiss-comma-Paul in the Manhattan phone book, she reported back to Mr. Reston. 'He didn't groan, tear his hair or -- more important, and the reason for my undying gratitude -- laugh at me,' Ms. Greenhouse said. 'He gently explained that Paul, Weiss was a New York law firm where Ted Sorensen was working, looked up the number and gave it to me.' It was perhaps this quality, this unfailing kindliness that constituted his special attractiveness. It enabled him to view the faults and frailties of the world with compassion and to carry on in the belief that the best in mankind would eventually win out over the worst. 'Stick with the optimists, Niftie,' he wrote in a column in February 1980, welcoming his new grandson, Devin Fitzgerald Reston, to the human race. 'It's going to be tough enough even if they're right.'

Mr. Reston is survived by his wife; his sons, Richard F. Reston of Martha's Vineyard, James B. Reston Jr. of Chevy Chase, Md., and Thomas B. Reston of Washington; his sister, Joanna Richey of Santa Cruz, Calif., and five grandchildren.

James Reston's father, also James, pictured on top of Dumbarton Rock.

Chapter 77

THE RAIL DISASTER

Lt James Bonnar, of the Argylls.

During more than half a century of reporting for newspapers, I have come to learn that almost every story has a local angle or aspect to it. The old saying that it is a small world we live in becomes ever truer. On the May 7 anniversary of the sinking of the Lusitania last year, I wrote about a Dumbarton woman and her two young children who had drowned after that great ship was cruelly torpedoed by a German submarine. Their names have been carved in their memory on a tombstone in Dumbarton Cemetery. I have now discovered that local soldiers perished in a disaster which was the railway equivalent in magnitude and horror of anything that happened at sea during the First World War. May 22, 1915, saw the 100th anniversary of the Quintinshill Train Crash at Gretna in Dumfries and Galloway.

Helensburgh man, Lt James Bonnar, of the 9th Argyll and Sutherland Highlanders was a passenger on the train. Lieutenant Bonnar, who was 27, was the only son of Provost James Dick Bonnar and his wife Isabella Crawford Bonnar, of Cairnsmore, 16 Queen Street. Two other officers of the 9th Argylls, Captain Robert S.Findlay of Boturich Castle, Balloch, and Lieutenant John Jackson, of Rockville, Dumbarton, also died. The *Helensburgh Heritage* website reveals: "They were all involved in the Second Battle of Ypres, which began at dawn on Monday, May 10. In his autobiography Rosneath man the Rev Charles L.Warr, at that time a Lieutenant in the Battalion, writes that he was seriously injured that day and the survivors had no respite until the 18th. - "Worn out through indescribable fatigue, the survivors lurched back from the trenches through Ypres to the transport lines near Poperinghe, and two days later, home leave was granted to four officers and a number of other ranks. The officers drew lots, and the apparently lucky ones were Captain R.S.Findlay, and three subalterns, Jackson, Bonnar and Kirsop."

Captain Findlay, second son of Robert E. Findlay, had been at the front for some time with his regiment and was coming home on a few days leave, having been in the trenches at Hill 60 for 44 days. Lieutenant Jackson, second son of Daniel Jackson, was 26 and had joined the Territorial Force four years earlier. He was at the front for some time and was invalided home suffering from shock from the sound of an explosion. After spending about a fortnight in hospital in London he was returning to Dumbarton on short leave. Lieutenant Purvis Kirsop, of Bearsden, who was in the same carriage as Lieutenant Bonnar, was seriously injured. He was asleep, and when the crash came he found himself pinned in between two mattresses. He was lying on the rails as the flooring of the carriage opened up in the collision. He assured the family that Lieutenant Bonnar's death was instantaneous. A contemporary book about the 9th Argylls in Flanders commented: "They had been granted short leave after a strenuous time, and it is strange to think they should meet with disaster in the homeland. These fine officers are a serious loss to the unit."

In Helensburgh there was huge sympathy for the Provost, his wife and daughters Helen and Florence. Another name that leapt out from the list of those killed was that of Lieutenant Christian Salvesen from the philanthropic trading and transport family. The Salvesen family lost many sons and nephews during the First World War and partly as a result of this they built several memorial housing developments for military veterans.

At 6.49 am on Saturday, May 22, 1915, a Liverpool-bound troop-train carrying nearly 500 members of the 7th (Leith) Battalion of the Royal Scots collided head on with a local passenger train. The passenger train had been side-lined facing north on the south-bound main line at Quintinshill, just North of Gretna, to allow a following express train to overtake it. Normally the local train would have been held in one of the loops at Quintinshill but both of these were already occupied by goods trains. The troop train overturned, mostly onto the neighbouring north-bound mainline track and, a minute later, the Glasgow-bound express ploughed into the wreckage causing it to burst into flame. The ferocity of the fire, and consequent difficulty of rescuing those trapped in the overturned and mangled carriages, was compounded by the fact that most of the carriages were very old, made of wood and lit by gas contained in a tank beneath them. Between the crash and the fire a total of 216 soldiers 12 others, mostly from the express but including the driver and fireman on the troop-train, died in, or as an immediate result of what was, and remains, Britain's worst railway disaster. It was a scene of unimaginable horror.

Many reports written in the press at the time of the accident suggested that some trapped soldiers, threatened with the prospect of being burnt alive, took their own lives or were shot by their own officers. These reports were long denied for lack of official reports. Now one hundred years later, Colonel Robert Watson, one of the most senior veterans of the Royal Scots has given his personal view of this in a BBC2 documentary about the crash which indicates this did happen. The troops were mainly from a Territorial battalion recruited mostly from Leith, then a separate Burgh from Edinburgh, had been mobilised at the start of The Great War and then employed on Coastal Defence duties on the Forth until April 1915 when they moved to Larbert, near Falkirk, to concentrate with 52nd Lowland Division before deploying to France. At the last moment orders were received changing the Division's deployment to Gallipoli.

Lieutenant Bonnar's body was taken back to Helensburgh, where he was buried with full military honours after a service at St Columba's Church of Scotland in Sinclair Street.

The Battalion was meant to leave Larbert on 21 May to board the troopship Aquitania in Liverpool but she ran aground in the Mersey and the move was delayed for 24 hours. The response to the accident was swift and spontaneous. The official record of events states: 'The survivors at once got to work to help their stricken comrades and soon the whole neighbourhood was alarmed, and motor cars from near and far hastened to the spot with medical and other help. The kindness shown on all hands will never be forgotten, especially by the people from the surrounding area and Carlisle who gave such valuable assistance to the injured. Their hospitals were soon overflowing, but all who needed attention were quickly made as comfortable as possible. The King and Queen early sent their sympathy and gifts to the hospitals."

Of the half-battalion on the train only sixty-two survived unscathed. It was a devastating blow to the Royal Scots and to the whole population of Leith - it was said that there was not a family in the town untouched by the tragedy, probably made worse by the fact that, out of the 216 who died in the disaster, or soon afterwards from their injuries, only 83 were ever identified. The remaining 133 bodies could not be identified or were, literally, cremated within the firestorm of the wreckage. Later 107 coffins were taken in procession for burial in a mass grave that had been dug in Rosebank Cemetery in Edinburgh. Lieutenant Bonnar's body was taken back to Helensburgh however where he was buried with full military honours after a service at St Columba's Church of Scotland in Sinclair Street.

A Board of Inquiry, convened three days after the crash, found a number of serious failings in procedure which, when combined, led to the disaster. The worst of these was the failure of the two signalmen on duty in the Quintinshill Box, now demolished, but which then immediately overlooked the crash site, to alert the troop-train to the local passenger train waiting in its path. Both signalmen were subsequently charged, appeared before the High Court in Edinburgh on 24 September, found guilty of culpable homicide and sentenced to periods of imprisonment, one of them with hard labour. The names of the dead are listed in a roll on the memorial at Rosebank and include 12 people from the from the Glasgow-bound express, listed as two RN officers, three officers from 9th Battalion The Argyll and Sutherland Highlanders, two civilians and a sleeping car attendant, together with a mother and her baby son on the local train.

The aftermath of the troop train disaster in which the Provost's son died.

Chapter 78

THE PROVOST

James McKinley, Provost of Dumbarton, railway finance executive

James McKinley, the son of a lowly Irish immigrant lamplighter who embraced a career in shipbuilding, the railways, the Catholic Church and politics and became Provost of Dumbarton, has died in Glasgow, aged 90, died in February 2016. He was a dour and determined old school Labour politician with a strong Catholic faith, both of which he wore on his sleeve. He was born at 19 Levenford Place overlooking the River Leven in Dumbarton to John and Grace McKinley (nee Callaghan). One of six surviving children, two sisters and three brothers, he also had a one step-brother as his mother remarried James Friel in 1941 after John's death. Jimmy's birth certificate gave his father's occupation as "corporation lamplighter," and he was proud of that. He was also proud of the fact that his parents, John McKinley and Grace Callaghan, had married 100 years ago in County Donegal.

Jimmy was a pupil at St Patrick's High School in Dumbarton for nine years until 1940 and was amongst the school's brightest pupils. His first job, whilst still at school, was on a milk round and then, on leaving school, he went to work at the famous Denny's Leven shipyard in Dumbarton, where he was an apprentice engineer. Jimmy was much involved in the Catholic Church where the parish priest was Monsignor Hugh Canon Kelly, who encouraged his young parishioners to take up the religious life. Jimmy tested his vocation to the priesthood, but he discerned it was not for him. His religion remained important throughout his life, as did his service and contribution to the Catholic Church in Dumbarton and further afield.

Jimmy spent the rest of his working life employed by British Rail working in many capacities from Station Master to finance executive, and retaining a lifelong interest in rail travel. He took many correspondence courses, including a three-year sabbatical to become a mature student at Strathclyde University, achieving an Economics degree in 1972. Education remained important to him, and in his retirement he took German classes - in recognition of the fact that some of his grandchildren were growing up in Germany - and in Catholic theology and catechesis through the Maryvale Institute in Birmingham.

During his time at British Rail he became involved in trades union affairs and with the Labour Party. He was first elected to Dumbarton Town Council in 1960. He was a Bailie, the Treasurer and then twice Provost (1975-77 and 1980-84). Dumbarton had one of the largest Irish immigrant populations in the middle of last century and a long history of division and sectarianism.

Jimmy McKinley was proud of the fact that he was the first Catholic Provost of the town since the Reformation. He was on the Education Committee and did a great deal to support Catholic schools, but also saw improving relationships between the different religious communities as a core issue. He encouraged closer co-operation between the Church of Scotland and the Catholic Church and was on good terms with the local clergy. It was during Jimmy's time that the traditional Kirkin' of the Council was changed to involve other churches of different denominations instead of just the Church of Scotland.

Mr McKinley was a director of the Dumbarton Equitable Co-operative Society, which was a power in the land at that time with almost every family possessing a "store number," to shop in departments that ranged from food to furniture. He worked his way up through the committees to become President of the DECS and was actively involved with the Dumbarton Old Folks Committee until his late seventies. The town of Dumbarton remained very important to him even when he latterly moved to Glasgow, and his service as a councillor was an inspiration to his family and those who knew him.

That family was always at the centre of his life. On August 4, 1953, Jimmy married Dumbarton woman Bridget Glover (1926-2002) at St Patrick's, Dumbarton. The service was celebrated by Father Richard O'Callaghan, with whom he and Bridget (Babs) were lifetime friends. His marriage to Bridget was the bedrock to his life and they had seven children – Ian, Marie, Kenneth (died at birth), Jim, Eileen, Pauline and Tony. Their five grandchildren – Jamie, Brian, Rebecca, Myriam, Judith – and two great-grandchildren – Ben and Alyssa – were Jimmy's pride and joy. Although Bridget sadly died in 2002, they were able to enjoy many happy years of retirement together, travelling the world to visit their children in the various countries to which some of them had gone to live and work.

Five years ago, due to failing health Jimmy moved to Glasgow, living first with his daughter Marie in Dennistoun, then moving into St Joseph's Care Home in Robroyston. He died there peacefully two weeks after his 90th birthday celebrations. His funeral Mass took place there followed by burial in Dumbarton Cemetery. Jimmy McKinley leaves an inspirational legacy of public service, rooted in a belief that community service is something everyone is called to. His daughter, Marie Cooke, said: "Alongside other aspects of his life such as his love for his family, his faith, dedication to learning, belief in others, this legacy will shape our memory of my father."

Chapter 79

QUEEN OF THE LOCH

Hannah Stirling MBE., who was dubbed Queen of the Loch.

BORN: 27 September, 1914, in Glasgow.
Died: 9 November, 2014, at Loch Lomond, aged 100.

Hannah Stirling earned her crown as Queen of Loch Lomond through the sheer force of her feisty determination to protect the iconic waters famed around the world, writes Alison Shaw in the Scotsman. Not only did she save the natural beauty of the landscape surrounding the loch from the scars of a hydro dam scheme, she went on to play a key role in the creation of Scotland's first National Park and become the first British recipient of a prestigious European award for her outstanding conservation work. She had lived overlooking the loch for just over a dozen years when the dam proposal reared its ugly head. Knowing the lure of Loch Lomond was worth fighting for, she and her friend Mrs Josephine Colquhoun resolved 'to do something about it'. They formed an action group which ultimately saw off the scheme and, as a result, visitors have continued to enjoy the

Lovely Loch Lomond looking towards Ben Lomond.
Picture by Bill Heaney

glorious views as she first fell in love with them almost half a century ago. Born in the West End of Glasgow not long after the start of the Great War, she grew up in Helensburgh from the age of seven and attended St Bride's Girls School, now Lomond School. She learned early the definition of responsibility, duty and care: she was just 17 when her mother died and had nursed her for several years whilst helping to raise her younger brother and sister. She then went to commercial college to learn secretarial skills before working in her father's solicitors' firm for several years. During the Second World War she joined the Women's Royal Naval Service and worked at the War Office's Censor Office in Glasgow editing letters to ensure sailors did not divulge sensitive details of shipping routes in mail to their loved ones. She also served in Inveraray, Troon and Dunoon. In 1945 she married Bill, a surgeon, and subsequently left the Wrens, accompanying her husband on a surgical tour of America. There she saw General Dwight Eisenhower, formerly Supreme Allied Commander in Europe, at a White House function in Washington, where she also met pastor and civil rights activist Martin Luther King at a garden party, before he became famous on the world stage. She would later return to America, on a coast-to-coast tour as an ambassador for the group she helped found to protect Loch Lomond, attending the Stone Mountain Highland Games in Georgia and being feted as a guest of honour at a lunch at Washington's National Geographic Society building. The Stirlings travelled widely, as far as Japan, China and India, before buying their home Auchendarroch on Loch Lomondside in 1965, following a spell living in Glasgow. It was in the spring of 1978 that the North of Scotland Hydro Electric Board's plans for a major hydro electric dam scheme on the eastern shores of Loch Lomond galvanised her into action. It threatened to blight the landscape with a storage reservoir, construction roads and power lines across the slopes. She wrote to a national newspaper inviting opponents of the scheme to get in touch and the move triggered a huge response – 200,000 people signed a petition against the proposal. The Friends of Loch Lomond, an independent conservation charity, was formed in Balloch that October and the Hydro Board scheme was eventually scrapped. The Friends continued to work in myriad ways to protect the area and improve opportunities for people to enjoy the loch and its surroundings. When the Forestry Commission announced plans to sell Ben Lomond, the charity launched another campaign and ownership of the much-loved Munro was transferred to the National Trust for Scotland. The group also lobbied for the creation of Scotland's first national park – which finally came into being in 2002, contributed to the debate on various planning issues and took the lead in practical improvements to enhance the area's natural and cultural heritage. Now known as The Friends of Loch Lomond and The Trossachs, the charity's work extends right across Loch Lomond, The Trossachs, Breadalbane and the Argyll Forest Park. In 1983 Mrs Stirling, who chaired The Friends, received a Queen Mother's Birthday Award.

This was followed, in 1993, by an honorary doctorate from the University of Strathclyde and in 1994 with an MBE. The band played The Bonnie Banks of Loch Lomond as she stepped forward to receive the honour from the Queen. Her work was also recognised in 1996 when she become the first Briton to be honoured with an award from Europa Nostra, a movement which safeguards Europe's cultural and natural heritage. Throughout the remainder of her life she retained an intense interest in the park and the welfare of people in the area, particularly the young. She continued to keep up with issues and was always on hand to encourage and guide – but never direct – others, whilst offering advice and contributing generously to ensure things went smoothly. Widowed some years ago, latterly she was president of the Friends and was delighted when, to mark her 100th birthday, they teamed up with boat operator Cruise Loch Lomond to launch a passenger vessel, the MV Lomond Hannah. The boat that bears her name will allow many more visitors to enjoy the spectacular views which had inspired her devotion to the loch.

The Lomond Queen shows visitors around Loch Lomond from its base at Tarbert.

The Cobbler at Arrochar and Rob Roy's Prison on the eastern shore of Loch Lomond.
Pictures by Bill Heaney

Chapter 80

THE SCOTCH WATCH

The Goose Girl, an oil painting by Sir James Guthrie.

A sea of liquid gold surrounds the Dumbuck House Hotel in Dumbarton. Worth many millions of pounds, the warehouses containing barrel after barrel of maturing Scotch whisky are guarded by a state of the art, 21st century security system. However, it is not so long since these precious stocks of spirits were protected by a line of defence effective since 390BC. Ballantine's famous gaggle of ferocious white geese – the Scotch Watch – have featured in international TV documentaries, magazine articles and even record covers.

The security value of these geese has been well known since Roman times when centurions and their legionnaires patrolled the Antonine Wall in the Old Kilpatrick Hills not far from here. The best known story of their efficiency dates from when enemy soldiers stealthily advanced towards Roman infantrymen as they slept in a hilltop fortress. The first invader was almost over the ramparts when the geese, kept by the Romans as sacred birds, began screeching to their masters to warn them of the imminent attack. It was this legend that sprang to mind when the security arrangements for the Dumbuck whisky complex were being drafted in the 1950s. The civil engineer in charge of the 14-acre site was Brigadier Ronald Cowan, who happened to be a keen ornithologist. Brigadier Cowan suggested that geese, with their acute hearing and eyesight, would make a perfect second line of defence against intruders. Fed from grain used in the distilling process, they would also prove much cheaper to keep than guard dogs. The original core of the Scotch Watch supplemented their diet by feeding off the grass lawns around the maturation houses.

The original goosekeeper was Alex Malcolm, who retired after 30 years tending his noisy regiment. In a ceremony attended by a bagpiper and the entire flock of geese, Alex passed on the responsibility by handing over his herding stick to his successor, fellow Dumbartonian Arthur Carroll. Geese have a lifespan of 60 years and minding them could be a tricky business.

'Even though I have had the odd nip or clout from their wings, I am going to miss them,' said Alex on the eve of his departure. The Scotch Watch was made up of around 70 Chinese white geese and Roman geese, which have a characteristic strutting walk and are well known for their sentry duties. Just as in the military after which they were named, the geese had a definite pecking order and certain birds left their mates in no doubt about who was in charge. They had been at Dumbuck for so long, guarding Ballantine's 17 Years Old and other Scotch whisky products that they had no urge to fly away. They were stood down permanently however after 40 of them were killed by foxes over a period of five years.

Geese continue to feature in the mythology of many countries across the world. The goose is commonly regarded as the bird that lays the golden egg, most probably because every part of it, right down to the feathers, can be put to good use. It features too in Aesop's Fables where the biggest egg was the sun, laid by Seb, father of Osiris.

How a gander managed to lay an egg was a point that Aesop overlooked, but that's another story best told at the bar of the Dumbuck House Hotel over a warming glass of whisky.

The Hiram Walker grain distillery, the biggest in Scotland, was built in Dumbarton in the 1930s.

Chapter 81

THE CHOCOLATE SOLDIER

Major Patrick Telfer Smollett and his wife, Gina, at Cameron House, Loch Lomond.

Loch Lomond laird, Patrick Tobias Telfer Smollett, was born in Derbyshire, son of Major General Alexander Telfer Smollett, a highly decorated soldier. The family are descended from a brother of Tobias Smollett, the celebrated eighteenth-century novelist, and Patrick's maternal grandfather was Herbert Strutt, a member of the wealthy cotton family who had mills at Belper in Derbyshire. As a result, Patrick was born into substantial wealth, his family having homes and estates in England as well as at Kingairloch in Argyll and Cameron House on Loch Lomond. Each summer his parents and their guests would sail up the west coast to Oban in the family yacht, first the Sanda, before the war, then the Galma. It was an indulged and privileged childhood. Patrick's academic career was far from impressive, but he came of an age when academic achievement was not considered as important as personal development He attended several schools, including Advreck at Crieff, but ultimately failed to pass the entrance exams for Harrow, Eton, and Stowe. A compromise was eventually reached, and he was sent abroad to learn French, before returning home to the Cameron House estate where the inevitable military career was mapped out for him.

In 1936 he was commissioned as a 2nd Lieutenant in the Highland Light Infantry and dispatched almost immediately to India. Among his fellow subalterns was the actor David Niven, with whom he forged a lasting friendship. In 1938 he was sent to Palestine and found himself in the midst of the Arab revolt. Shortly afterwards, following the outbreak of the Second World War, Telfer Smollett was serving in the 5th Indian Division with the HLI when he was sent to the Red Sea port of Massawa, in Eritrea. There he found himself in an absurd situation, where the British and Italian military commanders were in daily telephone communication with each other.

In Telfer Smollett's opinion, the ensuing battle was entirely unnecessary and a waste of human life, but for "dash and leadership in the face of enemy bombing" he was awarded the Military Cross. In 1942 he was sent to Egypt as part of the British Military Mission. Being only five years older, he gained the confidence of the young King Farouk, who had taken a dislike to Sir Miles Lampson, the British Ambassador. The King persuaded Telfer Smollett to return to the UK with a giant 130lb box of chocolates for the Princesses Elizabeth and Margaret from Princess Feriel, Farouk's daughter, accompanied by a letter from Farouk to King George demanding Lampson's withdrawal. The letter was duly noted by the Foreign Office, although Lampson stayed in place.

Immediately after the war, Telfer Smollett made an initial foray into politics, when he stood as an independent conservative candidate in the 1945 election, but then withdrew. From 1948 until 1951 he was stationed with Allied Command in Berlin, and in 1951 he married Georgina, daughter of Sir Gifford Fox, MP for Henley. They had one son, David, and one daughter, Gabrielle. David, who is based in in Devon, has widespread agricultural and business interests and Gabrielle, who lives in Rutland, is an artist. Serving with his regiment, Telfer Smollett was thereafter stationed in Cyprus from 1955 until 1956, then Egypt, before retiring in 1959.

In 1964 he was adopted as the official Conservative candidate for West Dunbartonshire, a safe Labour seat. His campaign was one of the first to involve media photo calls and included canvassing passengers on one of the newly introduced 'Blue trains' between Alexandria and Glasgow and seeking the votes of the members of a naturalist colony on the Loch Lomond island of Inchmurrin.

Cameron House Hotel on Loch Lomondside. *Picture by Bill Heaney*

He later stood in Glasgow Pollok, where he was also defeated. In common with other Scottish landowners at the time, he attempted to turn Cameron House into a visitor attraction. His great love of animals inspired him to create the Loch Lomond Bear Park. It was not a great success, and the property was sold in 1990 to become a luxury hotel. And it remains that to this day.

The Telfer Smolletts retreated to the adjacent Cameron Home Farm where he bred Highland cattle and started to write his memoirs. At the same time, he continued to play an active role in local affairs and served as president of the Balloch Loch Lomond Highland Games, Vice-Commodore of the Loch Lomond Rowing Club, and president of the Loch Lomond Motorcycle Club. He was also appointed Deputy Lord Lieutenant of Dunbartonshire, and was a member of the Royal Company of Archers (the Queen's Bodyguard in Scotland). A distinguished, elegant figure, Patrick Telfer Smollett had a keen sense of humour and an individual charm which won him many friends. He will be remembered as an enormously engaging character, an officer and a gentleman of a generation which is fast disappearing.

The wife of King Farouk, Queen Farida, with her three daughters; Princess Ferial, who sent the chocolates to Princess Elizabeth and Margaret via Major Telfer Smollett, Princesses Fawzia and Fadia. Pictures by courtesy of Smollett family.

Chapter 82

THE SWIMMING COACH

Tommy Baker

Born: Dumbarton, December 21, 1936
Died: Dumbarton, October 3, 2016

Tommy Baker, who taught hundreds of Dumbarton children to swim and whose family roots were in Inishbofin off the Connemara coast, has died after a long illness. He was 79. Tommy was born in Dennystown, Dumbarton, the first son of Lizzie and John Baker, who already had four daughters. Another son and two daughters followed into the Baker family. He was baptised in St Patrick's Church and went to school at St Patrick's High and Wee St Pat's in McLean Place. The Baker family home was in Brucehill, Dumbarton, where many of the residents were second and third generation Irish immigrants, some of them from

Connemara. There were so many Irish families in Dennystown that the area was known locally as Wee Dublin and the local football ground was named after the Phoenix Park. On leaving school, Tommy started work as an apprentice patternmaker in the Clyde shipbuilding industry in the Engine Works of world famous Denny's of Dumbarton. He carried on working in the shipyard after completing his National Service with the Royal Air Force, but when that industry slumped in the 'Sixties, Tommy adapted his many skills and became a joiner and kitchen-fitter. The family also set up a popular tearoom, The Gossip Shop, in Dumbarton High Street. In 1968, Tommy married Mary Lafferty from Cardross and they settled in Dumbarton, where they went on to have five children and were blessed by ten grandchildren. Canon Gerry Conroy, who conducted the well-attended funeral Mass in St Patrick's Church, said: "Many of you will remember Tommy as a swimming teacher. "Hundreds of children have been taught to swim by Tommy in the Brock Baths or at Notre Dame High School. For many years he was also a water-polo player, coach and referee." Tommy also owned a mini-bus and whilst a life-long Dumbarton FC supporter he enjoyed his fortnightly hire taking supporters of Glasgow Rangers to Ibrox Park. Canon Conroy added: "He also arranged trips to his beloved Connemara and loved every single minute of that. Anyone who chatted to Tommy for more than five minutes will certainly have been regaled with tales of Bofin, a small island in the Atlantic, seven miles off the Connemara coast, where his family originate from." Tributes from old friends were paid to Tommy Baker on social media, including this one from Dougie Blair, who wrote: "Sorry to hear about Tommy he was a true gent him and my dad Archie helped a lot of young swimmers in the Brock Baths. We fair miss a proper swimming pool in Dumbarton." Tommy Baker's grandfather, also Tom, was one of five men from Inishbofin who were lost in a drowning tragedy at the North Beach off the island in 1914. His wife, Lizzie Ward, emigrated to Dumbarton with her children but left one boy, Joe Baker, with the Lacey family in the West quarter of the island. Tommy Baker was a regular visitor to Cleggan and Inishbofin and had many friends on the island, where he brought his wife and family on holidays when they were children. Tommy, who is survived by his wife, Mary, and children Gerard, Karen, Marie-Jo, Clare and Kevin and ten grandchildren, was interred at Cardross Cemetery, Dunbartonshire.

Top picture: Dumbarton water polo team with Tommy Baker (back right) and from left Charlie Gallagher, Jim Kerr, Malcolm Dougall, and Jack Blair with Billy Blair and Stewart Thackeray in front. The team (bottom left) from 1963 includes Jim Kerr, Jim Brannan, Malcolm Dougall and Tommy Baker (front right). And the old Brock Baths on Dumbarton Common.

Chapter 83

THE BOOLER

John Milne Dow MBE

Born: 26 August, 1919, in Glasgow
Died: November 7, 2014, in Dumbarton.

National Health Service administrator, Queen's Park footballer, bowler and Burnsian John Milne Dow died, aged 95. Dow was born in Glasgow and moved at an early age with his parents Peter and Agnes Dow to Dumbarton, where he grew up with his four sisters. He attended Knoxland Primary School and Dumbarton Academy from 1924 to 1935 and was later was employed by Dumbarton Town Council in the Public Assistance Department between 1935 and 1946. During the Second World War years he served as a pilot with 179 Squadron Coastal Command, which took him to many locations in North America, training in Detroit, Florida, and Prince Edward Island, amongst others, and in the UK from Cornwall to the Outer Hebrides. In 1948 he joined the newly established National Health Service, which was to be the focus of his working career and beyond. Starting as an accountant to the Executive Council for Dunbartonshire, he became Clerk and Finance Officer to the Executive Council in 1953.

Studying at evening classes, he gained a Diploma in Public Administration from Glasgow University in 1950. Dow also served as the first Chairman of Dumbarton Burgh Children's Panel from 1970 to 1974. Following a major re-organization of the NHS in that year, his place of work moved to Paisley and until his retirement ten years later he occupied the post of Administrator, Primary Care for Argyll and Clyde Health Board. In the Queen's New Year's Honours list of 1985 he was appointed Member of the Order of the British Empire MBE, for 'Service to the NHS'.

Dow's link to the NHS continued after retirement. For 15 years from 1986 to 2001 - by which time he was 82 - he was Founder Chairman of the Argyll and Clyde Branch of the NHS Retirement Fellowship. At the same time, from 1990 to 1999, he was Chairman of the Federation of Scottish Branches of the Fellowship, becoming First President of the Federation in 1999. Dow maintained close links with the Retirement Fellowship until his final weeks.

He was for 23 years Treasurer of Dumbarton High and Riverside Churches, an Elder since 1954, and played an active role supporting the Rev. Jim Dunn in the context of the consolidation of the Dumbarton church landscape in the late 1960s, when, amongst others, the High and Parish Churches were amalgamated to form Riverside Church. He was founder secretary of Dumbarton Rotary Club in 1960 and its President in 1966. A member of Dumbarton Burns Club since 1969, he served as its President in 1978. His passion for the poetry of Robert Burns was a lifelong one, his many renderings of Tam o' Shanter unforgettable.

As a mature young man of 36 he had decided that bowling would be his sport and it became another lifelong passion. His heyday years as a bowler included a year as President of Dumbarton Bowling Club (1964) and winner of a whole range of trophies. He was Secretary of Dunbartonshire Bowling Association (1970-72) and its President (1990). In 2004, he was appointed Honorary President of Dumbarton Bowling Club and his Friday night visits with his friends to the

Bowling Club bar were a feature of recent years – that is, when he was in Scotland, and not in London, Australia or Germany, visiting one of his children. Fellow Burnsian Jimmy Hempstead's poem 'The Tam o' Shanter Mug", in which Johnnie Dow brings home an unsightly trophy to his wife, is a classic of Hempstead's humorous verse and nicely combines the Burns and bowling sides of John Dow:

'A booler ye can always tell,
Wi' badges pinned doon each lapel,
Like campaign medals they proclaim
The competitions he's won at hame.
And others on some foreign green,
Twixt Garelochhead and Aberdeen;
While special badges represent
Life member and ex-president.'

Before taking up bowling, however, Dow was a footballer, even making it as far as playing for Queen's Park in Glasgow. A recent event organized by the Dumbarton Academy Former Pupils Football Club featured a photograph, later published in the Lennox Herald, of the youngest member together with him as the oldest member present. His families were moved to learn that a minute's silence was observed in his honour before the kick-off of a game on Dumbarton Common. By half-time, however, with a score of Dumbarton 1 – Doune Castle 4, some of the most stalwart supporters were beginning to leave and shortly afterwards the score went to 5-1 down. How did it finish? 10-1 or worse? Not at all: it's reported that a 12th man may have been at work on the Dumbarton side: they scored five more goals and won 6-5!

John Dow was married to Pat for almost 65 years. They met in Cardiff during the War and they were able to do much together during the many years of their marriage. They have three children, John, Liz and Pam and are survived by them and their families in London, Australia and Germany. The depth of that relationship between John and Pat, who was President of the Dumbarton Inner Wheel, was demonstrated when Pat entered Langcraigs Residential Home. John dedicated the greater part of each day to being with her there in her final year.

His son, John, who delivered the eulogy at Dow's funeral service, conducted by the Rev Ian Johnson, in Dumbarton Riverside Parish Church, said: "It's a remarkable fact that he passed away peacefully exactly six years to the day after her, on 7 November, just after midnight. "Unbelievably in those six years he made three extended trips to Australia and to New Zealand and earlier this year he was considering yet another one. "It's unfortunate that he just missed the Comet landing – that would have inspired him, especially as he had himself visited the mission control centre in Darmstadt."

BILL HEANEY

The ladies of Dumbarton Inner Wheel Club of which Pat Dow was an enthusiastic member.

Chapter 84

BAND OF BROTHERS

The Rev Ian Millar and Renton's Archie Thomson unveil the memorial to the men who died in the Spanish Civil War.

In the sun-scorched hills outside Madrid there is a striking symbol of half a century of dictatorship, which I visited with a group from Dumbarton. I was in a party of pilgrims who had been to Salamanca and Avila to visit shrines to people who had done much good in this world – St Theresa of Avila, St John of the Cross – patron saint of journalists – and some magnificent churches and cathedrals. We decided on our way from Salamanca to the Spanish capital to call in at the Valley of the Fallen, a vast monument General Francisco Franco commissioned to commemorate his victory in the Spanish Civil War. It was there that our cheerful mood changed and a cold shiver ran down my spine at the thought of the thousands killed and the thousands more, political prisoners, who were enslaved into forced labour to build this dark and monstrous shrine to the dictator. Eighty years after that war began, there are finally plans to change this landmark, a move welcomed in the Scots village of Renton by the organisers of the International Brigade Memorial Day. One of the organisers, Drew MacEoghainn, said: 'This will be a day to take time to remember the ordinary men and women who left Scotland to fight against Franco and his fascists, ordinary men and women who became legends. At least 27 people left here to go to fight for justice. This is a day for all comrades from around the globe who appreciate the cause that saw our men and women go to Spain to fight for a cause they held dear.

The people of Spain will never forget these brave fighters neither will we.' These annual meetings are held at the John Connolly Centre, Main Street, Renton, where an iron statue of a Spanish bull was unveiled six years ago. This was to commemorate the five Communists from Renton and Dumbarton who joined the International Brigades to combat General Franco's fascist uprising against the country's democratically elected Republican government. The heroic efforts of Rentonian brothers Patrick, Tommy and Daniel Gibbons, along with James Arnott and Patrick Curley, was acknowledged when the Rev Ian Miller, of Bonhill Parish Church, paid a glowing tribute to the men and unveiled the statue. Danny Gibbons was wounded in the Battle of Jarama in February 1937, and was allowed to return home – but he made his way back to Spain, distressed that his brother Tommy had been killed in the battle for Brunete in July that same year. Danny was eventually captured by Franco's troops at the battle of Calaceite in March 1938. Drew MacEoghainn says Danny Gibbons and his comrades were kept in filthy conditions in a concentration camp, but were eventually exchanged in February 1939, for Italian and German prisoners. Patrick Joseph – 'Joe' – the third Gibbons brother, who volunteered as part of a Chicago-based battalion in Spain, was on a Barcelona-based ship which was torpedoed by an Italian submarine. Two hundred volunteers were lost at sea, but Joe bravely kept two colleagues, neither of whom could swim, afloat for hours until they could be rescued. He went on to fight the Falangists in numerous battles during the Civil War and was wounded after an enemy tank opened fire. Of the Renton five, James Arnott was repatriated and Patrick Curley was killed at Jarama – the same battle in which Danny Gibbons was wounded.

More than 500 Scots left their homeland to fight against Franco and 65 of them lost their lives. There were 31 in total from West

Dunbartonshire, including the five from Renton, and another 11 from Alexandria. The others came from Clydebank, Dumbarton, Duntocher and Dalmuir. Eighty years on from the end of the Spanish Civil War the statue in Renton, plus one of La Pasionaria in Glasgow, and memorial plaques have been erected throughout Scotland. Isidora Dolores Ibárruri Gómez – known as 'La Pasionaria' – was a Spanish Republican heroine of the Spanish Civil War and communist politician of Basque origin, known for her famous slogan *No Pasarán*! during the Battle for Madrid in November 1936.

There were terrible deeds done by both sides in this conflict. Jimmy Burns, an expert on Spanish affairs, states that 80 staff and students from a seminary much like the one at Cardross, where young men were formed for the priesthood, were abducted and shamefully treated after a raid by 60 armed anarchists on churches. The clergy in Republican-held territory in this part of Aragon and neighbouring Catalonia were treated brutally during the 1930s. For two weeks, 51 priests, brothers and seminarians were held in a cramped cell, on basic rations and limited water, struggling with dehydration in suffocating temperatures. They were subjected to simulated executions and verbal and physical abuse. Eventually they were taken away and shot without trial; their only offence, their refusal to renounce their religion. The final day of the executions was August 15, the Feast of the Assumption, one of the most important dates in the Spanish Catholic calendar.

The Spanish Civil War began after anti-clerical legislation, passed by the Madrid parliament, had fuelled an allegedly radical "extremist" campaign to purify Spain of all religion. Franco and other generals led a right-wing military uprising against the democratically elected Republican government, unleashing three years of brutal violence. This civil war was both bitter and brutal. In recent years, as in much of Europe, Spain has become an increasingly secularised state. The Catholic Church, previously dominant, has surrendered many of its privileges. Spaniards no longer kill each other when they disagree, however. The country is divided country and these divisions still surface in bars from Barcelona to Benidorm. Debate is uncivilised "but without blood reaching the river," according to Jordi Évole in the Catalan newspaper El Periódico. Just as happens here, people do most of their fighting on Facebook and Twitter.

The now democratic Spain has yet to agree on a shared narrative of what happened. Nor has it been decided finally who was to blame for the political and military choices taken and the violence that ensued. There is widespread criticism of the failure of today's party leaders to reach a consensus about what kind of government they want. And a widespread lamenting of the absence among politicians of any notion of the common good.

A group of visitors from Dumbarton at the monument in Spain.

The Franco-dedicated basilica in the Valley of the Fallen still stands. It was scooped out of the hills by labourers who worked until they dropped, and Franco himself is buried behind the altar, beneath a gravestone decorated with fresh flowers. This has long been a rallying point for the far right in Spain, built to exalt the armed nationalist uprising and Franco's 'glorious crusade'. Now the government is considering exhuming the dictator's remains in order to transform the site into a place of reconciliation, a delicate task. 'Spain's transition to democracy was an act of prudence after the deep wounds caused by the war and the dictatorship,' Ramon Jauregui, a Spanish socialist politician explained. 'We have dealt with the past little by little. Maybe we're tackling this site a little late, but prudence has been the key to our peaceful transition.'

Spain held no truth and reconciliation process after the war; there was no accounting for crimes, or punishment. The country agreed to 'forget' and look to the future, for the sake of peace. But as the fear has faded, that approach has been changing. In the 21st century, archaeologists and volunteers have been exhuming the remains of Republicans from unmarked graves. The bodies of most of those who died fighting for Franco were recovered long ago. Then in 2007, the government passed the Historical Memory Law, granting victims of the war and dictatorship formal rehabilitation and compensation.

All remaining monuments to Francoism were to be removed, including the basilica. But Spain's conservative opposition party, the PP, refused to back the bill. There was talk of opening up old wounds. 'There are people in Spain who are afraid of being confronted with the darkness of the past,' explains historian Angel Vinas. 'There were horrors committed here, massacres. But we're not unique in that and other countries have come to terms with it. I don't see why Spain should not.' For Vinas reforming the Valley of the Fallen is all part of the process.

Renton today, where the spirit of protest lives on. *Picture by Bill Heaney*

Chapter 85

THE HOTELIER

Petra McMillan, working to raise funds for Marie Curie.

The Dumbuck House Hotel is looking much better these days. It was quite frankly a terrible disgrace until 2014. The famous Dumbuck was yet another local institution that had been badly let down by its owners. To put it mildly, the Dumbuck House Hotel was a disaster. It has now undergone remarkable renovation, refurbishment and resuscitation and has come out of it looking like the first class establishment it was for so many years going all the way back to 1798. I know the hotel has been revitalised because, apart from the fact that the Old Lady has been given a smart new coat of white paint, I was asked to do some work for the new owners, journalist Petra McMillan and her husband, Tom, who wanted 'the Dumbuck' to be really local again. They had heard all the stories about the hotel's glory days. And they were determined to bring them back. People told them about former owners, the McManus family, Willie and Frances, and later the management of Alan Gay plus the excellent barmanship of the late Ned Ward, Fred McLaughlin and Jean, of course, everyone knew Jean. There were also many good times too under the management of the McGroarty family, James Junior and Agnes Mary. The McMillans heard too about the legendary ladies who served those magnificent meals in the Grand Hall at Rotary Club lunches, Burns Night dinners, staff nights out and weddings. Like hundreds of Dumbartonians, I had my own wedding reception at 'the Dumbuck' 44 years ago on April 10 when I married my wife, Bernie. As a young reporter, I was invited to all the major happenings in the hotel to write reports and organise photographs for the *County Reporter* and the *Lennox Herald*. This included covering civic receptions, reunions of all sorts and football and rugby club dinners. The golfers stuck to their clubhouses and some others to their own halls, but almost everything else was an occasion to be celebrated at 'the Dumbuck'. Some of these events are memorable although others, because of John Barleycorn's generous hospitality, are not so readily recalled. Petra McMillan, who is a journalist and marketing expert from Dundee, asked me would I put together some memorabilia about Dumbarton. How could I refuse? Petra's fund-raising activities for Marie Curie are legendary. Petra and Tom, who once played professional football for Dundee United, are dedicated to making Dumbuck House Hotel another successful venture to add to their extensive business portfolio. I am no artist and not much of a photographer and certainly no marketing guru. How best then to put the Dumbarton into the Dumbuck again? Petra and I both know a bit about newspapers though and so she asked for my assistance to launch a new one, *The Dumbuck Times*. This would be an in-house journal for the hotel and one of the pages had already been made up and was displayed on the wall outside the newly created honeymoon suite, the Thomson Suite. Petra and local woman Joan Baird, had put their heads together to come up with a remarkable story (and photographs) about Joan's mother, Mrs Thomson who had baked numerous wedding cakes for couples who got married both in times of rationing during and just after the Second World War. *The Dumbuck Times* is now up on the walls of the Glasgow Road establishment. It is on the display most of the main areas of the hotel. It's a *Down Memory Lane* sort of newspaper with vintage pictures and stories about many things local. There are pages dealing with the Clydeside shipbuilding industry and whisky distilling plus views of Loch Lomond and Glen Fruin.

It's all about local people's life and work over the past century. When the McMillan family took over The Dumbuck House Hotel in May 2014, they understood the enormity of the responsibility they bore as the new custodians of one of the oldest buildings in the local area, but little did they realise quite how ancient and decrepit the Dumbuck was. For more than two centuries, the Glasgow Road building - originally believed to have been built in 1825 - had been a striking landmark at the gateway to Dumbarton and was part and fabric of town life; first as a grand country home and then latterly as hotel and much-loved venue for likely thousands of weddings, parties, functions and gatherings covering every facet of life's great milestones from the cradle to the grave. But now, with her head bowed, this 'grand old dame' wore the evidence of years of neglect and her once-proud reputation at the heart of the community was in tatters too. Just 20 or so years before, such was her prestige that newly-engaged couples faced a three year waiting list for a wedding at the Dumbuck, but by 2014 the hotel had just a handful of bookings and a bleak future as a business ahead of her. Undeterred, and with a clear ambition to restore the Dumbuck to her former glory, the McMillans launched an ambitious £500,000 regeneration programme, which would renovate the existing building and, with the addition of extra suites and rooms, present the new Dumbuck as a hotel in step with 21st century guest expectations. One of the first projects to be tackled was the refurbishment of the 'top o' the house' - the second floor of the original building which faces onto Glasgow Road. Flooded in 2011 and left to decay, this 400-plus square feet of derelict space was in dire need of investment so a plan was hatched to turn what was previously five bedrooms into two luxurious 200ft suites which would offer more flexibility to the current collection of 18 bedrooms. One would become the new honeymoon suite and the other, a family suite which would cater for up to four guests.

Tommy and Petra at the Dumbuck and Petra and Gwen doing charity work for Marie Curie.

It was during this work that Petra and Tom spotted a beam in the rafters with a collection of numbers carved upside down in the wood. On closer inspection and once righted, the numbers clearly read '1 7 9 8' or '1798'. This date was a revelation since all previous records showed that the house was built in 1825 for a prominent local land owner, Lieutenant Colonel Andrew Geils and his family. Hidden but in plain view, could it be possible that the Dumbuck was built in 1798 and was in fact not an 19th century construction but an 18th century treasure? The idea of a 'lady' deliberately concealing her age appealed to the humour of the owners. Petra said: 'We understand it was common practise in the past to engrave the date of construction on central parts of buildings, such as a beam in the roof space so it is entirely possible in our minds that the Dumbuck is not 190 years old but 217 years old - a difference of 27 years. Normally a woman might be affronted at having her true age revealed but we like to think that given the attention we've paid to restoring her - facelift 'n all - she might forgive our indiscretion…'

Despite the best efforts of Christopher Cassels, an archivist with West Dunbartonshire Council, he too was unable to determine the true age of the Dumbuck. According to Sir William Fraser's book The *Chiefs of Colquhoun and Their Country*, it would appear that the lands and estate of Dumbuck were purchased by Lieutenant-General Thomas Geils of Ardmore from Sir Charles Edmonstone of Duntreath in August 1815 for the princely sum of £28,997 2s. 9d. Thomas Geils died just two months later on the 24th of October 1815 at which point Dumbuck passed to his son, Lieutenant-Colonel Andrew Geils. When Andrew died in 1843, the estate passed to John Edward Geils. John Edward had four elder brothers but they all drowned in a shipwreck on their way to Ceylon in 1815.

Soak up the history then. Take a trip 'around the horn' to the old Dumbuck Hotel for a super meal and a dram, see the newspaper for yourself – and taste the delicious cuisine, which includes tapas, while you are at it. Petra, a patron for Marie Curie, has made the Dumbuck a 'hub' for the charity locally and ensures that all funds raised by events at the hotel are used in the same area postcode to buy free professional nursing care at home for the terminally ill. They are already stacking up the industry awards.

Old Firm legends officially opened the Dumbuck House Hotel. Murdo Macleod of Celtic and Rangers' David Weir with owners, Tom and Petra McMillan.

Pictures by Colin Garvie

A signed photograph of motor racing legend Sir Jackie Stewart was sent to the Dumbuck Hotel by Sir Jackie Stewart. Manager Lauren Moffat and owner Petra McMillan are pictured showing it off.

The Dumbuck Hotel was always the favourite venue of Dumbarton Rugby Club which was formed in the town half a century ago. They held some memorable dinners there with speakers who included Scottish rugby international John Beattie, now of BBC Scotland. Right from the outset, they were keen lads who opted to play in all weathers, even – or especially – and make a point of their hardiness even when football matches were cancelled.

This team turned out in the snow – Front row (left to right) D. Callander, D. Lambe, J. Freshwater, L. Mathieson, B. Shearer, captain, D. Russell, R.Anderson, R. Eadie, A. Mathieson. Back row (left to right) D. Lockhart, I Matheson, K. Wade, D. Flackhard, E. Bain, K. Black, L. Adamson, A. Wingate, F. Calder, K. Stephen and P. Eadier. Two lads who didn't make it that day were V. Ritchie and I. McClenaghan.

This Dumbarton Rugby Club team from 1980 included a few well-known faces including Malcolm King, Dougie Lockhart, Gus McCuaig, Ian MacGregor and Calum Macdonald.

Chapter 86

THE BARBER

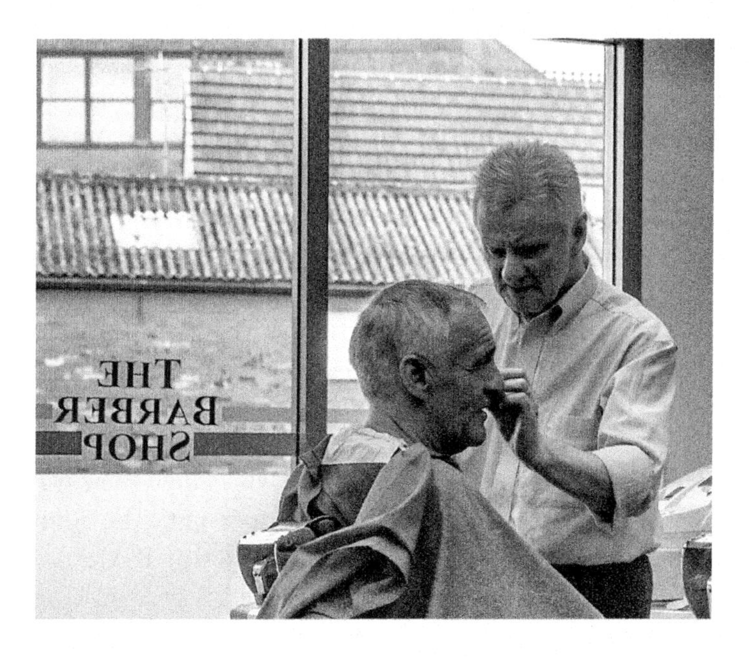

John McCann cuts the hair of former professional sprinter Pat McCafferty

Mohicans: I thought we had seen the last of them. But all those fashion conscious footballers on television have brought them back into vogue. We are talking haircuts here, men's haircuts. God be with days of the short back and sides, when men were men and society was content with that. There were no unisex salons in the middle of last century. In Dumbarton, the Vale of Leven and Helensburgh, men went to the barber's for a haircut. There were quite a few of them in the scissors and razor game then, and each barber had his own reputation that went before him. There was Jimmy McPherson and Jimmy Campbell and his son, Glen, in the High Street and Jimmy Nicol and Alex Murphy in the Vennel, and then Bruno Dynowsky came along to compete when he opened a shop in the old Artizan, near Denny's Engine Works. Peter McCann, who had worked for Alex Murphy in College Street, emigrated to Canada and came back and opened an all-American barber shop in the "new" town centre in the late Sixties. His shop was cutting edge new, smart and fashionable and his brother, John, went into an apprenticeship with him in College Way. The McCanns had to compete with Tommy McTaggart, who was in business in West Bridgend with his father, Matt, when crew cuts were all the rage and Tommy was a big hit with his teenage clientele. Then there was Jimmy Brown, the Salvation Army man, Alex Douglas, also in College Street, Chick McKernan, Jim Blair and many others who were popular, easy going guys from whom it was a pleasure to get a haircut. Sons of barbers, people like Glen Campbell and Andy Dynowsky, followed in their fathers' footsteps to demonstrate their skills at the barber's chair. In the Vale it was Willie Baxter that was the big name in barbering and his shop at the Fountain went like a fair with Willie Trotter and Alex Gallagher keeping the punters in trim. Charlie Daly kept everyone up to date on local politics and Jocky and Vince Flynn and Pat O'Brien were boxers who knew their way round the square ring. They did a very good upper cut. The Renton had two famous barbers – Johnny Antonelli and Jimmy Baxter. At the FE colleges, Tony Ventilla and ex-Commando Jack Kay from Dumbarton lectured youngsters in the art of hairdressing. Down in Helensburgh, a young Billy Rennie was cutting it with style and panache in a narrow shop across from the railway station in East Princess Street. We older, more mature guys are inclined to say that today's young men are far too fussy about their hair and that we were never like that. Dream on. Dedicated followers of fashion we were, slavishly copying the latest styles, whether it was a crew cut or a Tony Curtis. The mullet came later. There were hazards to overcome, of course, like the "coos' lick" we had inherited from our mothers being overzealous with the hair brush when we were still in the pram. Those were the days of the cock's comb; the centre parting, the side parting and the shed. Then there was the Bill Haley and the Comets kiss curl, pressed down on to the forehead when Rock Around the Clock was showing at the pictures and people were jiving in aisles. If the hair wouldn't succumb and stay put then the forces of Brylcreem (or margarine, yuk) were pressed into action. Currently there's the "all off" – the head shaved totally - but then there was the notorious Bobby Charlton comb over. It was important if you wanted a parting to ensure that it wasn't to the girl's side. I once a modelled for John McCann at a competition in the legendary Locarno Ballroom in Sauchiehall Street but he didn't win. I think my coo's lick ruined his chances. These days McCann still does his Sweeney Todd for everyone from sportsmen, schoolboys and pensioners and his customers include politicians and clergymen, including a chaplain to the Queen, Sir John Cairns. One of his great loves is boxing, and in his newly refurbished, super smart salon in Bridge Street he has a set of picture frames awaiting photographs of famous boxers and Italian singers, John McCluskey, Peter Keenan, Jim Watt, Cowboy McCormick or Dumbarton's own Donald McQueen and Wattie Glover, whose ring name was Frankie Narrow. John is also the oracle on football and can tell you the names of everyone locally who ever kicked a ball at any level, which team they played for, what they won -- and even which side they parted their hair on. He is celebrating 53 years as a barber this year. The long and the short of it is that he has never been counted out – and he has no intention of retiring to look after his grandchildren, including a new set of twins, which he and his teacher wife Anne are absolutely delighted about.

Bill Heaney, who once modelled for John McCann, and Sir Bobby Charlton of the infamous "comb over."

Chapter 87

SAINT PATRICK

St Patrick's Day falls on March 17 and the evidence to suggest Ireland's patron saint was born in West Dunbartonshire is becoming stronger, according to historian Billy Scobie. Vale of Leven man Billy, whose research was the catalyst for ecumenical services which are held annually on the Rock to mark the Feasts of St Andrew of Scotland, St Columba and St Patrick. Billy's research has led to links with St Patrick in the heraldry of the Earldom of Lennox. He maintains it is more than coincidence that the flag of Ireland, as incorporated in the Union Jack, bears the central feature of the heraldry of the Scottish earldom in which the patron saint of Ireland is traditionally believed to have been born. He points out that the flag of St Patrick itself includes the central aspect of the Lennox Arms – a red saltire, a diagonal or St Andrew's-type cross, on a white background, as adopted by the Earls of Lennox around the 12th or 13th century.

Billy, a retired local government officer, said: 'That red cross is the one incorporated into the Union Flag. It is the flag that is displayed on the ceiling above the central lobby of the House of Commons to represent

Ireland as the flag of St Patrick along side the flags of St George of England, St David of Wales and St Andrew of Scotland. But it will take a great deal more research to establish how this red saltire came to be part of the Lennox coat of arms which was used by the old Dunbartonshire County Council. Although the Office of the Lord Lyon has referred to a belief that the red saltire was adopted by an early Earl of Lennox because he had undertaken a crusade, they admitted that the real reason for the Lennox choice of that emblem remains a matter of speculation. It is a coat of arms not on general display in Dunbartonshire, but it is still in some public buildings, including the main chapel at Cardross Crematorium, Council Offices, Garshake, Dumbarton Police HQ and Hill Street Police Office, Alexandria. The flag and coat of arms of the current local authority for the area, West Dunbartonshire Council, includes the red saltire and an image of St Patrick.

History was made in 2014 when the first Christian service of worship since 1571 took place on the Rock and church and civic representatives gathered on the site of an ancient chapel dedicated to St Patrick to celebrate the life of St Andrew, Scotland's patron saint. Billy, who is the author of a history called *Upon This Rock*, told them that the Rock is the oldest recorded fortified site in Britain and that 'this has perhaps overshadowed the fact that it has also, since very early times, been a focus of Christian worship'.

It is probable that Christianity came first to the Dumbarton area through soldiers or merchants of the Roman Empire. There are a number of historians who believe that St Patrick was the son of a paymaster attached to the Roman Legions who are also connected with this area through the Antonine Wall, which is now an official World Heritage Site and runs into Old Kilpatrick. It could well be that St Patrick, who around 450 AD sent a letter condemning slavery to Coroticus, who is believed to have been a king ruling from Alt Clut (an ancient name for Dumbarton Rock), was born here and taken into captivity here and sold into slavery in Ireland. A chapel dedicated to St Patrick on Dumbarton Rock is said to have been founded by St Modwenna in the 6th century, then the earliest reference to Dumbarton as the birthplace of St Patrick was in an 11th century manuscript.

By the 12th century considerable numbers of pilgrims were visiting the saint's shrine at Kilpatrick, just a few miles from the Rock. By 1542 an English military document was referring to Dumbarton as the birthplace of St Patrick as a simple statement of fact. The reason for the choice of the red saltire as an Irish national flag is also a matter of debate. The strongest theory is that it was taken from the Order of St Patrick which was founded in 1783, and which adopted as its emblem a red saltire on white. But why was this symbol chosen by the Order of St Patrick? We would love to find out. Mr Scobie says logic suggests that, either the red saltire on white was an ancient symbol of St Patrick, which was adopted by the Earls of Lennox and subsequently by the Order of St Patrick, or the heraldry of the Lennox – the district of St Patrick's birth – was adopted as a symbol of the saint – and then of Ireland. Is all this simply coincidence, or was Patrick really a Son of the Rock?

* *Billy Scobie's book Upon This Rock by Alexander Tait is available for £7.99 from Books from Scotland.com*

Making history at Dumbarton Castle are (left to right) Billy Scobie, Archbishop Tartaglia, Bishop Duncan, the Rev Brian Mulraine, Provost Douglas McAllister, the Rev Kenny Macaulay, Gemma Doyle MP., Jackie Baillie MSP., Canon Gerry Conroy, the Rev Elaine McKinnon, Tim Rhead, Lord McFall and the Rev Ian Miller. *Pictures by Bill Heaney.*

Clergy taking part in the ecumenical service in honour of the saints on Dumbarton Rock.

Chapter 88

THE VICTORIA CROSS

Sergeant John Hamilton Brown VC was born in Dumbarton.

I have written a great deal over the past 50 years about serving soldiers and veterans – but never anything about the Dumbarton man who won the Victoria Cross. Lance Corporal John Brown Hamilton VC was born in Dumbarton on August 26, 1896, but little is known about his connections with the town. Unlike most other soldiers recruited in Dumbarton, John Hamilton did not join the Argyll and Sutherland Highlanders but was a member of the Highland Light Infantry, who were based at Maryhill Barracks in Glasgow. He later joined the Royal Pioneer Corps and took part not just in the First World War but the Second World War too. Hamilton, who was promoted to Sergeant, is officially listed as "a Scottish recipient of the Victoria Cross, the highest and most prestigious award for gallantry in the face of the enemy that can be awarded to British and Commonwealth forces."

He was just 21 years old, and a lance-corporal in the 1/9th Glasgow Highlanders Battalion of the HLI when he was awarded the Victoria Cross foe his actions during the Battle of Passchendaele. The citation states that on September 26, 1917, north of the Ypres-Menin Road, Belgium, great difficulty was experienced in keeping the front and support line supplied with small arms ammunition, owing to the intense artillery fire. At a time when this supply had reached a seriously low level, Lance-Corporal Hamilton on several occasions, on his own initiative, carried bandoliers of ammunition through the enemy's belts of fire and then, in full view of their snipers and machine-guns which were lying out in the front of our line at close range, he distributed the ammunition. Between the two world wars, Hamilton remained an active reserve and Territorial Army member. At the outbreak of the Second World War, he was in hospital and missed mobilisation, and luckily missed his unit being captured at St Valerie in the defence of Dunkirk. He eventually was promoted through the ranks and finished the war a Colonel in charge of an Italian prisoner of war camp in England.

His Victoria Cross is displayed at the National War Museum of Scotland, Edinburgh Castle having been delivered there by his daughter and grandson after he died in East Kilbride at the age of 76.

When war broke out in 1914, large numbers of young local men joined and the 9th Battalion of the Argylls was formed from the nucleus of the Territorial Army, which replaced the old Volunteers. Historian Dr Ian MacPhail tells us it was with "patriotic enthusiasm" that the Dumbarton terriers marched away, first to a spell of training in England and then to active service in France. Within a few months of arriving at the front line near Ypres, they tragically lost over 700 officers and men out of a strength of just over 1,000. Not all of those who volunteered or were conscripted – conscription was brought in only after 1916 – served in the Argylls and Hamilton was one of those. The long list of the Roll of Honour on the war memorial erected in Levengrove Park includes men of a great variety of regiments and corps. Dumbarton Castle, which looks down on Levengrove and which had no garrison since 1865, was once more occupied but never attacked during the course of the war. For those who stayed at home, the war meant a "black out" for fear of bombing by German zeppelins, rationing of food from 1916 onwards, long hours but high wages in the shipyards and engineering works.

Warships of all kinds except submarines and battleships were launched from Denny's and MacMillan's yards and, as often during wartime, boom conditions prevailed. But what did the local population have to put up with when the "war to end all wars" came to an end in November, 1918, and the demobbed soldiers gradually returned to their homes?

It was supposed to be a new improved world and "homes fit for heroes" after the "war to end all wars".

Demobbed and demoralised soldiers returned home to Dumbarton at the end of the First World War looking forward to better times. The Prime Minister, Lloyd George, made promises he could never keep to the bruised and battered battalions who had witnessed the horrors of the Somme, Ypres and Passchendaele Historian Dr Ian MacPhail tells us though that the post-war period brought many difficulties for people. Wage reductions led to strikes and lock-outs, such as the 1921 joiners' strike on Clydeside and the Strike in 1926 following the lock-out of the miners. The general strike affected all workers except those in essential services, and in Dumbarton for a time public transport came to complete halt. Occasional owner-drivers, who were immediately dubbed "scabs" by the striking workers, had to run the gauntlet of stones and other missiles at places at certain places like Dalreoch Quarry and West Bridgend.

My grandmother used to tell me a story, probably apocryphal, that one lady, upset by this behaviour which she classed hooliganism, had got one of her workmen to put a notice above where a crowd of workmen gather at the top of George Street in Dennystown. The notice which said The Sick, the Lame and the Lazy was said to have been placed there in time for a Royal Visit to dissuade the unemployed, poorly clad men from congregating there while the royal motorcade passed on its way to Helensburgh. Dr MacPhail has written that because of the strikes, poverty and unemployment, organised salmon-poaching on a large scale large scale took place regularly in the early 1920s on the River Leven. One of the favourite spots for the poachers was the old brickfield near Mains of Cardross, where there were huge mounds of sand. As the site was said to be very open, police and water-bailiffs were unable to effect a surprise raid and the poaching attracted hundreds of spectators who also acted as scouts and raised the alarm at the first sign of "the polis".

Then there was the ongoing problem of housing, the legacy of over rapid and unplanned housing such as the red brick Denny workers' rows and teeming tenements of Dennystown.

In 1911, nearly 12,000 people of 55 per cent of the population of Dumbarton lived in houses of just two rooms, almost all of which h lacked indoor toilets. Families had to share the outside lavatories and this greatly increased the risk of infection. Many of the houses were single-ends, solitary rooms, which were grossly over-crowded, dilapidated and condemned as unfit for human habitation.

Who remembers the sanitary inspectors and so-called Green Ladies who terrified dirty families into cleaning up their homes? If all politics is local then it took a national politicians to put legislation in place which made it mandatory for councils to prepare plans for re-housing working class tenants. Dumbarton's first housing scheme under the Addison Act of 1919 wasted a year later at Greenhead Road and the newly-formed streets of Alclutha Avenue, Strowans Road and Dunbritton Road. People who were allocated house in that part of Silverton became known as Ranchers because the lived on formerly green field sites which had been part of farms. The first slum clearance was of a small tenement at the foot of West Bridgend, inappropriately named Sunnybank. Financial difficulties which led the Government to set up the infamous Geddes Committee to enforce economies brought the house-building to an abrupt end. Politicians of today have a different word for that – austerity.

Anyway, the Wheatley Act, passed by the Labour Government of 1923-24 started off more council house building and the Brucehill scheme began to develop. This made possible the clearances of places such as Henryshott, part of an area which, because of its predominantly Irish population at one time, had been christened "Wee Dublin," the football pitch nearby acquiring in time the name "Phoenix Park". Phoenix Park is, of course, the largest public park in Dublin and the location of Áras an Uachtaráin, the home of the President of the Republic of Ireland.

Chapter 89

THE COUNCILLOR

Councillor Geoff Calvert was one of the "good guys" in the Labour Group when the council faced political turmoil in 2006.

Picture by Bill Heaney

Soldier, politician, community councillor
Born March 2, 1946 in Newcastle
Died February 20, 2015, in Kirkcudbright

Geoff Calvert, who was 68, has died suddenly of a heart attack at his home in Kirkcudbright, where he had retired to from the turbulent local government politics of West Dunbartonshire to become a community councillor in peaceful Dumfries and Galloway. From 1995 until 2012, Calvert had been the Labour member of West Dunbartonshire Council for Dumbarton through a period of unprecedented turmoil and faction fighting which saw the Public Accounts Commission for Scotland holding an inquiry into its affairs in November, 2006, in Clydebank Town Hall.

Calvert emerged as one of the "good guys" as senior Labour politicians launched a public broadside on their own party's leadership on West Dunbartonshire Council with the then local MP and MSP, John McFall and Jackie Baillie, calling for Holyrood ministers to send in a hit squad to force change. A series of astonishing accusations flowed at the inquiry by the local authority watchdog with allegations of widespread bullying and claims that a cabal of councillors had allocated £millions to favour their own wards. Not long afterwards Andrew White, the council leader, and his deputy, Jim Flynn, resigned from the council as the allegations piled up, including charges of contract fraud and irregular recruitment of members to rig candidate selection. It was left to Geoff Calvert and other senior Labour members to steady the ship and fight an upcoming election which they won against the odds in 2007.

The election, which was the first in Scotland using the single transferable vote system, ended with an administrative shambles. Labour won West Dunbartonshire in the end with ten seats to the SNP's nine. Independents took two of the remaining three seats and the Scottish Socialists one. Councillor Calvert polled 1292 votes in the Dumbarton ward beating Ian Robertson of the SNP and David McBride (Labour) into second and third place respectively. He resigned his seat in 2012 a few months prior to the May elections that year and left Dumbarton to return to Kirkcudbright where he had stayed after retiring from the Army.

Calvert had joined the Army in 1966 and been promoted through the ranks of the Blues and Royals and Royal Dragoons. He was to become the Regimental Sergeant Major of the 17/21 Lancers at Dundrennan Range, a weapons testing range on the Solway Firth, near Kirkcudbright. The range is part of the Kirkcudbright Training Area, 4,700 acres of farming land acquired by the Army in 1942 to train forces for the invasion of mainland Europe. Calvert also served in the Army in Germany and in Dorset before taking up his appointment in Kirkcudbright.

Geoff was a great walker whose hobby was hitch hiking and it was during a hike to the north of Scotland that he met his wife, Cath, a Clydebank woman whom he married in 1972. The couple lived in Kirkcudbright until 1989 when he retired from the Army to seek a job in Civvy Street, which wasn't an easy task since his only previous experience of work outside the Forces had been as a youthful civil servant.

He had joined the Civil Service after leaving St Cuthbert's secondary school in Newcastle, where he was born, the only son of George and Doris Calvert, in the city's West End.

In Dumbarton, the couple settled first in Argyll Avenue in Crosslet and later moved to a house in Mary Fisher Crescent which they left to return to Kirkcudbright in 2012. Geoff was a member of Kirkcudbright Community Council and introduced the Citizen of the Year Award there. His political career began in Dumbarton in 1995 when he represented the Bellsmyre ward and was proud of the progress he made on behalf of the community, forging close ties with the teachers, parents and pupils of St Peter's and Aitkenbar primary schools. When he moved into central Dumbarton, he campaigned tirelessly for improvements to the high flats at West Bridgend and strove to bring about improvements in the Town Centre, where there were battles to be fought on every front. He became the Roads and Technical Services Committee convener which kept him busy with so many changes taking place in the centre of the town and along the banks of the River Leven. Calvert was also chairman of the Licensing Committee, another stressful appointment, which saw him being reported to the Standards Commission for unlawfully opposing an application from Nightingales Night Club in Balloch, an accusation of which he was cleared.

Geoff Calvert and his wife, Cath, enjoyed the social side of his work too, particularly making presentations to couples celebrating their Golden Wedding – "He liked to surprise them by finding out interesting nuggets of information about them for his speech, things they thought he would never know about," said Cath.

One of the highlights of becoming the Deputy Provost was presenting the Freedom of West Dunbartonshire to the world famous Grand Prix racing driver Sir Jackie Stewart, who is a native of Dumbarton. Geoff's tragic death came when he collapsed at home while getting ready to take the family cat to the vet. Cath and a local doctor and members of the emergency services failed in their efforts to revive him and he died in the house. Geoff Calvert's funeral took place at St Andrew and St Cuthbert's Church in Kirkcudbright. He is survived by his wife, Cath, and their sons Neil, 41, and Martin, 31.

Chapter 90

THE CEMETERY

It was called God's Acre - old Dumbarton Cemetery.

Picture by Bill Heaney

Cemeteries hold a particular fascination for many of us. When my grandchildren were still in their pram, I enjoyed walking up to the quietest place in town to persuade them to go to sleep. Dumbarton Cemetery – or God's Acre, as it is sometimes known – is one of West Dunbartonshire Council's success stories. It is well kept and lovingly tended by the caring staff whose job it is to look after it. It's such a pity that that vandals and drunks, junkies and jakeys in modern parlance, vent their frustrations there from time to time. Out of their minds on cheap wine and barbiturates, they trample on graves and overturn headstones. They smash memorial stones and destroy lovingly laid flowers and those little mementoes people leave which were dear to their departed loved ones.

The new extension to the cemetery further up the brae in the hawk's field at Garshake is now complete. It too looks well, despite having the century old flourishing hawthorn boundary hedge cruelly and unthinkingly cut down and replaced with a wall and a gatehouse. Let's hope the vandals stay out of it. I have been digging up stories around cemeteries for the past 50 years and I recall handling the bones and skulls which came to the surface when workmen dug up the Old Parish Church graveyard to gain access to the distillery.

The history of the old cemetery is carefully laid out in a book, *God's Acre of Dumbarton*, published by Bennett and Thomson and printed on the presses of the old Lennox Herald office in Church Street. I have written about this book previously, but having another browse through it recently, I was amused at the chapter on Journalists. It begins: "The three gentlemen whose lives are given in this chapter were as pure in life as they were gifted in intellect." That didn't sound a bit like any of the journalists of today, the men and women whose job it is to write the first draft of history. And to shine a light in the darker corners of local government. Donald MacLeod, who wrote *God's Acre*, adds: "These virtuous, honourable, high-spirited journalists pursued the even tenor of their way unbiased by passion, prejudice or self-seeking; therefore their memories are worthy of the highest regard. The world owes much to such men."

My face was turning red with embarrassment at this point, even though this hagiography had been written long before my time. MacLeod added: "Fancy what state of matters might obtain were the press in the hands of unscrupulous, unprincipled conductors! These by its agency might pollute our moral atmosphere, and poison the wells of knowledge, and thereby make the press a curse rather than a blessing. Those who are conscious of the temptations many of which may beset the path of the active journalist, can ungrudgingly award the warmest praise to the pressmen who have scornfully brushed aside the allurements that would cripple or destroy."

It must have been truly difficult for local journalists in those days to resist the offer of a half and a beer in the Elephant and Castle or a ticket for the Big Green Burns' Supper. I am reminded of the Humbert Wolfe quote: "You cannot hope to bribe or twist (thank God!) the British journalist. But, seeing what the man will do unbribed, there's no occasion to."

Nowadays it's even harder to fend off the offer of a ticket to a visiting circus or a karaoke night in Balloch. Anyway, who were these great local journalists who trod those well-beaten paths to the Municipal Buildings for council meetings and Dumbarton Police Court to report on the drunk and incapables and petty housebreakers of a Monday morning? Thomas Bennett, who was born in Saltcoats in 1828, was the youngest of a large family who included his brother, Samuel, who started the *Dumbarton Herald* in 1851. This is said by MacLeod to have "opened up a congenial field for the literary workmanship of his younger brothers."

I am reminded at this point of writing that the New York-based journalist Joseph Mitchell, one of my heroes, who wrote that there was no bigger pain in the backside in a newspaper office than a reporter who thought himself a writer. Yet MacLeod says of Bennett: "His powers as a journalist were of a very high order, for his mind was clear, his judgement impartial, and his educational acquirements remarkable for solidity and thoroughness. On a wider area his originality of thought and terse reasoning would have given him a high place among the political and philosophic writers of the day; but the fates and his own too modest nature kept him from soaring too high, and led him to devote all his talents to the cultivation of his own little vineyard, in which he laboured zealously for more than a quarter of a century, and with no insignificant results." At this point in the book, my eyes began to mist over and I could take not much more in praise of my chosen profession. Bennett's story touched my heart. Thomas Bennett's memorial at Dumbarton Cemetery is about 50 yards to the left of the main gate on the breast of an incline, next to the much larger monument to his brother, Samuel.

It is written in rapidly fading letters on grey sandstone:
THOMAS BENNETT
Born in Saltcoats, 12th January, 1828
Died in Dumbarton, 28th May, 1880
For many years, editor of the Dumbarton Herald and ardent promoter and supporter of the social, benevolent and literary institutions of the Burgh. This memorial, by his many friends who long prized his honest work, revered his singleness of purpose and who now treasure the memory of his helpful, unselfish life, is here gratefully erected.

Samuel Bennett, who founded the *Lennox Herald*, was a Provost of Dumbarton. Born in Ardrossan, Bennett moved to Glasgow in the late 1830s intending to study for a career in the church. He undertook missionary work in the worst slums and helped set up the New Vennel School – perhaps the first of Scotland's "ragged" schools. Abandoning his ambitions to become a churchman, however, Bennett became a political activist in the Chartist movement. In 1842 he led 20,000 unemployed in a protest march from Glasgow Green to the west end of the city and in 1848 he organised a large Chartist demonstration on the Green. In 1851 Bennett moved to Dumbarton where he established the Dumbarton Herald and later its sister-newspaper, the Lennox Herald. He became Provost of Dumbarton in 1870.

The other two journalists who deserve to be name-checked here and whose graves are in Dumbarton Cemetery are, first, James Sutherland, who went on from working at the Lennox Herald to become the foreign editor of the Leeds Mercury, one of the most important British Provincial newspapers at that time, and later became editor of the Madras Times, the leading paper of South India. The second is Alexander Dingwall McRae, who served his apprenticeship in Church Street and went on to work for the Star newspaper in Glasgow. He was associated with teetotal societies in Dumbarton and Glasgow and went to work in New York where he became a sub-editor on the Scottish American Journal, a paper of considerable sectional interest. McRae was a promising poet and an excellent public speaker but in one dark fit of depression he destroyed all his poetic work. A total abstainer from alcohol, unlike so many of his journalistic colleagues, he became ill and came home to die in Dumbarton, aged just 24. Such is life, such is death.

New Dumbarton Cemetery at Garshake Road in Dumbarton.

A young Bill Heaney on the case after centuries-old skulls were exposed by workmen in the graveyard of the Old Parish Church in Dumbarton and vandalism was wrought in Old Dumbarton Cemetery at Garshake.

Old timers – the grave diggers at Dumbarton Cemetery in the 1920s.

Old Dumbarton Cemetery with snow covering the monuments.
Pictures by Bill Heaney

AFTERWORD

The power of the press. Does it really exist and what has its impact been in Dunbartonshire down through the years? What impression does a critical local newspaper have on the community it is there to serve? I have to go back to the 1850s when the town was under the influence of "the old fogeys". They were "if you always do what you always did then you always get what you always got" brigade. Old school politicians had hitched their wagon to the fading star of the past and were content to stay there. Not so the *Lennox Herald*, the leading local newspaper which, with the support of local traders and others, was determined Dumbarton should shake off its dusty past and become one of the most prosperous communities on Clydeside.

One of the first major improvements was the building of the railway, first between Balloch and Bowling, the terminus of the busy Forth and Clyde Canal. The railway was extended and a line was laid between Dalreoch and Helensburgh and Bowling to Glasgow. In return for permission to bridge the River Leven and run the line over the Common to Dumbarton East the town council was received £1,000 from the railway company. This plus the deepening of Dumbarton Harbour and an extension of the railway through Balloch to Stirling brought considerable benefits to this locality. As ever however there were drawbacks and one was that the steamer traffic to Dumbarton Quay – previously six steamers a day called there – dwindled. The Quay, off the High Street, was a "centre of activity and a popular rendezvous", according to Dumbarton historian Dr Ian MacPhail.

Because of the rapid growth of the town and the serious rioting which occurred in 1855 between Protestants and Catholics, and in 1856 over the lock-out of trade unionists, there was trouble. There were clashes between the factions in the High Street which resulted in one Catholic being carted off into the Denny/Rankine shipyard. This man was snatched back by his comrades as he was about to be consigned to a furnace. The final outcome was that the yard stopped employing Catholics to prevent sectarian trouble. There were very public disputes, which were carried on in the pages of the old *Lennox Herald*, including whether the Old Parish Church graveyard should close after a new cemetery had been opened at Stoneyflat. Progress cost money which took the form of rates and the "old fogeys" were reluctant to cough up. Dr MacPhail wrote: "It is almost impossible today to appreciate the fierceness of the criticism which these worthwhile and necessary improvements provoked." These diehards maintained that people like the Denny and other industrialist were simply out to line their own pockets. One of them was John Latta, a man of strong religious principles after whom a street off Bonhill Road is named. He was an implacable enemy of "Party of Progress," and as Treasurer of the town council for many years, he felt the large sums of money being invested in these new schemes was extravagant.

It was in the *Dumbarton Herald* – predecessor to the *Lennox Herald* – in 1851 that Samuel Bennett, a supporter of social reform, that the scheme of improvements was first outlined. In due course a rival newspaper called the Dumbarton Chronicle was produced by Bennett's political opponents. It proceeded to lampoon the progressive establishment who stood firm against the criticism and with the shipbuilding families dipping into their own pockets and the support of the community Dumbarton began to develop and stretch out. Dennystown was built at West Bridgend to house the shipyard workers and plans were laid for a new academy and burgh hall. Knoxland Square was donated to the town by the Dennys and rival shipyard owner John MacMillan bought the Levengrove estate for £20,000 – a vast sum at the time – making it a gift to the town as a public park.

Elections, both municipal and parliamentary, during this period were exciting affairs, even though the number of electors was usually small – 120 in 1851 and 300 in 1866. By the extension of the burgh franchise in Scotland in 1868 to all householders, working class men – not women, who did not get the vote until later – at last had a say in the town's affairs. In 1871, the appeal of *Lennox Herald* editor Samuel Bennett to the working classes resulted in a resounding victory for himself and his followers and the defeated party, headed by Provost Matthew Paul, resigned en bloc. Bennett's programme of "economy, retrenchment and progress" was intended to be in contrast to what he termed as the incompetent and extravagant administration of his predecessors, who had run into considerable trouble over the financing of the Black Linn reservoir.

Bennett however was not infallible. His own pet scheme for a pier at Dumbarton Castle, which was opened in 1874, proved to be a white elephant. At low tide steamers had difficulty making the pier and, at any rate, the railways were beginning to take away some of the steamer traffic on the River Clyde. Much of the pier was washed away in 1897 and the last remnants were removed in the 1890s. And so in the 21st century similar issues affect us here in the Lennox, the ancient capital of Strathclyde, the Vale of Leven, Helensburgh and Loch Lomondside. The role of journalists is not to make friends and influence people, it is to comfort the afflicted and afflict the comfortable. If you consider there is no need for us and that we are pests and an inconvenience to progress, consider this: "*Meum dictum pactum* – my word is my bond." It is the motto of the Institute of Bankers. It is to keep an eye on what the Nobel laureate Seamus Heaney called "party political jabberwocks" and provide information and news, challenging the establishment, the council and the government. And to persuade them to listen to the electorate and seek out conflicts of interest. Samuel Bennett followed that code as did Craig Jeffrey, David Callan and Donald Fullarton. Lord Cudlipp of *Publish and be Damned* fame did that too. My old school motto is *Tradamus Lampada* – We carry the Torch – and I have endeavoured to take up that torch for press freedom during my 55 years in newspapers, most of them in Dunbartonshire.

OTHER TITLES RECOMMENDED BY NEETAH BOOKS

All these titles can be found and ordered at discount and signed on the Neetah Books website – www.neetahbooks.com

Mightier than the Sword - by Alexander Tait, is a book about Scottish nationhood. It tells the dramatic story of William Wallace, the greatest warrior and martyr for Scotland s ancient liberty. It uncovers the fascinating history of the symbol which has for over 700 years represented the nation s heroic struggle for freedom. It provides a revealing record of the many chapters in the Scots relentless pursuit of self-determination, and, through the personal experience of the author, it illuminates what Scottish nationalism means in our own era. In September of this year, 2014, the Scots will decide democratically whether to remain within the 300-year-old union with England, or to re-join the community of nations as an independent state. For those who would understand the historical and emotional forces, the grievances and the vision, behind the independence campaign, Mightier than the Sword is an essential read. "Mightier than the Sword" is an essential read - Jack Paterson, Editor, Independence magazine.

Upon this Rock - by Alexander Tait. This book has it all, romance, subterfuge, and adventure. It is set amidst an important era of Scottish history and manages to both educate and excite. It is a book that every church goer should read. It is especially relevant in an age where religious bigotry still raises its head. Apart from being a thoroughly good read it is also an attempt to sensitively look at the Reformation against the broad sweep of Scottish history. As befits all good books the ending is especially worth waiting for !!!

Whisky in the Jar - by Alexander Tait, is an historical novel based on the illicit whisky distilling and smuggling activities that occurred around the eighteenth century on Loch Lomondside. Duncan Robertson is an heroic figure who finds himself ensnared in the conflict between the Highland people and the British military a generation after Culloden. It is also the story of the man who writes the novel. A man fighting his own battle against the mental oppression of agoraphobia, alcohol dependency and the threat of job loss. Where Duncan Robertson's weapons are the broadsword and the pistol, the author uses rock 'n' roll and eastern mysticism. These themes are as vibrantly interwoven as any Highland tartan, with richly colourful characters, romance, suspense and dry Scots humour.

The Cup – by Alexander Tait. In this richly varied collection of a dozen short stories, Alexander Tait draws from his skills of imagination and historical research to enable his readers to encounter Rock legends of the 'sixties, the court of King Arthur and a Roman centurion on the shores of Loch Lomond. Tait's characters are to be found on the Arctic Convoys, the beaches of Dunkirk, Blitz-torn Birmingham and the surface of the Moon. They have been crafted with understanding, warmth and humour, and demonstrate the great truth - that it is in the lives of the ordinary that the extraordinary is to be found. The tales, which range in time from the Crucifixion of Christ to the present day, all deal in their different ways with the eternal battle, within individuals and nations, between good and evil.

The Peck Chronicles – by Paul Murdoch. Talisman, Citadel and Tyrant are th first of a seven-book series. Inspired by the area around Alexandria and Loc Lomond, they feature an asthmatic boy-hero – James Peck and his crazy friends a they battle monsters and magic in an effort to save their families and severa planets along the way. "A fantastic adventure series for 'children', 9-90yrs Pratchett meets Tolkien…with Balloch [and Alexandria] clearly recognisable i the landscape." – Keith Charters, children's author.

Talisman

Citadel

Tyrant

The Tiffy & Toffy Picture-book Series – by Paul Murdoch (Sam Wilding)

Tiffy and Toffy – The Squashed Worm and Bramble Pie
Tiffy and Toffy – The Big Red Monster
Tiffy and Toffy – Annie Adder's Gold
Tiffy and Toffy – The Great Vole Rescue
Tiffy and Toffy – The Lucky Pellet

These colourful picture-books are brilliant for young children 3- 7yrs who love animals and adventure. There are items to find and count, hidden in the pages. The books have been used all over the world to help children with English and counting. (Used by UNICEF, Asthma UK, East Bali Poverty Project and Glasgow – The Caring City Charity)

Coming soon: **Sunny** – by Paul Murdoch. Racial prejudice and sectarianism come to the surface in a small Scottish town during the 1970's as Sunny Wilson tries to break through his school mates' narrow views and solve the mystery of a fatal crash.

Paul performs children's workshops all over the world in schools, libraries and festivals. www.paulmurdoch.co.uk

Lightning Source UK Ltd.
Milton Keynes UK
UKOW05f2211061116
287009UK00002B/37/P

9 781526 206374